Pennsylvania Almanac

Pennsylvania Almanac

Jere Martin

STACKPOLE
BOOKS

Copyright © 1997 by Stackpole Books

Published by
STACKPOLE BOOKS
5067 Ritter Road
Mechanicsburg, PA 17055

**This book is not an official publication of the State of
Pennsylvania, nor does its publication in any way imply
its endorsement by this agency.**

Cover: Capitol dome, Harrisburg, Pennsylvania
Photo by Socolow Photography
Cover design by Tracy Patterson

Printed in the United States of America

10 9 8 7 6 5 4 3 2 1

First edition

Library of Congress Cataloging-in-Publication Data

Martin, Jere.
    Pennsylvania Almanac / Jere Martin. — 1st ed.
        p.   cm.
    Includes bibliographic references and index.
    ISBN 0-8117-2880-3 (alk. paper)
        1. Pennsylvania—Miscellanea. 2. Almanacs, American—
Pennsylvania. I. Title.
F149.M39   1997
974.8—dc21   97-24386
                                                                         CIP

All in Pennsylvania

If you're off to Pennsylvania this morning
    And wish to prove the truth of what I say,
I pledge my word you'll find the pleasant land behind
    Unaltered since Red Jacket rode that way.

Still the pine woods scent the noon, still the catbird sings his tune,
    Still the autumn sets the maple forest blazing.
Still the grapevine through the dusk flings her soul-compelling musk.
    Still the fireflies in the corn make night amazing.

There are there, there, there with earth immortal
    (Citizens, I give you friendly warning),
The things that truly last when man and time have passed.
    They're all in Pennsylvania this morning!

—Rudyard Kipling

Contents

Acknowledgments

Every department of state government that is mentioned in this book provided some assistance to the author. Many went far beyond the call of duty.

The reference librarians at the Lancaster County Library, Franklin and Marshall College, Penn State–Harrisburg, and the staff of the Pennsylvania State Data Center were tremendously helpful.

Introduction

The *Pennsylvania Almanac* is the latest entry in a great Pennsylvania publishing tradition that began in 1685 when Samuel Atkins published the first book in Philadelphia, *Kalandarium Pennsilvaniense,* an almanac. By the time Benjamin Franklin published *Poor Richard's Almanac* in 1732, eight other almanacs had been printed. Franklin's almanac succeeded on such a grand scale that he was able to retire from publishing and devote full time to politics and his many other interests.

A variety of almanacs, concerned primarily with weather and matters agricultural, appeared throughout the 19th and early 20th centuries. The most successful of the modern era was the *Bulletin Almanac,* which began publication in Philadelphia in 1924. The fifty-second edition, published during the Bicentennial, was the last. It was 18 years before the *Philadelphia Almanac and Citizens' Manual* appeared to fill the void it left. Sponsored by the Library Company of Philadelphia, it was published for only three years.

While it would be presumptuous of us to compare this almanac with its esteemed predecessors, it does share their goal of providing useful information on a wide variety of subjects. The *Pennsylvania Almanac* is a compilation of the physical, natural, and cultural properties, institutions, and attractions of the state.

We attempted to produce the most comprehensive volume ever published about the Commonwealth of Pennsylvania. Thousands of items are grouped under 14 major headings, including history, government, arts and culture, natural resources, climate, media, tourist attractions, commerce, agriculture, education, and transportation.

The *Pennsylvania Almanac* has a statewide orientation. Prior publications were generally designed to appeal to a regional audience. The conventional wisdom was that Pennsylvanians were disinterested in regions outside their own. Phillip Klein, the distinguished historian, wrote, "We Pennsylvanians lack a real sense of identity, because traditionally people's allegiances have centered around their hometown rather than the total entity of the state." United States Senator Arlen Specter contends that campaigning in Pennsylvania is like visiting seven different states.

One of the goals of the *Pennsylvania Almanac* is to enable Pennsylvanians to see the larger picture of which they are a part, to develop a sense of the state as a whole, to recognize the factors that encourage regional orientation, and to appreciate their diversity and common interests.

We see the *Pennsylvania Almanac* as an ongoing venture. The nature of much of the information herein is changeable and we anticipate frequent revisions. The reader is invited to notify the publisher of omissions and errors in this first edition. We welcome suggestions as to other matters that have escaped our attention.

STATE SYMBOLS
The State Seal
The State Constitutional Convention in 1776 authorized the creation of a seal that would be affixed to all commissions. A seal was produced and designated as official by the General Assembly in 1791.

On the obverse of the seal, there is a shield with three symbols that were originally used in the seals of counties: a ship in full sail, the crest of Philadelphia County; the plow from the seal of Chester County; and sheaves of wheat from the crest of Sussex County, now

a part of Delaware. There is a cornstalk to the left of the shield and an olive branch to the right. The shield's crest is an eagle. The inscription "Seal of the State of Pennsylvania" encircles the design.

On the reverse, "Liberty," represented by a woman with a drawn sword in her right hand and a French symbol of liberty in her left, is depicted trampling upon a lion, the emblem of tyranny. The top half of the design has the inscription "Both Can't Survive." The State Seal is in the care of the secretary of the commonwealth. It is used to authenticate documents.

Coat of Arms
The coat of arms was designed by Caleb Lownes of Philadelphia in 1778. It has a shield with the three symbols from the State Seal—the ship, the plow, and sheaves of wheat—and an olive branch and a cornstalk crossed below them. An eagle is the shield's crest. Two black horses support the shield. At the bottom is the state's motto, "Virtue, Liberty, and Independence."

In 1874 a commission was appointed to study changes made to the original design over the years and to adopt an official coat of arms for the commonwealth. In 1875 the commissioners chose the original design.

State Flag

The State Flag was authorized by the General Assembly in 1799 and standardized in 1907. The flag is blue, the same shade as the blue in the flag of the United States. The State Coat of Arms is embroidered on it. The edges are trimmed with a knotted fringe of yellow, 2½ inches wide.

Official Symbols

The General Assembly has designated the following official symbols:

State Tree: hemlock
State Bird: ruffed grouse
State Flower: mountain laurel
State Animal: white-tailed deer
State Dog: Great Dane
State Fish: brook trout
State Insect: firefly
State Beverage: milk
State Fossil: *Phacops rana,* a small water animal
Official beautification and conservation plant: Penngift crownvetch
Flagship of Pennsylvania: the restored U.S. Brig *Niagara,* the ship of the hero of the Battle of Lake Erie, Oliver Hazard Perry

State Song

"Pennsylvania," written and composed by Eddie Khoury and Ronnie Bonner, became the official state song for all public events in 1990.

Verse 1
> Pennsylvania, Pennsylvania,
> Mighty is your name,
> Steeped in glory and tradition,
> Object of acclaim.
> Where brave men fought the foe of freedom,
> Tyranny decried,

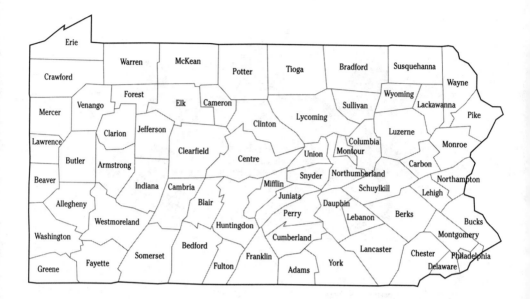

'Til the bell of independence
Filled the countryside.

Chorus
Pennsylvania, Pennsylvania,
May your future be,
Filled with honor everlasting
As your history.

Verse 2
Pennsylvania, Pennsylvania,
Blessed by God's own hand,
Birthplace of a mighty nation,
Keystone of the land.
Where first our country's flag
unfolded,
Freedom to proclaim,
May the voices of tomorrow
Glorify your name.

Chorus
Pennsylvania, Pennsylvania,
May your future be,
Filled with honor everlasting
As your history.

State Nickname
Pennsylvania is referred to as the Keystone State. Keystone is an architectural term referring to the central, wedge-shaped stone in an arch that holds the other stones in place. The origin of the reference to the state is lost. In the early 19th century, it came into use as an allusion to the geographical location of the state within the 13 original colonies. The modern reference is to Pennsylvania's key role in the development of the nation.

Pennsylvania History

EARLIEST INHABITANTS

Anthropologists have identified the Native Americans who inhabited what is now Pennsylvania at the time of the first European settlement as Stone Age people who had migrated from Asia sometime between 8000 and 6000 B.C. over a land bridge that existed across the Bering Strait.

Their artifacts were made of wood and stone, their homes of bark, and their clothing of animal skins. They traveled the streams and rivers by canoe; on land, they walked. They lived by hunting and food gathering, and on the crops of their rudimentary agriculture, especially corn. They were completely unaware of the existence of European culture until it descended upon them in the 17th century.

The three most important tribes were the Delaware (Leni-Lenape), the Susquehannock, and Shawnee. The Native Americans and the colonists never learned to live together harmoniously. Almost every aspect of their cultures conflicted. The vital difference was in how they viewed the ownership of the land. The Delaware, for example, thought that the land, air and water were owned by everyone and no one. When they signed treaties, they thought that they were simply agreeing to allow the white man to share the land. They never would have agreed to leave their land.

Those Native Americans that did not fall prey to war, disease, or the changing fortunes of the various colonial governments and armies with whom they made alliances eventually migrated north and west out of Pennsylvania.

COLONIAL PENNSYLVANIA

There are two aspects of the founding of Pennsylvania that set it apart from the other American colonies:

William Penn, the founder, was a Quaker, a religion which had been a persecuted minority sect in England, and provided for religious freedom for all in his First Frame of Government, which was adopted by the General Assembly in 1682.

Penn recognized the land rights of the Indians and insisted that they be paid for the lands taken from them by settlers. Two-thirds of the land in Pennsylvania was purchased by 1768; the entire commonwealth by 1789.

CHRONOLOGICAL HISTORY

1608 Capt. John Smith of Virginia, while traveling on the Susquehanna River, meets the Susquehannock, the first recorded European contact with Pennsylvania Indians.

1609 Henry Hudson, an Englishman exploring for the Dutch, enters Delaware Bay.

1610 Capt. Samuel Argall of Virginia names the Delaware Bay for Lord de la Ware, governor of Virginia.

1615 Étienne Brule, a French explorer, becomes the first white man to reach the interior of Pennsylvania.

1616 Capt. Cornelius Henderson of the Dutch ship *Onrust* visits the Schuylkill River and claims the land.

1623 The Dutch construct Fort Nassau on the New Jersey side of the Delaware River, the first recorded settlement.

1638 The Swedish West India Company, led by Peter Minuit, builds Fort Christiana, near present-day Wilmington, the first Swedish settlement.

1641 Settlers from Connecticut settle on the Schuylkill River. The settlement failed.

1643 Gov. John Printz establishes the capital of New Sweden on Tinicum Island, the first Swedish settlement in Pennsylvania. A Lutheran church, the first church in Pennsylvania, was consecrated on the site.

1644 Swedes found Upland, now Chester. William Penn is born in London.

1647 The Quaker religion is founded in England.

1648 The Dutch establish Fort Bevesrade, a trading post, along the Schuylkill River.

1653 The Iroquois destroy the Erie Indians.

1655 Gov. Peter Stuyvesant of New Netherlands seizes New Sweden.

1664 The Dutch settlements on the Delaware River are taken over by the English.

1673 The Dutch retake those Delaware River settlements.

1674 The English regain the Delaware River settlements under the Treaty of Westminster. The Duke of York appoints Sir Edmund Andros as governor of the settlements.

1675 The Iroquois crush the Susquehannock.

1680 William Penn petitions for a grant of land.

1681 The boundaries of Penn's province are established as the land between 39 and 42 degrees north latitude and from the Delaware River westward for 5 degrees of longitude. King Charles II signs the charter for Pennsylvania. Penn commissions William Markham, his cousin, deputy governor. Markham summons a council of nine men at Upland, beginning the government of Pennsylvania.

1682 Penn issues his First Frame of Government for the province. He departs England on the *Welcome* in September, arrives at Upland in October, and changes its name to Chester. In December, the First Assembly meets at Chester and enacts "The Great Law," which guarantees religious freedom in the province.

1683 Penn issues his Second Frame of Government with the cooperation of the Assembly. Francis Pastorius founds Germantown. Caleb Pusey builds a house in Chester that will survive to become the oldest building in Pennsylvania.

1684 William Penn goes back to England, not to return for fifteen years.

1685 Samuel Adkins publishes *Kalandarium Pennsilvaniense,* the first book published in Pennsylvania.

1688 The Germantown Society of Friends records the first vote condemning slavery in America.

1690 William Rittenhouse builds the first paper mill in America, on the Wissahickon Creek.

1692 Penn is deprived of his province by the English sovereigns King William and Queen Mary.

1694 The province is restored to Penn.

1699 Penn returns to Pennsylvania.

1701 Penn grants the Charter of Privileges, the constitution that governed Pennsylvania until 1776. Penn issues a charter to the city of Philadelphia. Penn returns to England, leaving the province in the hands of resident governors.

1703 Three lower counties establish a separate assembly, thereby establishing the state of Delaware.

1708 William Penn enters a gentlemen's debtors' prison in London—he is confined to an inn and his movement is restricted.

1710 The great migration of Germans and Scots-Irish to Pennsylvania begins.

1716 Thomas Rutter establishes the first ironworks in Pennsylvania, in Berks County.

1718 William Penn dies on July 30, at age 74.

1719 Andrew Bradford publishes the *American Weekly Mercury,* the first newspaper in Pennsylvania.

1723 Benjamin Franklin arrives in Philadelphia. The first paper money is issued by the provincial government.

1729 Franklin publishes the *Pennsylvania Gazette.*

1731 The Library Company of Philadelphia is founded.

1732 Conrad Beissel founds the Ephrata Cloister.

1737 The "Walking Purchase" of land from the Indians occurs: The Delaware Indians agree to sell a tract of land defined as the distance a man could walk in a day and half; the Provincial Government hires runners rather than walkers. Penn's sons, in promoting this, destroy all of the respect their late father earned for them.

1740 The University of Pennsylvania is founded.

1741 *American Magazine,* or *Monthly View,* America's first magazine, is published in Philadelphia.

1742 Henry Muhlenberg, a Lutheran leader, arrives in Pennsylvania.

1743 The American Philosophical Society is founded by Benjamin Franklin.

1747 Franklin organizes the Associates for the Defense of Philadelphia, financed by a public lottery.

1748 Linden Hall School for Girls opens in Lititz. James Hamilton becomes the first American-born governor.

1749 The French claim territory along the Allegheny River.

1751 Pennsylvania Hospital, the first in America, is chartered in Philadelphia.

1752 The Philadelphia Contributorship for the Insurance of Houses from Loss by Fire, the first insurance company in America, is chartered. Franklin performs his kite-flying experiment to discover the similarity between lightning and electric matter.

1753 George Washington is sent by the governor of Virginia to warn the French to leave Fort LeBoeuf.

1754 The French capture a fort on the Ohio River and complete construction of it as Fort Duquesne. Thus, the French and Indian War (1754–63) begins. Washington surrenders Fort Necessity to the French.

1755 French troops and Indians ambush General Braddock as his troops march to attack Fort Duquesne. The first Indian massacre occurs at Penns Creek.

1756 Col. John Armstrong destroys the Indian village of Kittanning.

1757 The first streetlights, designed by Benjamin Franklin, are installed in Philadelphia.

1758 Gen. John Forbes takes possession of Fort Duquesne, destroyed by the French as they retreated, and names the site Pittsburgh. Fort Pitt, the largest fortification in America, is erected.

1762 Anthracite coal is discovered in the Wyoming Valley.

1763 An Indian attack on Detroit marks the beginning of Pontiac's War. Indians capture Fort LeBoeuf and prepare to attack Fort Pitt. Col. Henry Bouquet, with a force of 500 men, defeats the Indians at Bushy Run, 20 miles from Fort Pitt, thereby ending the war.

1764 John Campbell lays out Pittsburgh.

1765 Philadelphia merchants protest the Stamp Act. The first medical school in America is established at the College of Philadelphia, now the University of Pennsylvania.

1766 The Stamp Act is repealed by Parliament, largely due to the efforts of Benjamin Franklin.

1767 Thomas Godfrey's *The Prince of Parthia,* the first play written by an American colonist, is produced in Philadelphia. John Dickinson's *Letters of a Pennsylvania Farmer,* which asked the English government for moderation in its dealings with the colonies, is published.

1768 Philadelphia merchants protest the Townshend Acts, taxes on imports, by agreeing not to import the taxed items. The boundary between New York and Pennsylvania is decided at Fort Stanwix by treaty with the Six Nations Indian tribes.

1769 Connecticut settlers arrive in the Wyoming Valley starting a long-term battle for territory known as the Yankee-Pennamite Wars.

1770 British repeal all taxes on imports, except those on tea.

1773 John Penn becomes resident governor.

1774 The First Continental Congress meets in Carpenters' Hall.

1775 The Second Continental Congress meets and appoints George Washington as commander-in-chief of the Army. The *Experiment,* the first boat of the Pennsylvania Navy, is launched.

1776 The Pennsylvania Navy forces the retreat of two British warships. The Declaration of Independence is adopted. The Pennsylvania Constitutional Convention assumes control of state government and passes a new constitution. The Provincial Assembly adjourns, ending proprietary government. The first arsenal of the United States is established at Carlisle. Washington crosses the Delaware River from Bucks County to defeat the British at Trenton on Christmas night.

1777 Congress adopts a national flag on June 14. Washington's forces are defeated at Brandywine and the Paoli Massacre. British troops under General Howe occupy Philadelphia. Congress meets in Lancaster on September 27, and in York beginning September 30. In October, British troops win the Battle of Germantown; Washington's forces take up winter quarters at Valley Forge.

1778 In June, British forces leave Philadelphia and Congress returns from York. British and Indian forces attack settlers in the "Wyoming Massacre." Congress adopts the Articles of Confederation.

1780 The General Assembly abolishes slavery in Pennsylvania. The Bank of Pennsylvania is formed.

1781 Pennsylvania Line (the military unit) mutinies over lack of pay. The Bank of North America is chartered.

1782 Indians destroy Hannastown, the county seat of Westmoreland County.

1783 The Revolutionary War ends.

1784 The *Pennsylvania Packet and Daily Advertiser,* the first successful daily newspaper in America, is published in Philadelphia.

1785 Dr. Benjamin Rush establishes the first dispensary, in Philadelphia.

1786 The *Pittsburgh Gazette,* the first newspaper west of the Alleghenies, begins publication.

1787 Pennsylvania is the second state to ratify the U.S. Constitution. The Pittsburgh Academy, the forerunner of the University of Pittsburgh, is chartered. Bethel African Methodist Episcopal Church is founded.

1789 Frederick A. Muhlenberg of Lancaster is elected the first speaker of the U.S. House of Representatives. The New York–Pennsylvania boundary is established at 42 degrees north latitude, its current location.

1790 State population: 434,373. Philadelphia is named capital of the United States. The second State Constitution is adopted; Thomas Mifflin becomes first governor. Benjamin Franklin dies.

1791 The Bank of the United States is established in Philadelphia. Philadelphia carpenters strike for a 12-hour workday.

1792 The U.S. Mint opens in Philadelphia. The U.S. government sells the land in the Erie Triangle to the state.

1793 The first iron furnace begins production in Pittsburgh.

1794 Western Pennsylvania farmers protest against a tax on distilled spirits; the "Whiskey Rebllion" is suppressed by federal troops led by President Washington.

1795 The Philadelphia-Lancaster Turnpike, America's first paved road, opens.

1798 "Hail Columbia," the first national song, is written by Joseph Hopkinson of Philadelphia.

1799 Southeastern Pennsylvanians protest against a new federal property tax; the "Hot Water Rebellion" is suppressed by state militia. Lancaster becomes the state capital.

1800 State population: 602,364. The U.S. capital is moved from Philadelphia to Washington, D.C.

1804 The first stagecoach line to the west is established. The first Pittsburgh bank opens.

1805 The Pennsylvania Academy of the Fine Arts establishes the first public art museum in Philadelphia.

1808 Judge Fell of Wilkes-Barre demonstrates the commercial value of anthracite coal.

1810 State population: 810,000

1811 The steamboat era begins when the *New Orleans* departs Pittsburgh for New Orleans.

1812 Harrisburg becomes the state capital. War with England, financed by Philadelphia entrepreneurs, begins.

1813 Oliver Hazard Perry defeats the British fleet in the Battle of Lake Erie, saving the Old Northwest and giving control of the Upper Great Lakes to the United States.

1818 Philadelphia's public school system begins operation.

1819 The first savings bank in the United States, the Philadelphia Savings Fund Society, is chartered.

1820 State population: 1,040,458. The Lehigh Canal opens between Mauch Chunk and Easton.

1822 The state capitol building in Harrisburg is completed at a cost of $135,000.

1824 The Historical Society of Pennsylvania—the Franklin Institute—is organized.

1829 The first locomotive in America, the *Stourbridge Lion,* begins operation between Honesdale and Carbondale. The Delaware and Hudson Canal is opened between Honesdale, Pennsylvania, and Kingston, New York.

1830 State population: 1,348,000

1831 Matthias Baldwin builds the first domestic locomotive.

1833 A national antislavery league is formed in Philadelphia.

1834 The Free School Law is enacted, the beginning of a great expansion of public schools.

1835 Pittsburgh's first public school opens.

1838 The third Constitution of Pennsylvania is adopted; it gives white voters more voice in government but disfranchises black voters.

1839 The Whig Party, predecessor to the Republican Party, nominates William Henry Harrison as its presidential candidate, at Zion Lutheran Church in Harrisburg.

1840 State population: 1,724,033. Harrison is elected president. A financial crash occurs; banks fail due to government overspending on public works, especially canals.

1841 Commercial production of coke begins, in Connellsville.

1842 The Philadelphia and Reading Railroad begins operation.

1844 Anti-Catholic religious riots take place among Native Americans in Kensington.

1845 Fire destroys about one-third of the city of Pittsburgh.

1846 The Pennsylvania and the Lehigh Valley Railroads are chartered. The first telegram is sent, from Harrisburg to Lancaster.

1847 The American Medical Association is founded in Philadelphia.

1848 James Gowen establishes the first agriculture school, in Mount Airy. The state legislature grants married women the right to own property.

1850 State population: 2,312,000. The first medical college for women, the Women's Medical College of Pennsylvania, is established.

1851 Riots occur in Christiana (Lancaster County) when citizens refuse to return runaway slaves.

1852 The Pennsylvania State Teachers Association is organized in Pittsburgh. The Pennsylvania Railroad reaches Pittsburgh.

1854 The Pennsylvania Railroad Main Line opens from Philadelphia to the suburbs. The city and county of Philadelphia are consolidated by an act of the General Assembly.

1855 The first State Normal School for the training of teachers opens in Millersville (Lancaster County). The Pennsylvania State University is established by the Land Grant Act.

1857 James Buchanan, the only Pennsylvanian to have achieved the presidency, is inaugurated.

1859 "Colonel" Drake drills the first productive oil well, near Titusville.

1860 State population: 2,906,215

1861 The Civil War begins. Five Pennsylvania militia companies are the first troops to arrive in Washington; ultimately over 350,000 Pennsylvanians will serve. Governor Curtin, the state's first Republican governor, is a major supporter of the war effort and of President Lincoln. The Camp Curtin training center, established in Harrisburg, becomes a major troop center.

1862 Confederates stage a lightning raid on Chambersburg.

1863 The Battle of Gettysburg takes place July 1–3; Lincoln's Gettysburg Address on November 19 dedicates the battlefield as a National Cemetery.

1864 The Confederates burn Chambersburg.

1865 John Stetson opens his hat company in Philadelphia.

1869 George Westinghouse organizes the Westinghouse Air Brake Company in Philadelphia.

1870 State population: 3,522,000. Judge Mellon establishes a private bank in Pittsburgh, T. Mellon & Sons.

1873 Financial panic, known as "the Panic of 1873," begins with the failure of a Philadelphia bank, Jay Cooke & Co.

1874 The fourth Constitution of Pennsylvania is adopted; it mostly provides for more elected officials.

1876 The Centennial International Exhibition in Philadelphia celebrates 100 years of independence. At the exhibition, Alexander Graham Bell demonstrates the telephone. Bell Telephone will open its first exchange two years later.

1877 Ten "Molly Maguires," militant coal miners, are hanged, in Pottsville and Mauch Chunk. The violent and destructive "Great Railroad Strike of 1877" against the Pennsylvania Railroad begins in Pittsburgh and spreads to Scranton and Reading.

1880 State population: 4,282,891

1881 A labor convention in Pittsburgh ultimately leads to the organization of the American Federation of Labor.

1883 Thomas Edison opens an electric lighting plant in Sunbury. The Philadelphia Phillies Baseball Club is founded.

1885 The University of Pittsburgh Medical School opens.

1886 The first successful electric streetcar system in America begins operation in Scranton.

1888 The Pittsburgh Reduction Company, which later becomes the Aluminum Company of America, is founded in Pittsburgh. Temple University is chartered.

1889 Johnstown is destroyed by flood; 2,209 die.

1890 State population: 5,258,000

1891 The secret ballot is adopted for Pennsylvania elections. Andrew Carnegie funds Carnegie Library, Music Hall, and the Museum of Natural History in Pittsburgh.

1892 The five-month-long Homestead Steel strike ends in November. The workers return defeated as the state militia opens the plant to strikebreakers. The strike was caused by an 18 to 26 percent cut in wages proposed by Carnegie Steel Works.

1893 The State Forestry Commission is established.

1895 The State Superior Court system, the Department of Agriculture, and the State Game Commission are established. The Compulsory Education Law is signed.

1897 The state capitol building is destroyed by fire.

1898 The Pennsylvania National Guard mobilizes at Mount Gretna for war with Spain. Pennsylvania units see action in Puerto Rico and the Philippines, but not in Cuba.

1900 State population: 6,302,115. The Philadelphia Symphony Orchestra is organized.

1901 Philadelphia City Hall is completed. The first Mummers Parade marches up Broad Street. United States Steel Corporation is formed.

1902 Andrew Carnegie funds Carnegie Technical School.

1903 Milton Hershey lays out the town of Hershey in Dauphin County and begins mass production of chocolate.

1904 Bethlehem Steel incorporates, after Charles Schwab merges his small steel company with U.S. Shipbuilding in 1903.

1905 The Pennsylvania State Police is created. H. J. Heinz incorporates.

The first all-motion-picture theater in the world opens in Pittsburgh.

1906 The new state capitol building, built and furnished at a cost of $13,000,000, is dedicated by President Theodore Roosevelt.

1907 The Market Street Subway in Philadelphia opens.

1910 State population: 7,665,000. The *Pittsburgh Courier*, which becomes an influential black newspaper, publishes its first edition. The Philadelphia Athletics baseball team wins the World Series this year, as well as in 1911 and 1913.

1911 Henry Bass, a Philadelphia Republican, is elected to the Pennsylvania Assembly, becoming the first black legislator.

1912 Leopold Stokowski becomes conductor of the Philadelphia Orchestra.

1913 The State Assembly approves the women's suffrage amendment, but it is defeated at the polls. This occurs again in 1915.

1915 The Workmen's Compensation Act is passed. The Philadelphia Phillies baseball team wins the National League pennant. The team will not win another pennant for 35 years or win a World Series for 65 years.

1917 The United States becomes involved in World War I. The first Pennsylvania troops sail for Europe in November; about 300,000 will eventually serve, including two generals who become successful chiefs of staff. The state's industrial complex provides massive amounts of war materiel.

1918 World War I ends. A worldwide influenza epidemic that killed a total of 20 million kills 12,000 in Philadelphia.

1919 Pennsylvania is the seventh state to ratify the 19th Amendment, giving women the right to vote. Major strikes in steel and coal industries occur.

1920 State population: 8,720,000. Radio station KDKA, Pittsburgh, produces the first scheduled radio broadcast in the world, with the results of the Harding-Cox election.

1923 The Administrative Code reorganizes state government.

1925 The United Mine Workers strike for 170 days into 1926, causing both immediate and long-term problems for consumers.

1926 The Delaware River Bridge opens. Philadelphia holds a Sesquicentennial Exposition.

1928 The Philadelphia Museum of Art and the Broad Street Subway open.

1929 The Fiscal Code reorganizes the state's financial affairs.

1930 State population: 9,631,350

1932 Industrial production in the state is 50 percent less than 1929 levels. Cox's jobless army leaves Pittsburgh for Washington.

1933 The Philadelphia Eagles Football Club is organized. With the repeal of Prohibition, all wine and liquor stores are put under state control.

1935 George Earle becomes first Democrat to hold the governorship in 45 years; U.S. senator Joseph Guffey becomes first Democrat elected to the Senate in 50 years.

1936 Governor Earle calls a special session of the State Assembly and launches his "Little New Deal." Floods in Pittsburgh, the worst in history, and in central Pennsylvania cause heavy damage and loss of 126 lives.

1938 The newly organized Congress of Industrial Organizations elects John L. Lewis its first president at its meeting in Pittsburgh.

1939 A pre–World War II industrial flurry begins to lift the state out of the economic doldrums.

1940 State population: 9,900,180. The Pennsylvania National Guard begins mobilization and the first registration for a military draft is held. The first section of the Pennsylvania Turnpike, the first superhighway in America, opens between Irwin and Carlisle.

1941 World War II begins; 1.25 million Pennsylvanians eventually serve, including 130 admirals and generals. Forty military bases are established in the state. The industrial complex of the state ranks sixth in war production, fifth in shipbuilding, and fourth in ordnance production.

1942 Rationing programs and statewide blackouts go into effect.

1944 Philadelphia transit workers strike over the issue of the hiring of black motormen; the federal government takes over the system for three days.

1945 Gov. Edward Martin proclaims a two-day holiday to celebrate the end of World War II on August 14. The State Council of Defense, which had organized 1.5 million civilians to help in the war effort, is dissolved.

1946 A huge postwar strike wave includes Pennsylvania workers in bituminous coal, steel, railroads, and Duquesne Power and Light Company.

1948 The Pennsylvania Turnpike reaches Philadelphia.

1950 State population: 10,498,012

1951 The Democratic Party wins control of Philadelphia for the first time since 1884; Joseph Clark is elected as mayor and Richardson Dilworth as attorney general.

1952 The first black state police officer is hired.

1953 The Salk vaccine, developed by Dr. Jonas Salk of the University of Pittsburgh, is formally certified to prevent polio; mass inoculations begin. The first successful open-heart surgery is performed at Jefferson Medical College, Philadelphia.

1954 Sen. George Leader is elected governor, the first Democrat since 1933. Genevieve Blatt is elected secretary of internal affairs, becoming the first woman to hold a constitutional office. The Philadelphia Athletics baseball team moves to Kansas City. The Philadelphia International Airport is dedicated. WQED, the first public television station, begins broadcasting in Pittsburgh.

1958 Anne Alpern is the first woman elected attorney general. Robert Nix, Jr., becomes the first African American elected to the U.S. Congress from Pennsylvania. The first nuclear power plant in the United States opens in Shippingport.

1960 State population: 11,319,366. The Pittsburgh Pirates win the World Series. The first statewide strike against the Pennsylvania Railroad results in the layoff of 3,000 workers. The General Assembly convenes its first annual session.

1961 Harness racing in Philadelphia and Sunday liquor sales in hotels are approved. A major school district consolidation law is enacted; fiercely fought, it would be amended in 1963, ultimately reducing the number of school districts from 2,500 to 500.

1962 Fire in an abandoned coal mine in Centralia proves impossible to extinguish and leads to the gradual abandonment of the town. Republican congressman William Scranton is elected governor; he will seek the Republican Party nomination for the presidency in 1964, fail, and serve as governor until 1967.

1963 Frank Rizzo is appointed police commissioner of Philadelphia.

1964 Rioting in North Philadelphia's black neighborhoods causes two deaths, 500 injuries, and $3 million property damage; 700 are arrested.

1965 Forty-one counties are declared drought disaster areas by the U.S. Department of Agriculture.

1967 Demonstrations are held against the Vietnam War, Dow Chemical, and the CIA at the University of Pennsylvania. Herbert Arlene is the first African American elected to the State Senate.

1968 The Constitution of 1968 is adopted; it allows the governor to serve two consecutive terms and contains a sex equality section, which the voters approve in 1972.

1970 State population: 11,793,909. United Mine Workers leaders Joseph Yablonski and his family are murdered in Clarksville. Philadelphia police battle Black Panthers. The Steelers win the first of their four 1970s Super Bowls. The first teachers' strike in Philadelphia closes the schools for four days.

1971 Police Commissioner Frank Rizzo is elected mayor of Philadelphia. The General Assembly passes the first state personal income tax, a graduated income tax, in March, repeals it in August, and replaces it with a flat-rate income tax. Robert Nix, Jr., becomes the first black justice of the Pennsylvania Supreme Court.

1972 Tropical storm Agnes causes the worst flooding ever; 50 die and 250,000 are left homeless. Voters ratify the Equal Rights Amendment. The first state lottery tickets are sold.

1973 Liquor store clerks strike for a new two-year contract; Philadelphia teachers strike for 52 days, win major increase in pay and benefits.

1974 Milton Shapp becomes first governor to succeed himself in the 20th century. Philadelphia Flyers win their first Stanley Cup in hockey. The Assembly retires the death penalty by overriding the governor's veto.

1975 Mayor Rizzo is reelected. Flyers win Stanley Cup again. Unionized state employees strike for higher wages, the first legal statewide public employees' strike in the nation's history. Legionnaires' disease causes the death of 23 people attending an American Legion convention in Philadelphia.

1976 The Liberty Bell is moved to Independence Mall in Philadelphia to accommodate Bicentennial crowds. John Heinz III is elected to the U.S. Senate. Volkswagen announces that it will build cars at the New Stanton plant abandoned by Chrysler.

1977 Johnstown flood number four leaves 50 dead and 50,000 homeless. Blessed John N. Neumann, fourth bishop of Philadelphia (1851–60), is canonized as a Roman Catholic saint. K. Leroy Irvins becomes the first black speaker of a state house of representatives in America.

1978 Legendary representative Daniel J. Flood is indicted for corruption; he

is allowed to resign his office in 1980. Philadelphia police storm MOVE headquarters; one policeman is killed, seven injured. Nine members of MOVE are ultimately convicted of third-degree murder in 1980.

1979 The Three Mile Island nuclear plant malfunctions, releasing radiation into the air and riveting the nation's attention.

1980 State population: 11,864,000. The Philadelphia Phillies win their first world championship. Three congressmen are indicted for bribery after an FBI undercover operation. Two are imprisoned; one, found not guilty, is reelected.

1982 Heinz is reelected to Senate. A lottery official and an accomplice are sentenced to seven years in prison for fixing the lottery in 1981.

1983 W. Wilson Goode is the first African American elected mayor of Philadelphia. An outbreak of avian influenza in poultry eventually forces farmers to destroy 16 million turkeys and chickens before a quarantine is lifted in 1984. An independent truckers' strike leads to terrorism and violence on the Pennsylvania Turnpike.

1984 Deputy Attorney General John Kerr is convicted of 139 counts of bribery in a job-selling scheme. The no-fault automobile insurance law is repealed.

1985 Tornadoes in the Lake Erie area kill sixty-four and destroy twenty-five hundred homes and businesses. Philadelphia police bomb MOVE headquarters in a private home after a two-day siege, killing 11, including five children, and destroying 60 homes in a three-block area. The Three Mile Island nuclear plant is reactivated.

1986 Robert Casey, former auditor general, wins governorship on his fourth try. State Treasurer R. Budd Dwyer is convicted of 11 counts of bribery. In 1988, Dwyer commits suicide at a televised press conference.

1987 Governor Casey undergoes quadruple bypass surgery. The New Stanton Volkswagen plant closes, leaving 5,000 unemployed.

1988 Summer drought and heat wave ruin crops. June to August have 54 days of 90 degrees or higher, with 11 days over 100 degrees. An Ashland Oil Company tank falls into the Monongahela River, causing a 1-million-gallon spill, which reaches the Ohio River. Environmental legislation is passed that includes mandatory recycling, hazardous waste cleanup, and the Pennvest program for water and sewer construction.

1990 State population: 11,882,000.

1992 Thirteen members of the 14th Quartermaster Detachment from Greensburg are killed by an Iraqi missile during Operation Desert Storm.

1993 Governor Casey undergoes a rare double-organ transplant in Pittsburgh. Sen. Arlen Specter undergoes brain surgery.

1994 Ernie Preate, state attorney general and 1994 candidate for governor, resigns and goes to prison for 14 months after a plea bargain over campaign contribution improprieties. Rolf Jensen, Supreme Court justice, is impeached for misusing the power of the bench.

1995 The Philadelphia Naval Shipyard closes. Widespread malfeasance by members of Philadelphia Police Precinct 39 leads to the overturning of many convictions and to lawsuits against the city.

COUNTY HISTORICAL SOCIETIES

The goal of county historical societies is to preserve and maintain the records and the history of the counties. They promote interest in each county's cultural and historic legacy, encouraging historical research and study. They collect and preserve books, newspapers, maps, letters, manuscripts, and material objects of historic interest. Some societies maintain historic buildings or have their headquarters in them.

Adams County Historical Society
    111 W. Confederate Ave.
    Gettysburg, PA 17325
Allegheny–Kiski Valley Historical
    Society
    224 E. Seventh Ave.
    Tarentum, PA 15084
Armstrong County Historical Society
    and Museum
    300 N. McKean St.
    Kittanning, PA 16201
Beaver County Historical Research and
    Landmarks Foundation
    Box 1
    Freedom, PA 15042
Bedford County–Pioneer Historical
    Society
    242 E. John St.
    Bedford, PA 15522
Berks County Historical Society
    940 Center Ave.
    Reading, PA 19601
Blair County Historical Society
    Box 1083
    Altoona, PA 16603
Bradford County Historical Society
    45 E. Corydon St.
    Bradford, PA 16701
Bucks County Historical Society
    130 Swamp Rd.
    Doylestown, PA 18901

Butler County Historical Society
  Box 414
  Butler, PA 16001
Cambria County Historical Society
  615 N. Center St.
  Ebensburg, PA 15931
Cameron County Historical Society
  102 W. Fourth St.
  Emporium, PA 15834
Carbon County Historical Society
  Box 273
  Jim Thorpe, PA 18229
Centre County Historical Society
  1001 E. College Ave.
  State College, PA 16801
Chester County Historical Society
  225 N. High St.
  West Chester, PA 19380
Clarion County
  18 Grant Ave.
  Clarion, PA 16214
Clearfield County Historical Society
  104 E. Pine St.
  Clearfield, PA 16214
Clinton County Historical Society
  362 E. Water St.
  Lock Haven, PA 17245
Columbia County Historical Society
  410 Main St.
  Orangeville, PA 17859
Crawford County Historical Society
  848 N. Main St.
  Meadville, PA 16335
Cumberland County Historical Society
  21 N. Pitt St.
  Carlisle, PA 17013
Dauphin County Historical Society
  219 S. Front St.
  Harrisburg, PA 17104
Delaware County Historical Society
  85 N. Malin Rd.
  Broomall, PA 19008
Elk County Historical Society
  109 Center St.
  Ridgway, PA 15853

Erie County Historical Society
  417 State St.
  Erie, PA 16501
Fayette County Historical Society
  Box 193
  Uniontown, PA 15401
Forest County Historical Society
  Box 405
  Marienville, PA 16239
Franklin County Heritage
  175 E. King St.
  Chambersburg, PA 17201
Fulton County Historical Society
  112 Lincoln Way East
  McConnellsburg, PA 17233
Greene County Historical Society
  S.R. 2026
  Waynesburg, PA 15370
Huntingdon County Historical Society
  106 Fourth St.
  Huntingdon, PA 16669
Indiana County Historical Society
  200 S. Sixth St.
  Indiana, PA 15701
Jefferson County Historical Society
  232 Jefferson St.
  Brookville, PA 15825
Juniata County Historical Society
  498 Jefferson St.
  Mifflintown, PA 17059
Lackawanna County Historical Society
  232 Monroe Ave.
  Scranton, PA 18505
Lancaster County Historical Society
  230 N. President Ave.
  Lancaster, PA 17603
Lawrence County Historical Society
  408 N. Jefferson St.
  New Castle, PA 16103
Lebanon County Historical Society
  924 Cumberland St.
  Lebanon, PA 17042
Lehigh County Historical Society
  501 Hamilton St.
  Allentown, PA 17042

Luzerne County–Wyoming Historical
and Geological Society
49 S. Franklin St.
Wyoming, PA 18644

Lycoming County Historical Society
888 W. Fourth St.
Williamsport, PA 17701

McKean County Historical Society
Courthouse
Smethport, PA 16749

Mercer County Historical Society
119 S. Pitt St.
Mercer, PA 16137

Mifflin County Historical Society
1 W. Market St.
Lewistown, PA 17044

Monroe County Historical Society
537 Ann St.
Stroudsburg, PA 18360

Montgomery County Historical Society
1654 DeKalb St.
Norristown, PA 19401

Montour County Historical Society
1 Bloom St.
Danville, PA 17821

Northampton County Historical Society
107 S. Fourth St.
Easton, PA 18042

Northumberland County Historical
Society
1150 N. Front St.
Sunbury, PA 17801

Perry County Historical Society
Box 73
Newport, PA 17074

Philadelphia County–Historical Society
of Pennsylvania
1300 Locust St.
Philadelphia, PA 19107

Pike County Historical Society
608 Broad St.
Milford, PA 18337

Potter County Historical Society
308 N. Main St.
Coudersport, PA 16915

Schuylkill County Historical Society
14 N. Third St.
Pottsville, PA 17901

Snyder County Historical Society
30 E. Market St.
Middleburg, PA 17842

Somerset County Historical and
Genealogical Society
R.D. 2
Somerset, PA 15501

Sullivan County Historical Society
Courthouse Square
Laporte, PA 18626

Susquehanna County Historical
Society
Box 174
Barnesboro, PA 15714

Tioga County Historical Society
120 Main St.
Wellsboro, PA 16901

Union County Historical Society
103 S. Second St.
Lewisburg, PA 17837

Venango County Historical Society
301 S. Park St.
Franklin, PA 16323

Warren County Historical Society
204 Fourth Ave.
Warren, PA 16365

Washington County Historical Society
49 Maiden St.
Washington, PA 15301

Wayne County Historical Society
810 Main St.
Honesdale, PA 18431

Westmoreland County Historical
Society
951 Old Salem Rd.
Greensburg, PA 15601

Wyoming County Historical Society
Box 309
Tunkhannock, PA 18657

York County Historical Society
250 E. Market St.
York, PA 17403

HISTORIC PLACES AND LANDMARKS

Pennsylvania currently has 2,575 sites on the National Register of Historic Places. This is the official list of the nation's cultural resources deemed worthy of preservation. It is part of a national program to coordinate and support public efforts to identify, evaluate, and protect our historic and archaeological resources. Properties listed in the National Register include districts, sites, buildings, structures, and objects that are significant in American history, architecture, archaeology, engineering, and culture. They must possess integrity of location, design, setting, materials, workmanship, feeling, and association and be associated with events that have made a significant contribution to the broad patterns of history or with the lives of persons significant in the past. Further, they must embody the distinctive characteristics of a type, period, or method of construction; represent the work of a master; possess high artistic value; or represent a significant and distinguishable entity whose components may lack individual distinction. They also must have yielded, or may be likely to yield, information important in prehistory or history.

The National Landmarks Program focuses on the National Register sites of nationwide significance. The National Historic Landmarks in Pennsylvania are listed here by name, location, and area of significance, by county.

Adams County

Eisenhower National Historic Site (period: 1950s)
Dwight D. Eisenhower Farmstead, southwest edge of Gettysburg National Military Park, Gettysburg
political and military history

Allegheny County

Allegheny County Courthouse and Jail (period: 1884–88)
436 Grant St., Pittsburgh
architecture
Forks of the Ohio
Point State Park, Pittsburgh
advance of the frontier
Kennywood Park (period: 1898–99)
4800 Kennywood Blvd., West Mifflin
recreation
Oakmont Country Club Historic District (period: 1903)
Hulton Rd., Oakmont
recreation and landscape architecture (Henry C. Fownes)
Smithfield Street Bridge (period: 1883–89)
Smithfield Street at the Monongahela River, Pittsburgh
engineering (Gustav Lindenthal)
Woodville: John Neville House (period: 1785)
PA Route 50, south of Heidelberg
political and military history

Beaver County

Old Economy Village (period: 1825–1905)
PA Route 65 at Ambridge, northwest of Pittsburgh
social and humanitarian movements
Beginning Point of the U.S. Public Land Survey (period: 1795)
west of Glasgow
political and military affairs (1783–1860) and recreation
Matthew S. Quay House (period: c. 1865)
205 College Ave., Beaver
politics

Bedford County

Bedford Springs Hotel (period: 1806–1935)
U.S. Business Route 220 and T408,

Bedford Township
*political and military affairs
(1783–1860) and recreation*
David Espy House (period: 1794)
123 Pitt St., Bedford
political and military history

Berks County
Gruber Wagon Works (period:
1882–1906)
PA Route 183, Tulpehocken Park,
Reading
engineering and transportation
Conrad Weiser House (period: 1729)
Womelsdorf
politics

Blair County
Allegheny Portage Railroad National
Historic Site (period: 1831–34)
U.S. Route 22, Cresson
engineering and transportation
Charles B. Dudley House (period: 1880s)
802 Lexington Ave., Altoona
science, commerce, and communications
Horseshoe Curve (period: 1854)
PA Route 193, 5 miles west of Altoona
engineering and transportation

Bucks County
Andalusia–Nicholas Biddle Estate
(period: 1794, 1934)
PA Route 32, 1.5 miles north of
Philadelphia
*politics and architecture (Thomas U.
Walter)*
Delaware Canal (period: 1827–1930)
west bank of the Delaware River,
Easton to Bristol
commerce, communication, engineering, transportation, and recreation
Fonthill (Mercer Museum, Moravian
Pottery and Tile Works) (period:
1907–16)

Doylestown
*art, industry, and architecture
(Henry C. Mercer)*
Green Hills Farm–Pearl S. Buck House
(period: 1835)
southwest of Dublin on Dublin Rd.
*literature, social and humanitarian
movements*
Honey Hollow Watershed (period: 1939)
PA Route 263, 2 miles south of the
Delaware River, near New Hope
conservation
Summerseat (period: c. 1770)
Clymer St. and Morris Rd.,
Morrisville
politics
Washington Crossing State Park (period:
1776)
between Yardley and New Hope on
the Delaware River
the War for Independence

Butler County
Harmony Historic District (period:
1805–14)
PA Route 68, Harmony
social and humanitarian movements

Cambria County
Cambria Iron Works (period: 19th and
20th centuries)
along Conemaugh River, Johnstown
*industry, ethnic heritage, architecture,
and engineering*

Carbon County
Asa Packer Mansion (period: 1852)
Packer Rd., Jim Thorpe
*architecture, commerce, and
industry*
St. Mark's Episcopal Church (period:
1865–69)
Race and Susquehanna Sts., Jim
Thorpe
architecture (Richard Upjohn)

Chester County

Cedarcraft (Bayard Taylor House)
(period: 1859)
Kennett Square
literature
Humphrey Marshall House (period:
1770–1811)
PA Route 162, 1407 S. Strasburg Rd.,
Marshallton
agriculture
Valley Forge National Historical Park
(period: 1777–78)
Valley Forge
the War for Independence
General Frederick Von Steuben Headquarters (period: 1778)
Valley Forge National Historical Park,
Valley Forge
the War for Independence
Waynesborough (period: 1724–91)
2049 Waynesborough Rd., Paoli
military history

Cumberland County

Carlisle Indian School (period:
1700–1918)
U.S. Route 11, east of Carlisle
*military history, education, sports,
social and humanitarian movements*
Old West, Dickinson College (period:
1804–22)
Dickinson College, Carlisle
architecture (Benjamin H. Latrobe)

Dauphin County

Simon Cameron House (period:
1764–66, c. 1863)
219 S. Front St., Harrisburg
politics
Harrisburg Central Railroad and Train
Shed (period: 1885–87)
Aberdeen St., Harrisburg
engineering
Milton S. Hershey Mansion (period:
1906–1908)

Mansion Rd., Hershey
*community planning, industry, and
architecture (Henry Herr)*

Delaware County

Brandywine Battlefield (period: 1777)
Chadds Ford
the War for Independence
The Printzhof (period: c. 1643)
Taylor Ave. and 2nd St., Essington
politics
1704 House (period: 1704)
Oakland Rd., Dilworthtown
architecture
Benjamin West Birthplace (period: 1724)
Swarthmore College Campus,
Swarthmore
art

Fayette County

Fallingwater (period: 1936–39)
west of PA Route 381, south of Mill
Run
architecture (Frank Lloyd Wright)
Albert Gallatin House (period: 1789)
PA Route 166, Point Marion
politics
Isaac Meason House (period: 1802)
U.S. Route 119, Dunbar
*architecture, landscape architecture
(Adam Wilson)*
Searights Toll House, National Road
(period: 1835)
west of Uniontown on U.S. Route 40
agriculture and transportation

Huntingdon County

East Broad Top Railroad (period: 1872)
U.S. Route 522, 1 mile northwest of
Orbisonia
transportation

Lackawanna County

Terence V. Powderly House (period:
1870–90)

614 N. Main St., Scranton
social and humanitarian movements

Lancaster County
James Buchanan House–Wheatland
(period: 1828)
1120 Marietta Ave., Lancaster
politics
Ephrata Cloister (period: 1740–46)
intersection of U.S. Routes 322 and
222, Ephrata
religion and philosophy
Robert Fulton Birthplace (period:
c. 1765)
8 miles south of Quarryville on U.S.
Route 222
engineering and transportation
Fulton Opera House (period: 1852)
12–14 N. Prince St., Lancaster
architecture (Samuel Sloan)
Stiegel-Coleman House (period:
1756–90)
intersection of PA Route 501 and U.S.
Route 322, Brickerville
commerce and industry

Lebanon County
Bomberger's Distillery (period: c. 1840)
PA Route 501, west of Newmanstown
agriculture and industry
Cornwall Iron Furnace (period: 1742)
Rexmont Rd. and Boyd St., Cornwall
commerce and industry

Lehigh County
George Taylor House (period: 1768)
Front St., Catasauqua
politics

Montgomery County
Augustus Lutheran Church (period:
1743)
7th Ave. E. and Main St., Trappe
architecture
Graeme Park (period: 1721–22)

Keith Valley Rd., Horsham
architecture
Grey Towers–William Welsh Harrison
House (period: 1893)
Easton Rd. and Limekiln Pike,
Glenside
architecture (Horace Trumbauer)
Merion Cricket Club (period: 1896–97)
Montgomery Ave. and Grays Lane,
Haverford
*architecture (Frank Furness) and
recreation*
Mill Grove (period: 1762–65)
Pawling Rd., Audubon
art, conservation, science, and recreation
M. Carey Thomas Library (period:
1807–1922)
Bryn Mawr College, Bryn Mawr
education
Washington's Headquarters–Isaac Potts
House (period: 18th century)
Valley Forge National Historical Park
the War for Independence

Northampton County
Gemeinhaus–De Schweinitz–Lewis
David Residence (period: 1733)
West Church St., Bethlehem
science
1762 Waterworks (period: 1762)
Bethlehem, Monocacy Creek Area
architecture

Northumberland County
Joseph Priestley House (period: c. 1794)
Priestley Ave., Northumberland
science

Philadelphia County
Academy of Music (period: 1857)
Broad and Locust Sts., Philadelphia
*architecture (Napoleon LeBrun and
Gustav Runge)*
American Philosophical Society Hall

(period: 1789)
Independence Square, Philadelphia
architecture (Samuel Vaughn)
Athenaeum of Philadelphia (period:
1845–47)
219 S. 6th St., Philadelphia
architecture (John Notman)
John Bartram House (period: 1731)
Eastwick Ave. and 54th St.,
Philadelphia
science
Boathouse Row (period: 1860–present)
1–15 Kelly Drive, Philadelphia
recreation
Carpenters' Hall (period: 1770–71)
310 Chestnut St., Philadelphia
architecture (Robert Smith)
Christ Church (period: 1727–54)
22–26 N. 2nd St., Philadelphia
architecture
Church of St. James the Less (period:
1846–50)
Hunting Park Ave. and Clearfield St.,
Philadelphia
architecture (C. G. Place)
Cliveden-Chew House (period: 1763)
6401 Germantown Ave., Philadelphia
*architecture, military and political
history*
Colonial Germantown Historic District
(period: 18th & 19th centuries)
Germantown Ave. between Windham
Ave. and Upsal St.
*architecture, industry, religion, and
philosophy*
Edward Drinker Cope House (period:
c. 1880)
2102 Pine St., Philadelphia
science
Thomas Eakins House (period: c. 1854)
1729 Mount Vernon Place,
Philadelphia
art
Eastern State Penitentiary (period:
1823–29)

Fairmount Ave. and 21st St.,
Philadelphia
social and humanitarian movements
Elfreth's Alley Historic District (period:
17th & 18th centuries)
Elfreth Alley, between 2nd and Front
Sts., Philadelphia
architecture
Fairmount Water Works (period:
1812–22)
East Bank of the Schuylkill River
*architecture (Frederick Graff),
engineering, conservation, invention,
landscape architecture, and sculpture*
First Bank of the United States (period:
1797)
120 S. 3rd St., Philadelphia
*architecture (Samuel Blodgett),
economics, law, politics, government,
and constitutional history*
Fort Mifflin (period: 1722–75, 1798)
Marina and Penrose Ferry Rds.,
Philadelphia
*architecture and engineering (Pierre
L'Enfant) and military history*
Founder's Hall, Girard College (period:
1833–47)
Corinthian and Girard Aves.,
Philadelphia
social, humanitarian movements
Furness Library, University of Pennsylvania (period: 1888)
34th St. near Walnut, Philadelphia
architecture (Frank Furness)
Germantown (Manheim) Cricket Club
(period: 1890–1907)
5140 Morris St., Philadelphia
*architecture (Charles F. McKim) and
recreation*
Frances Ellen Watkins Harper House
(period: 1870–1911)
1006 Bainbridge St., Philadelphia
*literature, social and humanitarian
movements, African-American history*
Hill-Physick-Keith House (period: 1786)

321 S. 4th St., Philadelphia
architecture and science
Institute of the Pennsylvania Hospital
(period: 1859)
111 N. 49th St., Philadelphia
social and humanitarian movements
Insurance Company of North America
Building (period: 1925)
1600 Arch St., Philadelphia
commerce
James Logan House (period: 1730)
Courtland and 18th Sts., Philadelphia
architecture and politics
Memorial Hall (period: 1876)
West Fairmount Park, Philadelphia
architecture (Herman Schwartzmann)
Mother Bethel A.M.E. Church (period
1889)
419 Sixth St., Philadelphia
*architecture, religion, philosophy,
social and humanitarian movements,
and African-American history*
Mount Pleasant (period: 1761)
Fairmount Park, Philadelphia
architecture
New Market (period: 1745)
S. 2nd St. between Pine and Lombard
Sts., Philadelphia
commerce and industry
Charles Willson Peale House (period:
c. 1750)
2100 Clarkson Ave., Philadelphia
art
Pennsylvania Academy of the Fine Arts
(period: 1871-76)
Broad and Cherry Sts., Philadelphia
architecture (Frank Furness)
Pennsylvania Hospital (period: 1756)
Spruce and 8th Sts., Philadelphia
social and humanitarian movements
Philadelphia City Hall (period: 1871-81)
Penn Square, Broad and Market Sts.
architecture
Philadelphia Contributorship (period:
1835)

212 S. 4th St., Philadelphia
commerce
Philadelphia Masonic Temple (period:
1873)
1 North Broad St., Philadelphia
architecture
Philadelphia Savings Fund Society
Building (period: 1932)
12 and Market Sts., Philadelphia
*architecture (George Howe and
William E. Lescaze)*
Edgar Allan Poe House (period: c. 1835)
530-532 N. 7th St., Philadelphia
literature
Reading Terminal and Train Shed
(period: 1891-93)
1115-1141 Market St., Philadelphia
engineering
Reynolds-Morris House (period:
1786-87)
225 S. 8th St., Philadelphia
architecture
Rittenhouse Town Historic District
(period: 1690-1850)
206-210 Lincoln Drive, Philadelphia
commerce
St. Mark's Episcopal Church (period:
1847-52)
1607-27 Locust St., Philadelphia
architecture (John Notman)
Second Bank of the United States
(period: 1824-36)
420 Chestnut St., Philadelphia
*architecture (William Strickland),
economics, law, politics, government,
and constitutional history*
Thomas Sully Residence (period: 1796)
530 Spruce St., Philadelphia
art
Henry O. Tanner House (period: 19th
century)
2908 W. Diamond St., Philadelphia
art
U.S. Naval Asylum (period: 1827-33, 1844)
Gray's Ferry Ave. at 24th St.,

Philadelphia
architecture (William Strickland)
USS *Becuna* (submarine) (period: 1944)
Penns Landing, Delaware Ave. and
Spruce St.
military and maritime history
USS *Olympia* (cruiser) (period: 1888)
Penns Landing, Delaware Ave. and
Spruce St.
military and maritime history
Wagner Free Institute of Science
(period: 1860–1940)
Montgomery Ave. and 17th St.,
Philadelphia
*education, science, social history, and
architecture*
Walnut Street Theatre (period: 1809,
1828)
9th and Walnut Sts., Philadelphia
theater
Wanamaker Store (now Lord and Taylor)
(period: 1902–10)
Juniper and Market Sts.,
Philadelphia
commerce and architecture
Woodford (period: 1734, 1756)
East Fairmount Park, Philadelphia
architecture
The Woodlands (period: 1770, 1778)
Woodland Ave. and 40th St.,
Philadelphia
architecture (William Hamilton)
Wyck House (period: 1690–1852)
6026 Germantown Ave., Philadelphia
architecture

Pike County
Grey Towers–Gifford Pinchot House
(period: c. 1886)
Milford
conservation

Venango County
Drake Oil Well (period: 1859)
PA Route 27 to Drake Well Memorial

Park, Titusville
industry

Washington County
Edward G. Acheson House (period:
1870s)
908 Main St., Monongahela
invention
David Bradford House (period: 1788)
175 S. Main St., Washington
*politics, government, and military
history*

Wayne County
Delaware and Hudson Canal (period:
1828)
1810 Main St., Honesdale
transportation and communication

Westmoreland County
Bushy Run Battlefield (period: 1763)
PA Route 993, Harrison City
military history

**THE PENNSYLVANIA
TRAIL OF HISTORY**
The Pennsylvania Trail of History consists of 27 historic sites and museums
owned and administered by the Pennsylvania Historical and Museum Commission. The sites preserve and interpret
the culture, history, and natural environment of the commonwealth. One of the
sites administered by the commission is
the State Museum of Pennsylvania in
Harrisburg, which contains the State
Archives.

The commission also owns 20 historic sites and museums administered
by local organizations. These sites have
varying hours of operation and should
be contacted prior to a visit.

The sites on the Trail of History
are listed in a logical geographic order,
beginning in Erie, with the flagship

Niagara, and ending in Bucks County at William Penn's country estate, Pennsbury.

Flagship *Niagara.* On this brig, after the stirring American victory over the British on Lake Erie in 1813, 28-year-old Capt. Oliver Hazard Perry declared, "We have met the enemy and they are ours!" The *Niagara* is located at the foot of Holland Street in Erie. The *Niagara* makes goodwill cruises on occasion. Call (814) 871-4596 to ensure that it is at home.

Drake Well Museum. The world's first oil-producing drilled well was established here by Edwin Drake in 1859. The Drake Well replica on the original site, the museum, and the working oil machinery throughout the 218-acre park depict the once-booming Pennsylvania oil industry. Drake Well is on PA Route 8, 3 miles south of Titusville, Venango County.

Old Economy Village. This restored village, build by George Rapp and his German followers between 1824 and 1830, was the home of the Harmonists, a mystical Christian society. They prospered in agriculture, textile manufacturing, and industrial investments, including oil production. The 6-acre site holds 17 historic buildings and 16,000 original artifacts. It is located in Ambridge, Beaver County, off PA Route 65.

Fort Pitt Museum. This museum recalls the fierce struggle between France and Britain for western Pennsylvania and the Northwest and tells the history of Fort Pitt, Fort Duquesne, and early Pittsburgh. It overlooks the "Gateway of the West" at Point State Park in downtown Pittsburgh.

Bushy Run Battlefield. Col. Henry Bouquet defeated the Indians here in 1763, opening western Pennsylvania to settlement. It is on PA Route 993, northwest of Greensburg.

Somerset Historical Center. The center and its grounds, a 4-acre site on PA Route 985 north of Somerset, exhibit the implements, furnishings, and crafts that supported southwestern Pennsylvania's rural life for two centuries.

Pennsylvania Military Museum. The Pennsylvania citizen-soldier at war is honored at this museum and park, home of the 28th Division Shrine. It is in Boalsburg, Centre County, on U.S. Route 322.

Pennsylvania Lumber Museum. The rough and rugged life of the lumber industry, once Pennsylvania's largest, is portrayed in a re-created lumber camp, railroad, and sawmill located at Denton Hill on U.S. Route 6 between Coudersport and Galeton, in Potter County.

Joseph Priestley House. The American home of the 18th-century theologian and scientist who discovered oxygen is located on Priestley Ave. in Northumberland, near the intersection of U.S. Route 11 and PA Route 147.

The State Museum of Pennsylvania/The State Archives. The State Museum presents the commonwealth's heritage, from earth's beginnings to the present, with exhibits of archaeological artifacts, minerals, paintings and decorative arts, animal dioramas, industrial and technological innovations, and military objects. A planetarium helps visitors understand the universe. The State Archives serves genealogists, scholars, and the public. Both are in Harrisburg, at 3rd and North Sts.

Cornwall Iron Furnace. In this furnace, which operated between 1742 and 1883, iron was smelted and implements were cast, including cannons for the Revolution. It is on PA Route 419 in Cornwall, Lebanon County.

Conrad Weiser Homestead. The stone home of colonial diplomat Conrad Weiser is featured in the midst of a 26-acre park. It is located 2 miles east of Womelsdorf, on U.S. Route 422, between Lebanon and Reading.

Ephrata Cloister. This community, noted for its music, decorative artwork, fraktur, and printing, was gathered by Conrad Beissel, a German mystic, in 1732. The Cloister's 12 restored medieval buildings are found in Ephrata, Lancaster County, at U.S. Route 322 and PA Route 272.

Landis Valley Museum. Twenty-two buildings on 40 acres tell the story of Pennsylvania German rural life, using tools, equipment, and decorative arts in living-history presentations. It is on PA Route 272, north of Lancaster.

Railroad Museum of Pennsylvania. A major collection of historic locomotives, railcars, and other artifacts of the once-dominant railroad industry is housed on PA Route 741, across from the Strasburg Railroad in Strasburg, Lancaster County.

Daniel Boone Homestead. The site of Daniel Boone's birth interprets both English and Germanic rural traditions on 579 acres of rolling countryside, which includes seven 18th-century structures and a beautiful recreation area. It is 1 mile north of Baumstown, Berks County, off U.S. Route 422.

The Pennsylvania Anthracite Heritage Museum. This museum, in its changing exhibits, explores work and life in the Anthracite Region of northeast Pennsylvania. It is next to the Lackawanna Mine Tour in McDade Park, off

Keyser Ave., Exit 57B of I-81 or Exit 38 of the Turnpike. It is part of the Anthracite Complex.

Scranton Iron Furnaces. Four massive stone stacks are the remains of the blast furnaces of the Lackawanna Iron and Coal Company, built between 1841 and 1857. It is on Cedar Ave. in downtown Scranton. It is part of the Anthracite Complex.

Museum of Anthracite Mining. The mining and processing of anthracite coal are the focus of this museum. It is located at 17th and Pine Sts., adjacent to the Pioneer Tunnel, an underground mine, in Ashland, a few miles west of Exit 36 of I-81, via PA Route 61. It is part of the Anthracite Complex.

Eckley Miners' Village. This 19th-century coal-mining town reveals a lifestyle that has all but vanished. Its 58 buildings, 100 acres, furnishings, and exhibits preserve the everyday life of the miner and his family. Eckley is 8 miles east of Hazleton, off PA Route 940 in Luzerne County. It is part of the Anthracite Complex.

Brandywine Battlefield. Here, General Washington tried to block the British occupation of Philadelphia in September 1777. Houses occupied by Washington and Lafayette are open, and a visitors center contains extensive exhibits. It is on U.S. Route 1 at Chadds Ford, Delaware County.

Pottsgrove Manor. In 1752, ironmaster John Potts built the principal part of this mansion with its stately classical features and lovely 18th-century furnishings. It is located on W. King St. in Pottstown, Montgomery County.

Morton Homestead. The 17th-century log home of the Swedish grandfather of John Morton, signer of the

Declaration of Independence, is located in Prospect Park, Delaware County, on PA Route 420 at Darby Creek.

Hope Lodge and Mather Mill. A Georgian house, grand in design and furnishings, was named for Henry Hope, whose family gave its name to the Hope Diamond. Nearby Mather Mill was an early-19th-century gristmill. They are located on Old Bethlehem Pike, off PA Route 309, near Fort Washington, Exit 26 of the Turnpike.

Graeme Park. This architecturally unusual and charming country house, built by Gov. William Keith in 1721–22 and sold to Dr. Thomas Graeme in 1739, is the only remaining colonial governor's residence in Pennsylvania. It is on County Line Rd., west of PA Route 611 near Horsham, Montgomery County.

Washington Crossing Historic Park. Washington's army crossed the Delaware River here and attacked the British forces on Christmas in 1776. The 500-acre park includes 13 historic buildings. Bowman's Hill Wildflower Preserve, open daily, offers woodlands and a 100-foot tower. In Bucks County, take PA Route 32 or 532.

Pennsbury Manor. The manor is a reconstruction of William Penn's country estate. Tours, programs, and classes are offered regularly. It is in Bucks County near U.S. Routes 1 and 13, south of Morrisville, east of Tullytown.

LOCALLY OWNED SITES

Additionally, the Pennsylvania Historical and Museum Commission owns several locally administered sites. Hours of operation for the properties vary.

Captain Phillips Ranger Memorial is an 18-acre site on PA Route 65, Ambridge, where a stone marker commemorates the massacre of 10 militia rangers by Indians on July 6, 1780.

French Azilum is a 27-acre site on the south shore of the Susquehanna River at Rummerfield. The site was developed by French immigrants escaping the French Revolution.

Old Stone House is a 77-acre site 12 miles north of Butler on PA Route 8. The house is a restored wayside tavern and is leased to Slippery Rock State University.

Admiral Perry Park is a 2-acre site on U.S. Route 22 at Cresson with a monument commemorating Perry's birth.

Curtin Village is an 8-acre site north of Bellefonte on U.S. Route 220 at Curtin. It is the site of the Eagle Furnace, which produced cast-iron products.

Old Chester Courthouse in West Chester is a Georgian/Colonial stone structure, built in 1724. It is regarded as the oldest public building in continuous use in the United States.

Peace Church is a limestone church built in 1789–99. It is located in Camp Hill at PA Route 641 and St. John's Rd.

Governor Printz Park, a 7-acre park in Essington, commemorates the contributions of Swedish colonists to the settlement of southeastern Pennsylvania.

Cashier's House is located at 413 State St. in Erie.

Judson House, built in 1820 in Waterford, is a Greek Revival house that was owned by merchant Amos Judson.

The Old Custom House at 409 State St. in Erie is leased to the Erie Art Museum. It once served as a branch of the Second Bank of the United States.

Searights Toll House, west of Uniontown, Fayette County, near U.S. Route 40, was built in 1835 by the U.S. government to collect tolls on the "National Road."

Old Browns Mill School is a limestone one-room school built in 1836. It is east of U.S. Route 11, near Marion.

Fort Loudon, near the village of the same name in Franklin County, was built by the provincial government during the French and Indian War.

Thomas Hughes House was built by a pioneer militiaman. It is an example of Post-Colonial architecture and is now the Greene County Public Library, located on Hatfield St. in Jefferson.

Tuscarora Academy, near Mifflintown in Juniata County, is a sandstone and frame structure built in 1839. There, men were trained for the ministry and women for the teaching profession.

Robert Fulton Birthplace commemorates the inventor of the first commercially successful steamboat. It is on U.S. Route 222, south of Quarryville in Lancaster County.

Johnston's Tavern, 6 miles south of Mercer on U.S. Route 19, is an 1831 fieldstone tavern restored to its original appearance by the Western Pennsylvania Conservancy. It is closed to the public.

McCoy House, the home of the Mifflin County Historical Society, is the brick boyhood home of Gen. Frank McCoy, soldier and diplomat. It is located at 17 N. Main St. in Lewistown.

The Highlands was built in 1796 as the country estate of a Philadelphia lawyer. It is on Sheaff Rd. in Fort Washington.

Bloody Spring, near Memorial Park in Sunbury, commemorates an ambush during the French and Indian War.

Fort Augusta, in Sunbury, is the site of a fort built during the French and Indian War. It is the current home of the Northumberland County Historical Society.

Sodom Schoolhouse is an octagonal, limestone school building, built in 1817. It is east of Montandon on PA Route 45.

Warrior Run Presbyterian Church was erected in 1835, the third structure with the Warrior Run name. The congregation was organized in 1767. It is north of McEwensville in Northumberland County.

Old Mill Village is a collection of buildings representative of the architecture of the northern counties of the commonwealth, with exhibits of area rural life. It is 1 mile south of New Milford on U.S. Route 11.

Pithole City, an 84-acre site off PA Route 227, north of Plumer in Venango County, is the site of an oil boomtown. A surviving photograph documents its existence.

David Bradford House is a stone house built by a leader of the Whiskey Rebellion (1790–94). It is at 175 S. Main St. in Washington, Washington County.

Nathan Denison House is a restored Colonial New England–style house built by a colonel in the militia who participated in the Wyoming Massacre. It is located at 35 Denison St. in Forty Fort, Luzerne County.

NATIONAL PARK SERVICE SITES

Allegheny Portage Railroad National Historic Site. Traces of the first railroad crossing of the Allegheny Mountains can still be seen here. An inclined-plane railroad, it permitted transportation of passengers and freight over the mountains, providing a critical link in the Pennsylvania Mainline Canal System and with the West. Built between 1831 and 1834, it was abandoned by 1857. P.O. Box 189, Cresson, PA 16630 (814) 886-6100.

Appalachian National Scenic Trail. The Appalachian Trail is a 2,097-mile continuous footpath along the crest of the Appalachian Mountains. It passes through 14 states between its south end at Springer Mountain, Georgia, and its northern end at Katahdin, Maine. Pennsylvania's segment is 228 miles through 11 counties, extending across the southeastern portion of the state from the Delaware Water Gap at the New Jersey State Line to Pen Mar on the Maryland border. (See also Hiking section.)

Delaware Water Gap National Recreation Area. This scenic and historic area preserves relatively unspoiled land on both sides of the Middle Delaware River. The river segment flows through the famous gap in the Appalachian Mountains. The park sponsors a craft village and several environmental education centers. (See also Water Resources section.)

Edgar Allan Poe National Historic Site. The life and work of this gifted American author are portrayed in the building where Poe lived in 1834–44. 532 N. 7th St., Philadelphia, PA 19123 (215) 597-8780.

Eisenhower National Historic Site. This was the only home ever owned by President Eisenhower. It was his retirement home. P.O. Box 1080, Gettysburg, PA 17325 (717) 334-1124.

Fort Necessity National Battlefield. Colonial troops commanded by Col. George Washington, then 22 years old, were defeated here in the opening battle of the French and Indian War on July 3, 1754. The National Pike, R.D. 2, Box 528, Farmington, PA 15437 (412) 329-5512.

Friendship Hill National Historic Site. This home on the Monongahela River belonged to Albert Gallatin, secretary of the treasury under Presidents Jefferson and Madison (1801–13). R.D. 1, Box 149A, Point Marion, PA 15474 (412) 725-9190.

Gettysburg National Military Park. The great Civil War battle fought here July 1–3, 1863, repulsed the second Confederate invasion of the North. Gettysburg National Cemetery adjoins the park. At the dedication of the cemetery, November 19, 1863, President Abraham Lincoln delivered his timeless Gettysburg Address. P.O. Box 1080, Gettysburg, PA 17325 (717) 334-1124.

Hopewell Furnace National Historic Site. This is one of the finest examples of a rural American 19th-century iron plantation. The buildings include a blast furnace, ironmaster's mansion, and auxiliary structures. Founded in 1771 by Mark Bird, the first ironmaster, it operated until 1883. 2 Mark Bird Lane, Elverson, PA 19520 (610) 582-8773.

Independence National Historical Park. The park includes structures and sites in central Philadelphia associated with the American Revolution and the founding of the United States: Independence Hall, Congress Hall, Old City Hall, the Liberty Bell Pavilion, the First and Second Banks of the United States, Franklin Court, and others. 313 Walnut St., Philadelphia, PA 19106 (215) 597-8787.

Johnstown Flood National Memorial. Over 2,200 people died in the Johnstown Flood of 1889. Clara Barton successfully led the American Red Cross in its first disaster relief effort. c/o Allegheny Portage Railroad National Historical Site, P.O. Box 189, Cresson, PA 16630 (814) 495-4643.

Middle Delaware National Scenic River. This segment of the river flows

40 miles through the Delaware Water Gap National Recreation Area. Swimming, boating, and fishing opportunities are available. c/o Delaware Water Gap National Recreation Area, Bushkill, PA 18324 (717) 588-2435. (See also Water Resources section.)

Potomac Heritage National Scenic Trail. This 700-mile trail includes portions in Maryland, Virginia, and Pennsylvania. The 75-mile Laurel Highlands Trail is the Pennsylvania segment. It extends from the upper end of the Conemaugh River Gorge south of Seward to the Youghiogheny Gorge in Ohiopyle State Park. (See also Hiking section.)

Steamtown National Historic Site. The former Delaware, Lackawanna & Western Railroad yard—including the remains of the historic roundhouse, switchyard, associated buildings, steam locomotives, and railroad cars—tells the story of 20th-century steam railroading. 150 S. Washington Ave., Scranton, PA 18503 (717) 340-5200.

Thaddeus Kosciuszko National Memorial. The life and work of this Polish-born patriot and hero of the American Revolution are commemorated at 301 Pine St., Philadelphia. c/o Independence National Historical Park, 313 Walnut St., Philadelphia, PA 19106 (215) 597-9618.

Upper Delaware Scenic and Recreational River. A 73-mile stretch of free-flowing river between Hancock and Sparrow Bush, New York, along the Pennsylvania–New York border. Public fishing and boating access are available. P.O. Box C, Narrowsburg, NY 12764 (914) 729-7135.

Valley Forge National Historical Park. Site of the Continental Army's winter encampment, 1777–78, the park contains General Washington's headquarters, original earthworks, a variety of monuments and markers, and recreations of log buildings and cannons. P.O. Box 593, Valley Forge, PA 19481 (610) 783-1000.

2

Government

The word *commonwealth* is used interchangeably with the word *state* in referring to Pennsylvania. The word is derived from Old English and refers to the common "weal," or well-being of the citizenry. The state has had five constitutions since 1776, and each refers to Pennsylvania as both a commonwealth and a state. There is no legal distinction between the two terms.

PENNSYLVANIA STATE CONSTITUTION

At a state convention convened by citizens impatient with the conservative Provincial Assembly, the Constitution of 1776 was adopted. It established an assembly with one house and a supreme executive council, in lieu of a governor. Many Pennsylvania leaders were opposed to this constitution. The members of the Constitutional Party, which governed the state until 1790, were considered to be radicals.

Conservative forces regained influence in the Assembly and a constitutional convention was called in 1790. Compromise was the order of the day. The rewritten document, the Constitution of 1790, provided for a second legislative house, the Senate, and a strong governor.

The Constitution of 1838 granted greater power to voters and protected citizens from government abuse of power. It also revoked the voting rights of blacks.

The fourth Constitution, the Constitution of 1874, created wider voting rights for citizens. It provided for the popular election of judges, the state treasurer, and the auditor general. Public education was guaranteed funding. The governor was limited to one term, but that term was increased from three to four years. The General Assembly was increased in number, but its power was decreased.

The fifth, and last, convention produced the Constitution of 1968. It revamped the judicial system, strengthened civil rights, allowed elected state officers to serve two terms, and provided that the General Assembly meet annually.

Through the 220 years that the commonwealth has been governed by a constitution, the basic Declaration of Rights, adopted in 1776, has remained essentially unchanged. Section 6, Trial by Jury, was amended in 1971. Section 9, Rights of Accused in Criminal Prosecutions, was amended in 1984. Section 10—Initiation of Criminal Proceedings;

PREAMBLE AND ARTICLE 1 OF THE CONSTITUTION OF THE COMMONWEALTH OF PENNSYLVANIA

PREAMBLE

WE, the people of the Commonwealth of Pennsylvania, grateful to almighty God for the blessings of civil and religious liberty, and humbly invoking His guidance, do ordain and establish this Constitution.

ARTICLE 1

Declaration of Rights

That the general, great and essential principles of liberty and free government may be recognized and unalterably established, WE DECLARE THAT—

Inherent Rights of Mankind

Section 1. All men are born equally free and independent, and have certain inherent and indefeasible rights, among which are those of enjoying and defending life and liberty, of acquiring, possessing and protecting property and reputation, and of pursuing their own happiness.

Political Powers

Section 2. All power is inherent in the people, and all free governments are founded on their authority and instituted for their peace, safety and happiness. For the advancement of these ends they have at all times an inalienable and indefeasible right to alter, reform or abolish their government in such manner as they think proper.

Religious Freedom

Section 3. All men have a natural and indefeasible right to worship Almighty God according to the dictates of their own consciences; no man can of right be compelled to attend, erect or support any place of worship or maintain any ministry against his consent; no human authority can, in any case whatever, control or interfere with the rights of conscience, and no preference shall ever be given by law to any religious establishments or modes of worship.

Religion

Section 4. No person who acknowledges the being of a God and a future state of rewards and punishments shall, on account of his religious sentiments, be disqualified to hold any office or place of trust or profit under this Commonwealth.

Elections

Section 5. Elections shall be free and equal; and no power, civil or military, shall at any time interfere to prevent the free exercise of the right of suffrage.

Trial by Jury

Section 6. Trial by jury shall be as heretofore, and the right thereof remain inviolate. The General Assembly may provide, however, by law, that a verdict may be rendered by not less than five-sixths of the jury in any civil case.

Freedom of Press and Speech; Libels

Section 7. The printing press shall be free to every person who may undertake to examine the proceedings of the Legislature or any branch of government, and no law shall ever be made to restrain the right thereof. The free communication of thoughts and opinions is one of the invaluable rights of man, and every citizen may freely speak, write and print on any subject, being responsible for the abuse of that liberty. No conviction shall be had in any prosecution for the publication of papers relating to the official conduct of officers or men in public capacity, or to any other matter proper for public investigation or information, where the fact that such publication was not maliciously or negligently made shall be established to the satisfaction of the jury; and in all indictments for libels the jury shall have the right to determine the law and the facts, under the direction of the court, as in other cases.

Security from Searches and Seizures

Section 8. The people shall be secure in their persons, houses, papers and possessions from unreasonable searches and seizures, and no warrant to search any place or to seize any person or things shall issue without describing them as nearly as may be, nor without probable cause, supported by oath or affirmation subscribed to by the affiant.

Rights of Accused in Criminal Prosecutions

Section 9. In all criminal prosecutions the accused hath a right to be heard by himself and his counsel, to demand the nature and cause of the accusation against him, to meet the witnesses face to face, to have compulsory process for obtaining witnesses in his favor, and, in prosecutions by indictment or information, a speedy public trial by an impartial jury of the vicinage; he cannot be compelled to give evidence against himself, nor can he be deprived of his life, liberty or property, unless by the judgment of his peers or the law of the land. The use of a suppressed voluntary admission or voluntary confession to impeach the credibility of a person may be permitted and shall not be construed as compelling a person to give evidence against himself.

Initiation of Criminal Proceedings; Twice in Jeopardy; Eminent Domain

Section 10. Except as hereinafter provided no person shall, for any indictable offense, be proceeded against criminally by information, except in cases arising in the land and naval forces, or in the militia, when in actual service, in time of war or public danger, or by leave of the court for oppression or misdemeanor in office. Each of the several courts of common pleas may, with the approval of the Supreme Court, provide for the initiation of criminal proceedings therein by information filed in the manner provided by law. No person shall, for the same offense, be twice put in jeopardy of life or limb; nor shall private property be taken or applied to public use, without authority of law and without just compensation being first made or secured.

Courts to Be Open; Suits Against the Commonwealth

Section 11. All courts shall be open; and every man for an injury done him in his lands, goods, person or reputation shall have remedy by due course of law, and right and justice administered without sale, denial or delay. Suits may be brought against the Commonwealth in such manner, in such courts and in such cases as the Legislature may by law direct.

Power of Suspending Laws

Section 12. No power of suspending laws shall be exercised unless by the Legislature or by its authority.

Bail, Fines and Punishments

Section 13. Excessive bail shall not be required, nor excessive fines imposed, nor cruel punishments inflicted.

Prisoners to Be Bailable; Habeas Corpus

Section 14. All prisoners shall be bailable by sufficient sureties, unless for capital offenses when the proof is evident or presumption great; and the privilege of the writ of habeas corpus shall not be suspended, unless when in case of rebellion or invasion the public safety may require it.

Special Criminal Tribunals

Section 15. No commission shall issue creating special temporary criminal tribunals to try particular individuals or particular classes of cases.

Insolvent Debtors

Section 16. The person of a debtor, where there is not strong presumption of fraud, shall not be continued in prison after delivering up his estate for the benefit of his creditors in such manner as shall be prescribed by law.

Ex Post Facto Laws; Impairment of Contracts

Section 17. No ex post facto law, nor any law impairing the obligation of contracts, or making irrevocable any grant of special privileges or immunities, shall be passed.

Attainder

Section 18. No person shall be attained of treason or felony by the Legislature.

Attainder Limited

Section 19. No attainder shall work corruption of blood, nor, except during the life of the offender, forfeiture of estate to the Commonwealth.

Right of Petition

Section 20. The citizens have a right in a peaceable manner to assemble together for their common good, and to apply to those invested with the powers of government for redress of grievances or other proper purposes by petition, address or remonstrance.

Right to Bear Arms

Section 21. The right of the citizens to bear arms in defense of themselves and the State shall not be questioned.

Standing Army; Military Subordinate to Civil Power

Section 22. No standing army shall, in time of peace, be kept up without the consent of the Legislature, and the military shall in all cases and at all times be in strict subordination to the civil power.

Quartering of Troops

Section 23. No soldier shall in time of peace be quartered in any house without the consent of the owner, nor in time of war but in a manner to be prescribed by law.

Titles and Offices

Section 24. The Legislature shall not grant any title of nobility or hereditary distinction, nor create any office the appointment to which shall be for a longer term than during good behavior.

Reservation of Powers in People

Section 25. To guard against transgressions of the high powers which we have delegated, we declare that everything in this article is excepted out of the general powers of government and shall forever remain inviolate.

No Discrimination by Commonwealth and Its Political Subdivisions

Section 26. Neither the Commonwealth nor any political subdivision thereof shall deny to any person the enjoyment of any civil right, nor discriminate against any person in the exercise of any civil right.

Natural Resources and the Public Estate

Section 27. The people have a right to clean air, pure water, and to the preservation of the natural, scenic, historic and esthetic values of the environment. Pennsylvania's public natural resources are the common property of all the people, including generations yet to come. As trustees of these resources, the Commonwealth shall conserve and maintain them for the benefit of all the people.

Prohibitions Against Denial or Abridgment of Equality of Rights Because of Sex

Section 28. Equality of rights under the law shall not be denied or abridged in the Commonwealth of Pennsylvania because of the sex of the individual.

Twice in Jeopardy; Eminent Domain—was amended in 1973. Section 27, Natural Resources and the Public Estate, was adopted in 1971, as was Section 28, Prohibition Against Denial or Abridgment of Equality of Rights Because of Sex.

THE LEGISLATIVE BRANCH

The Pennsylvania Legislature was established by the Constitution of 1776. It consisted of only one house. The second legislative house, the State Senate, was provided for in the Constitution of 1790.

The General Assembly now consists of a 50-member Senate and a 203-member House of Representatives. Each member represents a district of the commonwealth. By law, districts must be compact, contiguous, and nearly equal in population. Further, no county, city, town, borough, township, or ward is to be divided. Based upon 1990 U.S. Census Bureau figures, each senator represents 237,000 citizens; each representative, 58,000.

Elections for seats in the General Assembly are held every two years in even-numbered years. Representatives are elected every two years; senators, every four years. Half of the Senate runs for office every two years.

To run for the Assembly, a candidate must be 25 years of age for the Senate and 21 for the House, a citizen of the United States, a resident of the commonwealth for four years, and a resident of the district for one year.

The General Assembly term is divided into two one-year sessions.

Legislative procedures are determined by a variety of factors: constitutional mandate, legal statutes, rules of the house, agreement of the party caucuses, and tradition.

The conventional wisdom is that the Legislature makes the laws and the Executive Branch administers them, but the reality is that the two branches work together on shaping legislation. When there is a conflict, the two branches have checks upon each other's activities.

Procedures and Practices

A bill passes through many stages on its way to becoming a law. First, the bill is introduced on the floor of either the Senate or the House and referred to the appropriate committee. The committee considers the bill, after which it is reviewed by party caucuses; it is sent to the floor for three considerations and a vote is taken. If passed, the bill is then sent to the other house, where the procedure is repeated.

It is in committees that the real work on the bill is done. As of July 1995, there were 25 committees in the House and 22 in the Senate. Because of the large number of bills that are introduced, the committee system has evolved as the way to manage the workload. There were 5,126 bills introduced in the 1993–94 legislative session; only 354 passed both houses.

A committee may simply send a bill back to the floor exactly as it was submitted, amend the bill, recommend that it be passed or defeated, or do nothing with the bill.

The review of the bill by the party caucus helps party members learn what is in the bill and the effect it will have on their constituents. Caucuses review all of the bills daily; then the party leaders meet with the presiding officer of the House or Senate so that the officer can anticipate how the bill will be received on the floor. Generally, if the majority party is in complete agreement as to the value of the bill, passage or defeat is assured.

Every bill must be discussed on three different days. On the first day, it is simply reported from committee. On the second day, amendment and debate are permitted. On the third day, the bill can be amended, but it must be reprinted to include the amendment before the vote is taken. There is a Senate rule that no amendment may be made during the third consideration except by unanimous consent.

After debate and amendment, the presiding officer announces that the bill is ready for final consideration and calls for a vote. To pass, a bill needs a majority vote of both houses: 102 in the House and 26 in the Senate. (Some bills, such as an override of a governor's veto and some funding measures, require a two-thirds majority.)

If passed in one house, the bill is sent to the other house and the process is repeated. If the bill is defeated in the second house, it dies. If it is amended, it is returned to the first house for concurrence. Sometimes the first house will not accept what the second house has done to a bill. If not, a committee of six is appointed, two majority party members and one minority party member from each house, to work out an agreement. A conference committee report is written and sent to the house where the bill originated. Both houses must approve the report.

When a bill has been approved by both houses, it is sent to the secretary of state for recording. The State Department then sends it to the governor. If the governor signs it, the bill becomes known as an act. If the governor vetoes the bill, the General Assembly gets a chance to override the veto with a vote of two-thirds of the members of each house.

STATE HOUSE OF REPRESENTATIVES DISTRICTS

District Number	Counties Included
1, 2, 3, 4	Erie
5	Erie (part)–Crawford (part)
6	Crawford
7	Mercer
8	Armstrong-Butler-Mercer
9	Lawrence
10	Beaver-Butler-Lawrence
11, 12	Butler
13	Chester-Lancaster
14, 15	Beaver
16	Allegheny-Beaver
17	Crawford-Mercer
18	Bucks
19–24	Allegheny

STATE HOUSE OF REPRESENTATIVES DISTRICTS *(continued)*

District Number	Counties Included
25	Allegheny-Westmoreland
26	Chester
27–30	Allegheny
31	Bucks
32–36	Allegheny
37	Lancaster
38, 39	Allegheny
40	Allegheny-Washington
41, 42	Allegheny
43	Lancaster
44, 45	Allegheny
46	Beaver-Washington
47, 48	Washington
49	Fayette-Washington
50	Fayette-Greene-Washington
51	Fayette
52	Fayette-Westmoreland
53	Montgomery
54	Allegheny-Westmoreland
55–58	Westmoreland
59	Fayette-Westmoreland
60	Armstrong-Indiana
61	Montgomery
62	Cambria-Indiana
63	Armstrong-Clarion
64	Venango
65	Forest-McKean-Warren
66	Clearfield-Indiana-Jefferson
67	Cameron-McKean-Potter
68	Bradford-Tioga
69	Somerset
70	Montgomery
71	Cambria
72	Cambria-Somerset
73	Cambria

STATE HOUSE OF REPRESENTATIVES DISTRICTS *(continued)*

District Number	Counties Included
74	Centre-Clearfield
75	Clearfield-Elk
76	Centre-Clinton
77	Centre-Clearfield
78	Bedford-Fulton-Huntington
79	Blair
80	Bedford-Blair
81	Blair-Huntingdon
82	Juniata-Mifflin-Perry-Snyder
83, 84	Lycoming
85	Snyder-Union
86	Cumberland-Franklin-Perry
87, 88	Cumberland
89	Cumberland-Franklin
90	Franklin
91	Adams
92–95	York
96–100	Lancaster
101	Lebanon
102–6	Dauphin
107	Columbia-Montour-Northumberland
108	Northumberland
109	Columbia
110	Bradford-Susquehanna
111	Sullivan-Susquehanna-Wyoming
112–14	Lackawanna
115	Lackawanna-Wayne
116–21	Luzerne
122	Carbon-Luzerne
123	Schuylkill
124	Berks-Schuylkill
125	Schuylkill
126–30	Berks
131, 132	Lehigh
133	Lehigh-Northampton

STATE HOUSE OF REPRESENTATIVES DISTRICTS *(continued)*

District Number	Counties Included
134	Lehigh
135	Lehigh-Northampton
136, 137	Northampton
138	Monroe-Northampton
139	Pike-Wayne
140–45	Bucks
146–51	Montgomery
152	Bucks-Montgomery
153, 154	Montgomery
155–58	Chester
159–66	Delaware
167	Chester-Delaware
168	Delaware
169, 170	Philadelphia
171	Centre-Mifflin
172–77	Philadelphia
178	Bucks
179–82	Philadelphia
183	Lehigh-Northampton
184	Philadelphia
185	Delaware-Philadelphia
186	Philadelphia
187	Berks-Lehigh
188	Philadelphia
189	Monroe
190	Philadelphia
191	Delaware-Philadelphia
192	Philadelphia
193	Adams-York
194, 195	Philadelphia
196	York
197, 198	Philadelphia
199	Cumberland-York
200–203	Philadelphia

STATE SENATORIAL DISTRICTS

District Number	Counties Included
1, 2, 3	Philadelphia
4, 5	Montgomery-Philadelphia
6	Bucks
7	Philadelphia
8	Delaware-Philadelphia
9	Chester-Delaware
10	Bucks
11	Berks
12	Bucks-Montgomery
13	Lancaster-York
14	Luzerne
15	Dauphin
16	Lehigh-Northampton
17	Delaware-Montgomery
18	Monroe-Northampton
19	Chester
20	Luzerne-Monroe-Pike-Susquehanna-Wayne-Wyoming
21	Butler-Clarion-Lawrence-Venango
22	Lackawanna-Luzerne-Monroe
23	Bradford-Lycoming-Sullivan-Tioga-Union
24	Montgomery
25	Cameron-Clearfield-Elk-Erie-Forest-Jefferson-McKean-Potter-Venango-Warren
26	Delaware
27	Columbia-Montour-Northumberland-Snyder-Union
28	York
29	Carbon-Monroe-Schuylkill
30	Bedford-Blair-Fulton-Huntingdon
31	Cumberland-Perry-York
32	Fayette-Somerset-Washington-Westmoreland
33	Adams-Cumberland-Franklin-York
34	Centre-Clinton-Juniata-Mifflin-Perry

STATE SENATORIAL DISTRICTS *(continued)*

District Number	Counties Included
35	Cambria-Clearfield-Somerset-Westmoreland
36	Lancaster
37	Allegheny-Washington
38	Allegheny
39	Westmoreland
40	Allegheny-Butler-Westmoreland
41	Armstrong-Indiana-Jefferson-Westmoreland
42, 43	Allegheny
44	Berks, Chester, Lehigh, Montgomery
45	Allegheny-Westmoreland
46	Beaver-Greene-Washington-Westmoreland
47	Beaver-Lawrence
48	Berks-Lebanon-Lehigh
49	Erie
50	Crawford-Erie-Mercer

Source: The Pennsylvania State Data Center

THE EXECUTIVE BRANCH

The Executive Branch, one of the three branches of government as defined in the Constitution, is responsible for administering the laws of the commonwealth. "The supreme executive power shall be vested in the Governor, who shall take care that the laws are faithfully executed. . . ." The governor is also commander-in-chief of the military forces of the commonwealth, except when they are in the active service of the United States.

To be eligible for election as governor, a person must be at least 30 years old, a citizen of the United States, and a resident of the commonwealth for at least seven years before the election. The governor holds office for a four-year term and may serve one additional four-year term.

The Executive Branch consists of the governor, lieutenant governor, attorney general, auditor general, state treasurer, and numerous other departments, agencies, boards, and commissions. As head of the Executive Branch, the governor is the chief executive officer of the commonwealth. All executive and administrative agencies are under the governor's jurisdiction, except for certain elected officers: the attorney general, the auditor general, and the state treasurer.

Several executive departments, headed by a secretary, who is appointed by the governor and confirmed by the Senate, form the Cabinet. Some agencies have advisory boards or commissions; others are independent. The governor may appoint the members, but he has limited control over them. A few other agencies, including several public corporations, do not fall within the governor's jurisdiction, but by law, the governor sits on their boards.

The governor appoints the secretaries of departments and heads of other cabinet-level agencies, members of state boards, commissions, and councils. Some of these are subject to Senate approval, as are the district justices and other judicial officers the governor appoints.

The governor must annually present to the General Assembly a balanced operating budget for the ensuing fiscal year, as well as a financial plan for not less than the next five succeeding years.

The governor suggests measures that the Legislature may want to introduce in bill form. Any bill passed by the General Assembly (except for adjournment) must be submitted to the governor for approval. If the governor returns the bill, vetoing it, the General Assembly needs a two-thirds majority to override the veto and make the bill a law.

On extraordinary occasions, the governor may convene the General Assembly by proclamation for the transaction of executive business. One day after taking office, on January 17, 1995, Gov. Tom Ridge called a special legislative session on crime.

The governor serves as an ex officio member of many state boards and commissions and various educational institutions.

The governor's Executive Office includes the Office of Administration, Budget, Communications, General Counsel, Inspector General, Legislative Affairs, Policy, Public Liaison, Scheduling and Advance, and the Office of the First Lady.

The governor has five regional offices, located in Washington, D.C., Pittsburgh, Philadelphia, Erie, and Scranton.

The Lieutenant Governor

The major constitutional function of the lieutenant governor is to assume the governorship in the event that the governor is unable to perform the duties of office due to death, impeachment, resignation, or disability. In June 1993, Gov. Robert Casey underwent major surgery, and Lt. Gov. Mark Singel became acting governor from June 13 to December 21, 1993.

The lieutenant governor is also president of the Senate, presiding but voting only to break a tie vote. He is also chairman of the Board of Pardons.

The Attorney General

The commonwealth's chief legal and law-enforcement officer administers four divisions of the office: Criminal Law, Civil Law, Public Protection, and Drug Law.

The Auditor General

This "watchdog of the Treasury" reviews virtually every financial transaction of the commonwealth. The auditor general ensures that all money due the commonwealth is deposited in the State Treasury and that public money is disbursed properly and legally.

The State Treasurer

The treasurer handles the state's money, writes the checks on commonwealth funds, invests surplus funds, and manages securities in its custody.

Cabinet-Level Agencies

Department of Aging. Created in 1978, this department coordinates federal and state aging programs and, in general, promotes the older citizen's agenda. It is funded by proceeds from the lottery.

Department of Agriculture. This department encourages and promotes agriculture and related industries through four major programs: consumer protection, property protection, farmland preservation, and agribusiness development. It also has a Bureau of Dog Law Enforcement and oversees harness-racing and horse-racing activities.

Department of Banking. This department charters, licenses, regulates, and supervises banks and any other institutions directly involved in receiving deposits or lending funds to the public.

Department of Community and Economic Development. This department was created in 1996, when the Department of Commerce and the Department of Community Affairs were merged. It is responsible for the promotion and development of business and industry in the commonwealth. It administers and promotes economic development, tourism, and international trade in order to create or retain jobs for Pennsylvanians. It is the principal advocate within state government for the 2,600 municipalities in the commonwealth. It provides technical assistance and training to local governments and community-based organizations.

Department of Conservation and Natural Resources. Created in 1995, when the former Department of Environmental Resources was divided into the Department of Environmental Protection and this department, it oversees the public lands—the 114 state parks and 20 state forests—of the commonwealth. It protects all forest lands from fire, insects, and disease through advice to private woodland owners. It also provides grants and advice to help local governments administer local facilities and areas.

Department of Corrections. This department is responsible for the overall management and operation of the entire adult corrections system, including 21 prisons, 15 community corrections centers, and a motivational boot camp.

Department of Education. The secretary of education oversees all levels of education in the commonwealth, public schools from preschool to university level, and libraries at all levels, including the State Library.

Department of Environmental Protection. Created in 1995, when the former Department of Environmental Resources was divided into the Department of Conservation and Natural Resources and this department, it oversees the state's land, air, and water management programs, all aspects of environmental protection, and the regulation of mining operations.

Department of General Services. This department is the central construction, purchasing, publishing, and maintenance agency for the commonwealth. From constructing college buildings to purchasing vehicles for the State Police, it provides a multitude of services to all agencies of state government.

Department of Health. This complex department is responsible for protecting the health of the people of the commonwealth. The secretary of health is the chairperson of, or a member of, over 30 advisory boards and committees related to health issues.

Department of Labor and Industry. This multifaceted department serves the labor and industrial interests of the commonwealth by promoting the health, welfare, and safety of workers; working to reduce industrial strife; providing vocational rehabilitation, unemployment insurance, and disability insurance; promoting apprenticeship and job-training programs; assisting displaced workers; promoting economic development; and compiling statistical data on all of its activities.

Department of Military Affairs. The Adjutant General's Office is the headquarters of this department. The general is chief administrator of the Pennsylvania National Guard and state veterans programs, including the four veterans homes.

Department of Public Welfare. The largest state agency, Public Welfare administers a budget of $11.5 billion. In addition to the welfare program, this department provides services to the mentally ill and the mentally retarded, to families, and to children.

Department of Revenue. This department collects taxes and administers the Pennsylvania State Lottery fund.

Department of State. The secretary of state is responsible for all matters relating to elections in the commonwealth; records all public documents; regulates corporations and professional boxing and wrestling; and oversees licensing of 27 professional and occupational groups.

Pennsylvania State Police. The State Police have all the powers and prerogatives conferred by law upon members of the police force of cities of the first class and upon constables. The State Police also act as game protectors and as forest, fish, and fire wardens. They assist all police departments in Pennsylvania. They also patrol the Pennsylvania Turnpike.

Other Agencies
Other state agencies within the Executive Branch include the following: PA Council on the Arts; Civil Service Commission; Board of Claims; PA Commission on Crime and Delinquency; Emergency Management Agency; Environmental Hearing Board; State Ethics Commission; Fish and Boat Commission; Game Commission; PA Healthcare Cost Containment Council; PA Heritage Affairs Commission; State System of Higher Education; PA Higher Education Assistance Agency; PA Higher Educational Facilities Authority; Historical and Museum Commission; PA Housing Finance Agency; Human Relations Commission; Independent Regulatory Review Commission; Governor's Advisory Committee on Latino Affairs; Liquor Control Board; Medical Professional Liability Catastrophic Loss Fund; Milk Marketing Board; PA Municipal Retirement System; PA Infrastructure Investment Authority; Philadelphia Regional Port Authority; PA Board of Probation and Parole; State Public School Building Authority; Public School Employees' Retirement System; PA Public Television Network Commission; Public Utilities Commission; PA Securities Commission; State Employees' Retirement System; State Tax Equalization Board; PA Turnpike Commission; and the Commission for Women.

In addition, the state has entered into 21 interstate compacts and agreements.

STATE GOVERNORS

Name	Party	County	Term
Thomas Mifflin	None	Philadelphia	1790–99
Thomas McKean	D-R	Philadelphia	1799–1808
Simon Snyder	D-R	Northumberland	1808–17
William Findlay	D-R	Franklin	1817–20
Joseph Hiester	D-R	Berks	1820–23
John A. Shulze	D-R	Lebanon	1823–29
George Wolf	D-R	Northampton	1829–35
Joseph Ritter	Anti-Mason	Berks	1835–39
David R. Porter	D-R	Huntingdon	1839–45
Francis R. Shunk	D	Allegheny	1845–48
William F. Johnson	Whig	Armstrong	1848–52
William Bigler	D	Clearfield	1852–55
James Pollock	Whig	Northumberland	1855–58
William F. Packer	D	Lycoming	1858–61
Andrew G. Curtin	D	Centre	1861–67
John W. Geary	R	Westmoreland	1867–73
John N. Hartranft	R	Montgomery	1873–76
John N. Hartranft	R	Montgomery	1876–79
Henry M. Hoyt	R	Luzerne	1879–83
Robert E. Pattison	D	Philadelphia	1883–87
James A. Beaver	R	Centre	1887–91
Robert E. Pattison	D	Philadelphia	1891–95
David H. Hastings	R	Centre	1895–99
William A. Stone	R	Allegheny	1899–1903
Samuel W. Pennypacker	R	Philadelphia	1903–07
Edward S. Stuart	R	Philadelphia	1907–11
John K. Tener	R	Washington	1911–15
Martin G. Brumbaugh	R	Philadelphia	1915–19
William C. Sproul	R	Delaware	1919–23
Gifford Pinchot	R	Pike	1923–27
John S. Fisher	R	Indiana	1927–31
Gifford Pinchot	R	Pike	1931–35
George H. Earle	D	Montgomery	1935–39
Arthur H. James	R	Luzerne	1939–43
Edward Martin	R	Washington	1943–47

STATE GOVERNORS *(continued)*

Name	Party	County	Term
John Bell*	R	Philadelphia	1947
James H. Duff	R	Allegheny	1947–51
John S. Fine	R	Luzerne	1951–55
George M. Leader	D	York	1955–59
David L. Lawrence	D	Allegheny	1959–63
William W. Scranton	R	Lackawanna	1963–67
Raymond P. Shafer	R	Crawford	1967–71
Milton J. Shapp	D	Montgomery	1971–79
Dick Thornburgh	R	Allegheny	1979–87
Robert P. Casey	D	Lackawanna	1987–95
Tom Ridge	R	Erie	1995–

* Served out the term (19 days) of Governor Martin, who resigned to take a seat in the U.S. Senate.

THE JUDICIAL BRANCH
Courts of the Commonwealth

The Constitution of 1968 initiated many judicial reforms and reorganized the judiciary under a Unified Judicial System. It consists of the Supreme Court, Superior Court, Commonwealth Courts, Courts of Common Pleas, Philadelphia Municipal Court, Pittsburgh Magistrates Court, Philadelphia Traffic Court, and District Justice Courts. The Supreme Court administers all other state courts.

The Supreme Court

Established in 1722, the Supreme Court of Pennsylvania is the oldest appellate court in the nation, predating the U.S. Supreme Court by 67 years. The court is composed of seven justices elected for 10-year terms. The justice who has served longest presides as chief justice. The governor appoints new justices to the court when a vacancy occurs due to death, resignation, or retirement of a sitting justice, subject to Senate confirmation.

The Supreme Court hears appeals from orders of Common Pleas Court regarding the right to hold public office, any questions regarding the judiciary, death sentences, supersession of a district attorney by the attorney general or a court, rights of a political subdivision to issue bonds, the constitutionality of any statue or rule, and the right to practice law.

The Supreme Court also hears appeals from the final orders of the following agencies: Legislative Reapportionment Committee; the Minor Judciary Education Board; the Pennsylvania Board of Law Examiners; and the Disciplinary Board of the Supreme Court, which has the power to discipline attorneys.

The Supreme Court may assume jurisdiction of a case pending before any court involving an issue of immediate public importance.

The Superior Court

The Superior Court was created in 1895 to hear appeals. It is essentially a second major appellate court, reviewing final orders of Common Pleas Courts in those matters not within the jurisdiction of either the Supreme Court or Commonwealth Courts.

The 15 judges are elected to 10-year terms; the judges elect a president judge, who serves a five-year term.

The Commonwealth Court

The Commonwealth Court was created by the Constitution of 1968 both to serve as a third appellate court and to hear cases involving actions by or against the commonwealth. Its nine judges are elected to 10-year terms.

The Commonwealth Court has original jurisdiction in all civil actions for and against the commonwealth, eminent-domain proceedings, and actions where sovereign immunity has been waived.

It has appellate jurisdiction on direct appeals from final decisions of state administrative agencies; civil or criminal appeals from Common Pleas Courts involving the commonwealth; interpretation of General Assembly acts, home rule charters, and local ordinances or legislative acts governing local governments and appeals from local administrative agencies. This court also reviews arbitrators' awards in disputes between the commonwealth and its employees.

Courts of Common Pleas

Under the Constitution of 1968, Courts of Common Pleas have original jurisdiction in all cases except as may otherwise be provided by law, i.e., those in which the Supreme Court and the Commonwealth Court have original jurisdiction.

Courts of Common Pleas also hear appeals from final orders of the special courts and certain state and most local agencies. The Courts are organized into 60 judicial districts that generally follow county boundaries; seven districts are composed of two counties. Each district has from one to 95 judges. They are elected for 10-year terms.

Special Courts

Special courts are presided over by district justices, formerly known as justices of the peace. District justices have jurisdiction over summary offenses (except traffic offenses within the jurisdiction of a traffic court), landlord-tenant disputes, and other civil action where the amount claimed does not exceed $8,000. District judges may also preside at arraignments, fix and accept bail, except for offenses of murder and voluntary manslaughter, and issue warrants. As of 1995, there were 550 district judges. They need not be lawyers but must pass a course and take an examination before taking office.

Philadelphia does not have District Justice Courts. There the special courts are the Municipal Court and the Traffic Court. The Municipal Court, with 22 judges, has jurisdiction over all criminal offenses punishable by a term of imprisonment not exceeding five years. Civil actions are limited to cases involving amounts claimed of less than $5,000.

The Philadelphia Traffic Court, which has six judges who need not be lawyers, has jurisdiction over all summary offenses under the Motor Vehicle Code.

The city of Pittsburgh has seven magistrates in addition to district justices. They are appointed by the mayor and are the only nonelective judiciary in the state. The magistrates issue arrest warrants and hold arraignments and preliminary hearings for all criminal offenses occurring in the city. They hear criminal cases brought by the city police for violations of city ordinances, including health and housing code violations. These magistrates also sit on the Pittsburgh Traffic Court, which has jurisdiction similar to that of Philadelphia, and on the Pittsburgh Housing Court.

The number and boundaries of magisterial districts are based solely on population; each district contains one judge, elected to a six-year term.

There are no jury trials in the special courts.

U.S. CONGRESS

Pennsylvania has two U.S. senators and 21 representatives in Congress. The number of U.S. senators from a state is fixed, each state having two; the number of representatives is determined by a state's population.

The following are the Pennsylvania members in Congress as of 1997:

U.S. SENATORS

Arlen Specter (R)

Born:	Wichita, KS, 1930
Education:	B.A., University of Pennsylvania
Prior occupation:	district attorney, Philadelphia
Elected:	1980, 1986, 1992
Address:	530 Hart Bldg.
	Washington, DC 20510
Phone:	(202) 224-4254

Rick Santorum (R)

Born:	Winchester, VA, 1958
Education:	B.A., Penn State University;
	J.D., Dickinson Law
Prior occupation:	attorney
Elected:	U.S. House 1990, 1992
	U.S. Senate 1994
Address:	120 Russell Office Bldg.
	Washington, DC 20510
Phone:	(202) 224-6324

U.S. REPRESENTATIVES

1st District

Thomas Foglietta (D)

Born:	Philadelphia, PA, 1928
Education:	B.A., St. Joseph's College; J.D., Temple Law
Prior occupation:	attorney
Elected:	1980
Address:	31 Cannon HOB Washington, DC 20515
Phone:	(202) 225-4731

2nd District

Chaka Fattah (D)

Born:	Philadelphia, PA, 1956
Education:	University of Pennsylvania
Prior occupation:	government
Elected:	1994
Address:	1205 Longworth Cannon HOB Washington, DC 20515
Phone:	(202) 225-4001

3rd District

Robert A. Borski, Jr. (D)

Born:	Philadelphia, PA, 1948
Education:	B.A., University of Baltimore
Prior occupation:	stockbroker
Elected:	1982
Address:	2182 Rayburn HOB Washington, DC 20515
Phone:	(202) 225-8251

4th District

Ron Klink (D)

Born:	Canton, OH, 1951
Education:	high school
Prior occupation:	journalist
Elected:	1992
Address:	125 Cannon HOB Washington, DC 20515
Phone:	(202) 225-2565

U.S. REPRESENTATIVES *(continued)*

5th District

William F. Clinger, Jr. (R)

Born:	Warren, PA, 1929
Education:	B.A., Johns Hopkins;
	LL.B., University of Virginia
Prior occupation:	attorney
Elected:	1978
Address:	2160 Rayburn HOB
	Washington, DC 20515
Phone:	(202) 225-5121

6th District

Tim Holden (D)

Born:	St. Clair, PA, 1957
Education:	B.A., Bloomsburg State University
Prior occupation:	insurance and real estate
Elected:	1992
Address:	1421 Longworth HOB
	Washington, DC 20515
Phone:	(202) 225-5546

7th District

Curt Weldon (R)

Born:	Marcus Hook, PA, 1947
Education:	B.A., West Chester State University
Prior occupation:	business
Elected:	1986
Address:	2452 Rayburn HOB
	Washington, DC 20515
Phone:	(202) 225-2011

8th District

James C. Greenwood (R)

Born:	Philadelphia, PA, 1951
Education:	B.A., Dickinson College
Prior occupation:	government
Elected:	1992
Address:	430 Cannon HOB
	Washington, DC 20515
Phone:	(202) 225-4276

U.S. REPRESENTATIVES *(continued)*

9th District
Bud Schuster (R)
Born:	Glassport, PA, 1932
Education:	B.A., University of Pittsburgh;
	M.B.A., Duquesne University;
	Ph.D., American University
Prior occupation:	computer industry executive
Elected:	1972
Address:	2188 Rayburn HOB
	Washington, DC 20515
Phone:	(202) 225-2431

10th District
Joseph M. McDade (R)
Born:	Scranton, PA, 1931
Education:	B.A., Notre Dame;
	LL.B., University of Pennsylvania
Prior occupation:	attorney
Elected:	1962
Address:	2370 Rayburn HOB
	Washington, DC 20515
Phone:	(202) 225-3731

11th District
Paul Kanjorski (D)
Born:	Nanticoke, PA, 1937
Education:	B.A., Temple University;
	J.D., Dickinson Law
Prior occupation:	attorney
Elected:	1984
Address:	2429 Rayburn HOB
	Washington, DC 20515
Phone:	(202) 225-6511

12th District
John P. Murtha, Jr. (D)
Born:	New Martinsville, WV, 1932
Education:	B.A., University of Pittsburgh
Prior occupation:	government
Elected:	1974

U.S. REPRESENTATIVES *(continued)*

John P. Murtha, Jr., continued
    Address: 2423 Rayburn HOB
                             Washington, DC 20515
    Phone: (202) 225-2065

13th District
Jon D. Fox (R)
    Born: Philadelphia, PA, 1947
    Education: B.A., Penn State University;
                             J.D., Widener University
    Prior occupation: government
    Elected: 1994
    Address: 510 Cannon HOB
                             Washington, DC 20515
    Phone: (202) 225-6111

14th District
William J. Coyne (D)
    Born: Pittsburgh, PA, 1936
    Education: B.S., Robert Morris College
    Prior occupation: accountant
    Elected: 1980
    Address: 2455 Rayburn HOB
                             Washington, DC 20515
    Phone: (202) 225-2301

15th District
Paul McHale (D)
    Born: Bethlehem, PA, 1950
    Education: B.A., Lehigh University;
                             J.D., Georgetown University
    Prior occupation: attorney
    Elected: 1992
    Address: 217 Cannon HOB
                             Washington, DC 20515
    Phone: (202) 225-6411

16th District
Joseph R. Pitts (R)
    Born: Lexington, KY, 1939
    Education: A. B., Asbury College;
                             M. Ed., West Chester State University

---

U.S. REPRESENTATIVES *(continued)*

Joseph R. Pitts, continued
Prior occupation:	state assembly
Elected:	1996
Address:	504 Cannon HOB
	Washington, DC 20515
Phone:	(202) 225-2411

17th District

George W. Gekas (R)
Born:	Harrisburg, PA, 1930
Education:	B.A., Dickinson College;
	LL.B., J.D., Dickinson Law
Prior occupation:	attorney
Elected:	1982
Address:	2410 Rayburn HOB
	Washington, DC 20515
Phone:	(202) 225-4315

18th District

Mike Doyle (D)
Born:	Swissvale, PA, 1953
Education:	B.S., Penn State University
Prior occupation:	insurance
Elected:	1994
Address:	1218 Longworth HOB
	Washington, DC 20515
Phone:	(202) 225-2135

19th District

Bill Goodling (R)
Born:	Loganville, PA, 1927
Education:	B.S., University of Maryland;
	M.Ed., Western Maryland College
Prior occupation:	teacher/administrator
Elected:	1974
Address:	2263 Rayburn HOB
	Washington, DC 20515
Phone:	(202) 225-5836

20th District

Frank R. Mascara (D)
Born:	Belle Vernon, PA, 1930

U.S. REPRESENTATIVES *(continued)*

Frank R. Mascara, continued
Education:	California State University of Pennsylvania
Prior occupation:	accountant
Elected:	1994
Address:	1531 Longworth HOB Washington, DC 20515
Phone:	(202) 225-4665

21st District

Phil S. English (R)
Born:	Erie, PA, 1958
Education:	B.A., University of Pennsylvania
Prior occupation:	government
Elected:	1994
Address:	1721 Longworth HOB Washington, DC 20515
Phone:	(202) 225-5406

ELECTIONS

Both the Constitution of the United States and the Constitution of Pennsylvania contain provisions concerning the voter and elections. Article XV of the U.S. Constitution declares: "The right of citizens of the United States to vote shall not be denied or abridged by the United States or any state on account of race, color, or previous condition of servitude."

In the Bill of Rights, the Constitution of Pennsylvania states that elections are to be free and equal, and that no power, civil or military, shall interfere to prevent the free exercise of the right of suffrage. The Constitution also enumerates the qualifications for voting. Every citizen 18 years of age is eligible to vote if he or she has been a citizen of the United States for at least one month and has resided in the state for 30 days immediately preceding the election. (In 1971, the attorney general of Pennsylvania declared that college students are permitted to vote in the locality at which they are attending a college or university.)

Voter Registration

Voters must register in order to vote. This may be done in person at the county courthouse or by mail. Registration forms are widely available, at the courthouse, municipal buildings, libraries, and state liquor stores. Voters may also register when applying for a driver's license.

In order to vote for candidates in a primary election, voters must register by political party; those who do not designate a party may vote in the primary only on ballot issues.

To change one's name, address,

CONGRESSIONAL DISTRICTS

District Number	Counties Included
1, 2	Delaware-Philadelphia
3	Philadelphia
4	Allegheny-Beaver-Butler-Lawrence-Westmoreland
5	Armstrong-Cameron-Centre-Clarion-Clearfield-Clinton-Crawford-Forest-Jefferson-Lycoming-McKean-Potter-Tioga-Union-Venango-Warren
6	Berks-Montgomery-Northumberland-Schuylkill
7	Chester-Delaware-Montgomery
8	Bucks-Montgomery
9	Bedford-Blair-Centre-Clearfield-Franklin-Fulton-Huntingdon-Juniata-Mifflin-Perry-Snyder
10	Bradford-Lackawanna-Lycoming-Monroe-Pike-Sullivan-Susquehanna-Wayne-Wyoming
11	Carbon-Columbia-Luzerne-Monroe-Montour-Northumberland
12	Armstrong-Cambria-Clarion-Fayette-Indiana-Somerset-Westmoreland
13	Montgomery
14	Allegheny
15	Lehigh-Montgomery-Northampton
16	Chester-Lancaster
17	Cumberland-Dauphin-Lancaster-Lebanon-Perry
18	Allegheny
19	Adams-Cumberland-York
20	Allegheny-Fayette-Greene-Washington-Westmoreland
21	Butler-Crawford-Erie-Mercer

Source: The Pennsylvania State Data Center

or party affiliation, a voter must reregister.

Absentee Voting

Voters who will not be in the county on election day may vote by absentee ballot. Application must be made at the county courthouse no later than the Tuesday before the election. Absentee ballots must be mailed or delivered in person by voters themselves before 5 P.M. on the Friday before the election.

REGISTERED VOTERS
NOVEMBER 1996

County	Republicans	Democrats	Total*
Adams	22,630	14,102	40,308
Allegheny	228,385	517,580	808,503
Armstrong	16,734	19,110	38,443
Beaver	29,928	68,508	105,964
Bedford	15,193	9,660	26,114
Berks	77,820	84,574	179,734
Blair	35,777	21,865	62,480
Bradford	19,809	8,697	31,187
Bucks	172,519	124,270	337,139
Butler	43,067	36,961	88,050
Cambria	26,975	55,141	85,919
Cameron	1,665	1,453	3,277
Carbon	12,013	14,896	29,349
Centre	35,026	28,760	74,847
Chester	140,617	65,269	238,782
Clarion	10,855	9,110	21,156
Clearfield	18,897	19,905	41,276
Clinton	7,819	7,457	16,181
Columbia	14,328	15,672	32,802
Crawford	24,123	17,162	43,476
Cumberland	67,534	34,875	113,689
Dauphin	75,174	50,140	137,129
Delaware	223,946	93,686	346,217
Elk	6,907	10,064	18,262
Erie	62,019	84,445	156,477
Fayette	15,287	55,160	73,528
Forest	1,626	1,198	2,968
Franklin	35,900	20,079	61,307
Fulton	3,774	3,202	7,285
Greene	4,411	14,782	19,823
Huntingdon	12,488	7,718	21,857
Indiana	19,295	20,269	42,985
Jefferson	12,138	10,100	23,406
Juniata	6,338	4,543	11,448
Lackawanna	38,463	85,436	129,381

REGISTERED VOTERS *(continued)*
NOVEMBER 1996

County	Republicans	Democrats	Total*
Lancaster	142,170	56,036	224,162
Lawrence	18,742	30,296	52,185
Lebanon	36,310	16,991	58,412
Lehigh	70,507	73,186	159,113
Luzerne	63,614	101,503	173,280
Lycoming	31,630	22,184	57,588
McKean	14,185	7,362	23,188
Mercer	27,121	32,968	65,099
Mifflin	10,970	8,175	20,282
Monroe	27,727	25,352	61,795
Montgomery	253,409	139,401	443,042
Montour	4,817	3,998	9,712
Northampton	51,481	69,820	136,328
Northumberland	21,473	22,216	46,053
Perry	13,692	6,002	21,283
Philadelphia	201,064	689,880	939,815
Pike	11,639	6,935	21,735
Potter	6,072	3,272	9,806
Schuylkill	42,806	32,016	79,007
Snyder	11,539	3,985	16,738
Somerset	21,528	20,643	44,118
Sullivan	2,315	1,612	4,176
Susquehanna	13,689	7,346	22,528
Tioga	14,786	6,273	22,235
Union	9,667	4,303	15,267
Venango	16,240	11,437	29,700
Warren	13,290	9,753	25,031
Washington	33,962	77,977	120,050
Wayne	14,600	6,438	22,984
Westmoreland	64,751	130,346	210,217
Wyoming	9,676	4,815	15,485
York	95,652	68,293	184,449
Totals	2,910,614	3,336,933	6,805,612

*The difference between a county's total and the total of Democrats and Republicans is those voters registered either independent or in minority parties.

STATE PRESIDENTIAL VOTE, 1900–96

1900:	William McKinley	(R)	712,665
	William J. Bryan	(D)	424,232
1904:	Theodore Roosevelt	(R)	840,949
	Alton B. Parker	(D)	335,430
1908:	William Howard Taft	(R)	745,779
	William J. Bryan	(D)	448,782
1912:	Woodrow Wilson	(D)	395,637
	William Howard Taft	(R)	273,360
1916:	Charles E. Hughes	(R)	703,823
	Woodrow Wilson	(D)	521,784
1920:	Warren Harding	(R)	1,218,216
	James M. Cox	(D)	503,843
1924:	Calvin Coolidge	(R)	1,401,481
	John W. Davis	(D)	409,192
1928:	Herbert Hoover	(R)	2,055,382
	Alfred E. Smith	(D)	1,067,586
1932:	Herbert Hoover	(R)	1,453,540
	Franklin D. Roosevelt	(D)	1,295,948
1936:	Franklin D. Roosevelt	(D)	2,353,987
	Alf Landon	(R)	1,690,200
1940:	Franklin D. Roosevelt	(D)	2,171,035
	Wendell Willkie	(R)	1,889,848
1944:	Franklin D. Roosevelt	(D)	1,940,479
	Thomas E. Dewey	(R)	1,835,054
1948:	Thomas E. Dewey	(R)	1,902,197
	Harry S. Truman	(D)	1,752,426
1952:	Dwight D. Eisenhower	(R)	2,415,789
	Adlai E. Stevenson	(D)	2,146,269
1956:	Dwight D. Eisenhower	(R)	2,585,252
	Adlai E. Stevenson	(D)	1,981,769
1960:	John F. Kennedy	(D)	2,556,282
	Richard M. Nixon	(R)	2,439,956
1964:	Lyndon B. Johnson	(D)	3,130,954
	Barry Goldwater	(R)	1,673,657

STATE PRESIDENTIAL VOTE *(continued)*

1968:	Hubert Humphrey	(D)	2,259,405
	Richard M. Nixon	(R)	2,090,017
1972:	Richard M. Nixon	(R)	2,714,521
	George McGovern	(D)	1,796,951
1976:	James E. Carter	(D)	2,328,677
	Gerald R. Ford	(R)	2,205,604
1980:	Ronald Reagan	(R)	2,261,872
	Jimmy Carter	(D)	1,937,540
1984:	Ronald Reagan	(R)	2,584,323
	Walter F. Mondale	(D)	2,228,131
1988:	George Bush	(R)	2,300,087
	Michael Dukakis	(D)	2,194,944
1992:	Bill Clinton	(D)	2,239,164
	George Bush	(R)	1,791,841
1996:	Bill Clinton	(D)	2,206,241
	Robert Dole	(R)	1,793,568

LOCAL GOVERNMENT

There are 5,538 local government entities in Pennsylvania, including 67 counties, 56 cities, 966 boroughs, one incorporated town, 1,548 townships (91 first class, 1,457 second class), 501 school districts, and 2,399 authorities (some inactive). Each entity is independent of other local units, even if they overlap geographically or sometimes act in concert to perform their functions.

There are various classes of each of the general types of municipalities, except for boroughs, which are not classified. The General Assembly can legislate for each class. Each class of municipality operates under its own code of laws, which define the structure and powers of local government.

Local government entities have taxation authority over people and property within their jurisdiction. The two most commonly imposed taxes are the real estate tax and the earned income tax.

Home rule is an important aspect of Pennsylvania government. The Home Rule Charter and Optional Plans grant municipalities the right to select their own government structure and to decide which services they wish to provide. A home rule municipality is not subject to the state legislature's definition of its powers and organization. As of 1995, 68 municipalities had adopted home rule charters, including five counties, 18 cities, 18 boroughs, and 27 townships.

Counties

There are 67 counties in Pennsylvania, including the consolidated city-county

VOTE FOR GOVERNOR OF PENNSYLVANIA, 1902–94

1902:	Samuel Pennypacker	(R)	593,328
	Robert Pattison	(D)	450,978
1906:	Edwin Stuart	(R)	506,418
	Lewis Emery, Jr.	(D)	458,054
1910:	John Tener	(R)	415,614
	Webster Grim	(D)	129,395
1914:	Martin Brumbaugh	(R)	588,705
	Vance C. McCormick	(D)	453,380
1918:	William C. Sproul	(R)	552,537
	Eugene Bonniwell	(D)	305,315
1922:	Gifford Pinchot	(R)	831,696
	John McSparren	(D)	581,625
1926:	John S. Fisher	(R)	1,102,823
	Eugene Bonniwell	(D)	365,284
1930:	Gifford Pinchot	(R)	1,068,874
	John Hemphill	(D)	1,010,204
1934:	George Earle	(D)	1,476,467
	William Schnader	(R)	1,410,138
1938:	Arthur James	(R)	2,035,340
	Charles Jones	(D)	1,756,192
1942:	Edwin Martin	(R)	1,367,531
	F. Clair Ross	(D)	1,149,897
1946:	James Duff	(R)	1,828,462
	John Rice	(D)	1,270,947
1950:	John Fine	(R)	1,796,119
	Richardson Dilworth	(D)	1,710,355
1954:	George Leader	(D)	1,996,266
	Lloyd Wood	(R)	1,717,070
1958:	David L. Lawrence	(D)	2,024,852
	Arthur McGonigle	(R)	1,948,769
1962:	William W. Scranton	(R)	2,424,918
	Richardson Dilworth	(D)	1,938,627
1966:	Raymond Shafer	(R)	2,110,349
	Milton Shapp	(D)	1,868,719

VOTE FOR GOVERNOR *(continued)*

1970:	Milton Shapp	(D)	2,043,029
	Raymond Broderick	(R)	1,542,854
1974:	Milton Shapp	(D)	1,878,252
	Drew Lewis	(R)	1,578,917
1978:	Dick Thornburgh	(R)	1,966,042
	Pete Flaherty	(D)	1,737,888
1982:	Dick Thornburgh	(R)	1,872,784
	Allen E. Ertel	(D)	1,772,353
1986:	Robert P. Casey	(D)	1,717,484
	William Scranton III	(R)	1,638,268
1990:	Robert P. Casey	(D)	2,065,281
	Barbara Hafer	(R)	987,463
1994:	Tom Ridge	(R)	1,627,976
	Mark Singel	(D)	1,430,099
	Peg Luksik	(C)*	460,269

* Constitutional Party

of Philadelphia, and every resident is under the jurisdiction of one of them. For the purposes of legislation and regulation of their affairs, counties are divided into nine classes, based upon population. The State Constitution establishes a basic organization, but counties may adopt their own form of government. Five counties have adopted home rule charters: Delaware, Erie, Lackawanna, Lehigh, and Northampton.

The functions of county government include law enforcement, judicial administration, the conduct of elections, property assessment, regional planning, solid waste management, public health, welfare functions, and mental health. Counties may also establish housing and redevelopment authorities and community development programs, and can establish and maintain homes for the aged, hospitals, libraries, and community colleges.

County government operates without an executive. Counties are governed by a three-member board of commissioners. Certain county officials are popularly elected and are independent of the commissioners. These include the sheriff, district attorney, prothonotary, clerk of courts, registrar of wills, recorder of deeds and two jury commissioners, the controller or three auditors, and the treasurer. These officials appoint the other county officials and employees.

TAXATION AND FINANCE
Major General Fund Taxes

There are three state taxes in Pennsylvania, which account for about 90 percent of the total General Fund revenue: Sales and Use Tax (35%), Personal

Income Tax (33%), and Corporate Taxes (23%). The Inheritance Tax, Realty Transfer Tax, and Cigarette Tax are the only other taxes that account for more than 1% of general state revenue.

In addition to the General Fund, there are eight special funds of the commonwealth supported by taxes, generally called licenses and fees: Motor, Fish, Game, Banking Department, State Lottery, State Racing, Fire Insurance, and Municipal Pension. These fees are identified in the sections of the *Almanac* devoted to the activities or agencies that administer them.

Sales, Use, and Hotel Occupancy Tax. The rate is 6%. Philadelphia and Allegheny Counties levy an additional 1% tax on items subject to the state levy.

Personal Income Tax. The 2.8% rate is very close to being a flat tax. Allowable deductions are few, personal exemptions are not allowed, and losses in one category of income may not be used to offset gains in another.

Corporate Taxes. There are two major types: Net Income and Capital Stock and Franchise. The Net Income rate has been decreasing since 1994, when it was 11.99%. It was scheduled to reach 9.99% in 1997, and further cuts have been promised by the governor.

The Capital Stock and Franchise Tax rate is 12.75 mills based upon a formula valuation, with a $75,000 valuation exemption.

Inheritance Tax. The rate is determined by the relationship of the heir to the decedent. There is no tax on spousal transfers. Linear heirs—grandparents, parents, and children—are charged 6%. The rate for all other persons is 15%.

Realty Transfer Tax. The state tax of 1% is matched by the counties. Philadelphia County's rate is 4.23.

Cigarette Tax. At a rate of 1.55 cents per cigarette, the tax is 31 cents per package.

Liquor Tax. The state tax on liquor, which is sold legally only in state-owned stores, is 18%. The 6% sales tax is also charged on liquor purchases. Malt beverages, sold only in state-licensed distributorships, are taxed an additional 1 per cent per pint.

Personal Income Tax Information

The Pennsylvania Personal Income Tax became law in 1971. This tax is levied at a flat rate on gross income on eight classes of income. The tax rate, established by the Legislature, is currently 2.8%. The classes of income subject to tax are compensation, interest, dividends, profits from a business or farm, gain from disposition of property, rents, royalties, patents and copyrights, estate and trust income, and gambling winnings, except Pennsylvania Lottery winnings. All taxable income must be reported on a calendar year basis, from January 1 to December 31, unless a specific request is made to file on a fiscal year basis. There is no tax benefit to be gained by filing a joint tax return.

You may order any Pennsylvania tax form or schedule by calling (800) 362-2050 (within Pennsylvania) or (717) 787-8094 (outside the state). The Department of Revenue maintains five regional offices and 23 district offices to assist taxpayers:

Harrisburg Regional Office
    Lobby, Strawberry Square
    Harrisburg, PA 17128
    (717) 783-1404

Philadelphia Regional Office
210 State Office Bldg.
1400 Spring Garden St.
Philadelphia, PA 19130
(215) 560-2483

Erie Regional Office
Sumner Nichols Bldg.
155 W. 8th St.
Erie, PA 16501
(814) 871-4717

Pittsburgh Regional Office
1209A State Office Bldg.
300 Liberty Ave.
Pittsburgh, PA 15222
(412) 565-2450

Wilkes-Barre Regional Office
Samters Bldg.
101 Penn Ave.
Scranton, PA 18503
(717) 963-4080

District Offices should be contacted by phone:

Altoona, (814) 946-7310, serves Blair, Centre, Fulton, Huntingdon, and Mifflin Counties.

Bethlehem, (610) 861-2000, serves Lehigh and Northampton Counties.

Bradford, (814) 368-7113, serves Cameron, Elk, Forest, McKean, Potter, and Warren Counties.

Doylestown, (215) 443-2990, serves Bucks County.

Erie, (814) 871-4491, serves Erie and Crawford Counties.

Greensburg, (412) 832-5283, serves Westmoreland County.

Harrisburg, (717) 783-1405, serves Cumberland, Dauphin, and Perry Counties.

Indiana, (412) 357-7600, serves Armstrong, Clarion, Indiana, and Jefferson Counties.

Johnstown, (814) 533-2495, serves Bedford, Cambria, Clearfield, and Somerset Counties.

Lancaster, (717) 299-7581, serves Lancaster and Lebanon Counties.

Newtown Square, (610) 353-4051, serves Chester and Delaware Counties.

New Castle, (412) 656-3203, serves Beaver, Butler, Lawrence, Mercer, and Venango Counties.

Norristown, (610) 270-1780, serves Montgomery County.

Philadelphia, (215) 560-2056, serves Philadelphia County.

Pittsburgh, (412) 565-7540, serves Allegheny County.

Pottsville, (717) 621-3175, serves Carbon and Schuylkill Counties.

Reading, (610) 378-4401, serves Berks County.

Scranton, (717) 963-4585, serves Lackawanna, Monroe, Pike, Susquehanna, and Wayne Counties.

Sunbury, (717) 988-5520, serves Columbia, Juniata, Montour, Northumberland, Snyder, and Union Counties.

Washington, (412) 223-4550, serves Fayette, Greene, and Washington Counties.

Wilkes-Barre, (717) 826-2466, serves Luzerne and Wyoming Counties.

Williamsport, (717) 327-3475, serves Bradford, Clinton, Lycoming, Sullivan, and Tioga Counties.

York, (717) 845-6661, serves Adams, Franklin, and York Counties.

The Pennsylvania Lottery

The Pennsylvania Lottery was established on August 26, 1971, by legislative act, Title 91. The law specified that all proceeds were to be used to benefit older citizens, specifically, to provide property tax relief for the elderly.

Program benefits have since expanded to include rent rebates, free and reduced-fare public transit and reduced vehicle registration fees, a copayment prescription drug program (PACE), and funding for 67 Area Agencies on Aging services.

By law, the lottery must provide 30 cents of every dollar for benefits and 40 cents for prizes. In 1995, both of these minimums were surpassed, 40% of revenues being contributed to benefits, 51% to prizes. Retailers earn 5 cents for every $1 ticket they sell; overall administrative costs were 3.1% of gross revenues.

These percentages translated into significant amounts based upon 1995 sales of about $1.6 billion from six online and numerous instant games. Programs for the elderly received $631 million, players got $812 million back in prizes, retailers earned $81 million, and operating expenses were $50 million.

Since its beginning, the lottery has had sales of $20 billion. The largest prize ever awarded was $115.5 million.

Expenditures

Based upon the governor's fiscal year 1996–97 budget, the top departments or agencies are ranked by expenditures from the State General Fund:

Education	$6.9 billion
Public Welfare	$5.2 billion
Corrections	$916 million
Treasury	$608 million
Transportation	$291 million
Higher Education Assistance	$280 million
Revenue	$275 million
Health	$197 million
Legislature	$185 million
Judiciary	$177 million
Environmental Protection	$131 million
Economic and Community Development	$130 million
State Police	$122 million
Executive Offices	$93 million
General Services	$92 million
Conservation and Natural Resources	$72 million
Probation and Parole	$71 million
Military and Veterans Affairs	$69 million
Labor and Industry	$58 million
Attorney General	$56 million

Salaries

In 1995, the following salary schedule for public officials was enacted by the General Assembly:

Governor	$125,000
Lieutenant Governor	$105,000
Adjutant General	$90,000
Secretary of Aging	$95,000
Secretary of Agriculture	$90,000
Attorney General	$104,000
Auditor General	$104,000
Secretary of Banking	$90,000
Secretary of Community and Economic Development	$95,000
Secretary of the Commonwealth	$90,000
Secretary of Conservation and Natural Resources	$95,000
Secretary of Corrections	$100,000
Secretary of Education	$100,000
Secretary of Environmental Protection	$100,000
Secretary of General Services	$95,000
Secretary of Health	$100,000
Insurance Commissioner	$90,000

STATE GOVERNMENT EMPLOYEES (1996–97)

Department	Employees
Governor's Office	91
Executive Offices	2,218
Lieutenant Governor's Office	17
Aging	105
Agriculture	626
Banking	120
Civil Service Commission	181
Community and Economic Development	303
Conservation and Natural Resources	1,304
Corrections	12,178
Education	1,086
Emergency Management Agency	129
Environmental Hearing Board	22
Environmental Protection	3,169
Fish and Boat Commission	438
Game Commission	731
General Services	1,316
Health	1,395
Historical and Museum Commission	322
Infrastructure Investment Authority	22
Insurance	294
Labor and Industry	6,449
Liquor Control Board	2,969
Military and Veterans Affairs	1,805
Milk Marketing Board	36
Municipal Employees' Retirement	22
Probation and Parole Board	900
Public Television Network	20
Public Utility Commission	560
Public Welfare	25,625
Revenue	2,317
School Employees' Retirement System	289
Securities Commission	71

STATE GOVERNMENT EMPLOYEES *(continued)*

Department	Employees
State	385
State Employees' Retirement System	190
State Police	5,403
Tax Equalization Board	22
Transportation	12,405
Total All Departments	85,535

Source: Fiscal Year 1997–98 Governor's Executive Budget

Secretary of Labor and Industry	$100,000	Philadelphia Traffic Court Judge	$54,500
Secretary of Public Welfare	$100,000	District Justice	$51,500
Secretary of Revenue	$95,000	General Assembly,	
State Police Commissioner	$95,000	Representatives and	
Secretary of Transportation	$100,000	Senators	$57,367
State Treasurer	$104,000	salary plus $863 monthly	
Supreme Court, Chief Justice	$123,000	expenses. Officers and	
Supreme Court Justice	$119,750	leaders of the Assembly	
Superior Court, President Judge	$117,750	receive an additional	
Superior Court Judge	$116,000	expense allowance ranging	
Commonwealth Court, President Judge	$117,750	from $103 to $411 monthly.	
Commonwealth Court Judge	$116,000	Boards and Commissions:	
Court of Common Pleas, President Judge:		Board of Claims, Chairman	$84,800
Allegheny County	$106,000	Board of Claims Member	$80,800
Philadelphia County	$106,500	Public Utilities Commission, Chairman	$97,500
Other Districts	$104,000–105,000	Public Utilities Commission Member	$95,000
Court of Common Pleas Judge	$104,000	Liquor Control Board, Chairman	$50,800
Philadelphia Municipal Court, President Judge	$103,000	Liquor Control Board Member	$48,800
Philadelphia Municipal Court Judge	$101,250	Civil Service Commission, Chairman	$40,625
Philadelphia Traffic Court, President Judge	$55,000	Civil Service Commission Member	$40,625
		State Tax Equalization Board, Chairman	$17,500

State Tax Equalization Board Member	$16,250
Milk Marketing Board, Chairman	$16,250
Milk Marketing Board Member	$15,625
Securities Commission, Chairman	$16,250
Securities Commission Member	$15,000
Athletic Commission, Chairman	$13,125
Athletic Commission Member	$12,500
Board of Pardons Member	$11,500

These salaries are subject to an annual cost-of-living adjustment, effective December 1.

COUNTY PROFILES

The following addresses and phone numbers are for each county's courthouse. If only a phone number is listed. no street address is necessary for mailing correspondence.

ADAMS COUNTY

111 Baltimore St., Gettysburg, PA 17325 (717) 334-6781

Population: 78,724 (1990), 83,998 (1995)
Square miles: 520
Population per square mile: 151
Municipalities: 34 (13 boroughs, 21 townships)

The Scots-Irish who settled in the western part of York County in the 1740s, when the area was dominated by Germans, established a separate county in 1800, which they named in honor of President John Adams. Gettysburg, the county seat, was incorporated as a borough in 1806. It was named for a local landowner, James Getty.

Iron ore mining was one of the earliest industries in Adams County; it was superseded by limestone quarrying in the 1870s. The county has always been primarily agricultural. Only about 35 square miles of it is urban. Today, farming and tourism are the leading industries. "The Fruit Belt," where about half the Pennsylvania apple crop is grown, is part of both. The 1,100 farms in the county produce $140 million of cash receipts. Food processors are the major employers, which include the Knouse Food Cooperative; Gettysburg College, a historic institution, is the third largest.

Gettysburg's place in American history was established July 1–3, 1863, when Confederate and Union forces fought an epic battle here. Later that year, Abraham Lincoln delivered his immortal Gettysburg Address while dedicating the National Cemetery.

Gettysburg abounds in Civil War sites and memorabilia. The National Military Park attracted 1.7 million visitors in 1994. Further military interest centers around the Eisenhower National Historic Site, which includes the farm and retirement home of Dwight D. Eisenhower, the 33rd president of the United States and the supreme commander of the European armies in World War II.

Adams County is served by U.S. Route 30 east and west and U.S. Route 15 and PA Route 94 north and south.

ALLEGHENY COUNTY

436 Grant Street
Pittsburgh, PA 15219
(412) 350-5313
Population:
1,336,449 (1990), 1,309,821 (1995)
Square miles: 730
Population per square mile: 1,794
Municipalities: 128
(4 cities, 82 boroughs, 42 townships)

Allegheny County was created in 1788 from parts of Westmoreland and Washington Counties and was named for the Allegheny River; the county was reduced to its present size in 1800. Pittsburgh, the county seat, was named for William Pitt, a British statesman and prime minister. It was incorporated as a borough in 1794 and chartered as a city in 1816.

Long before "The Point" (where the Allegheny and Monogahela Rivers meet to form the Ohio River) was the site of a famous athletic stadium, it was of great strategic value in the struggle for possession of the Ohio Valley between the French and the British in the mid-1700s. On the recommendation of young George Washington, the British built Fort Pitt on the site, lost it to the French, and then regained it. The settlement that grew up outside its walls evolved into present-day Pittsburgh.

Early-19th-century industries of importance included boat building, iron making, and glass manufacturing. Through the period, Pittsburgh benefited from its location at the headwaters of a great water transportation system. It also had access to great fields of bituminous coal, limestone, and iron ore. The transportation that delivered raw materials to the city was always state-of-the-art: the Pennsylvania Canal, the railroads, the roads and turnpikes, and the Interstate Highway System, including I-79, I-279, and I-376, which were routed to meet Pittsburgh's needs.

Allegheny County evolved into an industrial colossus. Iron and steel were the core industries; other important industries, established by legendary entrepreneurs, included natural gas, petroleum, sand and gravel, electrical equipment, wood products, plate glass, paints, and food products.

In an era before government environmental regulation, this intense economic activity destroyed the land, air, and water, and the city became virtually uninhabitable. But Pittsburgh was reborn, beginning in the late 1940s, by combined political, industrial, and financial forces and, ironically, by a post–World War II economy that made other countries more attractive as places to do business. Along with its industry, the county lost 50% of its population between 1930 and 1990. The decline is excepted to continue into the year 2000.

The 40th-largest city in the country as of 1997, Pittsburgh is a vastly different place. While the county still has the largest number of manufacturing establishments (1,759) and the second-largest number of employees (over 89,000) in manufacturing in the state, and is the home of eight Fortune 500 companies, it is evolving into a high-technology and medical research center. Pittsburgh is now a center of finance, health services (with more than 50 hospitals), research and development, government, retail trade, and education (with 32 institutions).

Nevertheless, the area is not creating jobs on the scale needed to allow new workers to break into the market. Many young applicants must ultimately leave the area to find employment.

In 1985, Rand McNally rated Pittsburgh as the most livable city in America. One reason for this rating is its world-class cultural institutions, many of which were financed through gifts of the early entrepreneurs. They include the Carnegie Museum of Art, Carnegie Museum of Natural History, Carnegie Music Hall, Frick Art and Historical Center, Heinz Hall, and the Benedum Center for the Performing Arts. An exceptional selection of theater, dance, opera, and music is available.

ARMSTRONG COUNTY

Market St.,
Kittanning, PA 16201
(412) 543-2500
Population:
73,478 (1990), 74,569 (1995)
Square miles: 654
Population per square mile: 111
Municipalities: 45
(1 city, 16 boroughs, 28 townships)

Armstrong County was created in 1800 from three adjacent counties. It was named for Gen. John Armstrong, whose forces destroyed Kittanning, the largest Indian settlement west of the Alleghenies, in 1756, thereby making the area safer for settlers. Many of the Scots-Irish who later settled here were given their land as a reward for military service. The county seat, Kittanning, which means "at the great stream," was incorporated in 1821. It is located on the Allegheny River in the county's center.

Located about 40 miles northeast of Pittsburgh, in the heart of the Allegheny Highlands, Armstrong County is a land of vast rolling hills and fertile fields among placid lakes and streams. About 85% of the land is farmland or forest. The 740 farms produced $100 million of cash receipts in 1994. Only two of the 45 municipalities have over 5,000 residents.

The abundant resources found in the mines and quarries of the county contributed to the industrial development of western Pennsylvania. Iron and steel were produced here, as was plate glass, at the largest plate glass factory in the world.

Keystone Coal Company remains a major employer, but in general, the old industries are being replaced by high-tech companies, especially those related to the tool and die industry. Public agencies and utilities are major employers. The transition has been painful. County unemployment rates during the last 10 years have been above the commonwealth's average. Median household income dropped 13% between 1980 and 1990. Population peaked in 1960 and has been declining, although it is now growing slowly.

Nellie Bly is the most famous native of Armstrong County. An early feminist and newspaper reporter, she traveled around the world in 72 days in 1889 and 1890, beating the time of the protagonist in the Jules Verne novel *Around the World in 80 Days.*

U.S. Route 422 east and west links Kittanning to Indiana and Butler; PA Route 28 crosses the county northeast to southwest.

BEAVER COUNTY

Third St.,
Beaver, PA 15009
(412) 728-5700
Population:
186,093 (1990), 187,927 (1995)
Square miles: 435
Population per square mile: 419
Municipalities: 53
(2 cities, 29 boroughs, 22 townships)

Beaver County was created in 1800 from parts of Allegheny and Washington Counties and was named for the animal that sustained both the Indians and the early settlers. Beaver, the county seat, was incorporated as a borough in 1802. The county is on the Ohio border and is part of the Pittsburgh metropolitan area.

Agriculture and industry were the most important factors in the development of the county. Eventually, mining, metal, and metal products became important economic aspects. The fortunes of the county rose and fell with the Pittsburgh industrial colossus.

Devastated by the demise of the basic steel industry in the 1980s, especially by the closing of the mammoth Jones and Laughlin mill in Aliquippa, the county is struggling to reestablish its economic base. Household income declined 27% between 1980 and 1990. Population declined 9% during that period but is now growing slowly.

Service and retail trade are increasing in importance—medical centers are major employers, as is county government. Suburban shopping malls provide many retail jobs.

Beaver County is almost always rec-ognized in the national quality of life rankings in national magazines. *Money* magazine once ranked it the fourth most desirable area in the U.S. in which to live. In 1991, Century 21 Real Estate rated it the number one suburban location in the country. A low crime rate and the cultural opportunities in Pittsburgh were major factors in the high ratings.

Raccoon State Park in southern Beaver County is one of the largest state parks.

The Turnpike crosses the northeast corner of the county; U.S. Route 30 and PA Routes 51, 60, and 65 are the important roads.

BEDFORD COUNTY

203 S. Juliana St.,
Bedford, PA 15522
(814) 623-4833
Population:
47,919 (1990), 49,192 (1995)
Square miles: 1,015
Population per square mile: 48
Municipalities: 38
(13 boroughs, 25 townships)

Bedford County was created in 1771 from part of Cumberland County. It was named for Fort Bedford, which was named for the duke of Bedford. Bedford, the county seat, was laid out in 1776 on the site of the fort and incorporated as a borough in 1795.

From 1758, when Route 30, called "the Great Road," opened, Bedford was an important fort. It was meant to stabilize an area plagued by Indian massacres. George Washington spent a tour of duty here. He also established his headquarters at the fort during the Whiskey Rebellion. Route 30 and the fort also put Bedford on the route west.

Early industries included farming, sheep ranching, and iron production. Agriculture is still important. About 1,000 farms produced $64 million in cash receipts in 1994. Bedford Springs was a renowned health resort in the era of prescientific medicine. President James Buchanan established his Summer White House at the Springs.

Of the 14,000 nonfarm workers in the county, 30% are employed in manufacturing, 28% in retail trade, and 20% in services. Old Bedford Village, a living museum depicting life in the era from 1750 to 1850, is the center of tourism; there are three state parks and about 30,000 acres of state forestland.

A 35-mile stretch of the Turnpike crosses the county; U.S. Route 220 is the major north-south route. A major commercial complex has developed where the two routes intersect. Historic U.S. Route 30 is the scenic route of choice in this rural county on the Maryland border.

BERKS COUNTY

633 Court St.,
Reading, PA 19601
(610) 478-6134
Population:
336,532 (1990), 349,583 (1995)
Square miles: 859
Population per square mile: 407
Municipalities: 76
(1 city, 31 boroughs, 44 townships)

Berks County was created in 1752 from parts of Chester, Lancaster, and Philadelphia Counties and was named for Berkshire, England. Reading, the county seat, was named by Thomas Penn for Berkshire's county town. It was incorporated as a borough in 1783 and chartered as a city in 1847.

Berks County is a diamond-shaped area situated in southeastern Pennsylvania. Sections of the Blue and South Mountains, ridges of the Appalachian Mountain chain, form its northern and southern boundaries.

The foremost colonial industry was iron. The first iron forge in Pennsylvania was built in Berks County in 1716. When the iron industry declined, agriculture became the most important activity. The county was settled by almost every group that came to Pennsylvania— Swedes from the Delaware River area, Amish, Mennonites, Dunkers, Quakers, and French Huguenots.

The county prospered because of its location—roads and canals linked it with Philadelphia. Ultimately, these were surpassed by railroads; the Reading Railroad, of which Reading was the hub, ended the Canal Era and also provided work on the railroad and in its repair shops. From 1900 to 1915, the Duryea Power Company produced automobiles in Reading.

Today, about half the land in Berks County is devoted to agriculture. It is the third-leading producer of livestock and dairy products in the state. It is still an important industrial area, a center of textile, metal, and food production. Reading is a major center of outlet shopping. Albright College in Reading and Kutztown State University are the county's cultural centers.

Berks is well served by modern highways. The Turnpike, I-78 and I-176, and U.S. Routes 22, 222, and 422 provide con-

venient access to nearby urban areas—
Philadelphia, 55 miles away; Baltimore,
100 miles; and New York City, 125 miles.

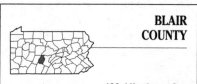

**BLAIR
COUNTY**

423 Allegheny St.,
Hollidaysburg, PA 16648
(814) 695-5541

Population:
130,542 (1990), 131,647 (1995)
Square miles: 526
Population per square mile: 250
Municipalities: 24
(1 city, 8 boroughs, 15 townships)

Blair County was created in 1846 from
parts of Bedford and Huntingdon Counties and was named for John Blair, a
prominent citizen. Hollidaysburg, the
county seat, was incorporated as a borough in 1836 and was named in honor of
the Holliday family, killed by Indians.

Early economic activity included
farming by German settlers in the fertile
valleys, iron and metal working (county
forges supplied the Continental Army
with over half of its lead), and an early
railroad in Hollidaysburg. The Portage
Railroad was an ingenious solution to
the problem of using canals to ship
goods across the mountains. Boats were
lifted from the Juniata Canal, hoisted
over the mountain, and set into the
Conemaugh River and Canal in
Johnstown.

The Pennsylvania Railroad ended this
activity and transformed Blair County
when tracks were laid across the mountain west of Altoona in 1852. The world-
famous Horseshoe Curve, a 2,375-foot
curve, rises at a rate of 91 feet per mile

to an elevation of 1,594 feet. The railroad
then built its shops, the largest in the
world, in Altoona, a village that it
founded and made into a city. By 1854,
the Pennsylvania Railroad was the
nation's most powerful rail system, and
Altoona and Blair County prospered with
it. The prosperity lasted for over a
century. In 1968, weakened by interstate
highways and trucks, air travel, and
the decline of Pennsylvania's industrial regions, the Pennsylvania Railroad
merged with the New York Central Railroad. The combined company died in
1970, the largest failure in American
business history. By 1990, the population
of Altoona had declined by 37% from its
peak in 1929.

The great railroad era left a historic
legacy. Horseshoe Curve and the Allegheny Portage Railroad Site have been
designated as National Historic Landmarks. Unfortunately for Blair County,
the U.S. National Railroad Park, Steamtown, was awarded to Scranton and
the Pennsylvania Railroad Museum to
Strasburg.

The leading employers today in Blair
County are hospitals and government
agencies. Brown Shoe Company is the
biggest manufacturing employer. A
major Penn State University Center is located in Altoona. The main campus
in University Park is only 43 miles
northeast.

U.S. Routes 22 and 220 cross the
county; the latter connects with the
Turnpike in Bedford County.

BRADFORD COUNTY

301 Main St.,
Towanda, PA 18848
(717) 265-1727
Population:
60,967 (1990), 62,260 (1995)
Square Miles: 1,151
Population per square mile: 54
Municipalities: 51
(14 boroughs, 37 townships)

Bradford County was created in 1810 from parts of Luzerne and Lycoming Counties and was originally named Ontario County. When it was formally organized in 1812, it was renamed Bradford to honor William Bradford, the attorney general in Washington's cabinet. Towanda, the county seat, was incorporated as a borough in 1828 and was named for the creek.

The first settlers, in 1771, were Germans from New York State. There was a strong Indian presence in the county; Wyalusing was a fortified village of the Iroquois and Munsee tribes. At Asylum (Azilum) in 1793, French exiles attempted to establish a haven in the New World from the revolutionary chaos in France. The Asylum Company bought 1,600 acres and built a village. Marie Antoinette and her two children were rumored to be coming to Asylum if they could escape from France. The venture failed; most of the settlers returned to France or went to the southern United States.

Agriculture, particularly dairy farming, has been an important industry since the beginning of Bradford County. Dairy, beef, and veal products are sold regionally. Cash receipts of $110 million in 1994 for farm products were the seventh highest in the state.

Major employers include Orsam Sylvania, with 1,400 employees at a chemical plant; DuPont, with 700 at a photochemical plant; and Masonite Corporation, with 600 at a wood products plant, all at Towanda. The largest employer in the county is a health-care system.

Bradford County lives up to is tourist office designation as a part of the "Endless Mountains" region of northern Pennsylvania. Rolling hills, deep stream valleys, and low plateaus abound. Hunting and fishing are important activities. The population peaked in 1980, but it is again growing, albeit slowly.

Towanda is 65 miles west of the nearest interstate highway interchange; the county is served by U.S. Routes 6 and 220 and five state routes.

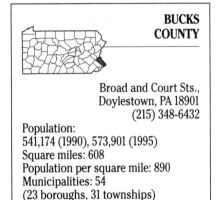

BUCKS COUNTY

Broad and Court Sts.,
Doylestown, PA 18901
(215) 348-6432
Population:
541,174 (1990), 573,901 (1995)
Square miles: 608
Population per square mile: 890
Municipalities: 54
(23 boroughs, 31 townships)

Bucks County was one of the original counties created by William Penn in 1682. Bucks is a contraction of Buckinghamshire, Penn's English shire. Doylestown, the county seat since 1812, when it replaced Newtown, was incorporated as a borough in 1838. It was named for William Doyle, an innkeeper.

Penn built his country estate, Pennsbury Manor, in Bucks County and commuted to Philadelphia by barge. About half of the Quakers who arrived on the good ship *Welcome* with Penn also settled in Bucks. More than 300 years later, James Michener, a native son, referred to the area as "a kind of residential paradise, with its winding roads, covered bridges and beautiful valleys."

George Washington crossed the Delaware from a site in Bucks County now called Washington Crossing on Christmas night 1776 to attack the British at Trenton, reviving hope when national morale was low. He sent his report of the victory to Congress from Newtown.

Most of the Delaware Canal is in Bucks County. Now a state park, the canal was once a major industrial highway, from Easton to Bristol, linking Philadelphia with the anthracite region.

As recently as 50 years ago, Bucks County produced one-third of the vegetables grown in the state. Its production ranked seventh in the nation. By 1994, it had fallen to 25th in the state. The population increased 13% between 1980 and 1990; by 1995, there were another 32,000 residents.

Manufacturing is important to the economy; much of it is in postindustrial sectors. The two largest employers in 1994 were the national and county governments. Household income ranks among the highest in the state.

Tourism has emerged as a major industry, contributing about $300 million annually to the economy. New Hope, a charming 18th-century village and artists' colony on the Delaware Canal, is a major draw. Doylestown has two concrete castles built by Henry Mercer,

which are now intriguing museums. Washington Crossing National Park, four state parks, and numerous vineyards are additional lures.

I-95, I-276, and U.S. Route 1 cross the developed southeast corner of the county.

BUTLER COUNTY

336 S. Main St.,
Butler, PA 16001
(412) 285-4731

Population:
152,013 (1990), 165,557 (1995)
Square miles: 789
Population per square mile: 210
Municipalities: 57
(1 city, 23 boroughs, 33 townships)

Butler County was created in 1800 from Allegheny County and was named for Gen. Richard Butler, a lawyer, legislator, Indian agent, and soldier who was killed in battle in 1791. Butler, the county seat, was laid out in 1803, incorporated as a borough in 1817, and chartered as a city in 1918.

Butler was a major participant in the Pennsylvania oil and gas boom in the 1870s. Its oil wells supplied 75% of the world's demand. There are still remnants of the industries, mostly specialty producers.

Butler was the home of John Roebling, inventor of the modern steel cable and designer of the Brooklyn Bridge. Butler also was home to a pioneering automobile manufacturer from 1912 to 1940. The American Bantam Car Company built small, open, light vehicles and built the first commercial jeep in 1946.

Butler County is directly north of Pittsburgh. The availability of land served by public utilities and a favorable tax structure caused it to grow rapidly from 1970 to 1990; population increased 19%, and housing units 47%. This growth came in spite of a 25% drop in manufacturing jobs. These losses were offset by gains in trade and services.

Two-thirds of the county is classified as rural. Farming is important. The 1,180 farms produced $47 million in 1995. The county is a leading producer of lamb. Only three of the 57 municipalities have a population in excess of 10,000. Semi-rural, small-town life can still be had here, less than an hour from Pittsburgh.

Residents often look to Pittsburgh for recreation and culture, but Slippery Rock State University and Moraine State Park are within the county's boundaries. The park, a 16,000-acre site near the intersection of I-79 and U.S. Route 422, Butler County's two major highways, was resurrected from environmental death in the 1960s.

CAMBRIA COUNTY

S. Center St.,
Ebensburg, PA 15931
(814) 472-5440
Population:
163,029 (1990), 160,531 (1995)
Square miles: 688
Population per square mile: 233
Municipalities: 64
(1 city, 33 boroughs, 30 townships)

Cambria County was created in 1804 from parts of three adjacent counties. Cambria is an ancient name for Wales.

Ebensburg, the county seat, was incorporated as a borough in 1825 and named for the son of a local minister.

The first permanent white settlement was a Welsh colony founded by an agent of Dr. Benjamin Rush. The county was a center of bituminous coal mining and iron and steel production, and was a transportation center from 1830 to 1860. The Pennsylvania Canal was an important element in each of these. The Portage Railroad between Holidaysburg and Johnstown, completed in 1834, connected the eastern and western segments of the canal. The Pennsylvania Railroad replaced it.

Iron ore manufacturing dates from the establishment of the Cambria Furnace in 1842. Before the Civil War, the area was one of the largest iron-producing areas in the state. The Cambria Iron Works produced the first steel rails in 1867.

The defining event in the history of Cambria County occurred on May 31, 1889, when a dam burst near Johnstown and 200 million tons of water roared through the valley, killing thousands and destroying everything in its path. The Johnstown Flood Museum, housed in a former public library building rebuilt by Andrew Carnegie in 1891, commemorates the event.

Recent technological changes have rendered Cambria County's industries obsolete. The transition to the new world order has been slow and painful. The county population declined precipitously from 1960 to 1995. The population of Johnstown has declined almost 60% since 1930. The unemployment rate is usually the highest in the state and wages are generally the lowest. Household income declined almost 20% between 1980 and 1990.

Prince Gallitzin State Park and adjacent state game lands are the principal natural attractions in the county. There is a branch of the University of Pittsburgh in Johnstown.

The county is crossed by U.S. Route 219 north and south, and U.S. Route 22 east and west.

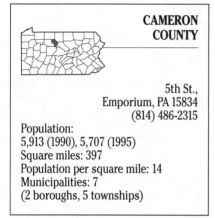

CAMERON COUNTY

5th St.,
Emporium, PA 15834
(814) 486-2315
Population:
5,913 (1990), 5,707 (1995)
Square miles: 397
Population per square mile: 14
Municipalities: 7
(2 boroughs, 5 townships)

Cameron County was created in 1860 from parts of four adjacent counties and was named for Simon Cameron, a U.S. senator, secretary of war in Lincoln's cabinet, and ambassador to Russia. Emporium, the county seat, was incorporated as a borough in 1864; its name means market or trade center.

Many of the early settlers were Revolutionary War veterans. Settlement of the area began around 1810. Lumbering and tanning industries grew up in the area, and in 1890, a powder plant opened in Emporium. Dynamite produced there was used to build the Panama Canal. As lumbering declined, some agriculture developed, but the area is 97% forest today.

Most of the population lives in Emporium Borough and Shippen Township. The population peaked in 1960 at 7,500, fell to 5,900 in 1990, and has continued its slow decline. The area has some manufacturing enterprises that produce fabricated metal products, cutlery, hand tools, and hardware.

There are three state parks and 131,000 acres of state forestland in the county. All of the roads are scenic; PA Route 120 is Bucktail State Park, perhaps the ultimate Pennsylvania scenic road.

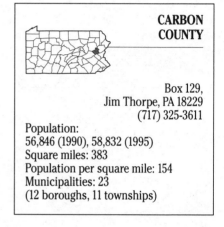

CARBON COUNTY

Box 129,
Jim Thorpe, PA 18229
(717) 325-3611
Population:
56,846 (1990), 58,832 (1995)
Square miles: 383
Population per square mile: 154
Municipalities: 23
(12 boroughs, 11 townships)

Carbon County was created in 1843 from parts of Northampton and Monroe Counties. Its name refers to its deposits of anthracite coal. Jim Thorpe, the county seat, was originally incorporated as Mauch Chunk (Bear Mountain) in 1850. It was renamed in 1954 to honor the famous Native American athlete, who was buried here.

Anthracite coal was discovered in Carbon County near Mauch Chunk in 1791, and ultimately the first large commercial coal operation was established on the site. Lumbering, milling, metals, and farming remained important industries in the county, but coal was its lifeblood.

The economy of Carbon County today has three major components: service industries, especially those that have developed around recreation sites in the three state parks and three ski areas; manufacturing, primarily women's apparel; and retail trade.

I-80 crosses the northern portion of the county; the Northeast Extension of the Turnpike runs the length of the county, north and south.

CENTRE COUNTY

Bellefonte, PA 16823
(814) 355-6700
Population:
123,786 (1990), 131,968 (1995)
Square miles: 1,108
Population per square mile: 119
Municipalities: 36
(11 boroughs, 25 townships)

Centre County was created in 1800 from parts of four counties. It was named for its location in the geographic center of the state. Bellefonte, the county seat, was incorporated as a borough in 1806. Its name refers to a large spring that Talleyrand, the French statesman, called *belle fonte,* beautiful spring, in French.

The discovery of iron ore in 1790 led to the establishment of an iron industry. The county was the iron center of the nation until the mid-1800s. Farming was the other major activity in the county, but the destiny of the area rested upon the establishment of an educational institution created in response to the Land Grant College Act signed in 1862 by Abraham Lincoln. The state legisla-

ture established its land-grant school, the Farmers Agricultural and Mechanical High School, in Centre County. This evolved into the Pennsylvania State University.

With about 60,000 students and 4,400 employees, the university is the center of Centre County. The football team is an industry unto itself, drawing 100,000 fans to the area five or six times a year.

Other major employers include the state government and the State College School District in the public sector, and Corning Glass and Murata Erie in the private sector.

The northwestern half of the county is a forested plateau divided by numerous fast-flowing streams. Philipsburg and Snow Shoe are the principal industrial, mining, and residential centers. The southeastern half contains the alternating ridges and valleys common to central Pennsylvania and is the agricultural center of the county. Light industrial and research and development centers are numerous in the State College and Bellefonte areas. State College is the largest municipality, with 40,000 residents.

Centre County offers many recreational opportunities: a state park, parts of four state forests, and two natural areas. State College is the site of the annual Central Pennsylvania Festival of the Arts.

I-80 and U.S. Routes 220 and 322 are the major roads.

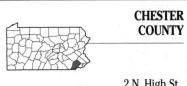

CHESTER COUNTY

2 N. High St.,
West Chester, PA 19380
(610) 344-6100
Population:
376,396 (1990), 404,945 (1995)
Square miles: 756
Population per square mile: 536
Municipalities: 73
(1 city, 15 boroughs, 57 townships)

Chester County, one of the three original counties, was laid out in 1682 by William Penn. Its name was derived from Cheshire, England, from whence many of its earliest settlers came. West Chester, the county seat, was incorporated as a borough in 1799 and named for the shire town of Cheshire.

Chester County began as a Swedish settlement along the Delaware River in 1643. That area is now the city of Chester in Delaware County. (Delaware County was created from part of Chester County in 1789.)

Chester County was the site of two important Revolutionary War battles: Brandywine and Valley Forge. Always an important agricultural area, the county developed a broad manufacturing base as well, particularly in iron and steel. The first rolling mill in America was built in Coatesville in 1793; two steel mills survive to this day.

The county's modern economy is a vibrant combination of agriculture, services, manufacturing, and trade. The county leads the state in crop production and was fourth in diary production in 1995. A mushroom-growing center in Kennett Square produces about 45% of U.S. mushrooms. The county's 1,550 farms produced cash receipts of $479 million in 1994. The overall unemployment rate is consistently below the state average; the median family income is the highest in the state.

There are six institutions of higher education, numerous museums and historic attractions, and 13 federal, state, and county recreation areas in the county. This is also horse country, and the Devon Horse Show is a major event.

The county is served by 26 miles of the Turnpike; U.S. Routes 1, 30, 202, and 322; and PA Route 100.

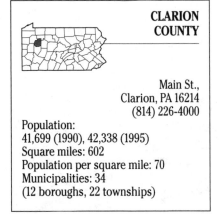

CLARION COUNTY

Main St.,
Clarion, PA 16214
(814) 226-4000
Population:
41,699 (1990), 42,338 (1995)
Square miles: 602
Population per square mile: 70
Municipalities: 34
(12 boroughs, 22 townships)

Clarion County was created in 1839 from parts of Venango and Armstrong Counties. The county was named for the Clarion river's clear sound of distant ripples. Clarion, the county seat, was incorporated as a borough in 1841.

Once known as "Iron County," Clarion prospered in the mid-1800s, when 31 stone blast furnaces were in operation. The industry collapsed during the Civil War when the technology changed. The timber industry was also important; settlers used the Clarion and Allegheny Rivers to transport timber to markets.

Cook State Forest is a vestige of the timber era with its large stand of virgin white pine and hemlock. By 1876, about 50 oil wells were operating in the county; natural gas and bituminous coal were also plentiful.

Today, Clarion State University is the largest employer and cultural center of the county. The economy also includes manufacturing, tourism, and farming. Other major employers include Owens-Brockway Packaging, Clarion Hospital, and state government; four modular housing production companies employ about 1,500.

Autumn foliage in the picturesque valleys carved from the mountains by the rivers draws many of the county's annual 250,000 visitors. Finally, there are about 500 farms with cash receipts of about $25 million, produced in livestock and dairy products.

I-80's six exits have produced a significant improvement in the county's commercial life. I-79 intersects I-80 50 miles west of Clarion; U.S. Route 322 parallels I-80.

Counties. Clearfield was designated as the county seat in 1805 and incorporated as a borough in 1840. The area was a wilderness when it was organized, and it functioned as a part of Centre County until 1822. The name was derived from the large surrounding fields cleared of undergrowth by buffalo wallows.

Early settlers included Revolutionary War veterans who were given grants of land, Quakers who settled in Grampton in 1805, Germans who settled in Luthersburg in 1820, and French settlers who established Frenchville in 1832.

Natural resources—timber, coal, clay, and iron ore—fueled the county's growth. A pioneer charcoal furnace was erected in 1814 on the Little Moshannon Creek. By 1840, lumbering had become the major industry. At one time over 400 sawmills operated in the county. Coal mining replaced lumbering around 1900. Twentieth-century industries also included surface mining of stone and sand, leather, metal, and food products. A state prison opened in Houtzdale in 1996.

The county has 97,000 acres of public forestland and two state parks. The West Branch of the Susquehanna River, once an industrial highway, is valued today as a scenic and recreational area.

Easy access to Clearfield County is available at six exits of I-80. These have proven to be a major stimulus to the retail trade sector. U.S. Route 219 is the major north-south road; U.S. Route 322 parallels I-80.

CLEARFIELD COUNTY

2 Market St.,
Clearfield, PA 16830
(814) 765-2641

Population:
78,097 (1990), 79,724 (1995)
Square miles: 1,147
Population per square mile: 70
Municipalities: 50
(1 city, 19 boroughs, 30 townships)

Clearfield County was created in 1804 from parts of Huntingdon and Lycoming

CLINTON COUNTY

Box 928,
Lock Haven, PA 17745
(717) 893-4000
Population:
37,182 (1990), 37,215 (1995)
Square miles: 891
Population per square mile: 42
Municipalities: 29
(1 city, 7 boroughs, 21 townships)

Clinton County was created in 1839 from parts of Centre and Lycoming Counties and named for De Witt Clinton, governor of New York, who was a promoter of the Erie Canal. Lock Haven, the county seat, was incorporated as a borough in 1840 and chartered as a city in 1870; it derived its name from its position on the West Branch Canal.

Clinton County had a strong Indian presence before the coming of Europeans. The Great Island, in the Susquehanna River just south of Lock Haven, was occupied by many Indian nations that followed trails from the Genesee, Ohio, Potomac, and Susquehanna Rivers. The Delaware and Shawnee stopped here for a time during their westward migration.

One of the major early settlements was led by a Moravian minister, who brought 200 Christian Mohicans and Delawares from Wyalusing to Friedensstadt in 1772.

The mountainous area had abundant natural resources—coal, clay, limestone, and flagstone—as well as excellent soil for farming. In Sugar Valley, great groves of sugar maple trees were the basis of a prosperous sugar and syrup enterprise.

By 1834, the West Branch Canal had reached Lock Haven; the Philadelphia and Erie Railroad followed. Lock Haven became a lumber and mill center. Renovo became a railroad town, with repair yards and shops.

Clinton County developed a strong industrial component during Pennsylvania's heyday; paper products, printing, textiles, leather, and meat packing were the cornerstones. Piper Aircraft was a major employer, especially during World War II, but it eventually moved to Florida.

The modern economy is heavy on retail trade. Residents of adjacent counties shop in Clinton. Services located at the exits of I-80, which crosses the southern portion of the county, have increased commerce. U.S. Route 220 links Lock Haven and Williamsport. PA Route 120, a route so scenic that it is a state park itself, runs from Lock Haven through the forested northern half of the county. There are three small state parks in the area, enormous state forest acreage, and two tracts of state game lands.

COLUMBIA COUNTY

35 W. Main St.,
Bloomsburg, PA 17815
(717) 389-5603
Population:
63,202 (1990), 64,492 (1995)
Square miles: 486
Population per square mile: 133
Municipalities: 33
(9 boroughs, 24 townships)

Columbia County was created in 1813 from part of Northumberland County.

Columbia is a poetic name for America. Bloomsburg, the county seat, was incorporated as a town in 1870 and named for Samuel Bloom, a Northumberland County supervisor.

The two major urban areas of Columbia County, Bloomsburg and Berwick, are located on the Susquehanna River. Bloomsburg grew during the 19th century with its iron industry. Deposits of limestone and iron ore were plentiful, and numerous furnaces were established. The industry lasted about 75 years. Bloomsburg then developed a major mill industry, producing carpets, hosiery, rayon, and undergarments. The mill industry is still important. Bloomsburg State University, with an enrollment of 8,000 students, is important to the town both economically and culturally.

Berwick used its access to the roads, railroads, and canals to develop a production center for the components of railways. The first all-steel railroad cars made in America were produced in Berwick. During World War II, the plants produced tanks. Anthracite coal was mined in the southern part of the county; farming was productive in the valleys.

Today, about 54% of the 2,400 workers in the county are employed in manufacturing, the highest percentage in the state.

The Bloomsburg Fair attracts 500,000 visitors to the area every September. The county is also home to Ricketts Glen State Park, a state park with national park scenic credentials, and 25 covered bridges.

I-80 and U.S. Route 11 parallel the river on their course through Columbia County. PA Route 487 traverses the area north and south.

CRAWFORD COUNTY

903 Diamond Park,
Meadville, PA 16335
(814) 336-1151
Population:
86,169 (1990), 89,173 (1995)
Square miles: 1,013
Population per square mile: 88
Municipalities: 51
(2 cities, 14 boroughs, 35 townships)

Crawford County was created in 1800 from part of Allegheny County and was named for Col. William Crawford, a frontier hero. Meadville, the county seat, was incorporated as a borough in 1823 and chartered as a city in 1866. It was named for David Mead, its founder. Crawford County is on the Ohio border, just south of Erie County and Lake Erie, both of which were attached to Crawford County until 1803.

The county was settled by veterans of the Revolutionary War. Lumber and agriculture were the pioneer industries. Titusville was the site of the first successful oil well in Pennsylvania, in 1859. The discovery of oil set off a boom; 10,000 wells were drilled in the next 15 years. By 1891, 31 million barrels of oil were being extracted. The drilling, refining, and marketing of petroleum had become a major industry. But the oil was being depleted, and except for a surge of production in the Bradford field in the 1930s, it was downhill from 1891. Titusville is left with a number of refineries manufacturing lubricating oils and grease. Oil Creek State Park was located in neighboring Venango County.

Meadville prospered in the 1920s and

30s on the basis of zipper manufacturing. The zipper was invented in Meadville, and it was the world's leading producer. It also was a center of textiles, silk yarns, and thread, including rayon.

Manufacturing of chemicals, plastics, food, and machinery has recently increased, but service jobs outnumber these about two to one. The top employers are the Meadville Medical Center, the state government, and the Meadville School District; 1,235 farms produce $81 million in cash receipts, mostly in dairy products and livestock.

The Pymatuning State Park, with its 17,088-acre lake, is a major recreational attraction; Conneaut, the largest natural lake in the state, is between Pymatuning Lake and Meadville.

The cultural centers of the county are the University of Pittsburgh–Titusville Campus and Allegheny College, founded in 1815, in Meadville, which President McKinley attended.

I-79 is the county's link with Pittsburgh and Erie. Other important routes include U.S. Routes 6, 19, and 322.

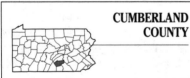

CUMBERLAND COUNTY

1 Courthouse Square,
Carlisle PA 17013
(717) 240-6150
Population:
195,257 (1990), 205,959 (1995)
Square miles: 550
Population per square mile: 374
Municipalities: 34
(12 boroughs, 22 townships)

Cumberland County was created in 1750 from part of Lancaster County and was named for Cumberland, England. Carlisle, the county seat since 1752, was incorporated as a borough in 1782. It was named for a county town in England. (Shippensburg was the county seat from 1750 to 1752.)

The Scots-Irish settled the county; Pennsylvania Germans appeared soon after. Because the county was on the frontier, Indians were a threat, and several forts were erected. Carlisle Barracks, the oldest military post in America, grew from a fort erected in 1750. During the Revolution, it was an armament and ordnance center. Carlisle assembled 15,000 troops to march against the whiskey rebels in 1794. Both Carlisle and Shippensburg were important way stations on the road to the western frontier. Mechanicsburg was named for the workers in the area's many machine shops and foundries.

About half of the present-day land is in crop and pastureland. The county is a part of the southeastern dairy region and is an important apple-growing area. About 30% of the land is forested.

The economy is heavily weighted toward services; government and medical facilities are major employers. There are three urban areas: Shippensburg on the southwest boundary, Carlisle in the middle, and the eastern portion, with seven boroughs and four townships.

Shippensburg is the site of a State University campus. Dickinson College in Carlisle, founded in 1783, was the 12th college chartered in America. It has a noted law school, which affiliated with Penn State in 1997. The now-defunct Carlisle Indian School was the scene of the legendary exploits of Jim Thorpe.

There are three state parks in the county, as well as the 36,000-acre Cumberland State Forest.

Thirty-eight miles of the Turnpike cross the county. It intersects I-81 about 20 miles west of the Susquehanna River. U.S. Routes 11 and 15 are heavily traveled local routes. Each day about 21,000 Cumberland residents use them to go to work in Harrisburg and Dauphin County. Cumberland County is part of the Harrisburg Metropolitan Area.

DAUPHIN COUNTY

Front St., Harrisburg, PA 17108 (717) 255-1360
Population: 237,813 (1990), 246,338 (1995)
Square miles: 525
Population per square mile: 469
Municipalities: 40
(1 city, 16 boroughs, 23 townships)

Dauphin County was created in 1785 from part of Lancaster County and was named for an heir to the French throne. Harrisburg, the county seat, was incorporated as a borough in 1791 and chartered as a city in 1860. It was named for its founder, John Harris, an early settler, trader, and entrepreneur. It became the state capital in 1812.

Dauphin County is located along the east bank of the Susquehanna River in south-central Pennsylvania. The southern half is located in the Kittatinny Valley, the northern half at the base of the Blue Mountains of the Appalachian Range. Slightly less than half of its land is forested and about one-third is agricultural.

Because of its location, Dauphin County was an important center of transportation and commerce. The Pennsylvania Canal was begun here in 1826, and the county became a railroad center in 1836. Its ferries and bridges made it an important crossing point on the Susquehanna River. Coal mining was important in the Lykens Valley area, and dredging operations were conducted on the river.

Because Harrisburg is the state capital, Dauphin County enjoys many advantages, 22,000 government jobs and major transportation systems being among the most important. It is also a cultural center, with many museums, archives, libraries, musical organizations, and the art and sculpture of its government buildings. When one tires of culture, Hersheypark and Hershey's chocolate are not far away. The infamous Three Mile Island nuclear power plant looms nearby.

The county's role as a transportation center continues today. It is served by four interstate highways—76, 81, 83, and 283; U.S. Routes 11, 15, 22, 322, and 422; and the Harrisburg International Airport in Middletown.

DELAWARE COUNTY

Government Center Bldg., Media, PA 19063 (610) 891-4259
Population: 547,651 (1990), 548,708 (1995)
Square miles: 184
Population per square mile: 2,982
Municipalities: 49
(1 city, 27 boroughs, 21 townships)

Delaware County was created in 1789 from part of Chester County and was named for the Delaware River, which had been named for Lord Delaware, governor of Virginia. Chester was the original county seat, having been the county seat of Chester County before 1788. In 1850, Media was chosen as the new county seat and incorporated as a borough.

The first permanent European settlement of Pennsylvania took place in what is now Delaware County in 1643, when Swedes established a fort at Tinicum. Later that year, Upland was founded. William Penn arrived 40 years later, changed the name of Upland to Chester, and organized Chester County.

Because of its location near Philadelphia and the building of the first railroad in America, Delaware County had the potential for prosperity from its beginning. Agriculture, textiles, and stone quarrying were early industries; oil refining and shipyards later became important. The county still has an industrial base—Boeing and Arco Chemical are major employers—but the economy is now more service oriented. There are 11 institutions of higher education in the county, including historic Swarthmore College.

Only 184 square miles, Delaware County, the commonwealth's third smallest, has the fourth-largest population. Its density is second only to Philadelphia's. The population decreased somewhat between 1980 and 1990 but recently has increased slightly. Most of the remaining available land is zoned for low-intensity development.

Delaware County is a bedroom community for both Philadelphia and Wilmington, Delaware. It has excellent access to King of Prussia, one of the fastest-growing areas in nearby Montgomery County. It has excellent road access: I-95 and I-476 have supple-

mented the early U.S. Routes 1, 13, 30, 202, and 322.

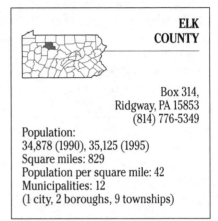

ELK COUNTY

Box 314,
Ridgway, PA 15853
(814) 776-5349
Population:
34,878 (1990), 35,125 (1995)
Square miles: 829
Population per square mile: 42
Municipalities: 12
(1 city, 2 boroughs, 9 townships)

Elk County was created in 1843 from parts of Jefferson, Clearfield, and McKean Counties. It was named for the elk that once roamed the area. Ridgway, the county seat, was laid out in 1833 and named for Jacob Ridgway, a local landowner. It was incorporated as a borough in 1881.

By the late 19th century, the elk were gone. Elk were imported from Wyoming and Montana to replace the native herds in 1913. The only elk herd in the state, estimated to number 254 in 1995, roams Elk and Cameron Counties. The herd is most often seen near St. Marys airport and in the Benezette area.

Elk County's first inhabitants were Seneca Indians. European settlers arrived in 1798, attracted by the abundant forestland. In 1842, a large settlement of Catholics came to St. Marys and settled on 3,500 acres. The first industry was lumbering, followed by paper production and leather goods. The world's largest tannery, Elk Tannery in Wilcox, processed an estimated 1 million buffalo hides between 1866 and 1876. In the

1940s, over 1,000 employees worked at the Johnsonburg paper mill.

Modern manufacturing enterprises include paper, metal, leather, rubber, powder, and wood products. Manufactured goods and services, both of which are growing slowly, each account for about half of the nonagricultural employment in the county.

More than half of Elk County is public recreation land, including part of the Allegheny National Forest, Elk State Forest, and Bendigo and Elk State Parks. Six tracts of state game lands total 73,000 acres. The elk is a protected animal and not hunted.

U.S. Route 219 is the major road in Elk County.

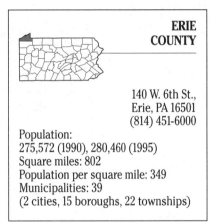

ERIE COUNTY

140 W. 6th St.,
Erie, PA 16501
(814) 451-6000

Population:
275,572 (1990), 280,460 (1995)
Square miles: 802
Population per square mile: 349
Municipalities: 39
(2 cities, 15 boroughs, 22 townships)

Erie County was created in 1800 from part of Allegheny County and was named for Lake Erie, which had been named for an Indian tribe. Erie, the county seat, was laid out in 1795, incorporated as a borough in 1805, and chartered as a city in 1851. Almost 40% of the population of the county resides in the city of Erie.

The French came to the area first, erected forts at Presque Isle and LeBoeuf, and held them until the British displaced them in 1759. The Senecas defeated the British; General Bouquet and the Americans defeated the Senecas. Pennsylvania ultimately purchased the area close to the New York border from the U.S. government in 1788 for 75 cents an acre. Serious settlement began around 1795.

Lake Erie was the scene of a historic naval battle in 1813, when Commodore Perry defeated the British fleet. Perry's flagship, the *Niagara,* has been restored and is open to the public.

Lake Erie influences everything in Erie County, beginning with the weather pattern. A long frost-free growing season and moderate temperatures make the growing of fruits and vegetables possible. The Lake Erie Plain produces about 85% of the state's grapes and is the second-leading vegetable-growing area. Also, the northwest section of the county produces chrysanthemums on a grand scale. Overall, the county ranked 10th in agricultural production in 1994. These crops have attracted food processors to the area, most notably H. J. Heinz and Keystone Foods, which have built plants close to the fields.

Because of its location on the lake and the flatness of the plain, Erie has always been a transportation center. It is closely linked with Cleveland, Buffalo, and Pittsburgh. Canals were built between Erie and Pittsburgh in 1844 and Erie and Buffalo in 1846. The railroads and the major highways were built to exploit the raw materials from the lake and the markets on each side of it.

The lake is now the center of the tourist and recreation industry, which has become the county's second-largest economic sector. Presque Isle State

Park, a 3,000-acre peninsula, and the county's 44 miles of lake shoreline are major attractions.

Erie has traditionally been a heavy industry town. Modern manufacturing sectors include electronics, instruments, paper products, and transportation equipment. General Electric Transportation Systems was awarded a contract in 1995 to build 92 engines for Amtrak. About 650 plants employ about one-third of the workforce.

A Penn State Center and Edinboro State University are the major cultural centers. Governor Ridge is a native.

FAYETTE COUNTY

61 E. Main St.,
Uniontown, PA 15401
(412) 437-4525

Population:
145,351 (1990), 146,827 (1995)
Square miles: 790
Population per square mile: 186
Municipalities: 42
(2 cities, 16 boroughs, 24 townships)

Fayette County was created in 1783 from part of Westmoreland County and was named in honor of the Marquis de Lafayette. Uniontown, the county seat, was laid out in 1776; the name refers to the federal Union. It was incorporated as a borough in 1796 and chartered as a city in 1913.

The southern border of Fayette County forms a section of the Mason-Dixon Line with West Virginia and Maryland. The county is divided by mountains and lowlands; the eastern portion is mountainous, with Chestnut Ridge rising to 2,000 feet. West of the mountains, rolling hills form a gradual slope to the Monongahela River. The center of the county, near the city of Uniontown, is about 45 miles south of Pittsburgh.

Most of Fayette County's early growth can be traced to Monongahela River traffic and the construction of the Great Cumberland National Road through the area in the early 1800s. Spur railroads were built after the Civil War to serve the resource industries. The coal mines and the allied coke industry were centered in Fayette County. The first glass factory in western Pennsylvania was built in New Geneva. Between 1881 and 1917, the county boomed.

But changing technology ended this. The county has not benefited from the new world order; population declined about 9% between 1980 and 1990, although it has now stabilized. The median household income decreased almost 20% during that time.

Health services are now the largest employer. The county is looking to tourism to improve its economic outlook. Ohiopyle State Park, 19,000 acres of rugged beauty, is a major attraction. Fallingwater, Frank Lloyd Wright's masterpiece, and the Fort Necessity National Battlefield Site, where young Col. Washington fought the first engagement of the French and Indian War, are interesting diversions.

U.S. Route 40, northwest and southeast to Maryland; U.S. Route 119, north and south to West Virginia; and PA Route 51 to Pittsburgh all pass through Uniontown, the hub of the county's highway system.

FOREST COUNTY

Box 423,
Tionesta, PA 16353
(814) 755-3526
Population:
4,802 (1990), 5,001 (1995)
Square miles: 428
Population per square mile: 12
Municipalities: 9
(1 borough, 8 townships)

FRANKLIN COUNTY

157 Lincoln Way, East,
Chambersburg, PA 17201
(717) 264-4125
Population:
121,082 (1990), 126,444 (1995)
Square miles: 772
Population per square mile: 164
Municipalities: 22
(7 boroughs, 15 townships)

Forest County, named for its forests, was created in 1848 from parts of Jefferson County, to which it remained attached until 1857. Part of Venango County was added in 1866, at which time Tionesta became the county seat. (Marienville was the county seat from 1857 to 1866.) Tionesta is an Indian word, meaning, roughly, "it penetrates the land."

Forest County, located in northwest Pennsylvania, is the least populated county in the commonwealth. Recreation is a major industry. The county has about five times as many seasonal homes as permanent ones. About two-thirds of the land is publicly owned. Over 100,000 acres of the Allegheny National Forest and part of the Cook Forest State Park are within Forest County.

Lumbering was the reason for the development of the county. It peaked around 1900. Some oil and natural gas were discovered in the county, and there was an oil boom in 1882–83.

Services, lumber, and wood products contribute to the current economy. The county is declining in most nonagricultural employment categories.

U.S. Route 62 is the major road.

Franklin County was created in 1784 from part of Cumberland County and was named for Benjamin Franklin. Chambersburg, the county seat, was founded in 1764 by Ben Chambers, a Scots-Irish settler. It was incorporated as a borough in 1803.

Indian attacks drove off the early settlers. Four forts were subsequently built for protection, but raids continued until after the Revolutionary War. During the Civil War, both armies passed through on their way to Gettysburg. The Confederates burned Chambersburg and Thaddeus Stevens's charcoal furnace at Caledonia, which is now a state park.

Farming has always been the major endeavor in Franklin County. The county is part of the southeastern Pennsylvania dairy region. The county ranks second in both milk production and apple production. Overall, the 1,450 farms produced cash receipts of $208 million in 1994.

The present-day economy is based upon service, including tourism, retail trade, and manufacturing. The county tourist business benefits from the popularity of Gettysburg in neighboring

Adams County, and Franklin County has three state parks and 40,000 acres of state forestland.

There is a Penn State Center at Mont Alto.

Proximity to the Washington-Baltimore area helped the county population grow 20% from 1970 to 1990. It is one of the most affordable areas in the commonwealth, has low property taxes, and provides an attractive rural experience for urban refugees.

The Lincoln Highway, U.S. Route 30, crosses the center of the county east and west; the Turnpike crosses the northern end for 15 miles. The major commuter route is I-81, north to Harrisburg and south to Hagerstown, Maryland, and beyond.

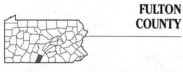

FULTON COUNTY

201 N. 2nd St.,
McConnellsburg, PA 17233
(717) 485-4212
Population:
13,837 (1990), 14,362 (1995)
Square miles: 438
Population per square mile: 33
Municipalities: 13
(2 boroughs, 11 townships)

Fulton County was created in 1851 from part of Bedford County and was named for Robert Fulton, inventor of the steamboat. McConnellsburg, the county seat, was laid out by Daniel McConnell in 1786 and incorporated as a borough in 1814.

Early settlement, which began about 1740, was sparse and precarious. The settlers were harassed by Indians, who completely wiped out one of the major

early settlements. Fort Littleton, an important frontier fort, was built in Fulton County to protect the settlers.

The county was on the main route west, but it never had a railroad line. It is a mountainous area with numerous high ridges separating fertile valleys. Agriculture, grist milling, and bituminous coal mining were the principal economic activities of the 19th century.

About one-third of the work force is employed in manufacturing. Jobs declined in the Franklin-Fulton Labor Market Area in 1994, continuing the trend of the 1990s. Almost every sector of nonagricultural employment showed a decrease in the 1990–94 period.

Fulton County has about 500 farms, which produced $25 million in cash receipts in 1994.

Recreational facilities in the county include Cowan Gap State Park and Buchanan State Forest.

The Turnpike crosses the northern part of the county; I-70 runs north and south along the western border; U.S. Route 30 crosses the middle of the county.

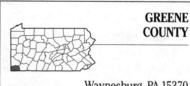

GREENE COUNTY

Waynesburg, PA 15370
(412) 852-5283
Population:
39,550 (1990), 41,114 (1995)
Square miles: 576
Population per square mile: 71
Municipalities: 26
(6 boroughs, 20 townships)

Greene County was created in 1796 from part of Washington County and named for Gen. Nathanael Greene. Waynesburg, the county seat, was named for Gen. Anthony Wayne. It was laid out in 1796 and incorporated as a borough in 1816.

Greene County, at the southwest corner of the commonwealth, was the subject of a boundary dispute in 1776. The Virginia State Assembly annexed the region. In 1784, a joint commission ruled for Pennsylvania and established the present boundary.

The economy of the area has been based, at various times, upon agriculture (especially sheep ranching), bituminous coal mining, oil, and natural gas production. Coal mining is the current major employment area; about 22% of the nonagricultural jobs in 1994 were in mining, and three coal companies were among the county's five largest employers. Government is the largest single employer, primarily due to the presence of two state correctional institutions in the county.

The county is 89% rural and is slowly declining in population; between 1980 and 1990, it lost about 3% and the median household income decreased by 21%. About 20% of the county population lives below the poverty line.

The cultural center of the county is Waynesburg College, established in 1851. The recreational center is Ryerson Station State Park, a 1,164-acre park about 8 miles from the West Virginia border on U.S. Route 21.

I-79 runs north and south through the center of the county; U.S. Route 21 runs east and west.

HUNTINGDON COUNTY

223 Penn St.,
Huntingdon, PA 16652
(814) 643-3901

Population:
44,164 (1990), 44,933 (1995)
Square miles: 875
Population per square mile: 51
Municipalities: 48
(18 boroughs, 30 townships)

Huntingdon County was created in 1787 from part of Bedford County. Huntingdon Borough, the county seat, was incorporated in 1796. Dr. William Smith, provost of the University of Pennsylvania, who owned the land, laid out the town of Huntingdon and named it to honor the countess of Huntingdon, England, who was a benefactor of the university.

Huntingdon County lies slightly south of the geographic center of the state, within the scenic ridge and valley section. It is rural and three-quarters forestland. Early settlement was fostered by its proximity to Bedford, a principal route to the west, and its own good location on the Juniata River, which was a route to the northwest. Eventually, the Pennsylvania Canal and the Pennsylvania Railroad came through Huntindgon County.

An iron industry developed, with about 50 furnaces in operation. Clay, stone, and bituminous coal were mined. Today, services, manufacturing, and government are major employers. All manufacturing sectors had double-digit decreases in employees in the past four years. Unemployment exceeds the state average, generally ranging around 10%.

Tourism is important in the area; Raystown Lake attracts about 1.5 million visitors annually. "Raystown Country" has three small state parks, part of a state forest, and extensive state game lands. A seasonal-housing boom is taking place in the county, constituting one-third of all new housing construction.

Juniata College, a four-year liberal-arts college established in 1876 in Huntingdon Borough, is the cultural center of the county.

The Turnpike grazes the southeast corner of the county. U.S. Routes 22 and 522 and PA Route 26 are the major highways.

INDIANA COUNTY

825 Philadelphia St.,
Indiana, PA 15701
(412) 465-3860

Population:
89,994 (1990), 90,604 (1995)
Square miles: 830
Population per square mile: 109
Municipalities: 38
(14 boroughs, 24 townships)

Indiana County was created in 1803 from parts of Westmoreland and Lycoming Counties and was named for the territory of Indiana. The county seat, Indiana, was incorporated as a borough in 1816.

Early European settlement was sporadic and precarious because of the presence of hostile Indians. The area was a complete wilderness, and life was primitive. The Kittanning Path, the trail used by the Delaware and Shawnee nations, passed through the area. With the Purchase of 1776, Indian attacks ended and the region was settled by farmers, mostly Scots-Irish from Cumberland County.

Mineral resources also attracted attention. Salt was mined along the Conemaugh River at Saltsburg. Production peaked in 1830, then declined rapidly to extinction. Other 19th-century industries included coal mining, natural gas production, and limestone mining. From 1829 to 1860, Blairsville was a main point on the Pennsylvania Canal.

The economy of the county today includes agriculture, education, energy production, and commerce. The Indiana State University has 14,000 students and employs over 1,700. Indiana County electric generating plants supply electricity to 21 million customers and employ 1,100. Indiana bills itself as "the Christmas Tree Capitol of the World"; over 1 million trees are shipped from the county annually. Actor Jimmy Stewart was a native son. His statue stands on the courthouse lawn, and a cottage tourist industry has grown around him. The Jimmy Stewart Airport Terminal Building and the Jimmy Stewart Museum opened in May 1995.

Since 1990, Indiana County has lost almost one-third of its manufacturing base; mining employment has declined by almost half. Overall, nonagricultural employment has declined about 7%.

Indiana Borough is 60 miles from Pittsburgh, and a segment of the population is drawn from that area. Access is excellent, via U.S. Routes 119 and 22.

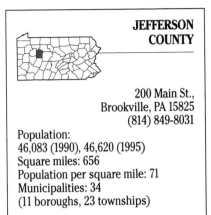

JEFFERSON COUNTY

200 Main St.,
Brookville, PA 15825
(814) 849-8031

Population:
46,083 (1990), 46,620 (1995)
Square miles: 656
Population per square mile: 71
Municipalities: 34
(11 boroughs, 23 townships)

Jefferson County was created in 1804 from part of Lycoming County and was named for President Thomas Jefferson. It was not formally organized until 1830. Brookville, the county seat, was laid out in 1830 and incorporated as a borough in 1834. It was named for the numerous brooks and streams in the area.

Many of the early settlers were Revolutionary War veterans. From the time that the first European settlers built a sawmill on Sandy Lick Creek in 1797, lumber was Jefferson County's basic industry. In the 1830s, companies and individuals from New England and New York arrived, built the first lumber railroad in Pennsylvania, and cut down every tree in sight.

Small mineral industries replaced the exhausted lumber industry—coal mining, stone, and natural gas were the main resources. Coal mining has endured; in 1994, 1.6 million tons of bituminous coal were mined.

The forests regenerated, and today about three-quarters of the county is covered by woodlands, including two state parks, Clear Creek and Cook Forest. The world-renowned weather prognosticator, Punxsutawney Phil, the groundhog, resides in the area.

I-80 crosses the center of Jefferson County, taking about the same route as U.S. Route 322.

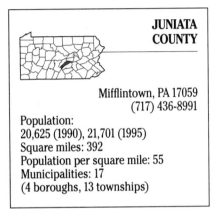

JUNIATA COUNTY

Mifflintown, PA 17059
(717) 436-8991

Population:
20,625 (1990), 21,701 (1995)
Square miles: 392
Population per square mile: 55
Municipalities: 17
(4 boroughs, 13 townships)

Juniata County was created in 1831 from parts of Mifflin County and was named for the Juniata River, an Indian name meaning "people of the standing stone." Mifflintown, the county seat, was laid out in 1781 and incorporated as a borough in 1833. It was named for Gov. Thomas Mifflin.

Early settlement of the county was discouraged by the presence of hostile Indians who did not wish to surrender their lands. The Provincial Government was able to buy some land in 1754, but even this did not end all the attacks, which continued until about 1764.

In addition to agriculture, early industry grew along the river—an iron forge, gristmills, sawmills, and a paper mill. The early settlers were mainly Scots-Irish. The county was along the route of the Pennsylvania Canal and the railroad that replaced it.

This quiet rural area, 12 miles wide and 52 miles long, now has an Amish and Mennonite aspect to its agriculture. Dairy, poultry, and fruit are the major farm products. The workforce is about equally divided between service and manufacturing employment, but the former is growing and the latter is declining. Major employers include food processors and apparel manufacturers.

U.S. Routes 22 and 322 cross the county east and west near its center.

LACKAWANNA COUNTY

200 Adams Ave., Scranton, PA 18503 (717) 963-6800

Population: 219,039 (1990), 215,688 (1995)
Square miles: 459
Population per square mile: 469
Municipalities: 40
(2 cities, 17 boroughs, 21 townships)

Lackawanna County was created in 1878 from part of Luzerne County and was named for the Lackawanna River, an Indian name meaning "stream that forks." It was the last county formed in Pennsylvania. Scranton, the county seat, was incorporated as a borough in 1856 and chartered as a city in 1866. It was named for its founders, the Scranton family.

Both the northwest and southeast thirds of the county are generally rural areas of woodland and dairy and vegetable farms. Together they contain one-quarter of the population. The majority of the population lives in the middle third of the county, the Lackawanna Valley.

It was in this valley that anthracite coal was discovered in the 1820s. The mines, railroads, ironworks, and textile mills that came to constitute the "coal region" transformed the area into an urban center that stretched from Scranton on the north to Carbondale on the south. The extraction of coal dominated every aspect of existence in the area. When it died as an industry, anthracite mining left the economy and the land in utter ruin.

Today, diversified manufacturing, corporate back-office operations, and service industries form the basis of the county's economy. Industrial and office parks are being developed throughout the county. Defense contracts also are very important to the economy.

Tourism is becoming another economic force. The Steamtown National Historic Site, Lackawanna Coal Mine Tour, and Montage Mountain Ski Resort and Outdoor Performing Area are major attractions. A State Heritage Park, the Lackawanna Heritage Valley, is an ambitious project that will, if successful, have an enormous impact on the county.

Due to the efforts of a legendary congressman, Daniel J. Flood, the county has an excellent highway system, which includes I-81, I-84, and I-380; the Northeast Extension of the Pennsylvania Turnpike; scenic U.S. Route 6; and U.S. Route 11. These roads, and the county's location near the markets of New York and New England, have helped it to solidify its position as a transportation center.

LANCASTER COUNTY

50 N. Duke St.,
Lancaster, PA 17603
(717) 299-8300
Population:
422,822 (1990), 447,521 (1995)
Square miles: 949
Population per square mile: 472
Municipalities: 60
(1 city, 18 boroughs, 41 townships)

Lancaster County was created in 1729 from Chester County. It was the fourth county established in the state. It was named for Lancashire, England, the birthplace of a local surveyor. At that time, it included all of the unclaimed western Pennsylvania lands. As settlers moved west, more counties were formed. Lancaster reached its present boundaries in 1813. The city of Lancaster became the county seat in 1730, was incorporated as a borough in 1742, and was chartered as a city in 1818.

From the beginning, Lancaster County was the premier farming area in the state and one of the best in the country. The soils and climate mixed perfectly with the legendary work ethic of the German farmers who have turned it into the most productive nonirrigated land in America. The county leads the state in production of most crops and all livestock except sheep. Dairy production is the main agricultural activity. About 60% of the land is farmed.

Agriculture is even more important to the county than the impressive farm production indicates. The picturesque and culturally distinct landscape of farming communities attracts about 5 million tourists annually to the county, mostly from the nearby urban centers of New York, New Jersey, Maryland, and Philadelphia.

Many of these tourists are drawn to the county by the "Plain People"— Amish, Mennonite, and Brethren—who own about 40% of the farms. With their characteristic dress and a lifestyle that eschews many modern conveniences for home and farm, they give Lancaster County a strong identity.

Lancaster County ranks fifth in both the number of manufacturing establishments in the state—897—and the number of employees—61,000. The major employer is Armstrong World Industries, a floor-covering producer that employs 3,500. R. R. Donnelley is a steadily expanding printing operation.

This economic activity, combined with steady population growth, has crammed the county's roads. The Turnpike crosses the county too far north to help with the congestion; U.S. Routes 30 and 222 traverse the county, and PA Route 283 connects it with Harrisburg.

LAWRENCE COUNTY

Court St.,
New Castle, PA 16101
(412) 658-2541
Population:
96,246 (1990), 96,604 (1995)
Square miles: 360
Population per square mile: 268
Municipalities: 27
(1 city, 10 boroughs, 16 townships)

Lawrence County was created in 1849 from parts of Beaver and Mercer Counties and was named for Capt. James Lawrence, a naval hero. New Castle, the county seat, was laid out in 1802, incorporated as a borough in 1821, and chartered as a city in 1869. It was settled by former residents of New Castle, Delaware.

New Castle lies at the confluence of three rivers and was an important Iroquois and Delaware Indian settlement. White settlers arrived in 1798. They eventually established a charcoal iron industry, which supplied the demands of Pittsburgh's industry. The iron industry evolved into steel mills in the 1890s. The Pittsburgh and Erie Canal passed through the county, as did the railroads. Glass manufacturing, pottery, woolen goods, and machine shop operations, usually small-scale, abounded in the area.

Lawrence County's fortunes were closely tied to Pittsburgh; they declined together. Household income in Lawrence County declined by 20% between 1980 and 1990; the population also declined. New Castle peaked at 50,000 residents in 1930; it now has 28,000.

Hospitals, government, public agencies, and public utilities are the major employers today. Chinaware is produced in New Castle; chemicals, leather goods, lumber, and agriculture all contribute to the economy.

I-76 crosses the southwest corner of the county; I-79 runs parallel to the eastern boundary; I-80 runs just to the north; PA Route 60 runs north and south through the center of the county and links I-76 and I-80.

LEBANON COUNTY

400 S. 8th St.,
Lebanon, PA 17042
(717) 274-2801

Population:
113,744 (1990), 116,789 (1995)
Square miles: 362
Population per square mile: 323
Municipalities: 26
(1 city, 7 boroughs, 18 townships)

Lebanon County was created in 1813 from parts of Lancaster and Dauphin Counties. Lebanon is a biblical name meaning "white mountain." Lebanon, the county seat, was laid out in 1750, incorporated as a borough in 1821, and chartered as a city in 1885.

Lebanon County's early growth was fueled by its natural resources: iron ore, timber, and limestone. The Cornwall Iron Furnace, established in 1742, operated around the clock until 1883. It produced pig iron and domestic products, as well as cannons, shot, and shells for the Revolutionary Army. Local mining operations continued until the early 1970s, capitalizing on the largest iron ore deposits east of Lake Superior.

Agriculture has always been the county's core industry, and about half of the land is farmland. But suburbanization is cutting into it. The county's close proximity to urban areas and its rural charms make it attractive to commuters. About 30% of the residents commute to a worksite outside the county.

The largest employers in Lebanon County are hospitals and government agencies. The best-known product of modern-day Lebanon is Lebanon bologna, sweet or spicy sausagelike meat made from beef, herbs, and spices.

Lebanon Valley College in Annville is the cultural center of the area. Penn National Race Course is located in Grantville. The area has two state parks and 25,000 acres of state game lands. The Indiantown Gap Military Reservation is open to the public for recreation on a limited basis.

U.S. Route 422, which links Reading and Harrisburg, crosses the center of the county; nearly two-thirds of the county's residents live within 3 miles of this route. I-76, I-78, and I-81 also run through the county.

LEHIGH COUNTY

Allentown, PA 18105
(610) 820-3050
Population:
291,130 (1990), 297,838 (1995)
Square miles: 347
Population per square mile: 858
Municipalities: 24
(1 city, 8 boroughs, 15 townships)

Lehigh County was created in 1812 from part of Northampton County and was named for the Lehigh River. Lehigh is derived from the German word *lecha,* which in turn is a derivation of an Indian word meaning "where the streams fork."

Lehigh County is in east-central Pennsylvania, 100 miles west of New York City and 60 miles north of Philadelphia. The Lehigh River forms part of the eastern boundary; the Blue Mountains form the northern boundary. South Mountain is a major ridge, south of Allentown. A limestone belt that has formed prime farming soil and provides material for the cement and crushed stone industries lies along the central valley.

Swiss and German farmers settled in the area as early as 1715. During the Revolutionary War, when the British occupied Philadelphia, the Liberty Bell was hidden in Zion Reformed Church in Allentown. Historically, the principal industrial products of Lehigh County have been cement, silk, textiles, mining machinery, iron, and steel.

Among the largest employers in the county today are AT&T and Pennsylvania Power and Light. Dixie cups and Crayola crayons are produced in Allentown. The change from manufacturing to service and trade continues, and about two-thirds of the region's jobs are nonmanufacturing.

Most of the economic growth has occurred in industrial and business parks in Hanover and Upper Macungie Townships. The region's largest shopping centers are in Whitehall Township. Yet Allentown has maintained its population. It is one of only three Pennsylvania cities with more than 50,000 people that gained in population between 1980 and 1990; it is one of two Pennsylvania cities (along with nearby Bethlehem) that have a population higher in 1990 than it was in 1930.

I-78 provides easy access to New York City. The Northeast Extension of the Turnpike connects the county with Philadelphia and the Wilkes-Barre–Scranton area. U.S. Route 22 serves the county east and west.

LUZERNE COUNTY

600 N. River St.,
Wilkes-Barre, PA 18711
(717) 825-1509

Population:
328,149 (1990), 326,063 (1995)
Square miles: 891
Population per square mile: 366
Municipalities: 76
(4 cities, 36 boroughs, 36 townships)

Luzerne County was created in 1786 from part of Northumberland County and was named for the Chevalier de la Luzerne, French minister to the United States. Wilkes-Barre, the county seat, was laid out in 1772 and named for members of the English Parliament, John Wilkes and Isaac Barre, who were advocates of American colonial rights. It was incorporated as a borough in 1806 and chartered as a city in 1871.

Located in northeastern Pennsylvania, Luzerne County is 100 miles west of New York City and 100 miles northwest of Philadelphia. It has two urban areas: greater Wilkes-Barre, along the Susquehanna River in the Wyoming Valley in the north, and the greater Hazleton area, near the southern boundary. The suburban and rural townships of these areas are growing. The population of the cities of Wilkes-Barre and Hazleton declined sharply with the decline of the mining industry.

Luzerne County was a major center of Indian life; Shawnee and Delaware Indians lived here under the control of the Iroquois. In 1753, settlers came from Connecticut, claiming that the land had been granted to them prior to William Penn's grant. The two groups fought often for the land, until the Pennsylvania claim was upheld by a federal commission.

The modern history of the area lies in its tie to anthracite coal. From around 1825, when coal was shown to be a practical fuel, until 1917, when production peaked, the county prospered. The gradual decline of the industry, as anthracite coal became technologically obsolete, devastated the county. The long, painful transition to the present-day economy, featuring services and manufacturing, especially apparel and textiles, retail trade, government work, and transportation, is a prototype of American social and economic history.

Both Hazleton and Wilkes-Barre have Penn State Centers. Private colleges include King's, Wilkes, and Misericordia.

Lehigh Gorge and Frances Slocum State Parks, state forests, state game lands, and the nearby Pocono Mountain resort area provide recreational opportunities.

I-80, I-81, and the Northeast Extension of the Turnpike are the major roads.

LYCOMING COUNTY

48 W. Third St.,
Williamsport, PA 17701
(717) 327-2314

Population:
118,710 (1990), 120,194 (1995)
Square miles: 1,235
Population per square mile: 97
Municipalities: 52
(1 city, 9 boroughs, 42 townships)

Lycoming County was created in 1795 from part of Northumberland County and was named for Lycoming Creek. The name is derived from an Indian word meaning "sandy or gravelly creek." Williamsport, the county seat, was laid out in 1796, incorporated as a borough in 1806, and chartered as a city in 1866.

Lycoming County is located in north-central Pennsylvania and, at 50 miles wide and 35 miles long, is the largest county in the state. It boasts 2,220 miles of rivers and streams. Williamsport is the major metropolitan center of the north-central region; nevertheless, it has lost almost one-third of its population in the past 60 years.

Williamsport's years of glory were 1835 to 1893, during the height of the Pennsylvania lumber boom. Millions of logs were floated down the Susquehanna to Williamsport for milling. The city once had the most millionaires per capita in America. These lumber barons built opulent mansions, some of which have survived. When the industry moved on because the forests upriver were depleted and shipping by rail became possible, Williamsport languished.

Lumber-related industries account for only about 12% of current employment. The largest employers in Lycoming County are health centers, a bank, and Brodart, a library supply company; government at all levels is also a major employer.

As a rural area close to the major urban areas of the East Coast, the county has great tourist appeal, particularly to hunters and fishers, and visitors have been building second homes or retiring to the area in increasing numbers.

Little League Baseball originated in Williamsport, and the city is the site of a world series every August.

I-80, 17 miles to the south, just misses the southern boundary of the county, but I-180 links Williamsport to it, as does U.S. Route 220 to the west. U.S. Route 15 crosses the center of the county north and south.

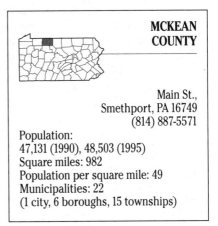

MCKEAN COUNTY

Main St.,
Smethport, PA 16749
(814) 887-5571

Population:
47,131 (1990), 48,503 (1995)
Square miles: 982
Population per square mile: 49
Municipalities: 22
(1 city, 6 boroughs, 15 townships)

McKean County was created in 1804 from parts of Lycoming County and was named for the second governor of Pennsylvania, Thomas McKean. Smethport, the county seat, named in honor of two Dutch bankers, was incorporated as a borough in 1853.

The first white settlers, who came from New York, New England, and southeastern Pennsylvania, were attracted by the dense forests of virgin white pine, northern hardwoods, and hemlock. In 1888, 225 million board feet of hemlock were harvested in the county. Loggers did miss one tract of fine black cherry trees.

Following the discovery of oil in 1859, petroleum and gas operations flourished. Bradford, the largest town in McKean County, was named the oil capital of the world in 1875. Between 1875 and 1881, oil production increased from 36,000 to 23 million barrels annually. About 9,000 wells were drilled during that period.

As of 1994, about one-third of the workforce was employed in manufacturing, primarily in wood, glass, and clay products; chemicals; powder and explosives, and oil products. Today the service economy dominates, as transportation, public utilities, and federal government jobs are increasing. Tourism is another aspect of the service economy. The Allegheny National Forest covers the western quarter of the county. The Kinzua Bridge, a railroad bridge that is a National Engineering Landmark, also attracts visitors.

U.S. Route 6 is the major road in McKean County. In the recent past, both *Car and Driver Magazine* and the Harley-Davidson Company have designated the Pennsylvania portion of this transcontinental highway as an outstanding scenic route. North-south traffic uses U.S. Route 219 and PA Route 46.

MERCER COUNTY

S. Diamond St.,
Mercer, PA 16137
(412) 662-3800

Population:
121,003 (1990), 122,254 (1995)
Square miles: 672
Population per square mile: 182
Municipalities: 48
(3 cities, 14 boroughs, 31 townships)

Mercer County was created in 1800 from part of Allegheny County and was named for Gen. Hugh Mercer, who was wounded at the Battle of Princeton and died in 1777. Mercer, the county seat, was incorporated as a borough in 1814.

In the late 1700s, Mercer County was an isolated area covered with heavy forests that made settlement difficult. The county eventually grew slowly and followed the classic pattern: Settlers farmed, hunted, and trapped to survive. Then they established sawmills, gristmills, and distilleries.

Transportation was always an important aspect of the economic life of the county, situated as it was, 75 miles north of Pittsburgh and 65 miles south of Lake Erie. It was served by canal and rail routes when these modes of transportation were important. In 1821, the Mercer Pike was an important part of the Pittsburgh-Erie route; 100 years later, U.S. Route 19 linked the two cities, as I-79 does today.

Coal was discovered in the 1830s, and 50 mines opened between 1837 and 1876. This coal was important in the development of the iron industry. By 1874, the area had 30 blast furnaces, some with rolling mills. Some of these furnaces evolved into steel mills; U.S. Steel took over the Sharon plant in 1902.

Despite all this activity, the county remained basically rural. Dairy farming is still important, and some of the area's 1,160 farms are owned by the Amish.

Modern-day Mercer County has diversified to include high-tech manufacturing, health services, and tourism along with its metal-related industries. Hospitals, schools (including the Penn State–Shenango Campus in Sharon), and government are major employers.

MIFFLIN COUNTY

20 Wayne St.,
Lewistown, PA 17044
(717) 248-6733
Population:
46,197 (1990), 47,066 (1995)
Square miles: 411
Population per square mile: 115
Municipalities: 16
(6 boroughs, 10 townships)

Mifflin County was created in 1789 from parts of Cumberland and Northumberland Counties and was named for the sitting governor, Thomas Mifflin. Lewistown, the county seat, was laid out in 1790, incorporated as a borough in 1795, and reincorporated in 1811. It was named for William Lewis, a pioneer ironmaster.

The first English traders visited the area in 1731, and the first trader settled in 1754. At the time, Lewistown, called Ohesson by the Indians, was an important village on a crossroad of Indian trails. The Juniata Path joined the Tuscarora Path at Port Royal and followed the Juniata River to meet Kittanning Path at Mount Union. The Warriors Path from Sunbury also passed through the county. Routes 322 and 522, the Pennsylvania Canal, which reached Lewistown in 1829, and the Pennsylvania Railroad were run along these same paths.

Agriculture has always been a major enterprise in Mifflin County. The principal products today are dairy and livestock. There is a significant Amish presence in the area near Belleville. Health services and retail trade have become the major economic activities in

the county; Lewistown Hospital is the largest employer. There is a significant manufacturing sector as well; Standard Steel and New Holland America are large employers.

In addition to Reeds Gap State Park, which is adjacent to the 200,000-acre Bald Eagle State Forest, there are four state parks just over the county line. There are also numerous privately owned recreational operations in the area. Most of the mountains in the county are forest covered.

Lewistown is 32 miles southeast of State College, which is easily reached via U.S. Route 322.

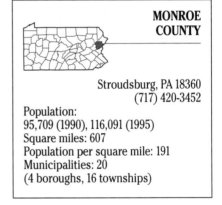

MONROE COUNTY

Stroudsburg, PA 18360
(717) 420-3452
Population:
95,709 (1990), 116,091 (1995)
Square miles: 607
Population per square mile: 191
Municipalities: 20
(4 boroughs, 16 townships)

Monroe County was created in 1836 from parts of Northampton and Pike Counties and was named for President James Monroe. Stroudsburg, the county seat, was incorporated as a borough in 1815 and named for Jacob Stroud, a settler.

Monroe County is in northeastern Pennsylvania and has the Blue Mountains, the Delaware River, and the Lehigh River as partial boundaries. It is the site of some of the most beautiful natural areas in the state, including the Pocono Mountains and the Delaware Water Gap.

The first settlers were from Holland and settled at Shawnee, near Stroudsburg. They farmed and worked copper mines. There were Indian problems— some of the county was within the area covered by the "Walking Purchase"— until the Revolutionary War.

Monroe is the second-fastest-growing county in the state. The population increased by 38% between 1980 and 1990.

In addition to generating $500 million in revenue annually, the tourist business also attracts a large seasonal population. Consequently, 27% of the housing units in the county are seasonal.

Monroe County has the lowest percentage of jobs in the goods-producing sector in the state, and the number is decreasing, mainly due to defense cutbacks.

East Stroudsburg State University, with 5,500 students, is the cultural center of the county.

I-80 and I-380 cross the county; U.S. Route 209 runs southwest to northeast into New York.

was named for Gen. Richard Montgomery, a soldier-patriot. Norristown, the county seat, was laid out in 1784 and incorporated as a borough in 1812. It was named for Isaac Norris, a landowner.

The first settlers in the county were Welsh who bought the land from William Penn. German settlers followed and established the agricultural base that remains to this day. The county became one of the state's major manufacturing centers. At Hatboro, hats for the Revolutionary Army were produced. The tradition continued during World War II, when county industries produced iron, rubber, and textile products for the military.

Montgomery County is one of the places to which Philadelphia's population and economic life moved after World War II. Land use in the county is diverse, ranging from older, stately bedroom communities near Philadelphia to productive farms in the western portion. Three major employment centers have developed: King of Prussia, Fort Washington, and North Penn. King of Prussia is also the site of a world-class shopping mall. Many Fortune 500 companies are located in Montgomery County: Merck, GE, Ford, Unisys, and Prudential Insurance, the county's largest employer. Residents have the highest per capita income in the commonwealth, $26,358 in 1994.

The county is home to 21 institutions of higher education, including branch campuses of Penn State and Temple, six theological seminaries, and some nationally recognized liberal arts colleges, notably Bryn Mawr, Haverford, and Ursinus. Another important institution is the State Correctional Institution at Graterford, the largest in the state.

MONTGOMERY COUNTY

Swede & Airy Sts.,
Norristown, PA 19404
(610) 278-3000

Population:
678,111 (1990), 705,178 (1995)
Square miles: 483
Population per square mile: 1,460
Municipalities: 62
(24 boroughs, 38 townships)

Montgomery County was created in 1784 from part of Philadelphia County and

The county has two state parks that combine history and outdoor recreation: Fort Washington, on the site where troops built a fort in 1779 before moving on to Valley Forge, and Evansburg, in eastern Montgomery County, where remnants of 18th- and 19th-century Mennonite settlements survive. Valley Forge National Historical Park is the premier tourist spot in the county.

The Pennsylvania Turnpike touches the southwest corner of the county; the Northeast Extension crosses the center. U.S. Route 202 and PA Route 29 are also important roads.

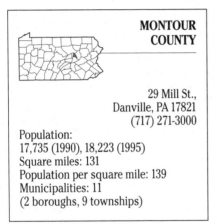

MONTOUR COUNTY

29 Mill St.,
Danville, PA 17821
(717) 271-3000
Population:
17,735 (1990), 18,223 (1995)
Square miles: 131
Population per square mile: 139
Municipalities: 11
(2 boroughs, 9 townships)

Montour County was created in 1850 from part of Columbia County and was named for Madame Montour, a woman of French and Indian descent who was prominent in Indian affairs. Danville, the county seat, was incorporated in 1849. It was laid out in 1792 and was the county seat of Columbia County from 1813 to 1846. In 1846, Bloomsburg, Danville's arch rival, became the county seat of Columbia County. The ill will that this change wrought led to a movement to create another county so that Danville

could regain county seat status. Thus, Montour County, at 131 square miles the smallest county in the commonwealth, was born.

Montour is strategically located on the Susquehanna River. Consequently, Danville became an important way station between Sunbury and the upper Susquehanna Valley. The river valley served as a natural route for roads, railroads, and the Pennsylvania Canal System.

Danville's importance grew with the discovery of iron ore nearby. A thriving iron industry developed. In 1845, the Montour Iron Works rolled the first iron T-type rail ever produced. The transition to steel rails in the 1860s led to the decline of the iron industry.

Modern-day Danville has become a regional medical center. It is home to the Geisinger Medical Center, a private 577-bed, state-of-the-art facility, and the Janet Weis Children's Hospital.

I-80 crosses the county.

NORTHAMPTON COUNTY

669 Washington St.,
Easton, PA 18042
(610) 559-3195
Population:
247,105 (1990), 256,796 (1995)
Square miles: 374
Population per square mile: 686
Municipalities: 38
(2 cities, 19 boroughs, 17 townships)

Northampton County was created in 1752 from part of Bucks County and was named for Northamptonshire, England, where Thomas Penn's father-in-law, the earl of Pomfort, lived on his estate, Easton. Easton, the county seat, was incorporated as a borough in 1789 and chartered as a city in 1886.

Northampton County was part of the frontier at the time of its creation. English and Scots-Irish settlers came first, but German settlers followed in such great numbers that the area assumed a definite German character. Easton, at the junction of the Delaware and Lehigh Rivers, became a principal trading area for interior Pennsylvania. It had been a center of Indian activity prior to white settlement. Moravians settled in Bethlehem in 1741. It was the site of the first pharmacy in America and had the first fire engine and the first municipal waterworks.

The county is located about 60 miles north of Philadelphia and 80 miles west of New York. The Delaware River forms the eastern boundary with New Jersey, and the Blue Mountains form the county's northern boundary. The central valley, which includes the county's two cities and most of its urban development, contains a limestone belt that formed excellent soil for farming and provides material for the cement industry. Northampton, with 6.7 million tons of non-coal mining production, generally ranks second only to Lancaster County in that activity.

The county was a major player in the great iron and steel industry of Pennsylvania. As recently as 1974, the Bethlehem Steel plant produced 3 million tons of steel. Production declined after that, and in 1995, the mighty Bethlehem Steel plant shut down.

Manufacturing is still important in the county, but retail trade and services play an increasingly important role in the economy. New industrial and business parks in Hanover, Bethlehem, and Forks Townships have helped to diversify the economic base. Lafayette and Moravian Colleges are historic institutions that remain cultural centers of the area as well as major employers.

The Delaware Canal State Park is the major tourist and recreational attraction in the county.

I-78 provides excellent access to New York City; U.S. Route 33 connects Easton with I-80 and the Pocono Mountain resorts; U.S. Route 22 and PA Route 611 are important local roads.

NORTHUMBERLAND COUNTY

Sunbury, PA 17801
(717) 988-4281

Population:
96,771 (1990), 96,260 (1995)
Square miles: 460
Population per square mile: 209
Municipalities: 36
(2 cities, 11 boroughs, 23 townships)

Northumberland County was created in 1772 from parts of five counties and was named for an English county. Sunbury, the county seat, was laid out in 1772, incorporated as a borough in 1797, and chartered as a city in 1921. It was named for an English village near London.

Sunbury, at the junction of the North and West Branches of the Susquehanna River, was once the site of the great Indian town of Shamokin. Shikellamy, the great Oneida chief, the chief negotiator between the Indians and the Provincial

Government, lived in Shamokin from 1728 to 1748.

Sunbury was the last proprietary town of the Penns. A Moravian mission in 1742 was the first settlement. Settlements were subject to frequent attacks from British troops and Indians during the Revolution. One such attack, known as the "Wyoming Massacre," in 1778 drove all of the settlers from the area.

An early turnpike linked Sunbury to Reading and Williamsport. The Pennsylvania Canal, on the North Branch of the Susquehanna River, and the Pennsylvania Railroad also went through Sunbury. Consequently, the county shared in the prosperity that came with the great lumber industry in the region.

Northumberland became a major anthracite-producing area after 1850. The towns of Shamokin and Mount Carmel developed around mining; the coal was shipped down the Susquehanna.

Recent population growth in the area has been very slow; after about a 2% growth from 1980 to 1990, it has been flat for the past five years. About 40% of the labor force is engaged in manufacturing. Food processing is the major activity in that sector. State government is the fifth-largest employer, mainly at the State Correctional Institution in Coal Township.

Although the acreage is small, the land along the Susquehanna River is among the richest farmland in the state. The county has about 660 farms, which raise mostly corn and soybeans.

I-80 and I-180 pass through the northern part of Northumberland County, intersecting near Milton. PA Route 61 is the major east-west road; PA Route 147 and U.S. Route 11 follow the Susquehanna River.

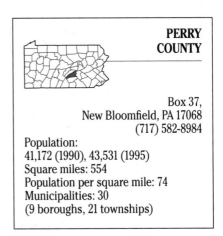

PERRY COUNTY

Box 37,
New Bloomfield, PA 17068
(717) 582-8984
Population:
41,172 (1990), 43,531 (1995)
Square miles: 554
Population per square mile: 74
Municipalities: 30
(9 boroughs, 21 townships)

Perry County was created in 1820 from part of Cumberland County and was named in honor of Adm. Oliver Perry, the hero of the Battle of Lake Erie. New Bloomfield, the county seat after 1827, was open farmland when the construction of county buildings began—on blooming fields of clover. It was incorporated as a borough in 1831. The first county seat (1820–27) was Landisburg.

Because of the abundant water power available, a large number of mills were established in Perry County. Iron forges and furnaces followed. The county became an important producer of charcoal iron in the mid-19th century. But Perry County was a crossroads on the way to the western and northern frontier, rather than a destination. The Susquehanna and Juniata Rivers were major highways in the settlement of the county. Turnpikes, canals, and railroads all played their role.

Perry County is part of the Harrisburg Metropolitan Area, which includes Dauphin and Cumberland Counties.

About 62% of the county is forestland. Perry does not have an urban center toward which the population gravitates. The residents live in nine small boroughs that are reminiscent of times gone by and in large agricultural townships. The county ranks 50th in population in the state.

The service sector dominates the county economic activity, particularly retail stores. There are about 40 manufacturing enterprises. Seventy percent of the residents work in other counties. This is the highest percentage of commuters in the state.

There are three small state parks in Perry County and about 40,000 acres of public forestland. The major roads, U.S. Routes 22/322 and 11/15, provide easy access to Harrisburg.

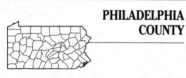

PHILADELPHIA COUNTY

City Hall,
Philadelphia, PA 19107
(215) 686-3462
Population:
1,585,577 (1990), 1,498,971 (1995)
Square miles: 135
Population per square mile: 11,103
Municipalities: 1
(1 city)

Philadelphia County was one of the three original counties created by William Penn in 1682. The name means "city of brotherly love." It was chartered as a city in 1701, and rechartered in 1789. In 1854, all the municipalities within the county were consolidated with the city; in 1952, county offices merged with city government.

The First Continental Congress met in Philadelphia in 1774, and independence from the crown was declared in 1776. By the time of the American Revolution, Philadelphia was the second-largest English-speaking city in the world. It was the nation's capital from 1790 to 1800. Visitors can relive these momentous times at Independence National Historical Park, where two of the nation's monuments to freedom, the Liberty Bell and Independence Hall, are located.

Philadelphia, with a population of 1.5 million, is now the second-largest city on the East Coast, although the population has been declining dramatically for the past 45 years. It is situated between the major cities of the Middle Atlantic states and New England. Major airlines operate from Philadelphia International Airport, and Amtrak Northeast Corridor Service includes the city. Several interstate highways pass through or run nearby. A comprehensive system of public transportation includes buses and subways within the city and regional rail lines serving the suburbs.

Despite suburbanization, Philadelphia is still the employment center of the region, although the workforce has declined in numbers and the nature of the employment has changed dramatically, manufacturing having been replaced by services. Nine of the 10 biggest employers in 1994 were public agencies; Bell Atlantic Telephone was the 10th.

The new world order has produced some horrific side effects in Philadelphia. Twenty percent of the population is below the poverty line, large sections of the city are run-down and neglected, and city services are often inadequate, thus perpetuating a large population of urban poor.

Still, bright areas do exist. Center City is an attractively rebuilt business and residential area, and a new Convention Center opened in 1993. Its spectacular grand hall is contained within the historic train shed of the Reading Railroad Terminal. Some of the city's cultural and architectural treasures line the boulevard that links the center of Philadelphia with Fairmount Park, the largest landscaped urban park in the world. Along the Benjamin Franklin Parkway are the Philadelphia Museum of Art, the Franklin Institute Science Museum, the Academy of Natural Sciences, and the Rodin Museum. The city is also home to the Philadelphia Orchestra, which performs in the historic and magnificent Academy of Music. Opera, dance, world-class libraries, and the University of Pennsylvania are available to residents and to tourists, which are coming in increasingly large numbers.

To attempt to describe the multifaceted city is to confront the problem faced by the mythical blind man in describing the elephant.

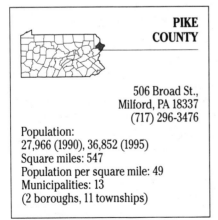

PIKE COUNTY

506 Broad St.,
Milford, PA 18337
(717) 296-3476
Population:
27,966 (1990), 36,852 (1995)
Square miles: 547
Population per square mile: 49
Municipalities: 13
(2 boroughs, 11 townships)

Pike County was created in 1814 from part of Wayne County and was named for Gen. Zebulon Pike, a hero of the War of 1812, who had discovered Pike's Peak in 1806. Milford, the county seat, was incorporated as a borough in 1874 and was named for Milford Haven in Wales.

Located in the northeastern corner of Pennsylvania, Pike County meets New Jersey and New York at the tristate boundary marker on the banks of the Delaware River. It lies 70 miles northwest of New York City. Dutch settlers from New York who settled near what is now Milford were the first white inhabitants of Pennsylvania. The county's demographic composition, as well as its community character, has been closely linked to that of nearby urban areas since then.

The first major industry in Pike County was lumbering. Early railroads and canals were developed to service that industry. Later, the Delaware and Hudson Canal was built to carry coal to New York City. Pike County has long relied upon its recreational attractions for its economic viability. The tourist trade, the service sector, and second-home construction are the major elements of the modern economy.

The county's growth rate, 135 percent between 1980 and 1990, is the highest in Pennsylvania. In addition to growth in its permanent population, Pike County experiences tremendous increases in seasonal population. In 1990, about 60% of the housing units were second homes. The theoretical peak of second-home population in the county is 60,000, which is almost double the permanent population.

More than one-third of the county's 350,000 acres is in public land, the best known of which is the Delaware Water Gap National Recreation Area, 70,000 acres along a 40-mile stretch of the river.

Notable Pike countians include former governor and conservationist Gifford Pinchot and western novelist Zane Grey, who wrote the first of his novels while living in Lackawaxen from 1905 to 1918. The homes of both are now museums.

I-84 bisects the county east to west, joining the New York State Thruway to the east and I-81 to the west at Scranton. Scenic U.S. Route 6 crosses the northeast portion of the county.

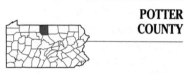

POTTER COUNTY

1 E. Main St.,
Coudersport, PA 16915
(814) 274-8290

Population:
16,717 (1990), 17,090 (1995)
Square miles: 1,081
Population per square mile: 16
Municipalities: 31
(6 boroughs, 25 townships)

Potter County was created in 1804 from part of Lycoming County and was named for Gen. James Potter, a soldier of the American Revolution and noted Indian fighter. It was not fully organized until 1835. Coudersport, the county seat, was laid out in 1807 and incorporated as a borough in 1848. It was named for an Amsterdam banker, Samuel Couderc, who had directed some investment into the land company that laid out the town.

Potter County is located in the center of what is called the Northern Tier of Pennsylvania on the New York boundary. Its location on a highly dissected plateau with narrow, steep-sided valleys made early travel difficult and settle-

ment hesitant. In 1852, world-renowned concert violinist Ole Bornemann (Ole Bull) founded Oleona, where he tried to establish a new, free Norway on 11,000 acres. There were 800 settlers, but the colony failed for financial and legal reasons, the prime reason being that the seller did not own the land he sold to the settlers.

The lumber industry brought development to the area. At first, logs were floated down the Allegheny River to mills, but in the 1880s, the Goodyear Lumber Company built local mills. The company did not reforest, and the last hemlocks were gone by 1920, as was the company. Today, almost 80% of the county is forested; most of the southern half is public land. The Pennsylvania Lumber Museum in Galeton is an excellent place to learn about the timber industry in the 19th century.

In the county, about 2 miles north of the point where Allegheny, Sweden, and Ulysses Townships join, on a relatively flat hill about 800 feet long and 400 feet wide, and at an altitude of 2,520 feet above sea level, is the divide between waters going west to the Ohio and Mississippi Rivers, and thence to the Gulf of Mexico; those going north to Lake Ontario and the St. Lawrence River; and those going east to the Susquehanna River and the Chesapeake Bay. Few places have a site showing so precisely the separation of three major drainage systems.

The present-day Potter County economy is based on services, particularly health services, transportation, and retail trade. Natural gas, farming, and outdoor recreation have always been important.

Scenic U.S. Route 6 is the major east-west route through the county; PA Route

44 passes from the southeast to the northwest corner, through the Susquehannock State Forest.

SCHUYLKILL COUNTY

401 N. Second St.,
Pottsville, PA 17901
(717) 628-1204
Population:
152,585 (1990), 153,616 (1995)
Square miles: 779
Population per square mile: 197
Municipalities: 67
(1 city, 30 boroughs, 36 townships)

Schuylkill County was created in 1811 from parts of Berks and Northampton Counties; parts of Columbia and Luzerne Counties were added to it in 1818. Schuylkill is a Dutch word meaning "hidden stream." Orwigsburg was the original county seat; Pottsville was designated county seat in 1851 and was chartered as a city in 1910. John Potts laid out the town.

Anthracite coal mining was the chief industry of Schuylkill County from the time its value as a fuel was established. Mining operations brought roads, canals, and eventually railroads to the area, as well as an ethnically diverse population of miners. The area was the scene of historic labor-management disputes, the most famous involving the "Molly Maguires," some of whom were hanged in the courtyard of the Schuylkill County Prison in Pottsville. The county has the largest reserve of anthracite coal in the world beneath it, but only small strip miners are extracting it.

Agriculture is still important here. About 650 farms generated $40 million in cash receipts in 1995. Large employers include Morgan Knitting Mill, Cressona Aluminum, and Good Samaritan Regional Hospital. The new growth industry is prisons. Within 5 miles of Frackville, two state prisons have opened in the last 10 years. Ten miles away, near Minersville, a federal prison with 1,360 inmates opened in 1991. Although they were opposed by residents, the prisons have revitalized the area economically.

Tourist attractions include the Museum of Anthracite Mining and the Pioneer Tunnel Coal Mine Tour in Ashland. The county also has the oldest continuously operating brewery in the United States, D. G. Yuengling & Son. The Schuylkill County Fairgrounds is the site of the Kutztown Folk Festival, which runs for nine days in July.

Schuylkill County is accessible via I-81, which runs northeast and southwest through the county and connects with I-78 and I-80 just beyond its boundaries. PA Route 61 is the main state route.

SNYDER COUNTY

Middleburg, PA 17842
(717) 837-4208
Population:
36,680 (1990), 37,845 (1995)
Square miles: 331
Population per square mile: 114
Municipalities: 21
(6 boroughs, 15 townships)

Snyder County was created in 1855 from part of Union County and was named to honor the third governor of Pennsylvania, Simon Snyder. Middleburg, the county seat, was laid out in 1800 and incorporated as a borough in 1860. The name came from its location on Middle Creek, in the middle of the county.

Snyder County is part of the Ridge and Valley Province in the Middle Susquehanna River Valley; the river is its eastern boundary.

The last major events in Snyder County involved Indians and settlers. In 1755, Indians massacred settlers along Penns Creek. In 1768, Frederick Stump, a settler, murdered 10 Indians near Selinsgrove. The army arrested Stump and was holding him for travel to Philadelphia to stand trial, when a mob released him from jail. He was never recaptured.

Farming is the principal economic activity in Snyder County; 740 farms use 43% of the land and generate $56 million in cash receipts. Other industries include textiles, lumber, and wood products, including furniture.

Susquehanna University in Selinsgrove, founded in 1894, is the major cultural institution in the county and the third-largest employer.

The county is located between Williamsport and Harrisburg via U.S. Routes 11 and 15. PA Route 522 runs southwest and northeast through the county.

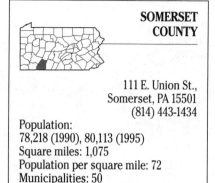

SOMERSET COUNTY

111 E. Union St.,
Somerset, PA 15501
(814) 443-1434

Population:
78,218 (1990), 80,113 (1995)
Square miles: 1,075
Population per square mile: 72
Municipalities: 50
(25 boroughs, 25 townships)

Somerset County was created in 1795 from part of Bedford County and was named for Somersetshire, England. Somerset, the county seat, was laid out in 1795 and incorporated as a borough in 1804.

The county is located in the southwestern corner of Pennsylvania and is part of the Johnstown Metropolitan Statistical Area. Most of the county is a high plateau located between the crest of the Allegheny Mountains on the east and Laurel Hill on the west. The highest point in Pennsylvania, Mount Davis, is in Somerset County.

America literally passed through Somerset County on its way west. George Washington supervised the building of the first road. Gen. John Forbes and Col. Henry Bouquet marched through during their campaigns. Stage and freight lines used the early turnpikes. The Great Cumberland Road or National Pike, now U.S. Route 40, touched the southwest corner of the county. The railroad came in the 1870s.

The Baltimore and Ohio Railroad opened up markets for the rich bituminous coalfields in the county. These fields are still producing over a million tons annually, which are used in America and abroad for power production. Natural gas production dates from the 1950s with the discovery of the Johnstown and Boswell Fields.

Agriculture is important to the county's economy. Dairy, hay, corn, and oats, the last a crop in which Somerset led the state in 1995, are the main products. Tourism, especially outdoor recreation, and a second-home industry have developed around two state parks and parts of two others, state forests, and ski areas.

The Pennsylvania Turnpike and I-70 make the area very accessible to Pittsburgh and the Baltimore-Washington area.

SULLIVAN COUNTY

Laporte, PA 18626
(717) 946-5204
Population:
6,104 (1990), 6,184 (1995)
Square miles: 450
Population per square mile: 14
Municipalities: 13
(4 boroughs, 9 townships)

Sullivan County was created in 1847 from part of Lycoming County and was named for state senator Charles Sullivan, who championed its creation. Laporte, the county seat, was incorporated as a borough in 1853 and was named for John La Porte, who was surveyor general of Pennsylvania at that time.

The first settlers came from Wyoming County. They were originally from

Connecticut and claimed the land under a grant from the king of England. The proprietors of Pennsylvania had these people driven from the area or arrested. New settlers arrived, but they were driven out by the Indians, who remained until they were dispossessed in the Indian wars.

In 1786, white settlers returned to stay. The dense forest made settlement slow and difficult, however. Lumbering and tanning supported some of the people. A woolen mill was established in 1802; it prospered through government contracts to sell cloth to the army during the War of 1812 and survived until 1916, when it was destroyed by a flood.

Sullivan County today is one of the least-populated counties in the commonwealth, and 85% of the land is in forest, including two state parks and the Eagles Mere resort area. Local industry and commerce are small-scale and personal.

The county is served by U.S. Route 220, which connects with I-80 about 40 miles to the southwest, near Williamsport, and numerous rural roads.

SUSQUEHANNA COUNTY

Montrose, PA 18801
(717) 278-4600
Population:
40,380 (1990), 41,800 (1995)
Square miles: 823
Population per square mile: 51
Municipalities: 40
(13 boroughs, 27 townships)

Susquehanna County was created in 1810 from a part of Luzerne County, to which it remained attached until 1812. Montrose, the county seat, was incorporated as a borough in 1824. Its name is a combination of the French word for "mountain" and rose, for Dr. Robert Rose, a Philadelphian who owned 100,000 acres in the county and whose influence attracted many Quakers to the area.

Susquehanna County is located in the northeast corner of the state along the New York border. It is now part of the Binghamton, New York, metropolitan area. The county was not settled until after the Revolutionary War. The first settlement was an encampment of the army en route to an Indian war in New York. The county was part of the area settled by New Englanders who claimed ownership through a competing royal charter.

The county has rolling hills with lakes and streams throughout. It is ideal grazing land. The leading agricultural activities are dairy farming and veal production. The 790 farms have an average of 239 acres, the third highest in the state. About 65% of the county is forestland. Mineral resources include sand and gravel, sandstone, and bluestone.

Health care, education, and government are major employers; the largest noninstitutional employer is an electronic components assembly plant in Hallstead.

Outdoor activities, especially hunting and fishing, are major attractions. Salt Springs State Park is a focal point of these activities.

I-81 runs north and south through the middle of the county, linking it with Scranton, 49 miles south, and Binghamton, 31 miles north. Ten state routes crisscross the area.

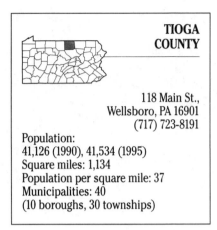

TIOGA COUNTY

118 Main St.,
Wellsboro, PA 16901
(717) 723-8191

Population:
41,126 (1990), 41,534 (1995)
Square miles: 1,134
Population per square mile: 37
Municipalities: 40
(10 boroughs, 30 townships)

Tioga County was created in 1804 from part of Lycoming County and was named for the Tioga River. The name is derived from an Indian word meaning "the forks of a stream." Wellsboro, the county seat, was incorporated as a borough in 1830. It was named for the locally prominent Wells family.

The county was covered with dense forests; logging was the major early industry. Little of the virgin forest remains, but Leonard Harrison and Colton Point State Parks are beautiful wooded areas. Pine Creek Gorge, the "Grand Canyon of Pennsylvania," is the county's main attraction. About two-thirds of the land is in forest. Only four small lumber companies and a leather tannery remain. Mineral resources include coal, sand and gravel, oil, and gas. A bituminous coal mine near Blossburg produced the first coal in the state.

The largest employer in Tioga County is the Ward Foundry in Blossburg. Hitachi recently bought the company and is expanding operations by building a new plant in Lawrence Township. The Laurel Health System, a multifaceted health services provider, is the second-largest employer. Mansfield State University is the leading cultural resource and a major economic influence. The Penn College of Technology, an affiliate of Penn State, offers a higher-education program.

U.S. Routes 6 and 15 are the major roads in the county, which is also served by ten state routes. The nearest interstate, I-81, is 60 miles from Wellsboro.

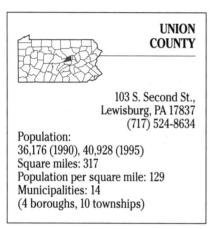

UNION COUNTY

103 S. Second St.,
Lewisburg, PA 17837
(717) 524-8634
Population:
36,176 (1990), 40,928 (1995)
Square miles: 317
Population per square mile: 129
Municipalities: 14
(4 boroughs, 10 townships)

Union County was created in 1813 and was named in honor of the federal Union, which was new and significant in 1813. Lewisburg, the county seat after 1855, when Snyder County was created from part of Union County, was named for its founder, Lewis Derr. It was incorporated as a borough in 1822. (New Berlin was the Union County seat from 1813 to 1855.)

Union County is located in the Susquehanna Valley of central Pennsylvania, 60 miles north of Harrisburg. The West Branch of the Susquehanna River is its eastern boundary. It is mostly wooded mountains and open space. It has two state parks and a large tract of state forestland. The commercial devel-

opment areas are located along U.S. Route 15 and PA Route 45, in Lewisburg and Mifflinburg.

Union County was the ninth-fastest-growing county in the state between 1980 and 1990. Recreational opportunities, seasonal homes, and safe, lower-cost retirement have attracted new residents.

Though manufacturing employs a large number of people in the production of furniture, fixtures, lumber, and wood products, agriculture is the vital force in the lifestyle and culture of Union County. The 510 farms produce about $50 million annually.

Lewisburg is the site of the two major institutions in the county, Bucknell University and a U.S. penitentiary, which are the largest single employers.

VENANGO COUNTY

Franklin, PA 16323
(814) 432-9543
Population:
59,381 (1990), 59,057 (1995)
Square miles: 675
Population per square mile: 87
Municipalities: 31
(2 cities, 9 boroughs, 20 townships)

Venango County was created in 1800 from parts of Allegheny and Lycoming Counties. Its name is a derivative of the Indian name for French Creek. Franklin, the county seat, was laid out in 1795 at Fort Franklin, which was built by the army in 1787 and named for Benjamin Franklin. It was incorporated as a borough in 1828 and as a city in 1868.

The early history of Venango County is a story of conflicting territorial claims—Virginia, the French, and the Indians all claimed sovereignty in the late 18th and early 19th centuries. Forts were built and destroyed, settlements developed and abandoned, settlers chased off the land or killed. Finally, the Americans established dominion over the area and settlers came to stay. Many were Revolutionary War veterans granted free land as a service benefit.

At first, the forest supported them. Eventually, between 1830 and 1850, 26 iron furnaces were established, earning Venango the title "Iron County."

In 1859, just inside the county line near Titusville, "Colonel" Drake discovered crude petroleum and changed the life of the county and the world. Oil was discovered near Franklin in 1860, natural gas in 1885.

A small-scale petroleum industry and manufacturing related to it are still part of the economy. Quaker State Corporation is headquartered in Oil City; Pennzoil Products Company is a major employer. Manufacturing employment has declined sharply in the last four years, mainly due to the closing or the downsizing of plants. Service and trade employment is increasing, and the population is decreasing as a result. Oil City has lost half of its population since 1930; Franklin is the only other population center. Most of the rest of the county is farmland and small rural villages.

Oil Creek State Park, state forestland, and state game lands provide recreational opportunities, as does the Allegheny River. An Oil Region Heritage Park Program is in development.

I-80 crosses the extreme southern part of the county; local traffic uses PA Route 8 and U.S. Route 322.

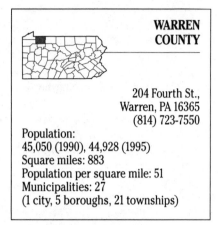

WARREN COUNTY

204 Fourth St.,
Warren, PA 16365
(814) 723-7550

Population:
45,050 (1990), 44,928 (1995)
Square miles: 883
Population per square mile: 51
Municipalities: 27
(1 city, 5 boroughs, 21 townships)

Warren County was created in 1800 from parts of Allegheny and Lycoming Counties and was named for Gen. Joseph Warren, who was killed at the Battle of Bunker Hill. It was not formally organized until 1819. Warren, the county seat, was laid out in 1795, incorporated as a borough in 1832, and designated a city in 1989.

The county is located in the midst of the Allegheny National Forest and is bordered on the north by New York State. Most of the land in the eastern and southern portions of the county is broken and hilly; the northwest was carved by glaciers. Hardwood trees once covered the western portion. Large stands of pine and hemlock grew in the creek valleys and southwest of the Allegheny River. The Allegheny and its three main tributaries were natural waterways for the rafting of lumber. Thus, lumbering was the main industry from 1800 to 1870.

The discovery of oil at nearby Titusville in 1859 and the arrival of the railroad at about the same time led to a boom in Warren County. Some oil production and refining still exist, but Warren's economy today is heavily weighted toward service, especially retail trade, health services, and tourism. The completion of the Kinzua Dam and the Allegheny Reservoir in 1965 intensified the tourist industry. The major employer in retail trade is a clothing warehouse and outlet.

Scenic U.S. Route 6 is the major road. It is the road of choice for fall foliage viewing.

WASHINGTON COUNTY

100 W. Beau St.,
Washington, PA 15301
(412) 228-6700
Population:
204,584 (1990), 208,017 (1995)
Square miles: 857
Population per square mile: 243
Municipalities: 67
(2 cities, 33 boroughs, 32 townships)

Washington County was created in 1781 from part of Westmoreland County and was named for George Washington, as was the county seat, which was laid out in 1781, incorporated as a borough in 1810, and chartered as a city in 1924.

Washington County is located in southwestern Pennsylvania on the West Virginia border. It is part of the Pittsburgh–Beaver Valley Standard Metropolitan Statistical Area. Its northern boundary is just 10 miles south of Pittsburgh and a few minutes from the Pittsburgh Airport.

The county has a proud heritage. It was roamed by French fur traders in early colonial times; George Washington campaigned through the area during the French and Indian War; it was the focal point of the "Whiskey Rebellion"; and one of its residents, William Holmes McGuffey, authored the McGuffey *Readers.* Historic landmarks include 25 well-maintained covered bridges, a courthouse that is a fine example of Italian Renaissance architecture, and U.S. Route 40, America's first federally built highway.

The county has a nonfarm economy about equally weighted between manufacturing and mining, retail trade and service. Some of the traditional southwestern Pennsylvania industries, such as glassmaking and coal mining, endure; Corning Glass is a major employer.

Agriculture is also important. The county has the third-highest number of farms in the state and leads in number of sheep. About 75% of the harvest cropland is in hay, primarily alfalfa.

The California State University and Washington and Jefferson College are cultural centers. Hillman State Park and the Meadows racetrack are recreation centers.

I-70 and I-79 both cross the county and provide excellent access to Pittsburgh and neighboring states, as do U.S. Routes 19 and 40 and PA Route 18.

WAYNE COUNTY

925 Court St.,
Honesdale, PA 18431
(717) 253-5970
Population:
39,944 (1990), 44,070 (1995)
Square miles: 729
Population per square mile: 60
Municipalities: 28
(6 boroughs, 22 townships)

Wayne County was created in 1798 from part of Northampton County and was named for Gen. Anthony Wayne, a military hero of the western frontier. Honesdale, the county seat, was named for Phillip Hone, president of the Delaware and Hudson Canal Company. It is the fourth county seat, preceded by Wilsonville (1799–1802), Milford (1802–1805), and Bethany (1805–1841). Honesdale was laid out in 1827 and incorporated as a borough in 1831.

Wayne County is located in the northeast corner of Pennsylvania. Its proximity to New York City and neighboring urban areas has been a major factor in the county's development. It was among the territory claimed by Connecticut and New York in pre-Revolutionary times. Although Pennsylvania ultimately prevailed in the dispute, some of the land claims of Connecticut settlers were honored.

Lumbering and coal were important early industries. Wayne County was involved in many schemes to ship anthracite coal to market. In the glory days of the Delaware and Hudson Canal Company, Honesdale stored and shipped millions of tons of coal brought in by train from Carbondale and loaded on canal boats.

Today, about 82% of the workforce is employed in retail trade or services, especially related to tourism. Seven of the top 10 employers in 1994 were public agencies. The Waymart Correctional Institution is located here, making state government the largest single employer. From 1990 to 1994, Wayne County lost about 33% of its manufacturing jobs, mainly due to plant closures.

There are 110 lakes in Wayne County. The largest is Lake Wallenpaupack—14 miles long and 3 miles wide, with 56 miles of shoreline.

Wayne County is growing rapidly by Pennsylvania standards: 13% between 1980 and 1990. The second-home phenomenon is very strong here.

Major highways include I-84 and I-380, which brushes the southwest tip; and U.S. Route 6.

WESTMORELAND COUNTY

301 Courthouse Square,
Greensburg, PA 15601
(412) 830-3000
Population:
370,321 (1990), 376,501 (1995)
Square miles: 1,023
Population per square mile: 368
Municipalities: 65
(6 cities, 38 boroughs, 21 townships)

Westmoreland County was created in 1773 from part of Bedford County and was named for a county in England, whose name meant "land of the western moors." Hannastown, the original county seat, was destroyed by an Indian raid in 1782. Greensburg, 5 miles south, was named county seat in 1785, incorporated as a borough in 1799, and chartered as a city in 1928. It was named for Gen. Nathanael Greene.

The history of Westmoreland County can be divided into two major eras. The first was the battle for the western frontier. Fort Ligonier, Bushy Run Battlefield, and Hannastown are historic sites of that struggle. The military road built by Gen. John Forbes in 1758 was the forerunner of U.S. Route 30.

The second era involved bituminous coal and industry. A native son, Henry Clay Frick, made the manufacture of coke from bituminous coal the major industry. After the Civil War, when Frick and Andrew Carnegie became partners, the steel mills of Pittsburgh, fueled by coke, boomed. The boom spread to Westmoreland. Steel, aluminum, and glass plants were built, and towns grew around them. Westmoreland County was part of the Pittsburgh metropolitan area long before the Census Bureau designated it as such.

The great industrial base has not disappeared altogether—Alcoa, Westinghouse, and Elliot Turbomachinery are still visible. Lenox Crystal, in Mount Pleasant, Latrobe Steel, and Allegheny Ludlum continue the historic industries, but at a greatly downsized level. The top employers in 1994 were the state and county governments and hospitals.

The population has declined, but not as sharply as it might have. The industrial slowdown has been partially offset by suburbanization. The suburban and rural areas of the county are attractive to city residents. Good highways make the trip convenient. These include I-70; the Pennsylvania Turnpike; U.S. Routes 22, 30, and 119; and PA Route 66.

There are five state parks, two colleges, two branches of major universities, and a community college in the county. Latrobe is the birthplace of two modern American icons, Arnold Palmer and Mister (Fred) Rogers.

WYOMING COUNTY

1 Courthouse Square,
Tunkhannock, PA 18657
(717) 836-3200
Population:
28,076 (1990), 29,316 (1995)
Square miles: 397
Population per square mile: 74
Municipalities: 23
(5 boroughs, 18 townships)

Wyoming County was created in 1842 from part of Luzerne County and was named for the Wyoming Valley. Wyoming was an Indian word meaning "extensive meadow." Tuckhannock ("small stream"), the county seat, was incorporated in 1841.

Wyoming County is a part of the Scranton–Wilkes-Barre metropolitan area and is about a 30-minute drive from both cities.

The county was the scene of numerous Indian battles, including one that broke the power of the mighty Iroquois tribe from New York. Settlers from Pennsylvania and Connecticut also fought periodically between 1769 and 1789 for control of the valley.

Dairying and agriculture in general

flourished here on the banks of the North Branch of the Susquehanna River and its tributaries. Through the 1800s, the area was a hub for the floating of logs down the river. In the mid-1800s, when the railroad arrived, the area became a major shipping point for livestock, lumber, grain, and flagstone.

Primarily rural, with vast open spaces and great natural beauty, the county provides some of the best boating and fishing in the state. Points of interest include Lakes Carey and Winola, and the Tunkhannock Viaduct, which, at 240 feet, was one of the highest railroad bridges in the world when it was built in 1915.

The major employers are Procter and Gamble paper products, Keystone Junior College, and the Tunkhannock School District.

U.S. Routes 6 and 11 and six state highways serve the area. The nearest interstate interchange is 26 miles from Tunkhannock.

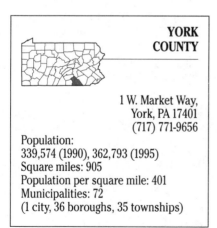

YORK COUNTY

1 W. Market Way,
York, PA 17401
(717) 771-9656
Population:
339,574 (1990), 362,793 (1995)
Square miles: 905
Population per square mile: 401
Municipalities: 72
(1 city, 36 boroughs, 35 townships)

York County was created in 1749 from part of Lancaster County and was named for either the duke of York or York, England. The city of York, the county seat, was laid out in 1741, incorporated as a borough in 1787, and chartered as a city in 1887.

York County is located in south-central Pennsylvania on the Maryland border. Lord Baltimore insisted that the York area was part of Maryland, and border disputes were common. After the Revolution, the Mason-Dixon survey party set the border between the two states and settled the issue.

The iron industry was York's most important early industry. York was also on the road west, and thousands of pioneers used its ferries and turnpikes. The Susquehanna River is its eastern border. Hanover was the scene of the first Civil War battle in the North, a cavalry battle that delayed J. E. B. Stuart on his way to Gettysburg.

York County has been an area of dynamic growth since 1960; the population increased from 238,000 to an estimated 362,000 in 1995. About half of the population lives in the city of York and adjacent municipalities. The area around the borough of Hanover in the southwestern part of the county is another growth area. I-83 and the Turnpike have attracted residents from Harrisburg and Baltimore to the region.

The county has a diverse economy, with manufacturing, agriculture, and a growing tourism industry all contributing. About 46,000 are employed in manufacturing. Some of York's best-known companies are Harley-Davidson, York Barbell, Pfaltzgraff pottery, and Caterpillar Tractor. Caterpillar announced that it will be closing the York plant, which employs 2,000. A bitter, long, unresolved strike ended in 1996.

The number of farms in York County is second only to that of Lancaster County. Cash receipts in 1994 were $114 million. The tourism business is based in part on the history of the county. York hosted the Continental Congress from September 1777 to June 1778 and 20,000 Confederate troops in 1863. It has many elegant historic buildings.

MUNICIPALITIES

Every resident of a Pennsylvania county also lives in a municipality—a city, borough, or township. These local entities provide police and fire protection, maintenance of local roads, water supply, sewage collection and treatment, parking and traffic control, local planning and zoning, parks and recreation, trash collection, health services, libraries, licensing of businesses, and code enforcement.

Cities

Philadelphia is Pennsylvania's only first-class city—one with a population exceeding 1 million. Pittsburgh is the only second-class city—one with a population of 250,000 to 1 million residents. Scranton is the only second-class A city—one with a population of 80,000 to 250,000 residents.

In each of these three cities, the mayor is the dominant political force and has control of the administration of the city. The mayor has broad appointive and removal powers, prepares the annual budget, and proposes and has veto power over legislation. Each of these cities has adopted a home rule charter.

The remaining 53 cities are third-class—ones with populations under 80,000—or have not elected to become second-class cities. Twenty of these cities are governed by a commission form of government, the commission consisting of a mayor, who acts as president, and four other council members. Each member is in charge of one of the five major city departments. With the exception of an elected controller or treasurer, the council appoints all officers and employees.

Eleven cities have selected a mayor-council form government, which may include a five-, seven-, or nine-member council. The mayor is the chief executive of the city and enforces ordinances of the council, supervises the work of all city departments, and submits an annual city budget.

Five cities have adopted a council-manager form in which all authority is vested in a five-, seven-, or nine-member council. The council appoints a city manager as chief administrative officer to execute its ordinances and appoint and remove department heads.

Eighteen cities have adopted home rule charters, or optional plans, which permit them to determine for themselves which structure the government will adopt and the services it will perform.

Boroughs

Boroughs are governed by councils, a weak mayor, and three elected officials—the tax collector, tax assessor, and auditor—who are independent of the council. Other officials are appointed by the council. The powers of the council, usually a body of seven, are all-encompassing. In about 200 boroughs, the council appoints a manager to carry out policies and enforce ordinances.

COUNTIES, COUNTY SEATS, AND
NUMBER OF MUNICIPALITIES (1996)

County	County Seat	Total	Cities	Boroughs	Townships
Adams	Gettysburg	34	—	13	21
Allegheny	Pittsburgh	128	4	82	42
Armstrong	Kittanning	45	1	16	28
Beaver	Beaver	53	2	29	22
Bedford	Bedford	38	—	13	25
Berks	Reading	76	1	31	44
Blair	Holidaysburg	24	1	8	15
Bradford	Towanda	51	—	14	37
Bucks	Doylestown	53	—	22	31
Butler	Butler	57	1	23	33
Cambria	Ebensburg	64	1	33	30
Cameron	Emporium	7	—	2	5
Carbon	Jim Thorpe	23	—	12	11
Centre	Bellefonte	36	—	11	25
Chester	West Chester	73	1	15	57
Clarion	Clarion	34	—	12	22
Clearfield	Clearfield	50	1	19	30
Clinton	Lock Haven	29	1	7	21
Columbia	Bloomsburg	33	—	9	24
Crawford	Meadville	51	2	14	35
Cumberland	Carlisle	34	—	12	22
Dauphin	Harrisburg	40	1	16	23
Delaware	Media	49	1	27	21
Elk	Ridgway	12	1	2	9
Erie	Erie	39	2	15	22
Fayette	Uniontown	42	2	16	24
Forest	Tionesta	9	—	1	8
Franklin	Chambersburg	22	—	7	15
Fulton	McConnellsburg	13	—	2	11
Greene	Waynesburg	26	—	6	20
Huntingdon	Huntingdon	48	—	18	30
Indiana	Indiana	38	—	14	24
Jefferson	Brookville	34	—	11	23
Juniata	Mifflintown	17	—	4	13
Lackawanna	Scranton	40	2	17	21

COUNTIES, COUNTY SEATS, AND
NUMBER OF MUNICIPALITIES *(continued)*

County	County Seat	Total	Cities	Boroughs	Townships
Lancaster	Lancaster	60	1	18	41
Lawrence	New Castle	27	1	10	16
Lebanon	Lebanon	26	1	7	18
Lehigh	Allentown	24	1	8	15
Luzerne	Wilkes-Barre	76	4	36	36
Lycoming	Williamsport	52	1	9	42
McKean	Smethport	22	1	6	15
Mercer	Mercer	48	3	14	31
Mifflin	Lewistown	16	—	6	10
Monroe	Stroudsburg	20	—	4	16
Montgomery	Norristown	62	—	24	38
Montour	Danville	11	—	2	9
Northampton	Easton	38	2	19	17
Northumberland	Sunbury	36	2	11	23
Perry	New Bloomfield	30	—	9	21
Philadelphia	Philadelphia	1	1	—	—
Pike	Milford	13	—	2	11
Potter	Coudersport	31	—	6	25
Schuylkill	Pottsville	67	1	30	36
Snyder	Middleburg	21	—	6	15
Somerset	Somerset	50	—	25	25
Sullivan	Laporte	13	—	4	9
Susquehanna	Montrose	40	—	13	27
Tioga	Wellsboro	40	—	10	30
Union	Lewisburg	14	—	4	10
Venango	Franklin	31	2	9	20
Warren	Warren	27	1	5	21
Washington	Washington	67	2	33	32
Wayne	Honesdale	28	—	6	22
Westmoreland	Greensburg	65	6	38	21
Wyoming	Tunkhannock	23	—	5	18
York	York	72	1	36	35
Totals	—	2,570	56	966	1,548

Source: The Pennsylvania State Data Center

Townships

Two classes of township exist in Pennsylvania. There are 91 first-class townships—ones with a population density greater than 300 per square mile. They are the more urban townships located in metropolitan areas. The 1,457 second-class townships are primarily rural. Many townships that meet the population density requirement to become first-class remain second-class nevertheless.

The governing bodies of the two classes differ. First-class townships are governed by elected commissioners, from five to 15, depending on whether elections are conducted by wards. Commissioners serve overlapping four-year terms.

The governing body of second-class townships is composed of either three or five supervisors, who are elected at large for six-year terms.

Other elected township officials include the tax assessor, tax collector (second-class), three auditors or a controller, and a treasurer (first-class). Appointed officials include the secretary, township manager (optional), chief of police, fire chief, engineer, and solicitors.

Twelve first-class townships and 15 second-class have adopted home rule charters.

Authorities

Authorities are a special kind of local unit. They are defined as "a body corporate and politic authorized to acquire, construct, improve, and maintain and operate projects and to borrow money and issue bonds to finance them." Projects include school buildings, transportation facilities—highways, parkways, airports, parking places—waterworks, sewage treatment plants, playgrounds, hospitals, and industrial developments. An authority may be organized by any municipality or school district either singly or in partnership with another. As of January 1995, there were 2,399 authorities in Pennsylvania.

3

Natural Resources and Outdoor Recreation

STATE PARKS

The 114 Pennsylvania state parks represent some of the state's most valuable resources. They offer a wide variety of outdoor activities year-round, special events and programs, and opportunities to learn about nature and critical environmental issues in every area of the state. One of the heroes of the state park system, Maurice K. Goddard, secretary of the Department of Forests and Waters and its successor, the Department of Environmental Resources, accomplished his goal of establishing a state park within 25 miles of every resident.

The state park descriptions here are intended to give a general idea of the nature of each park. Maps and pamphlets for individual parks can be obtained by writing to the Bureau of State Parks, P.O. Box 8551, Harrisburg, PA 17105-8551. For park information, call (800) 63-PARKS. Reservations are made by calling the individual park offices.

State parks are open year-round from 8:00 A.M. to sunset. Snackbars, swimming pools, and boat rentals normally operate only from Memorial Day weekend to Labor Day.

Park Resources and Regulations

Hunting. Most state parks contain areas for hunting. Areas closed to hunting are posted. In many cases, state forests and state game lands, where hunting is permitted, are nearby. Pennsylvania game laws are in effect.

Fishing. Fishing is permitted in state parks in accordance with current Pennsylvania Fish and Boat Commission laws.

Swimming. Swimming is available in those state parks that have designated beaches and pools. It is permitted only where and when lifeguard protection is provided. Some pools charge an admission fee. Hours are usually from 11:00 A.M. to 7:00 P.M. Swimming may be limited the two weeks after Memorial Day and two weeks prior to Labor Day, depending on the availability of lifeguards. Snorkels and scuba equipment are prohibited. Children under nine years of age must be supervised.

Picnicking. Picnic facilities are provided in most parks, complete with tables, drinking water, and a limited number of charcoal grills. (It is preferable to bring your own grill.) In many parks, pavilions and picnic groves can be rented for group affairs.

Boating. Boating is permitted at 54 parks throughout the year, but overnight mooring of boats is available by permit only from April 1 to November 1. Marina seasons vary. Very few state parks permit boats with unlimited horsepower motors. Those that do include Elk, Presque Isle, Bald Eagle, Susquehanna, Shikellamy, Beltzville, and Neshaminy.

Boats must be registered, either with the Fish and Boat Commission (boats with motors must be so registered), another state, or with the state parks, which issue a special launching permit.

Boat rentals are available at 41 parks, but no guarantee of availability is made. It is best to check on availability at the park office before your visit.

Hiking. Hiking is a widespread activity and maps of trails are available in the parks. Many parks serve as trailheads for backpacking trails on other public lands.

Special Regulations for Day-Use Areas. Pets must be kept on a leash no longer than 6 feet. Pets must be attended at all times, must be cleaned up after, and are not permitted in swimming or overnight areas.

Alcoholic beverages are not permitted in any park.

Plants, animals, minerals, historic sites, structures, and exhibits must not be disturbed.

Overnight Facilities. *Cabins.* Eleven state parks provide 147 family vacation cabins that were built in the 1930s of wood and stone. Most of the cabins have indoor fireplaces or woodburning stoves, beds, chairs, tables, modern electric ranges, refrigerators, and lights. Extra cots are not available. Firewood is provided when available but is not guaranteed. Kooser, Parker Dam, Linn Run, and Worlds End State Parks rent rustic cabins year-round. The other seven, Clear Creek, Cook Forest, S. B. Elliot, Promised Land, Black Moshannon, Cowans Gap, and Ralph Stover, rent cabins from the second Friday in April until the Friday of the week of regular antlerless deer season. Cabins are rented only by the week, Friday to Friday, during the summer.

Fourteen state parks provide 132 modern cabins constructed by the Pennsylvania Conservation Corps. They have a living and dining area, shower and toilet, and two or three bedrooms. All rooms are furnished. They are available for year-round use.

Three state parks have cabins that are accessible to people with disabilities: Keystone, Moraine, and Pymatuning.

Costs of renting a state park cabin depend upon the length of the stay and type of cabin. Rates for rustic cabins vary from $90 to $210 weekly for residents, $110 to $230 for nonresidents; modern cabins are $250 or $310 weekly for residents, $275 or $335 for nonresidents. Off-season daily rates range from $23 to $50 for residents for rustic cabins, $60 or $78 for modern cabins; nonresidents pay $27 to $55 for rustic cabins, $70 or $85 for modern cabins.

Group Camping. Group camping areas have drinking water and pit or flush toilets, and are normally located in isolated areas of the park. One responsible adult leader, 18 years or older, is required for each 10 campers in a youth organization.

Five parks—Blue Knob, French Creek, Hickory Run, Laurel Hill, and Raccoon Creek—provide rustic, dormitory-type cabins for organized nonprofit groups. These areas accommodate groups up to 150 people. Rental periods range from one night to a season.

Family Camping. Fifty-five state park campgrounds offer about 7,000 sites. The maximum camping period is 14 consecutive nights during the summer season. Some parks allow camping for 21 consecutive nights at other seasons.

A few areas are limited to tent camping only. Most campgrounds have sites available for any type of camping equipment; some have electric hookups. Site occupancy at all parks is limited to one family unit or one nonfamily unit with five or less people per site, including a responsible individual eighteen years of age or older. Reservations are available at some state park family campgrounds.

Environmental Education and Interpretation. Summer environmental and interpretive activities are offered in many state parks; some also offer spring and fall programming. These include guided walks, evening and daytime programs, and environmental education activities. Historical programs on past lifestyles and early industries, such as ironmaking, lumbering, and milling, are offered at many sites. Visitor centers are located at many state parks. Self-guided trails and various publications provide different do-it-yourself activities. Group programs can be arranged in advance.

Northwest

Bendigo State Park. This is a small, day-use park consisting of 100 acres located 4 miles northeast of Johnsonburg on Legislative Route 24201, which branches off U.S. Route 219 there. The developed area of the park is approximately 20 acres, half of which is a large, shaded picnic area. There is a swimming pool and a designated sledding slope in the park. The East Branch of the Clarion River flows through the park and is stocked with trout.

Chapman State Park. This 805-acre park is located in Warren County near Clarendon, off U.S. Route 6, in the midst of about 517,000 acres of Allegheny National Forest and state game lands. It includes a 68-acre lake on the West Branch of Tionesta Creek. Chapman is an ideal starting point for backpacking trips into the national forest.

Clear Creek State Park. This is a 1,209-acre area in Jefferson County that occupies a scenic portion of the Clear Creek Valley from PA Route 949, accessible from Exits 12 or 13 of I-80, to the Clarion River. The river provides excellent canoeing, especially during spring and fall. It is a Class C waterway, with an average downward flow of 4 miles per hour. A popular canoe trip is the 10-mile run to Cook Forest State Park. Clear Creek has a small, man-made lake with a swimming beach. The southern boundary of the Allegheny National Forest is just north of the park.

Cook Forest State Park. This park encompasses 6,668 acres in Clarion, Forest, and Jefferson Counties. Bordered by the Clarion River, the park is famous for virgin white pine and hemlock timber stands. Classified as a National Natural Landmark by the National Park Service, Cook is often referred to as the "Black Forest" of Pennsylvania. The park is located on PA Route 36, best accessed from I-80, Exit 13 from the east or Exit 8 from the west, via PA Route 66. A trail system of 27 miles goes through the magnificent timber stands. All the outdoor activities and extensive camping opportunities exist here.

Elk State Park. This park consists of 3,192 acres, including the 1,160-acre East Branch Lake. It is located approximately 8 miles east of Wilcox on State Route 1006 and 9 miles south of Clermont on

State Route 2001. Unlimited-horsepower boating is permitted on the lake; swimming is not. It is stocked with both warm- and cold-water fish.

Kinzua Bridge State Park. This park is located 4 miles north of U.S. Route 6 at Mount Jewett on State Route 3011. It features a 2,053-foot railroad bridge that has been designated a National Engineering Landmark. Built in 1882, it was the highest railroad bridge in the world at 301 feet. It was rebuilt in 1900. The Knox, Kane, Kinzua Railroad meanders 97 miles through the awesome peaks and valleys of the Allegheny National Forest and over the Kinzua Bridge to and from Marienville.

M. K. Goddard State Park. This 2,856-acre park in northeast Mercer County includes the 1,860-acre Lake Wilhelm. Crossed by I-79 and U.S. Route 19 about 13 miles south of Meadville, the park has a major marina and seven boat launches around the lake. The upper portion of the lake, 420 acres, is part of State Game Lands No. 270. All winter sports, including sledding, are permitted. Reportedly, the larger fish caught in Lake Wilhelm are taken through the ice.

Oil Creek State Park. This 7,075-acre park is off PA Route 8, 1 mile north of Rouseville. It adjoins Drake Well Museum and the city of Titusville at its northern end, and Oil City is 4 miles from the southern end. The park tells the story of the early petroleum industry by identifying oil boomtowns, important well sites, transportation points, and cemeteries. The events of the exciting 1860s receive special emphasis. Recreational opportunities include a 10-mile paved bicycle trail through Oil Creek Gorge, a major hiking trail of 36 miles, a canoeing stream suitable for beginners,

and a 26-mile excursion on the Oil Creek and Titusville Railroad, from May to October.

Parker Dam State Park. This 968-acre park is located in Clearfield County, 17 miles north of Clearfield and only 6 miles north of S. B. Elliott State Park, off PA Route 153. It is in the Moshannon State Forest and entirely wooded. It offers picturesque areas of forest and swamp meadows, pine plantations, typical mixed hardwood and oak second-growth timber, and a section of the largest tornado blowout ever to strike Pennsylvania. A 20-acre lake is the focal point for much of the recreational activity in the park. It is the western trailhead of the Quehanna Trail System, which has 75 miles of hiking without backtracking. It also connects with the Susquehannock Trail System.

Presque Isle State Park. This park is a 3,200-acre peninsula extending 7 miles into Lake Erie. It is reached via PA Route 832. A 14-mile road system within the park forms a loop that is popular for sightseeing. The park offers every form of outdoor recreation and affords ecologists, historians, geologists, biologists, and bird-watchers a unique venue. It is a National Natural Landmark.

Pymatuning State Park. This park is located near the Crawford-Mercer County line about 1 mile northwest of Jamestown. About 75% of the 17,088-acre lake is located in Pennsylvania; the rest is in Ohio. The park is accessible via U.S. Routes 6 and 322 and PA Routes 18, 58, and 285. Millions of visitors use this park annually. Water sports, hunting, fishing, and one of the largest camping areas in the commonwealth are the attractions. An organized camping area is available for groups up to 400; there are

657 family camping sites and a cluster of modern two- and three-bedroom family cabins.

S. B. Elliott State Park. This 318-acre park is located in Clearfield County off PA Route 153, just north of Exit 18 of I-80, 9 miles north of Clearfield. Named in honor of a pioneer of forest conservation, the park, in the Moshannon State Forest, is entirely wooded. Fishing in the small mountain streams surrounding the park offers sport for those who like to walk and fish in uncrowded streams for native and stocked trout. Parker Dam State Park is nearby.

North-Central

Bald Eagle State Park. This 5,900-acre tract was developed around the Foster Joseph Sayer Dam in Centre County, just off PA Route 150, midway between Milesburg and Lock Haven. The park was named for Chief Bald Eagle of the Leni-Lenape nation, who inhabited the area near Milesburg until about 1720. Recreational activities are centered around the 1,730-acre lake, which has a 1,200-foot sand and turf beach and a marina with 354 dock spaces.

Bucktail State Park. This park is actually a 75-mile scenic drive from Emporium (Cameron County) along PA Route 120, through Renovo, to Lock Haven (Clinton County). It passes through a narrow valley called the Bucktail Trail, named after a famous Civil War regiment of woodsmen, the Bucktail Rangers. PA Route 120 is a former Indian trail to and from the eastern continental divide between the Susquehanna and Allegheny Rivers. The valley is mostly forestland, bounded as it is by over 500,000 acres of the Elk and Sproul State Forests. In October, when the leaves are turning, and in spring, when the mountain laurel is in bloom, the drive is awesome.

Cherry Springs State Park. This 48-acre park, located along PA Route 44 in Potter County, is named for the large strand of native black cherry trees in the park. Surrounded by the Susquehannock State Forest, it is nearly as remote and wild today as it was a century ago. It is a haven for campers who like to rough it and who can appreciate the fine scenic drive on the way. There is an airport nearby for those who might not appreciate the drive. An annual Woodsmen's Carnival is held here in August.

Colton Point State Park. This 368-acre tract is on the western rim of the Grand Canyon of Pennsylvania, 5 miles south of U.S. Route 6 at Ansonia. Trails in the park lead hikers to and along the bottom of the gorge and to scenic overlooks. The leaves of the hardwood trees in the park turn all shades of red, yellow, and purple in early autumn.

Denton Hill State Park. This is a ski resort in Potter County. Easy access from PA Route 6 is important in the middle of the snow belt. Lyman Run State Park is nearby.

Hills Creek State Park. This 406-acre park is located in north-central Tioga County, just north of U.S. Route 6 between Wellsboro and Mansfield. The focal point of the park is a 137-acre lake that was developed by impounding Hills Creek. There are three boat-mooring areas, with a capacity of 65 boats, two of which double as launching areas. Hunting is not permitted in the park, but the rugged 13,000 acres of State Game Lands No. 37 are within walking distance.

Hyner Run State Park. This 180-acre park is located in Clinton County, 6 miles east of Renovo on PA Route 120, and 3 miles north of Hyner on Hyner Run Road. It is entirely surrounded by Sproul State Forest. The terrain of the park is generally level; it occupies the small valley created by Hyner Run. There are steep mountains on both sides. The park serves as the eastern trailhead for the 50-mile Donut Hole Trail System and as a trailhead for the 64-mile Hyner Mountain Snowmobile Trail.

Hyner View State Park. This is a 6-acre picnic area at Hyner Run Park that features a scenic overlook wall. It was once the site of a flaming foliage festival, which moved down to the foot of the mountain.

Kettle Creek State Park. This park consists of 1,793 acres along Kettle Creek in western Clinton County along State Route 4001, 7 miles north of Westport and PA Route 120. It is situated in a valley surrounded by the mountainous terrain of Sproul State Forest. The 160-acre Kettle Creek Reservoir is a U.S. Army Corps of Engineers Flood Control Project. The 7-acre Kettle Creek Lake, below Bush Dam, is in the southern end of the park. The park has an equestrian trail and a mountain-biking trail.

Leonard Harrison State Park. This is a 585-acre park on the eastern rim of the Grand Canyon of Pennsylvania, 10 miles west of Wellsboro on PA Route 660. The leaves of the hardwood trees in this park turn every shade of red, yellow, and purple in early October. Trails lead hikers to and along the bottom of the gorge and to scenic overlooks. The Grand Canyon was carved by glacial action at the end of the last ice age. A moraine blocked Pine Creek, reversing

its flow by accumulating a volume of water great enough to seek another outlet. The creek gouged a channel some 800 feet deep.

Little Pine State Park. This is a 2,158-acre park located on State Route 4001 in Lycoming County. It is 4 miles north of Waterville on PA Route 44, and 8 miles south of English Center on PA Route 287. It is in one of the most beautiful mountain sections of the Tiadaghton State Forest in the Appalachian Mountain Region. It has a 94-acre lake. A special attraction of the park is its trail system; the Mid-State Trail passes through the park, providing hiking for all levels of skill, but especially for seasoned hikers.

Lyman Run State Park. This is a 595-acre tract of forested mountain land carved from Susquehannock State Forest. It is located 7 miles west of Galeton in Potter County. A 45-acre lake was created by a dam on Lyman Run and is used by swimmers, boaters, and fishers. The Susquehannock Trail System crosses the western edge of Lyman Run. All winter sports are available.

McCall Dam State Park. This park occupies the site of an abandoned dam constructed about 1850 on White Deer Creek. It is located at the northeast tip of Centre County, 4 miles from R. B. Winter State Park along McCall Dam Road, which runs from PA Route 192 to Eastville near PA Route 880. Organized tent camping, picnicking, and fishing are popular here.

Milton State Park. This is an 82-acre island on the Susquehanna River, between the boroughs of Milton and West Milton, with access via PA Route 642 off PA Route 147 from the east and U.S. Route 15 at West Milton. The park is strictly a day-use area that provides picnic facilities, hiking trails, and a play area with a ballfield and soccer fields. The southern half remains wooded for hiking and nature study. A launch area on the east side of the island is for small boats only.

Ole Bull State Park. This park consists of 125 acres along the Kettle Creek Valley, surrounded by the Susquehannock State Forest. It is located along PA Route 144, 18 miles south of Galeton and 26 miles north of Renovo. The area is referred to as the "Black Forest" because of its dense tree cover, mountainous terrain, and wilderness habitat. Campers love the area. The park is named for a 19th-century Norwegian violinist who failed in his attempt to establish a Norwegian colony in this area in 1852.

Patterson State Park. This former state forest picnic area, located in a remote area off PA Route 44, still has two rustic picnic pavilions. It provides a trailhead for the Susquehannock Trail, which passes through the park.

Prouty Place State Park. This park, located in a remote area southeast of Coudersport, is another small roadside picnic area. It is on Long Toe Road, off PA Route 44 near Patterson State Park. The Susquehannock Trail leads into the park's tent camping area.

Ravensburg State Park. This park is situated on 78 acres in Clinton County on PA Route 880, 8 miles southeast of Jersey Shore. It is in a steep-walled, rocky gorge carved by Rauchtown Creek on the side of Nippenose Mountain. The park, 1,100 feet above sea level, is within Tiadaghton State Forest. Tent camping, hiking, fishing, and picnicking are available. Hunting is not permitted.

Sinnemahoning State Park. This 1,910-acre park is located in Cameron and Potter Counties, on PA Route 872, 8 miles north of its junction with PA Route 120 near Sinnemahoning. Located on the first fork of the Sinnemahoning Creek, it is situated in the midst of Elk State Forest and offers a picturesque view of the surrounding peaks and deep valleys. The diverse habitat supports the bald eagle, black bear, and white-tailed deer. Pontoon boat rides on Stevenson Reservoir during the summer allow a closer look at lake wildlife. A rental cottage along Brooks Run is available year-round.

Sizerville State Park. This 386-acre park is located 7 miles north of Emporium on PA Route 155 in Cameron and Potter Counties. It provides a gateway to the Elk and Susquehannock State Forests and is a trailhead for the Bucktail Trail. The park has beautiful white pines and hemlocks, spring wildflowers, a butterfly garden, and flaming fall foliage in early October.

Susquehanna State Park. This park, on U.S. Route 220 at the west end of Williamsport, emerged from a flood control project on the shore of the West Branch of the Susquehanna River. Operated by the Williamsport Chamber of Commerce, the park's primary attraction is the riverboat *Hiawatha*, a modern paddlewheeler that operates May through October.

Upper Pine Bottom State Park. This is a small, roadside picnic site that provides access to all of the activities of the nearby Little Pine State Park and Tiadaghton State Forest.

Northeast

Archbald Pothole State Park. The main attraction of this 150-acre park, 9 miles south of Scranton on U.S. Route 6, is a pothole that formed during an ice age 15,000 years ago. It is 38 feet deep, and its largest diameter is 42 feet. A loop hiking trail is a good route to take to see the pothole and the parent sandstone from which it was cut.

Big Pocono State Park. This park, off PA Route 715 near Tannersville, near Exit 45 of I-80, consists of 1,306 acres of rugged terrain on the slopes and summit of Camelback Mountain. From the summit, there is a great view of eastern Pennsylvania, New York, and New Jersey. A 1½-mile scenic drive encircles the mountaintop. The park is located near the famous Pocono Mountain resort area.

Frances Slocum State Park. This is a 1,035-acre park in Luzerne County, 5 minutes from Dallas and 10 minutes from Wilkes-Barre via U.S. Route 309. Frances Slocum Lake forms a horseshoe covering 165 acres. The park was named for a Quaker girl from the area who was kidnapped by Indians at the age of five, in 1778, and subsequently spent her entire life living among the Indians. The visitors center highlights Native American culture. Lackawanna and Ricketts Glen State Parks are nearby.

Gouldsboro State Park. This park is just south of Gouldsboro off PA Route 507, which intersects I-380 2 miles south. The 2,800-acre park has a 250-acre lake. Activities on the lake include boating, fishing, ice fishing (at its coldest), ice skating, and swimming. Lake Wallenpaupack is nearby.

Hickory Run State Park. This 15,500-acre park is in Carbon County, in the western foothills of the Pocono Mountains. It can be reached via PA Route 534 and is 6 miles west of Exit 41 of I-80. The Lehigh River flows along the western boundary; an elaborate 37-mile trail system is a prime attraction. The main fea-

ture is the Boulder Field, a National Natural Landmark, which has remained relatively unchanged for 20,000 years. It covers an area 400 feet by 1,800 feet. Some of the boulders measure 26 feet long.

Lackawanna State Park. This park is located 10 miles north of Scranton and is easily accessible from I-81 via PA Route 524. The 1,411-acre park with a 210-acre lake is popular with canoers, hikers, and campers.

Mount Pisgah State Park. This 1,302-acre park is located midway between Troy and Towanda in Bradford County, only 2 miles north of U.S. Route 6, the major route through the Northern Tier. It is situated along Mill Creek at the base of Mount Pisgah, elevation 2,260 feet. Stephen Foster Lake, named after the famous composer and former local resident, is formed by a dam on Mill Creek. The lake is 75 acres and is used for fishing, boating, and skating. The park also has a 5,676-square-foot swimming pool.

Nescopeck State Park. This is a 2,981-acre area administered by the Pennsylvania Game Commission. State Game Lands No. 187 surround the park, which is touched by I-80 on its southern boundary, near White Haven.

Promised Land State Park. This 2,971-acre park is located in Pike County, 10 miles north of Canadensis, along PA Route 390. It is in the Pocono Mountains, 1,800 feet above sea level, and surrounded by 8,000 acres of state forest and natural area. Two lakes, Promised Land Lake (422 acres) and Lower Lake (173 acres), add to the scenic beauty. Camping, hiking, boating, and swimming are the main activities. Nearby Bruce Lake Natural Area also has two lakes and a swamp.

Ricketts Glen State Park. This park encompasses 13,050 acres in three counties. It is located 30 miles north of Bloomsburg on PA Route 487. A 245-acre lake provides all water sports. The Glens Natural Area, a Registered National Natural Landmark, has a trail along a series of 22 wild, free-flowing waterfalls, each cascading through a portion of rock-strewn cleft in this ancient hillside. The highest is 94 feet. Trees in the area are over 500 years old and reach 100 feet in height.

Salt Springs State Park. This is a 400-acre, mostly undeveloped wooded park located 7 miles north of Montrose, off PA Route 29. A small picnic area is located at the base of a mountain along a stream stocked with trout. Virgin hemlock, estimated to be 600 to 700 years old, and the waterfalls of Fall Brook, a stream that flows into Silver Creek, are park highlights.

Tobyhanna State Park. This 440-acre park is located 2 miles north of Tobyhanna on PA Route 423. The focal point of the park is a 170-acre lake, a popular trout-fishing spot. Nights are chilly here at 2,100 feet above sea level, even in summer.

Worlds End State Park. This 780-acre park is located on PA Route 154, about 5 miles north of its intersection with U.S. Route 220, in a narrow, S-shaped valley of the Loyalsock Creek just south of Forksville, Sullivan County. The first road through the valley was high on the steep slope of the mountain, and the precipitous journey made early travelers think that they were surely at the "end of the world." The Canyon Vista and High Knob Overlook provide outstanding views of the region, especially during the June mountain laurel bloom and fall foliage periods.

Southwest

Blue Knob State Park. This park consists of 5,614 acres of woodland, located off PA Route 869 in the northwestern tip of Bedford County, west of U.S. Route 220 and 20 miles north of Exit 11 of the Turnpike. The park is named for the majestic quartzite peak Blue Knob, at 3,416 feet above sea level the second-highest point of land in the state. Ski Blue Knob offers the highest vertical drop in Pennsylvania skiing, 1,050 feet; average annual snowfall is about 12 feet. Snowmobile routes, cross-country ski trails, and hiking trails are extensive; one 17-mile trail traverses the park.

Hillman State Park. This is a 3,664-acre tract of undeveloped land administered by the State Game Commission. It lies just south of Raccoon Creek State Park and is located near the intersection of U.S. Route 22 and PA Route 18.

Keystone State Park. This park consists of 1,169 acres in Westmoreland County along PA Route 981, north of Latrobe. Camping, modern cabins, trails of all sorts, and a lake with a swimming beach are popular here, within easy driving distance of Pittsburgh.

Kooser State Park. This 250-acre wooded area, with a 4-acre lake, is located on PA Route 31, midway between the Donegal and Somerset exits of the Turnpike. The park's design stresses rustic values in site and building materials and in their application: native stone, rough sawn and stained wood surfaces, log and timber members. Kooser is bounded on two sides by Forbes State Forest and is a good place to begin a trip on the Laurel Highlands Hiking Trail.

Laurel Hill State Park. This park consists of 3,935 acres of mountainous terrain in Somerset County near Exits 9 and 10 of the Turnpike. The 63-acre Laurel Hill Lake is the focal point of the park. Hiking trails lead through a diversity of plants and wildlife.

Laurel Mountain State Park. This is a ski area, along the western slope of Laurel Ridge.

Laurel Ridge State Park. This 13,625-acre park stretches along Laurel Hill from the Youghiogheny River at Ohiopyle to the Conemaugh Gorge near Johnstown. It spans Cambria, Fayette, Indiana, Somerset, and Westmoreland Counties. The Laurel Highlands Hiking Trail is the main feature of the park. The map and guide to the state park includes a map and a guide to the trail.

Laurel Summit. This is a small scenic area in Westmoreland County that provides a commanding view of Laurel Ridge and the surrounding region from an elevation of 2,739 feet. This scenic picnic area is south of Linn Run State Park on Linn Run Road.

Linn Run State Park. This is an area of 571 acres within Forbes State Forest, about 4 miles south on PA Route 381 from its intersection with U.S. Route 30. The varied topography, Linn Run stream, and mixed hardwood and evergreen forests appeal to campers, hikers, and picnickers.

McConnell's Mill State Park. This park, near the intersection of U.S. Routes 19 and 422, is north of Portersville, in the deep gorge of Slippery Rock Creek. The restored mill, one of the first rolling mills in the country, may be toured free of charge. A covered bridge is open to pedestrian and vehicle traffic. There are two rock-climbing and rappelling areas.

Moraine State Park. This park, at the intersection of I-79 and U.S. Route 422 in western Butler County, has all of the features of a good state park: a 3,225-acre lake with fishing, swimming, and boating; 1,200 picnic tables; hiking trails through interesting terrain; mountain and trail biking; hunting; and winter sports. What sets Moraine apart from other parks is its history. It was developed on a site desecrated by coal mines, strip mines and their residue, and 422 abandoned oil wells. Acid mine drainage polluted many of the streams in the area. The reclamation of this land by two state agencies is simply miraculous.

Ohiopyle State Park. This park is located primarily in Fayette County, about 4 miles north of Farmington, on PA Route 381, which traverses the park. It encompasses 19,046 acres of rugged natural beauty, including more than 14 miles of the Youghiogheny River Gorge. The "Yough" provides some of the best whitewater rafting in the East. Various overlooks provide spectacular views of the river and falls. Ferncliff Peninsula, a Registered National Natural Landmark, contains 4 miles of easy hiking trails and several overlook areas.

Point State Park. This park is located at the tip of Pittsburgh's "Golden Triangle" and commemorates the strategic and historic role of the area during the French and Indian War. Paved walks lead along the riverfront and to dramatic views of the city, the waterways, and the hillside scenery. There is a majestic fountain at the headwaters of the Ohio River, from which water rises to a height of 150 feet.

Prince Gallitzin State Park. This 6,249-acre park is located in the scenic Allegheny Plateau region of northern Cambria County. It can be reached via PA Routes 36 and 53 and U.S. Route 219. Glendale Lake covers 1,600 acres and has a 26-mile shoreline. Named after a beloved Russian prince turned Catholic priest who served the area during the years 1799 to 1840, the park has many activities available on a vivid landscape. The park has a 437-site tent and trailer campground, 10 modern cabins, and a 120-person-capacity primitive tenting area for groups.

Raccoon Creek State Park. This 7,323-acre park features the beautiful 101-acre Raccoon Creek Lake. It is located in southern Beaver County; PA Route 18 passes through the park. The Wildflower Reserve and Visitor Center, on the park's eastern boundary, contains a unique stand of native wildflowers. The historic Frankfort Mineral Springs, site of a nationally known health spa during the 1800s, is located in the park. Spectacular ice formations may be seen there in the winter.

Ryerson Station State Park. This 1,164-acre park is located in Greene County, near the West Virginia border, on State Route 3022, just off PA Route 21. The area has steep slopes, grand vistas, and the 62-acre Duke Lake, which is stocked with trout.

Nearby are charming small towns and villages.

Shawnee State Park. This park consists of 3,983 acres along U.S. Route 30, 10 miles west of Bedford. The focal point of the park is the 451-acre Shawnee Lake, named for the Indians who lived in the area for a short time during their migration from the Potomac in the early 1700s. The park is known for its long sand-and-turf beach.

Yellow Creek State Park. This 2,981-acre park is located along one of the first "highways" in the state, the Kittanning Path, a trail used by the Delaware and Shawnee Indians and by early settlers. U.S. Route 422 roughly follows that path and provides the main access

to the park from Indiana and Ebensburg. The park has a 720-acre lake with an 800-foot guarded beach. The rolling terrain provides easy walking trails.

South-Central

Big Spring State Park. This 45-acre park is located about 5 miles southwest of New Germantown, Perry County, along PA Route 274. It is named for a nearby spring that forms the Sherman Creek, which runs through the park. Big Spring is adjacent to the Tuscarora State Forest and serves as a trailhead for snowmobiling there. It also provides access to the Iron Horse Trail, which is designed for both day and overnight hiking.

Black Moshannon State Park. This park is located 9 mines east of Philipsburg, on PA Route 504. The park covers 3,394 acres, including a 250-acre lake. The Moshannon State Forest surrounds the park. The name Moshannon, which the Indians gave the stream that runs through the park, means "moose stream." A boardwalk provides access to the Black Moshannon Bog Natural Area on the west side of the lake, which includes many rare plants found in sphagnum bogs.

Buchanan's Birthplace Historical State Park. This 18-acre park is nestled in a gap of the Tuscarora Mountains in Franklin County, between McConnellsburg and Mercersburg, along PA Route 16. A monument honoring James Buchanan, the state's only president, marks the site of his birth and the place where he lived the first 6 years of his life. The park has two picnic pavilions and native brook trout fishing. Nearby Cowans Gap State Park offers the full range of state park recreational opportunities.

Caledonia State Park. This park is located in Adams and Franklin Counties midway between Chambersburg and Gettysburg, on U.S. Route 30. The park is named for Thaddeus Stevens's charcoal iron furnace, which began operation here in 1837 and was destroyed in 1863 by Confederate cavalry. There is a large swimming pool, fishing in three creeks, a golf course, camping, hiking, and summer stock theater. The Appalachian Trail crosses the park.

Canoe Creek State Park. This is a 958-acre day-use facility with a 155-acre lake, located on U.S. Route 22, 7 miles east of Hollidaysburg. The panoramic view of the lake when cresting the hill of the entrance road is awesome. One of the largest bat colonies in the eastern United States lives here. The park has the ruins of several limestone quarry operations. They are the focus of historical and interpretive programs and displays. The site is part of an Industrial Heritage Project.

Codorus State Park. This 3,326-acre park is located in the southwest corner of York County, near Hanover, along PA Route 216. The 1,275-acre Lake Marburg has 26 miles of shoreline, and a variety of mooring spaces are available. There are seven launch ramps around the lake; the main launch area, off Sinsheim Road, is a lighted facility, open 24 hours year-round. All warm-weather species, plus rainbow and brook trout, have been stocked in the lake. Waterfowl hunting is popular, and the duck blinds are awarded by a lottery held on the third Saturday in September.

Colonel Denning State Park. This park is located in Doubling Gap in Cumberland County, along PA Route 233. The Gap is so named for the S turn here,

where Blue Mountain doubles back on itself. The park includes 270 acres of woodland and a 3-acre lake. The general topography is hills and ridges, with elevations varying from 500 to 1,650 feet above sea level. A 2-mile trail rises to Flat Rock and a beautiful view of the Cumberland Valley.

Cowans Gap State Park. This 1,085-acre park is located in a beautiful valley of the Tuscarora Mountains in Fulton County, between Chambersburg and McConnellsburg. There are several hiking trails in the park and on the adjacent state forestland, including the 105-mile Tuscarora Trail. The cabin colony is on the National Register of Historic Places; it is charming, but it lacks indoor plumbing.

Fowlers Hollow State Park. This park is located 7 miles south of Blain, off PA Route 274. From the picnic area at the edge of the Tuscarora State Forest, the trail system (and Hemlock Road) goes to the Hemlock Natural Area. The picnic area was the site of a late-1800s sawmill.

Gifford Pinchot State Park. This 2,338-acre park, along PA Route 177 between Rossville and Lewisberry, in northern York County, consists of reverting farm fields and wooded hillsides. The 340-acre lake, which has 345 mooring spaces, also has 340 campsites at its southern end. Pinchot Lake is designated as a big bass lake; special rules are in effect for fishing.

Greenwood Furnace State Park. This 406-acre park, nestled in northeastern Huntingdon County off PA Route 305, has the usual amenities of a mountain park with a lake: swimming, fishing, family camping, and winter sports. The park also has a historical aspect: An iron furnace operated here from 1834 to 1904 in a company town that consisted of 127 buildings, where about 300 employees lived and worked. They produced iron for the national railway system. Six of the original buildings and the community cemetery remain.

Little Buffalo State Park. This 830-acre park in Perry County, 2 miles west of Newport on Little Buffalo State Park Rd., off PA Route 34, embraces the Little Buffalo Creek, dammed to form an 88-acre lake. The park also has a half-acre swimming pool. Historic features include an "un"covered bridge, a fully restored 18th-century gristmill, an old tavern, and remnants of a narrow gauge railroad, including one of the original cars.

Mont Alto State Park. This 24-acre park is just east of the town of Mont Alto, on PA Route 233, near Michaux State Forest. Activities including fishing, hiking, snowmobiling, and especially, picnicking.

Penn Roosevelt State Forest Picnic Area. This park is in an isolated area of Centre County in the Seven Mountains region known locally as Stone Kettle Creek. It is surrounded by a massive tract of state forestland. The best park entries are from Crowfield Rd. or Stone Creek Rd., off U.S. Route 322 east of Potters Mills. Picnicking, hiking, and camping are the main activities; there is a small, unstocked lake.

Pine Grove Furnace State Park. This 696-acre park is located in a beautiful mountain setting off PA Route 233 in the heart of the Michaux State Forest. There are two lakes: 25-acre Laurel Lake and 2-acre Fuller Lake. The park was the site of the Pine Grove Iron Works, established in 1764. Historic buildings include the ironmaster's mansion, a gristmill, an inn, and several residences. The Appalachian Trail passes through.

Poe Paddy State Park. This park is located 4 miles east of Poe Valley State Park at the confluence of Big Poe Creek and Penns Creek. Family camping, organized group camping, and fishing are the major attractions. The Mid-State Trail passes through the park, and hikers on that trail hike through the 250-foot-long Paddy Mountain Railroad Tunnel. Only 23 acres, the park is near other parks and in the midst of vast forests.

Poe Valley State Park. This 620-acre park, with a 25-acre lake, is nestled in a rugged mountain valley in Centre County and is surrounded by the Bald Eagle State Forest. Many outdoor activities can be enjoyed here year-round. The park is located about 27 miles east of Potters Mills and U.S. Route 322. Marked state forest roads, mostly gravel, lead from the Seven Mountain Scenic Area for about 10 miles to the Poe Valley.

R. B. Winter State Park. This park, on PA Route 192 in Union County, 18 miles west of Lewisburg, is situated on 695 acres within the Bald Eagle State Forest. It is in a narrow valley 1,500 feet above sea level and is surrounded by oak forests on steep mountain ridges. Natural features include dense thickets of rhododendron and mountain laurel. Easy trails encourage hiking, cross-country skiing, and snowmobiling.

Reeds Gap State Park. This 220-acre park, located along the banks of Honey Creek in the Amish country of Mifflin County, joins two sections of Bald Eagle State Forest. The park is on New Lancaster Valley Rd. (State Route 1002), best reached from U.S. Route 322 at Reedsville or Milroy. The area has excellent hunting and fishing, interesting large boulders, and is a popular spot for snowmobiling and cross-country skiing.

Shikellamy State Park. This 131-acre park, named for an Iroquois chief, is divided into two sections, which are located in different counties. The 78-acre tract in Union County is situated on Blue Hill across the Susquehanna River from Sunbury, north of Shamokin Dam on U.S. Route 11. The 53-acre tract in Northumberland County is located between the borough of Northumberland and Sunbury on PA Route 147. The two areas are separated by Lake Augusta, a 3,060-acre lake formed by a dam 3 miles downriver. Scenic views of Sunbury and the lake are superb.

Trough Creek State Park. This park is situated along a scenic gorge where the creek cuts through Terrace Mountain on its way to Raystown Lake. This 541-acre park is along PA Route 994 in Huntingdon County, 5 miles east of PA Route 26 near the village of Entriken. It is surrounded by Rothrock State Forest and has several notable geological features.

Warriors Path State Park. This park lies very near the famous path used by the Iroquois in their wars. The 334-acre park is located in Bedford County, about 2 miles south of Saxton via PA Route 913. The finger of land on which the park sits is bounded on three sides by the Raystown Branch of the Juniata River, which empties into Lake Raystown 1 mile downstream. Unique habitats exist as a result of the river formation. A freshwater swamp follows the long axis of the park adjacent to the river bottomland. Weathered shale cliffs near the swamp have unique trees, plants, and animals associated with this environment.

Whipple Dam State Park. This park is located 12 miles south of State College off PA Route 26. The highlight of the park is the 22-acre Whipple Lake, where boating, fishing, swimming, and ice sports are popular. Hunting in the park is limited, and camping is not permitted. Greenwood Furnace State Park and Penn Roosevelt State Forest Picnic Area are nearby.

Southeast

Beltzville State Park. This 2,972-acre park in Carbon County is located along U.S. Route 209, near Exit 34 of the Northeast Extension of the Turnpike. It features Beltzville Lake, a 949-acre lake with a shoreline of almost 20 miles. Water sports, including unlimited-horsepower boating, and hunting are the most popular activities. The adjacent Beltzville Wildlife Management Project is also open to hunting.

Delaware Canal State Park. This is the only remaining continuously intact remnant of the great towpath-canal-building era of the early and mid-19th century. It remains today with most of its original features. During its century of operation, the canal transported cargo, mostly anthracite coal, from Easton to Bristol. Mule-drawn canal boat rides and the Lock House Visitor Center are located in New Hope. The canal is a National Historic Landmark and the towpath is a National Heritage Trail.

Evansburg State Park. This is a day-use area off Germantown Pike between Norristown and Collegeville in Montgomery County. Its main feature is Skippack Creek, which has shaped the land into ridges and valleys and is also a fine trout stream. This narrow valley was first settled by Mennonites. Mill remnants, mill buildings, and houses remain in the park and provide insight into early American life. The 18-hole Skippack Golf Course is one of only two in the state park system.

Fort Washington State Park. This park consists of 493 acres between the towns of Fort Washington and Flourtown along Bethlehem Pike and Skippack Pike, about 2 miles from Exit 26 of the Turnpike. Wissahickon Creek passes through the park. Soldiers of the American Revolutionary Army built a fort here in 1777, and 12,000 of them camped here from November 2 to December 11, 1777. They then marched 15 miles to their destiny at Valley Forge.

French Creek State Park. This park is located on the Berks-Chester County line 3 miles east of Exit 22 (Morgantown) of the Turnpike. PA Route 345 runs through the park and continues on to the east and south entrances of the adjoining Hopewell Furnace National Historic Site. More than 30 miles of trails cover a large portion of the park's 7,339 acres. There are two small lakes for fishing, a swimming pool, and two disc golf courses.

Lehigh Gorge State Park. This park follows the Lehigh River from the Francis Walter Dam at the northern end to Jim Thorpe at the southern end. Exit 40 of I-80 provides easy access to the northern end; U.S. Route 209 goes to Jim Thorpe. The Lehigh River traverses the park in a stretch of steep-walled canyon. It is one of the most scenic rivers in America and features Class III whitewater rafting. The 4,548 acres of parkland along the river provide opportunities for hiking, bicycling, cross-country skiing, and snowmobiling.

Locust Lake State Park. This park is located in Schuylkill County near the junction of I-81 and PA Route 54, about 7 miles north of Pottsville, 3 miles south of Mahanoy City, and 6 miles west of Tuscarora State Park. It is in the western end of Locust Valley near the headwaters of Locust Creek. The park encompasses 1,144 acres, including a 52-acre lake. With the exception of 60 acres located in the immediate area of the dam, the entire park is forested. This is a secluded area—hunting, fishing, hiking, camping, and swimming are the primary activities.

Marsh Creek State Park. This 1,705-acre park is located in the rolling hills of north-central Chester County, 2 miles west of the village of Eagle and PA Route 100. The 535-acre lake is especially popular with sailboaters, and races are held frequently. Birding and nature photography are also popular, especially during the spring and fall waterfowl migrations.

Memorial Lake State Park. This is a 230-acre day-use area with an 85-acre lake on the Fort Indiantown Gap Military Reservation in Lebanon County, near Exit 29 of I-81. It has facilities for picnicking, boating, fishing, hiking, and winter sports.

Neshaminy State Park. This is a 330-acre park along the Delaware River in Bucks County. It is easily reached from the PA Route 132 (Street Road) exit of I-95. It is named for the Neshaminy Creek, which joins the Delaware River at this site. There is a marina with 181 slips for larger boats for rent on a seasonal basis. (There is a waiting list.) Although the river flows for another 116 miles from here to the Atlantic Ocean, the park is at sea level, and when the tide comes in along the New Jersey shore, the water rises here also. Because of this tidal activity, the river here is like an estuary.

Nockamixon State Park. This park covers 5,283 acres of woodlands and fields in northern Bucks County, on PA Route 563, 5 miles east of Quakertown. It can be reached via Route 309, 313, or 412 (from Route 611). Nockamixon's 1,450-acre lake has four public launching areas, docking facilities for 576 boats, and a 76-space dry storage area for boats on trailers. (There is a waiting list.) Swimming is not permitted in the lake, but there is a swimming pool.

Ralph Stover State Park. This 45-acre park, along the Tohickon Creek, is 2 miles northwest of Point Pleasant on State Park Rd. and Stump Rd. in eastern Bucks County. When high-water conditions exist, the creek offers a challenging course for closed-deck canoes and kayaks. There is a rock-climbing area for expert climbers.

Ridley Creek State Park. This is a 2,600-acre area of gently rolling terrain bisected by Ridley Creek, which is stocked with trout. It is located 14 miles west of Philadelphia off PA Route 3. Designated the Ridley Creek Historic District on the National Register of Historic Places, the park contains a small 18th-century village that grew up around a gristmill. The miller's house, the office, the library, and several small workers' houses are still intact. Another park attraction is the Colonial Pennsylvania Plantation, a living museum that portrays life on a Quaker farm around 1776. Bordering the southern end of the park is the John J. C. Tyler Painter Arboretum, with its horticultural collections and historic buildings.

Samuel S. Lewis State Park. This park is located south of Wrightsville in York County, west of PA Route 624, on land donated to the state by Mr. Lewis. The park is a 71-acre tract on top of a 885-foot ridge separating the Kreutz

Creek and East Prospect Valleys. The highest point in the area, the park provides panoramic views of the Susquehanna River and the fertile farmlands that surround it. Kite fliers congregate on this windy hill.

Susquehannock State Park. This park lies atop a wooded plateau overlooking the Susquehanna River in southern Lancaster County. It is off PA Route 372 southwest of Buck. The primary attraction of the 224-acre park is the panoramic view from the 380-foot-high cliffs above the river. Mount Johnson Island was the world's first bald eagle sanctuary.

Swatara State Park. This park consists of 3,500 undeveloped acres of rolling fields and woodlands along I-81 at Exit 30, between the Second and Blue Mountains, 14 miles north of Lebanon. The Appalachian Trail touches the southern portion of the park.

Tuscarora State Park. This park is at the southern end of the Anthracite Coal Region, 2 miles west of Tamaqua, reached by going north on PA Route 309, then west on PA Route 54. It is set in a deeply wooded valley against a backdrop of Locust Mountain on the undeveloped south shore of a 96-acre lake. Fishing, boating, swimming, and hunting are the major activities in the park. Camping is available in nearby Locust Lake State Park, 6 miles upstream.

Tyler State Park. This 1,711-acre park is in Bucks County, adjacent to Bucks Community College. Take I-95 north to the Newtown-Yardley exit; then head west around Newtown on the four-lane bypass (PA 413) to Swamp Road. The Neshaminy Creek zigzags its way through the park, providing a nice canoeing area. The park features a youth hostel, a playhouse, many play areas, and multipurpose trails.

White Clay Creek Preserve State Park. This 1,253-acre park is in southern Chester County on PA Route 896, 3 miles north of Newark, Delaware. The land was donated to Pennsylvania and Delaware by the Dupont Company to preserve the diverse animal and plant species found here, as well as the rich cultural heritage of the area. The preserve is part of a larger tract of land sold to William Penn by a Lenape chief in 1683. Points of historical interest include a millhouse; a Baptist meetinghouse, c. 1729, with a stone walled cemetery; a stone farmhouse; and some monuments marking points along the Mason-Dixon Line. Day-use activities in the preserve include hiking, biking, horseback riding, hunting, fishing, and cross-country skiing. The only land in the state park system designated as a preserve, it is adjacent to Delaware's Walker S. Carpenter State Park.

STATE FORESTS

The Pennsylvania Bureau of Forestry is responsible for managing the state's 2,073,093 acres of public forestland within its 20 state forests. The land is managed under a multiple-use concept in which timber production, water supply, natural diversity protection, low-density recreational pursuits, and oil and gas development all coexist.

Special areas within the forest are designated as either natural or wild areas. The 61 natural areas cover 69,182 acres set aside for scientific observation of natural systems, to protect examples of typical or unique plant and animal communities, and to preserve outstanding examples of natural beauty. The 16 wild acres, encompassing 145,359 acres,

are managed to retain the undeveloped character of the area for the enjoyment of hunters, fishers, and hikers.

Northwest

Cornplanter State Forest. This is a 1,354-acre forest in Forest County. It has one natural area (96 acres), 2 miles of designated hiking trails, and 8 miles of cross-country ski trails.

Kittanning State Forest. This is a 13,299-acre forest located in Forest, Jefferson, and Venango Counties. It has 13 miles of roads, 47 miles of designated hiking trails, 11 miles of cross-country ski trails, and 18 miles of snowmobile trails.

North-Central

Elk State Forest. This 197,815-acre forest is located in Elk and Cameron Counties. It has 138 miles of roads, one wild area (48,186 acres), five natural areas (19,032 acres), 100 miles of designated hiking trails, 23 miles of cross-country ski trails, 96 miles of snowmobile trails, and a picnic area.

Moshannon State Forest. This is a 185,885-acre forest located in Centre and Clearfield Counties. It has 188 miles of roads, one wild area (48,186 acres), one natural area (917 acres), 244 miles of designated hiking trails, 12 miles of cross-country ski trails, and 168 miles of snowmobile trails.

Sproul State Forest. This 279,636-acre forest is located in Centre and Clinton Counties. It has 353 miles of roads, two wild areas (7,139 acres), four natural areas (16,859 acres), 257 miles of designated hiking trails, 15 miles of horse trails, 14 miles of cross-country ski trails, 238 miles of snowmobile trails, 32 miles of ATV trails, and a picnic area.

Susquehannock State Forest. This is a 261,784-acre forest in Potter County. It has 184 miles of roads, one wild area (30,253 acres), one natural area (1,521 acres), 85 miles of designated hiking trails, 30 miles of cross-country ski trails, 218 miles of snowmobile trails, and 35 miles of ATV trails.

Tiadaghton State Forest. This 214,973-acre forest is located in Lycoming County. It has 235 miles of roads, three wild areas (19,072 acres), six natural areas (5,690 acres), 200 miles of designated hiking trails, 60 miles of cross-country ski trails, 292 miles of snowmobile trails, and 14 miles of ATV trails.

Tioga State Forest. This 162,923-acre forest is located in Bradford and Tioga Counties. It has 178 miles of roads, one wild area (3,070 acres), three natural areas (13,773 acres), 34 miles of designated hiking trails, 7 miles of cross-country ski trails, 175 miles of snowmobile trails, and three picnic areas.

Wyoming State Forest. This is a 42,820-acre forest in Sullivan County. It has 77 miles of roads, one wild area (2,600 acres), three natural areas (1,066 acres), 50 miles of horse trails, 15 miles of cross-country ski trails, 60 miles of snowmobile trails, and a picnic area.

Northeast

Delaware State Forest. This 80,056-acre forest is located in Monroe and Pike Counties. It has 41 miles of roads, six natural areas (6,432 acres), 150 miles of designated hiking trails, 121 miles of snowmobile trails, 21 miles of ATV trails, and two picnic areas.

Lackawanna State Forest. This is a 8,816-acre forest in Lackawanna and Luzerne Counties. It has 14 miles of

roads, 23 miles of designated hiking trails, 14 miles of cross-country ski trails, 24 miles of snowmobile trails, and a picnic area.

Southwest

Forbes State Forest. This is a 51,701-acre forest in Fayette, Somerset, and Westmoreland Counties. It has 76 miles of roads, one wild area (4,675 acres), two natural areas (3,671 acres), 69 miles of designated hiking trails, 38 miles of cross-country ski trails, 78 miles of snowmobile trails, and two picnic areas.

South-Central

Bald Eagle State Forest. This 196,015-acre forest is located in Centre, Snyder, and Union Counties. It has 349 miles of roads, one wild area (3,935 acres), eight natural areas (7,442 acres), 58 miles of designated hiking trails, 24 miles of cross-country ski trails, 471 miles of snowmobile trails, 7 miles of ATV trails, and five picnic areas.

Buchanan State Forest. This is a 70,386-acre forest in Bedford, Franklin, and Fulton Counties. It has 150 miles of roads, one wild area (11,596 acres), two natural areas (1,971 acres) 87 miles of designated hiking trails, 5 miles of cross-country ski trails, 80 miles of snowmobile trails, 26 miles of ATV trails, and four picnic areas.

Gallitzin State Forest. This is a 15,337-acre forest in Bedford, Cambria, Indiana, and Somerset Counties. It has ten miles of roads, one wild area (2,791 acres), one natural area (384 acres), 51 miles of designated hiking trails, 7 miles of cross-country ski trails, 22 miles of snowmobile trails, and a picnic area.

Michaux State Forest. This 84,633-acre forest is located in Adams, Franklin, and Cumberland Counties. It has 126 miles of roads, four natural areas (1,601 acres), 65 miles of designated hiking trails, 4 miles of cross-country ski trails, 131 miles of snowmobile trails, 33 miles of ATV trails, and a picnic area.

Rothrock State Forest. This 94,349-acre forest is in Centre, Huntingdon, and Mifflin Counties. It has 226 miles of roads, two wild areas (6,589 acres), six natural areas (2,701 acres), 46 miles of designated hiking trails, 38 miles of cross-country ski trails, 186 miles of snowmobile trails, and two picnic areas.

Tuscarora State Forest. This 91,105-acre forest is in Cumberland, Franklin, Huntingdon, Juniata, Mifflin, and Perry Counties. It has 121 miles of roads, one wild area (5,363 acres), three natural areas (1,411 acres), 49 miles of designated hiking trails, 12 miles of cross-country ski trails, 120 miles of snowmobile trails, and a picnic area.

Southeast

Valley Forge State Forest. This 845-acre forest is in Chester County. It has four wild areas (891 acres) and 5 miles of designated hiking trails.

Weiser State Forest. This 19,361-acre forest is in Berks, Carbon, Dauphin, and Schuylkill Counties. It has 65 miles of roads, one natural area (70 acres), nine miles of designated hiking trails, 20 miles of snowmobile trails, and two picnic areas.

NATIONAL FORESTLAND
There is one national forest in Pennsylvania—the Allegheny National Forest, which covers more than a half-million acres of land in the north-central portion of the state, in Elk, Forest, McKean, and Warren Counties. The area is char-

acterized by flat, rolling plateaus, frequently dissected by stream valleys, which can be quite steep. The land is primarily timbered and helps to support local industries with fine hardwoods, such as black cherry, ash, and oak.

The watersheds provide high-quality water for local communities. There are several reservoirs and over 500 miles of waterways within the forest, including the Allegheny and Clarion Rivers and Kinzua, Bear, and Tionesta Creeks. The focal point of the forest is the 12,000-acre Allegheny Reservoir, on the upper Allegheny River. Developed recreational facilities include four beaches, six boat launches, three overlooks, and nine picnic areas. Of the 17 campgrounds in the forest, 10 are located on the shore of the reservoir.

Recreational opportunities consist mainly of hunting, fishing, hiking, and driving the scenic roadways. (One spectacular 29-mile loop near the reservoir has been designated by the Forest Service as a National Scenic Byway.) The forest has a 600-mile trail system, including about 200 miles for snowmobile trails. There are three areas exclusively for ATVs, including motorcycles and four-wheelers.

Within the forest, there are several specially designated areas: the Allegheny National Recreational Area, 23,000 acres along the Allegheny Reservoir and River; the Hickory Creek Wilderness Area and the Allegheny Islands Wilderness Area, which include a total of almost 10,000 acres. There also are two scenic areas: the Tionesta Area, 2,018 acres of virgin beech-hemlock forest, and the Hearts Content Area, 122 acres of white pine, hemlock, and mixed hardwoods, some of which are 300 to 400 years old.

At least 49 mammal species inhabit the forest, including black bears and elk, as well as small game and predators.

For more information, contact the Allegheny National Forest Supervisor's Office, (814) 723-5150; Elk County Visitors Bureau, Box 838, St. Marys, PA 15857, (814) 834-3711; Travel Northern Alleghenies, Box 804, Warren, PA 16365, (800) 624-7802; or Seneca Highlands Association, Drawer G, Custer City, PA 16725, (814) 368-9370.

OTHER RECREATION AREAS

The U.S. Fish and Wildlife Service administers two additional areas that provide recreational opportunities.

Erie National Wildlife Refuge. In the northwest corner of the state (on PA Route 198, east of Meadville), this refuge consists of 6,116 acres of open fields, woods, upland areas, swamps, and marshland that provide habitat for waterfowl, white-tailed deer, red fox, and beaver. Photography, cross-country skiing, hiking, and nature study are excellent here. Hunting, fishing, and trapping are permitted in designated areas.

Tinicum National Environmental Center. This 1,200-acre freshwater tidal marsh in Philadelphia and Delaware Counties is the largest remaining area of wetlands in the Pennsylvania stretch of the Delaware Estuary. It provides a unique opportunity to study wildlife in its natural habitat in the metropolitan Philadelphia area.

ENVIRONMENTAL EDUCATION CENTERS

There are four year-round environmental education centers in the state.

Jacobsburg Environmental Education Center. This facility is located on 1,168 acres at the foot of the Blue Mountains in Northampton County, adjacent to Jacobsburg State Park. It is accessible from PA Route 33 at the Belfast exit. Its mission is to provide discovery learning and problem-solving activities for students, preschool through graduate, and in-service workshops and training sessions for educators. It provides a wide variety of community programs to adult groups, civic groups, and the general public. The Jacobsburg National Historic District, which focuses on the Henry family and their small-arms industry, is within the center. A 12-mile network of multipurpose trails through fields, woodlands, and along streams is open to the public.

Jennings Environmental Education Center. The center is located near the intersection of PA Routes 173 and 528 and U.S. Route 8 in Butler County, adjacent to Moraine State Park. It was originally established by the Western Pennsylvania Conservancy to save a beautiful prairie flower, the blazing star. How did an area forested since the time of the Roman Empire remain in a prairie ecosystem? At Jennings Center, they know. Early August is the best time to view the blooming of the blazing star. Diverse habitat, varying terrain, and several miles of walking trails provide opportunities to view and photograph 366 species of plants, 134 species of birds, and many animals.

Kings Gap Environmental Education and Training Center. The center consists of 1,439 acres of forested land on South Mountain, Cumberland County, on the north edge of the Michaux State Forest. It is on Pine Road (State Route 3006), off Route 233, from Exit 11 of I-81. Fifteen miles of hiking trails, including seven self-guided nature trails, connect the three main day-use areas of the center. Kings Gap includes a training center for the commonwealth, providing meals and overnight lodging for state agencies.

Nolde Forest Environmental Education Center. Located on PA Route 625 south of Reading, the center covers 665 acres of deciduous woodland and coniferous plantations. A network of trails makes the center's streams, ponds, and diverse habitats accessible to both students and casual visitors.

WATER RESOURCES
Rivers and Streams
State Water Plan Subbasins. The six river basins in the commonwealth are the Delaware, Susquehanna, Ohio, Potomac, Genesee river basins, and the Lake Erie basin. The six basins are divided into 20 subbasins.

The Upper Delaware River Subbasin is located in the northeastern portion of the commonwealth and includes all of Pike County, almost all of Wayne County, two-thirds of Monroe County, one-third of Northampton County, and very small portions of Susquehanna and Lackawanna Counties. The land area totals 1,816 square miles, which is 28% of the Pennsylvania portion of the Delaware River Basin. The subbasin also contains the Lackawaxen River, Lake Wallenpaupack, Brodhead Creek, and both Bushkill Creeks (one in Pike and Monroe Counties, the other in Northampton County).

The *Central Delaware River Subbasin* is located in east-central and southeastern Pennsylvania. It includes most of Bucks, Lehigh, and Carbon Counties; the western half of Northampton; the western third of Monroe and small portions of Lackawanna, Luzerne, Schuylkill, Berks, and Montgomery Counties. The subbasin covers 1,943 square miles or approximately 30% of the state's

portion of the Delaware River Basin. The subbasin consists primarily of the Lehigh River Basin and also includes Tohickon Creek and Neshaminy Creek.

The *Lower Delaware River Subbasin* is located in southeastern Pennsylvania and includes all of Philadelphia and Delaware Counties; most of Chester, Montgomery, and Berks Counties; and small portions of Carbon, Lehigh, Bucks, Lancaster, and Lebanon Counties. The drainage area is 2,708 miles, or 42% of the state's portion of the Delaware River Basin. It includes the Schuylkill River Basin and other tributaries to the lower Delaware, including Brandywine, Chester, Ridley, Crum, and Darby Creeks.

The *Upper Susquehanna River Subbasin* is located along Pennsylvania's northern border and includes all of Bradford, Susquehanna, and Wyoming Counties; about half of Tioga County; and portions of Potter, Sullivan, Luzerne, and Lackawanna Counties. The land area totals 3,286 square miles. In addition to the North Branch of the Susquehanna River, this subbasin contains the Cowanesque and Tioga Rivers and Towanda, Waylusing, and Tunkhannock Creeks.

The *Upper Central Susquehanna River Subbasin* is located in northeastern Pennsylvania and includes almost all of Luzerne and Columbia Counties, most of Lackawanna, and portions of Schuylkill, Northumberland, Montour, Lycoming, and Sullivan Counties. The land area is 1,759 square miles. In addition to the North Branch of the Susquehanna River, the subbasin includes the entire Lackawanna River Basin, Fishing Creek, Wapwallopen Creek, Nescopeck Creek, and Catawissa Creek.

The *Lower Central Susquehanna River Subbasin* is located in east-central Penn-

PENNSYLVANIA'S WATER RESOURCES

Major water basins	6
State water plan subbasins	20
Miles of rivers and streams	53,962
Number of lakes, reservoirs, and ponds	3,956
Number of significant publicly owned lakes	160
Acres of lakes, reservoirs, and ponds	161,445
Acres of significant publicly owned lakes	96,203
Square miles of estuaries and bays	
Delaware Estuary	17
Presque Isle Bay	6
Miles of Great Lake shoreline	63
Acres of freshwater wetlands	403,924
Acres of tidal wetlands	512

sylvania and includes almost all of Snyder County, half of Northumberland County, one-third of Dauphin and Union Counties, one-fourth of Centre County, and small portions of Mifflin, Juniata, Perry, Schuylkill, and Columbia Counties. The land area of the subbasin is 1,448 square miles. In addition to the North Branch of the Susquehanna River, the subbasin includes Penns, Middle, Shamokin, Mahanoy, Mahantango, and Wiconisco Creeks.

The *Lower Susquehanna River Subbasin,* located in south-central Pennsylvania, includes all of Cumberland, Lancaster, and York Counties; most of Lebanon County; half of Adams, Dauphin, and Perry Counties; and small portions of Chester, Berks, Franklin, and Schuylkill Counties. The subbasin covers 4,158 square miles. This subbasin consists of the lower main stem of the Susquehanna River and a number of major tributaries: Sherman, Codorus, Conodoguinet, Swatara, Yellow Breeches, Conewago, Conestoga, and Octoraro Creeks.

The *Upper West Branch Susquehanna River Subbasin* is located in the central portion of the commonwealth. It includes all of Cameron County; most of Clearfield County; large portions of Centre, Cambria, Elk, and Potter Counties; and small parts of Indiana, Clinton, and Blair Counties. The drainage area is 2,631 square miles. The subbasin includes Chest, Clearfield, Moshannon, and Sinnemahoning Creeks.

The *Central West Branch Susquehanna River Subbasin* is located in north-central Pennsylvania and includes almost all of Clinton County, half of Centre County, and one-third of Potter, Lycoming, and Tioga Counties. The drainage area is 2,539 square miles. The subbasin includes Kettle, Bald Eagle, and Pine Creeks.

The *Lower West Branch Susquehanna River Subbasin,* in north-central Pennsylvania, includes almost all of Sullivan County; two-thirds of Lycoming, Montour, and Union Counties; and small portions of Columbia, Tioga, Wyoming,

Bradford, and Clinton Counties. The land area is 1,809 square miles. Major waterways include the West Branch of the Susquehanna and Lycoming, Loyalsock, Muncy, Buffalo, and Chillisquaque Creeks.

The *Upper Juniata River Subbasin* is located in the south-central portion of the state and includes all of Blair County, the northern two-thirds of Bedford County, the western half of Huntingdon County, and small parts of Fulton, Cambria, and Centre Counties. The subbasin encompasses 1,943 square miles. It is made up of the Raystown and Frankstown Branches of the Juniata River and the Little Juniata River.

The *Lower Juniata River Subbasin* in south-central Pennsylvania drains 1,462 square miles. It includes almost all of Mifflin and Juniata Counties, the northern half of Perry County, the southeastern third of Huntingdon County, and small parts of Snyder, Centre, Fulton, and Franklin Counties. Included in this subbasin are the main stem Juniata River and its tributaries, including Aughwick, Kishacoquillas, and Tuscarora Creeks.

The Pennsylvania portion of the *Potomac River Basin,* the Potomac River Subbasin, lies in the extreme southcentral portion of the state on the Maryland border. It includes the southwestern half of Adams County, the lower third of Bedford County, the southeast corner of Somerset County, and all but the northern third of Fulton and Franklin Counties. The subbasin covers 1,584 square miles, 11% of the total Potomac River drainage. It includes Wills, Evitts, Tonoloway, Licking, Conococheague, Marsh, and Rock Creeks.

The *headwaters of the Genesee River* form the Genesee River Subbasin in north-central Pennsylvania on the New York border. The subbasin is located in the north-central portion of Potter County and covers only 99 miles.

The *Lake Erie Drainage Subbasin* is located in the extreme northwest corner of Pennsylvania and includes the northwest half of Erie County and the northwest corner of Crawford County. The subbasin drains about 511 square miles of land in the state.

The *Upper Allegheny River Subbasin* is located in northwestern Pennsylvania and borders New York. The Allegheny River originates in Pennsylvania, flows into New York, and returns to Pennsylvania. This subbasin includes all of Warren County; most of McKean, Venango, and Crawford Counties; the southeastern half of Erie County; the western two-thirds of Forest County; and small parts of Potter, Mercer, Butler, Clarion, and Elk Counties. It drains about 4,474 square miles in Pennsylvania. In addition to the Upper Allegheny, the subbasin includes Oswayo, Portage, Brokenstraw, Tionesta, Oil, and French Creeks.

The *Central Allegheny River Subbasin* is located in west-central Pennsylvania and covers 2,930 acres. It includes all of Jefferson County, almost all of Clarion and Armstrong Counties, and parts of Elk, Indiana, Butler, Forest, McKean, and Clearfield Counties. In addition to a portion of the Allegheny River main stem, it includes the Clarion River Basin and Redbank, Mahoning, and Crooked Creeks.

The *Lower Allegheny River Subbasin* drains 2,394 square miles in southwestern Pennsylvania. It includes approximately half of Allegheny, Indiana, Cambria, Somerset, and Westmoreland Counties and small parts of Butler and Armstrong Counties. It includes a portion of the Allegheny River main stem and the Kiskiminetas River Basin, the Conemaugh River, and Loyalhanna Creek.

The *Monongahela River Subbasin* is located along the southwestern border of Pennsylvania and is adjacent to Maryland and West Virginia. It includes all of Fayette County; most of Greene, Washington, Somerset, and Westmoreland Counties; and a small portion of Allegheny County. The Pennsylvania portion drains approximately 2,737 square miles. It includes the Monogahela River and its major tributaries: Dunkard, Tenmile, and Redstone Creeks and a small segment of the Cheat River, as well as the Youghiogheny River with its major tributaries, the Casselman River and Sewickley Creek.

The *Ohio River Subbasin* is located in extreme western Pennsylvania along the Ohio–West Virginia border. It includes all of Beaver and Lawrence Counties, most of Mercer, two-thirds of Butler, about half of Allegheny and Washington Counties, and small portions of Greene and Crawford Counties. The subbasin covers 3,080 square miles and includes the main stem Ohio River and its tributaries, Chartiers and Raccoon Creeks from the south. The northern part of the subbasin includes the Beaver, Mahoning, and Shenango Rivers, as well as Neshannock, Slippery Rock, and Connoquenessing Creeks.

Wild and Scenic Rivers. Pennsylvania's many miles of streams and rivers are among its most valuable recreational resources. Efforts to protect these waters and to assure their future availability for recreational use are being conducted at both the national and state levels.

The National Wild and Scenic Rivers System has two components in Pennsylvania:

• A 37-mile stretch of the Middle Delaware River between Milford and the Delaware Water Gap. This lies wholly within the Delaware Water Gap National Recreation Area and is managed by the National Park Service.

• A 73-mile stretch of the Upper Delaware River between Hancock, New York, and Sparrowbush, New York. This is the Pennsylvania–New York border in Wayne County. This is designated as a scenic and recreational river, and is managed by the National Park Service.

The Pennsylvania Scenic Rivers System encompasses a total of 502 miles, which carry designations of wild, scenic, recreational, pastoral, or a combination thereof.

Scenic river designation of a commonwealth waterway invokes only limited protection from adverse developments. In reality, it is only the first step in a long-term process of river conservation, education, and planning, involving citizens, landowners, and local governments. The Department of Environmental Resources, Pennsylvania Rivers Conservation Program, provides grants to local groups that assume responsibility for the process.

Water Quality. The Pennsylvania Department of Environmental Protection assesses water quality in the state as required by the Federal Clean Water Act. The 1996 assessments were conducted on 24,482 miles of Pennsylvania streams.

A total of 19,984 stream miles, or 81.6%, were assessed as fully supporting water uses—they were fishable and swimmable and met the state's water-quality standards. Partial support of uses was reported for 1,850 stream

SCENIC RIVERS

River	Length in miles	Designation
Bear Run	4.3	pastoral, modified recreational
French Creek	42.75	scenic
LaTort Springs Run	7.6	pastoral, modified recreational
Lehigh River	64	wild, scenic
Lick Run	23	wild, scenic
Lower Brandywine	65.85	scenic, pastoral
Octoraro Creek	36.5	scenic, pastoral
Pine Creek	24.2	scenic, wild
Schuylkill River	124.8	pastoral, recreational, or modified recreational
Stony Creek	16	wild
Tucquan Creek	8	wild, scenic
Tulpehocken Creek	28.8	pastoral, recreational
Yellow Breeches Creek	56	recreational, scenic, pastoral

miles, or 7.6 percent. This means that some violations of water-quality standards were found, there was an impairment of fish and aquatic life, or fish flesh was contaminated. Nonsupport of stream uses was reported for 2,647 stream miles, or 10.8 percent, of the miles assessed. These streams are polluted.

The single biggest source of surface water contamination is resource extraction. It is responsible for at least 2,575 of the 4,479 miles reported as impaired, or 57.3 percent. The primary source is abandoned mine drainage, from both anthracite and bituminous mining.

Other major sources of use impairment are agriculture (633 miles), industrial point sources (237 miles), municipal point sources (186 miles), and on-site wastewater systems (107 miles). Natural conditions and undetermined sources account for the remainder.

Wetlands

Wetlands are transitional zones between purely terrestrial and aquatic environments. They are defined as areas inundated or saturated by surface water or groundwater adequate to support vegetation adapted for life in saturated soil conditions. Wetlands include swamps, marshes, bogs, and similar areas. Generally, swamps are dominated by woody plants and marshes by nonwoody plants. Both have water systems flowing through them with defined inlets and outlets. Bogs lack flowing water and usually have a combination of woody and nonwoody vegetation.

These areas perform the primary vital functions of water-quality maintenance, flood control, groundwater maintenance, and assistance in atmospheric balance. They provide habitat for wildlife, including rare and endangered species, food resources, extractable resources, education and research sites, and opportunities for recreation.

Pennsylvania has 403,924 acres of wetlands and 412,905 acres of deep-water habitats, excluding farmed wetlands and smaller rivers and streams that do not show up on aerial photos. About 1.4% of the state's land surface is wetlands, 97% of which is classified as palustrine wetlands, meaning aquatic beds, emergent, scrub-shrub, and forested. Forested and scrub-shrub wetlands account for three-quarters of the palustrine wetland areas. Lacustrine wetlands, mainly the shallow water zone of Lake Erie, represent abut 2% of the state's total; riverine wetlands make up the remaining 1%. Pennsylvania has 512 acres of tidal wetlands in the Delaware Estuary. The state has no marine systems.

Wetlands are most abundant in the glaciated regions of the northeastern and northwestern portions of the commonwealth. Crawford, Erie, Mercer, Monroe, Pike, Wayne, and Luzerne Counties contain 40% of the state's wetlands. Pike and Monroe Counties have the highest percentages of land area covered by wetlands, with 6.7% and 6.4%, respectively. Other counties with 2% or more of their land surface in wetlands are Crawford (5.2%), Erie (4.8%), Wayne (4.4%), Mercer (3.7%), Lackawanna (3.2%), Luzerne (3.0%), Bucks (2.6%), Wyoming (2.5%), Susquehanna (2.3%), McKean (2.2%), Sullivan (2.2%), Warren (2.2%), Adams (2.1%), Bradford (2.0%), and Lawrence (2.0%).

In the early 1970s, the U.S. Forest Service inventoried Pennsylvania wetlands and compared them with wetlands that had been inventoried in 1954. The study showed a 22% loss of wetland acreage and a 17% reduction in the size of the remaining wetlands. The chief factors were strip mining in western counties; development in the northeast, particularly with subdivided lots for second-home development in the Pocono area; and the construction of impoundments, primarily reservoirs.

The loss of wetlands can also occur as the result of many other development activities, such as highway building across wetland areas or the channelization of rivers and streams, which results in the loss of riparian wetlands by eliminating stream meanders, floodplains, swamps, and marshes.

Wetlands are dynamic areas. For example, timber harvesting might change a forested wetland to a scrub-shrub wetland. Thus, all wetland classifications experience gains and losses.

Lakes

There are 160 publicly owned lakes encompassing 96,203 acres that the commonwealth has defined as significant. Many are found within state parks; other owners include the Pennsylvania Fish and Boat Commission and the U.S. Army Corps of Engineers.

The U.S. Army Corps of Engineers, as a by-product of its projects designed to improve navigation, control beach erosion, and provide drainage and flood control, has increased water-based recreation in Pennsylvania considerably. The 24 multipurpose Corps reservoir projects total 140,000 acres, most of which are used for recreation. Eight of these projects adjoin state parks, and two are in the Allegheny National Forest. The Corps reservoirs are the major lakes within Pennsylvania that permit unlimited-power boating.

PUBLICLY OWNED LAKES

Lake	County	Acres
Barmore Lake	Mercer	25
Barneston Dam	Chester	7
Beaver Run Reservoir	Westmoreland	1,125
Beechwood Lake	Tioga	67
Belmont Dam	Lackawanna	7
Belmont Lake	Wayne	172
Beltzville Lake	Carbon	947
Bernharts Dam	Berks	13
Birch Run Dam	Adams	1,500
Black Moshannon Lake	Centre	250
Blue Marsh Lake	Berks	1,150
Brookville Dam	Jefferson	6
Bruce Lake	Centre	48
Buhis Park Dam	Mercer	4
Canoe Lake	Blair	155
Canonsburg Lake	Washington	76
Chapman Dam	Warren	68
Chapman Lake	Lackawanna	98
Chartiers Creek #4	Washington	125
Clarion River Reservoir	Elk	1,160
Cloe Dam	Jefferson	30
Colyer Lake	Centre	77
Conemaugh River Lake	Indiana-Westmoreland	300
Conneaut Lake	Crawford	929
Cowanesque Lake	Tioga	1,090
Cowans Gap Lake	Fulton	42
Coxes Dam	Somerset	252
Cranberry Glade Lake	Somerset	72
Crooked Creek Lake	Armstrong	350
Cross Creek Lake	Washington	244
Curwensville Lake	Clearfield	540
Decker Pond	Pike	119
Donegal Lake (Fourmile Run Dam)	Westmoreland	90
Duck Harbor Pond	Wayne	122
Duman Lake	Cambria	22

PUBLICLY OWNED LAKES *(continued)*

Lake	County	Acres
Dutch Fork Lake	Washington	91
East Branch Lake (Clarion)	Elk	1,160
Edinboro Lake	Erie	240
Egypt Meadow Lake	Pike	60
Faylor Lake	Snyder	140
Ford Lake	Lackawanna	72
Foster Joseph Sayers Lake	Centre	1,730
Frances Slocum Lake	Luzerne	165
Francis E. Walter Reservoir	Luzerne-Carbon	90
Furnace Creek Dam	Berks	15
George B. Stevenson Reservoir	Cameron	142
Glade Dam Lake	Butler	400
Glade Lake (on Glade Run)	Butler	62
Glendale Lake	Cambria	1,600
Gouldsboro Lake	Susquehanna	250
Green Lake Reservoir	Montgomery	814
Green Lick Reservoir	Fayette	25
Hammond Lake	Tioga	680
Harveys Lake	Luzerne	659
Hereford Manor Lake	Beaver	55
Hereford Manor Lake—Upper	Beaver	23
High Point Lake	Somerset	342
Hills Creek Lake	Tioga	137
Hopewell Lake	Berks	68
Howard Eaton Reservoir	Erie	245
Hunters Lake	Sullivan	36
Indian Run Dam	Berks	5
Ironworks Reservoir	Bucks	172
Kaercher Creek Lake	Berks	32
Kettle Creek Lake	Clinton	160
Keystone Lake	Westmoreland	78
Keystone Lake (Plum Creek Reservoir)	Armstrong	880
Kinzua Lake	Warren	12,100
Kyle Dam	Jefferson	143
Lackawanna Lake	Lackawanna	210

PUBLICLY OWNED LAKES *(continued)*

Lake	County	Acres
Lake Antietam	Berks	16
Lake Arthur	Butler	3,225
Lake Carey	Wyoming	263
Lake Galena	Bucks	365
Lake Gordon	Bedford	135
Lake Heritage	Adams	146
Lake Jean	Luzerne-Sullivan	245
Lake Koon	Bedford	192
Lake Ladore	Susquehanna	255
Lake Latonka	Mercer	320
Lake Luxembourg	Bucks	174
Lake Marburg	York	1,275
Lake Meade	Adams	291
Lake Minisink	Pike	34
Lake Nephawin	Bradford	28
Lake Nessmuk	Tioga	60
Lake Nockamixon	Bucks	1,450
Lake Ontelaunee	Berks	1,080
Lake Rose	Luzerne	47
Lake Scranton	Lackawanna	225
Lake Somerset	Somerset	253
Lake Wallenpaupack	Pike-Wayne	5,760
Lake Warren	Bucks	15
Lake Wilhelm	Mercer	1,860
Lake Winola	Wyoming	190
Laurel Lake	Cumberland	25
Laurel Hill Lake	Somerset	63
Laurel Run Reservoir	Elk	2
Lily Lake	Luzerne	108
Little Buffalo State Park Lake	Perry	88
Little Pine Dam	Lycoming	94
Lock Alsh Dam	Montgomery	9
Locust Lake	Schuylkill	52
Long Pine Run Reservoir	Adams	500
Lower Woods Pond	Wayne	91
Loyalhanna Lake	Westmoreland	210

PUBLICLY OWNED LAKES *(continued)*

Lake	County	Acres
Mahoning Creek Lake	Armstrong	170
Marilla Brook Reservoir	McKean	20
Marsh Creek Lake	Chester	535
Memorial Lake	Lebanon	84
Middle Creek Waterfowl Management Lake	Lancaster	365
Minsi Lake (Martins)	Northampton	121
Octoraro Lake	Lancaster-Chester	669
Oneida Reservoir	Butler	155
Opossum Lake	Cumberland	59
Parker Dam	Clearfield	20
Pecks Pond	Pike	300
Pinchot (Conewago) Lake	York	340
Poe Valley Lake	Centre	25
Promised Land Lake—Lower	Pike	173
Promised Land Lake—Upper	Pike	422
Prompton Reservoir	Wayne	280
Pymatuning Reservoir	Crawford	14,500
Quemahoning Reservoir	Somerset	900
Raccoon Creek Lake	Beaver	101
Raystown Lake	Huntingdon-Bedford	8,300
Rock River Reservoir	Chester	65
Rocky Glenn Pond	Lackawanna	37
Rose Valley Lake	Lycoming	389
Ryerson Station Lake	Greene	62
Sand Spring Lake	Carbon	11
Scotts Run Lake	Berks	21
Shawnee Lake	Bedford	451
Shenango River Lake	Mercer	3,560
Shohola Lake	Pike	1,130
Sones Pond	Sullivan	20
Speedwell Forge Lake	Lancaster	106
Springton Reservoir	Delaware	375
Stephen Foster Lake	Bradford	79
Stevens Lake	Wyoming	72

PUBLICLY OWNED LAKES *(continued)*

Lake	County	Acres
Stillwater Lake	Monroe	348
Struble Lake	Chester	146
Sweet Arrow Lake	Schuylkill	100
Tamarack Lake	Crawford	556
Thorn Run Reservoir	Butler	49
Tioga Lake	Tioga	470
Tionesta Lake	Forest	480
Tobyhanna Lake	Monroe	170
Township Line Dam	Chester	65
Trout Run Reservoir	Berks	65
Tuscarora Lake	Schuylkill	96
Twin Lake—Lower	Westmoreland	30
Twin Lake—Upper	Westmoreland	20
Union City Lake	Erie	2,290
Virgin Run Lake	Fayette	32
Walker Lake	Snyder	239
Whipple Dam	Huntingdon	22
Wisecarver Run	Greene	18
Yellow Creek Lake	Indiana	740
Youghiogheny River Lake	Fayette-Somerset	2,840

Water Quality. Current information on trends in lake water quality is not readily available. The Department of Environmental Protection is monitoring selected lakes in an attempt to correct this deficiency; about 90 lakes are scheduled for annual sampling. Lakes included are selected on the basis of size, public access, intensity of use, or availability of historic data.

Hydroelectric Projects

The 21 operating hydroelectric projects licensed in Pennsylvania by the Federal Energy Regulatory Commission are required to provide opportunities for recreational activities such as fishing, boating, swimming, and shoreline activities such as hiking, camping, picnicking, and hunting. Major projects providing recreational opportunities include the following:

Lake Lynn Project, on the Cheat River, on the West Virginia border, 8 miles northeast of Morgantown: 1,729 acres of water with a 26-mile shoreline.

Conowingo Project, on the Susquehanna River, near the Maryland border, 8 miles northeast of Havre de Grace,

Maryland: 9,000 acres of water with a 38-mile shoreline.

Muddy Run Project, on Muddy Run Creek, 15 miles south of Lancaster: 386 acres of water with a 19-mile shoreline.

Holtwood Dam, on the Susquehanna River, 10 miles south of Lancaster: 2,400 water acres with a 16-mile shoreline.

Safe Harbor Dam, on the Susquehanna River, 10 miles west of Lancaster: 7,360 acres of water with a 21-mile shoreline.

York Haven Project, on the Susquehanna River, 10 miles south of Middletown: 1,490 acres of water with a 9-mile shoreline.

Wallenpaupack Project, on Wallenpaupack Creek, 10 miles south of Honesdale: 5,700 acres of water with a 52-mile shoreline.

Piney Project, on the Clarion River, 2 miles southwest of Clarion: 545 acres of water with a 32-mile shoreline.

U.S. Soil Conservation Service Projects.

The U.S. Soil Conservation Service (SCS) plans, constructs, and shares the cost of flood prevention and multipurpose dams for water supply, fish and wildlife, and recreation. In some areas, SCS develops shoreline facilities. The local sponsor assumes responsibility for the completed project.

The 19 Soil Conservation Service projects within Pennsylvania have a total water surface area of 5,704 acres for water-based recreation.

HUNTING

The hunting and trapping of animals and birds is a popular pastime and a big business in Pennsylvania. In 1995, 2.4

million hunting licenses were sold. The Game Commission estimates that hunters spent about $1.8 billion, generated $38 million in taxes, and supported 24,000 jobs.

The Game Commission maintains 1,376,456 acres of state game lands in 292 tracts located in 65 of the state's 67 counties. An additional 4,489,314 acres of privately owned land are enrolled in public-access programs. Sportsmen are also welcome to hunt on the 2,200,000 acres of state forestland, selected state parks, the Allegheny National Forest, and several sizable federal properties administered by various agencies.

Game animals that may be hunted in the state are the black bear, elk, white-tailed deer, cottontail rabbit, snowshoe hare, woodchuck (groundhog), and red, gray, black, and fox squirrels. Bear, elk, white-tailed deer, and wild turkey are defined as big game.

Furbearers, which may be hunted or trapped, are the badger, beaver, bobcat, coyote, fisher, mink, muskrat, opossum, otter, pine marten, raccoon, red and gray foxes, skunk, and weasel.

Game birds in the state are the bobwhite, quail, Hungarian partridge, grouse, snipe, woodcock, pheasant, wild turkey, mourning dove, sora, Virginia rail, gallinules, coot, mergansers and other wild ducks, brant, geese, and swans. Although not considered to be a game bird, hunting regulations also apply to the crow.

Descriptions of several game animals and birds can be found in the chapter on plants and wildlife.

Licensing

The general hunting license is valid from July 1 to the following June 30.

LICENSE FEES*

Type of License	Ages	Fee
Resident junior hunting	12–16	$5.75
Nonresident junior hunting		$40.75
Resident junior furtaker	12–16	$5.75
Nonresident junior furtaker		$40.75
Resident adult hunting	17 and up	$12.75
Nonresident adult hunting		$80.75
Resident adult furtaker	17 and up	$12.75
Nonresident adult furtaker		$80.75
Resident senior hunting	65 and up	$10.75
Resident senior furtaker	65 and up	$10.75
Resident senior lifetime hunting	65 and up	$50.75
Resident senior lifetime furtaker	65 and up	$50.75
Nonresident 7-day small game	12 and up	$15.75
Archery license		$5.75
Muzzle loader**		$5.75
Resident bear license		$10.75
Nonresident bear license		$25.75

*Excluding issuing fees
**Must be purchased by 6/30

Special licenses must be obtained to hunt antlerless deer or to use either a muzzle-loading gun or a bow and arrow during designated seasons. These weapons may be used during the regular hunting season without the special license. A special license is required to hunt bear during a three-day season. A Federal Duck Stamp is required to hunt waterfowl.

Nonresidents pay significantly higher fees for a license to hunt in Pennsylvania. For the purposes of hunting, a resident is defined as a person who has lived in the state for 30 consecutive days prior to application.

Licenses may be purchased from issuing agents in commercial businesses, county treasurers, Game Commission headquarters, and six regional field offices. The bear licenses and the lifetime senior licenses are available only at Game Commission offices. Antlerless deer licenses are available only by mail from county treasurers. The Pennsylvania Game Commission is located at 2001 Elmerton Ave., Harrisburg, PA 17119, telephone (717) 787-4250.

FISHING AND BOATING

The statistics on fishing and boating in the commonwealth are awesome:

Approximately 1 million fishing licenses are sold annually, and these anglers enjoy about 21 million fishing trips each year. The Pennsylvania Fish and Boat Commission operates 15 fish culture stations, provides small fish and guidance to 175 cooperative nurseries operated by sportsmen's groups, and protects and manages the commonwealth's fishery resources, including reptiles and amphibians. Over 10 million trout and 650 million warm-water fish are stocked each year to augment the natural fish population.

The Fish and Boat Commission owns or controls 38,000 acres of property, including 71 lakes, dams, and reservoirs; owns or leases 39 miles of streams; and owns or has under easement 318 fishing and boating access areas.

There were 330,000 registered boats in Pennsylvania in 1995. These boaters participated in about 20 million days of boating activities, contributing $1.7 billion to the economy for equipment, supplies, and fuel. Fishers contributed an additional $1.1 billion.

Fishing Licenses and Regulations

Persons 16 years of age or older must have a license to fish in Pennsylvania, and it must be displayed on an outer garment while fishing. There are more than 1,700 license-issuing agents in the state, including most sporting-goods stores, bait and tackle shops, many variety and specialty stores, and all county treasurers. Nonresidents may order by mail from the Pennsylvania Fish Commission, Box 1673, Harris-

---

SEASONS AND DAILY LIMITS

Bass—smallmouth, largemouth, and spotted	mid-June to mid-April	6
Bass—striped	year-round	2
Shad	year-round	6
Muskellunge, northern and Amur pike	early May to March 14	2
Chain pickerel, walleye, and sauger	early May to March 14	14
Trout—wild	mid-April to day after Labor Day	8
Trout—stocked	mid-April to last day of February	3

Sunfish, yellow perch, crappies, catfish, rock bass, eels, carp, white bass, and baitfish may be taken year-round. The daily limit is 50 fish combined from the group.

Dates vary from year to year. A summary of fishing regulations is provided with each fishing license.

burg, PA 17105. In 1996, 972,204 licenses were sold; it was the first time since 1976 that sales failed to reach one million.

1997 LICENSE FEES

Resident adult	$16.25
Senior resident (age 65+)	4.00
Lifetime resident (age 65+)	16.00
Nonresident (annual)	35.00
Seven-day tourist license	30.00
Three-day tourist license	15.00
Trout and salmon permit	5.00
Lake Erie surcharge	3.50
Issuing agent fee	0.75

Boating Regulations and Fees

Pennsylvania law requires that all motorboats, including those powered by electric motors, be registered. Most county treasurers, marine dealers, and sporting-goods stores may register boats. Registration may also be done by mail. Form Rev. 336, "Application for Pennsylvania Boat Registration," with proof of ownership and the proper fees, may be sent to the Pennsylvania Fish and Boat Commission, Boat Registration Division, P.O. Box 68900, Harrisburg, PA 17106-8900. Proof of payment of sales tax is required to complete registration. Pennsylvania has a two-year registration system; registrations expire on March 31 of the second year. The two-year registration costs $20 for boats less than 16 feet, $30 for boats 16 feet to less than 20 feet, and $40 for boats over 20 feet. Unpowered boats are registered under a voluntary system. The registration fee is $10.

Renewals can be done by mail in the same manner as motor vehicle registration. An application for renewal will be sent by the Commission.

A boat with a registration from any state may operate in any other state or in Canada for a maximum of 60 days.

Beginning in 1972, the federal government required that all boats manufactured for sale in the U.S. have a Hull Identification Number (HIN). The HIN is located on the outside of the transom (rear) on the starboard (right) side. If the boat is homemade, if it was manufactured prior to 1992, or if the HIN cannot be found, one will be assigned by the Commission.

Boaters are responsible for making certain their boats are equipped with proper safety equipment. A review of legal and safety requirements may help avoid a fine or, worse, an emergency on the water.

In 1996, the Commission initiated alcohol checkpoints on the Susquehanna River similar to those conducted by the State Police on the highways. The same .10% blood alcohol level standard applies on the water. Although open containers of alcohol are permitted on boats, operating a boat while under the influence is not. In Pennsylvania, about one-third of all boating fatalities involve alcohol.

WHITEWATER RECREATION

There are three major areas of whitewater activity in Pennsylvania; all are in state parks.

The major attraction of **Lehigh Gorge State Park** is whitewater boating. This section of the Lehigh River is Class III whitewater and is popular for rafting, kayaking, and canoeing. The best time for these activities is usually mid-March through June, but conditions vary greatly. River flow is controlled by the U.S. Army Corps of Engineers at the Francis Water Dam and by streams flowing into the river through the park. Flow rates from the dam may be obtained by calling (800) 431-4721.

Inexperienced boaters should not attempt to run the Lehigh River without a qualified guide. Outfitted trips are available from concessionaires, who provide transportation to and from the river, rafts, guides, and safety equipment. A list of licensed commercial outfitters is available at the park office.

There are three basic trips: White Haven to Rockport, about 9 miles; Rockport to Jim Thorpe, 15 miles; and White Haven to Jim Thorpe, which is 24 miles and will take 10 to 12 hours when water levels are low.

Ohiopyle State Park contains two segments of the Youghiogheny River that are used for whitewater activities. The famous lower river run begins below the Ohiopyle Falls and has numerous Class III and IV rapids that require sturdily constructed rubber rafts, kayaks, or closed-deck canoes. The upper section, toward Confluence, has Class I and II whitewater. Four concessionaires provide guided river tours on the lower segment. They also rent equipment to individual boaters. A permit from the park office is required for all unguided whitewater trips.

Pine Creek which flows through **Leonard Harrison and Colton Point State Parks,** offers the whitewater experience without the white knuckles. The water is not in the same class as the Lehigh or Youghiogheny Rivers, but it

does include a ride through the Grand Canyon of Pennsylvania. The best conditions prevail in the Owassee and Split Rock Rapids, a 20-mile stretch from Blackwell to Ansonia, from March to June, when water levels are high. The Tioga County Tourist Promotion Agency in Wellsboro, telephone (800) 332-6718, can provide further information.

SKIING

In a state where the highest point, Mount Davis, has an elevation of 3,213 feet and the approximate mean elevation is 1,100 feet, skiing does not have a Rocky Mountain feeling. Nevertheless, selective skiers of all ability levels can enjoy a fair number of challenging runs. Ski mountain elevations range from 528 feet at Spring Mountain to 3,152 feet at Blue Knob.

Pennsylvania is an especially good environment in which to learn to ski. The fear that the mere presence of nearby towering peaks can instill in beginners is absent. The mountains offer a chance to grow and to improve upon newly acquired techniques on slopes appropriate to skill levels.

There are 28 downhill resorts in Pennsylvania, 11 of which are clustered in the Pocono Mountains in the northeast corner of the state; five others are nearby. The seven resorts in the central counties extend from the New York to the Maryland border. Four of the five western ski areas are in the southern half of the state; one is near Lake Erie.

Unless otherwise noted, all of the areas have ski school, night skiing, snowboarding, snow-making equipment, and equipment rentals.

PENNSYLVANIA SKI AREAS

Pocono Mountains

Alpine Mountain
　　Route 447, Analomink, PA 18320
　　(717) 595-2150, (800) 233-8240

snow report:	(717) 595-2150
elevation:	1,150 feet
vertical:	500 feet
longest run:	2,640 feet
total slopes and trails:	18
	25% difficult, 50% intermediate, 25% easy
chairlifts:	1 double, 2 quad

　　no night skiing

Blue Mountain
　　P.O. Box 216, Palmerton, PA 18071
　　(610) 826-7700

snow report:	(800) 235-8100
elevation:	1,600 feet
vertical:	1,082 feet
longest run:	5,200 feet
total slopes and trails:	20
	32% difficult, 37% intermediate, 31% easy
chairlifts:	4 double, 1 T-bar, 1 detach

Camelback
　　Exit 45 of I-80, Tannersville, PA 18372
　　(717) 629-1661

snow report:	(800) 233-8100
elevation:	2,050 feet
vertical:	800 feet
longest run:	1 mile
total slopes and trails:	31
	22% difficult, 40% intermediate, 38% easy
chairlifts:	7 double, 2 triple, 1 quad, 2 HS detach quad

Fernwood
　　U.S. Route 209 N., Bushkill, PA 18324
　　(717) 588-9500

snow report:	(717) 588-9500
elevation:	1,200 feet
vertical:	225 feet

PENNSYLVANIA SKI AREAS *(continued)*

Fernwood, continued

longest run:	1,500 feet
total slopes and trails:	2
	50% difficult, 50% easier
chairlifts:	1 double

Mount Airy Lodge
Mount Pocono, PA 18344
(717) 839-8811

snow report:	(717) 839-8811
elevation:	1,200 feet
vertical:	280 feet
longest run:	2,300 feet
total slopes and trails:	7
	42% difficult, 58% easier
chairlifts:	2 double

Mount Tone Ski Resort
Off Route 47, Lake Como, PA 18437
(717) 798-2707

snow report:	(717) 798-2707
elevation:	1,500 feet
vertical:	450 feet
longest run:	2,500 feet
total slopes and trails:	11
	20% difficult, 40% intermediate, 40% easy
chairlifts:	1 triple, 1 T-bar, 2 rope

Shawnee Mountain
Exit 52 of I-80, Shawnee-on-Delaware, PA 18356
(717) 421-7231

snow report:	(800) 233-4126
elevation:	1,350 feet
vertical:	700 feet
longest run:	5,100 feet
total slopes and trails:	23
	25% difficult, 50% intermediate, 25% easy
chairlifts:	1 triple, 8 double

Split Rock Resort
Lake Harmony, PA 18624
(717) 722-9111

PENNSYLVANIA SKI AREAS *(continued)*

Split Rock Resort, continued

snow report:	(717) 722-9111
elevation:	1,950 feet
vertical:	250 feet
longest run:	1,700 feet
total slopes and trails:	7
	35% difficult, 65% easy
chairlifts:	1 triple, 1 T-bar

Tanglewood
Lake Wallenpaupack, Tafton, PA 18464
(717) 226-9500

snow report:	(717) 226-9500
elevation:	1,750 feet
vertical:	415 feet
longest run:	1.25 miles
total slopes and trails:	10
	30% difficult, 45% intermediate, 25% easy
chairlifts:	2 double, 2 T-bar, 1 rope

The Big Two: Big Boulder
P.O. Box 702, Blakeslee, PA 18610
(717) 722-0100

snow report:	(800) 475-SNOW
elevation:	2,175 feet
vertical:	475 feet
longest run:	2,900 feet
total slopes and trails:	13
	25% difficult, 35% intermediate, 40% easy
chairlifts:	2 triple, 5 double

Jack Frost Mountain
P.O. Box 703, Blakeslee, PA 18610
(717) 443-8425

snow report:	(800) 475-SNOW
elevation:	2,000 feet
vertical:	600 feet
longest run:	2,700 feet
total slopes and trails:	20
	40% difficult, 40% intermediate, 20% easy
chairlifts:	1 quad, 4 double, 2 triple

PENNSYLVANIA SKI AREAS *(continued)*

Eastern

Blue Marsh
P.O. Box 447, Bernville, PA 19506
(610) 488-6399

snow report:	(717) 488-6399, 488-6396
elevation:	580 feet
vertical:	300 feet
longest run:	3,500 feet
total slopes and trails:	11
	25% difficult, 50% intermediate, 25% easy
chairlifts:	1 triple, 1 double, 1 T-bar, 1 handle tow

Doe Mountain
101 Doe Mountain Lane, Macungie, PA 18062
(610) 682-7108

snow report:	(800) 282-7107
elevation:	1,100 feet
vertical:	500 feet
longest run:	1.5 miles
total slopes and trails:	15
	30% difficult, 40% intermediate, 30% easy
chairlifts:	1 triple, 3 double, 2 rope, 1 T-bar

Elk Mountain
RR #3, P.O. Box 338, Union Dale, PA 18470
(717) 679-2611

snow report:	(800) 233-4131
elevation:	2,693 feet
vertical:	1,000 feet
longest run:	1.75 miles
total slopes and trails:	25
	45% difficult, 30% intermediate, 25% easy
chairlifts:	1 quad, 5 doubles

Montage
1000 Montage Mountain Rd., Scranton, PA 18505
(717) 969-7669

snow report:	(800) GOT-SNOW
elevation:	2,000 feet
vertical:	1,000 feet
longest run:	1 mile

PENNSYLVANIA SKI AREAS *(continued)*

Montage, continued
 total slopes and trails: 20
           33% difficult, 45% intermediate, 22% easy
 chairlifts: 1 quad, 3 triple, 1 double, 2 tow

Spring Mountain Ski Area
 P.O. Box 42, Spring Mount, PA 19478
 (610) 287-7900
 snow report: (610) 287-7900
 elevation: 528 feet
 vertical: 420 feet
 longest run: 2,200 feet
 total slopes and trails: 7
           20% difficult, 40% intermediate, 40% easy
 chairlifts: 3 doubles, 1 triple, 1 rope

Central

Crystal Lake
 RR #1, P.O. Box 308, Hughesville, PA 17737
 (717) 584-2698
 snow report: (717) 584-4209
 elevation: 2,100 feet
 vertical: 250 feet
 longest run: 1,300 feet
 total slopes and trails: 4
           10% difficult, 60% intermediate, 30% easy
 chairlifts: 1 poma, 1 rope, 1 pony

Whitetail Resort
 13805 Blairs Valley Rd., Mercersburg, PA 17236
 (717) 328-9400
 snow report: (717) 328-9400
 elevation: 1,800 feet
 vertical: 935 feet
 longest run: 4,900 feet
 total slopes and trails: 17
           25% difficult, 53% intermediate, 22% easy
 chairlifts: 3 quad, 1 tow, 1 double, 1 HS detach quad

Ski Denton
 U.S. Route 6, Coudersport, PA 16915
 (814) 435-2115

PENNSYLVANIA SKI AREAS *(continued)*

Ski Denton, continued

snow report:	(814) 435-2115
elevation:	2,885 feet
vertical:	650 feet
longest run:	1 mile
total slopes and trails:	20
	33% difficult, 32% intermediate, 35% easy
chairlifts:	1 triple, 1 double, 1 handle, 2 poma

Ski Liberty
PA Route 116 & Sanders Rd., Fairfield, PA 17320
(717) 642-8282

snow report:	(717) 642-8282
elevation:	1,186 feet
vertical:	600 feet
longest run:	5,300 feet
total slopes and trails:	14
	30% difficult, 40% intermediate, 30% easy
chairlifts:	3 quad, 3 double, 1 J-bar, 1 handle

Ski Roundtop
925 Roundtop Road, Lewisberry, PA 17339
(717) 432-9631

snow report:	(717) 432-9631
elevation:	1,355 feet
vertical:	600 feet
longest run:	4,100 feet
total slopes and trails:	14
	35% difficult, 30% intermediate, 35% easy
chairlifts:	1 quad, 1 triple, 4 double, 2 pony, 2 J-bar

Ski Sawmill Mountain Resort
P.O. Box 5, Morris, PA 16938
(717) 353-7731

snow report:	(800) 532-SNOW
elevation:	2,215 feet
vertical:	515 feet
longest run:	4,100 feet
total slopes and trails:	8
	20% difficult, 30% intermediate, 50% easy
chairlifts:	1 double, 2 T-bar

PENNSYLVANIA SKI AREAS *(continued)*

Tussy Mountain Ski Area
P.O. Box 559, State College, PA 16804
(814) 466-6810

snow report:	(814) 466-6810
elevation:	1,680 feet
vertical:	515 feet
longest run:	2,700 feet
total slopes and trails:	10
	25% difficult, 50% intermediate, 25% easy
chairlifts:	1 quad, 3 T-bar, 1 poma, 1 handle

Western

Blue Knob Recreation Area
P.O. Box 247, Claysburg, PA 16625
(814) 239-5111

snow report:	(800) 822-3045 in PA;
	(800) 458-3403 out of state
elevation:	3,152 feet
vertical:	1,072 feet
longest run:	2 miles
total slopes and trails:	21
	38% difficult, 33% intermediate, 29% easy
chairlifts:	2 triple, 2 double, 3 platters

Boyce Park Ski Area
675 Old Frankstown Rd., Pittsburgh, PA 15239
(412) 733-4656

snow report:	(412) 733-4665
elevation:	1,272 feet
vertical:	172 feet
longest run:	1,200 feet
total slopes and trails:	9
	60% intermediate, 40% easy
chairlifts:	2 double, 2 T-bar, 1 poma

Hidden Valley
4 Craighead Dr., Hidden Valley, PA 15502
(814) 443-2600

snow report:	(800) 443-SKII
elevation:	3,000 feet
vertical:	610 feet

PENNSYLVANIA SKI AREAS *(continued)*

Hidden Valley, continued
longest run:	1 mile
total slopes and trails:	17
	30% difficult, 35% intermediate, 35% easy
chairlifts:	1 quad, 2 triple, 3 double, 2 pony

Edinboro Ski Area
P.O. Box 447, Edinboro, PA 16412
(814) 734-1641

snow report:	(814) 734-1641
elevation:	1,550 feet
vertical:	320 feet
longest run:	2,800 feet
total slopes and trails:	11
	15% difficult, 75% intermediate, 10% easy
chairlifts:	2 T-bar, 1 handle, 1 poma

Seven Springs Resort
R.D. 1, Champion, PA 15622
(814) 352-7777

snow report:	(800) 523-7777
elevation:	2,990 feet
vertical:	750 feet
longest run:	1.25 miles
total slopes and trails:	31
	15% difficult, 45% intermediate, 40% easy
chairlifts:	2 quad, 7 triple, 2 double, 7 rope

HIKING

Most hiking trails in Pennsylvania are located within public lands; however, a number of long trails traverse the countryside between them, connecting parks, forests, and game lands. Among these are the Appalachian National Scenic Trail; the Donut Hole Trail; the Horseshoe Trail; the Laurel Highlands Hiking Trail, which is part of the Potomac Heritage National Scenic Trail; the Mason-Dixon Trail; the Mid-State Trail System; the Susquehannock Trail System; and the North Country Trail, a third National Scenic Trail currently in progress.

The **Appalachian National Scenic Trail** enters Pennsylvania (north to south) in the southern end of the Delaware Water Gap National Recreation Area and follows a southwestern route for 228 miles to Pen Mar on the Maryland state line.

From the Delaware Water Gap, the

trail climbs over 1,000 feet, affording fine views of the Delaware River. The trail continues south, remaining, for the most part, on the ridgeline. After crossing Wind Gap, it climbs onto the Blue Mountain Ridge and into State Game Lands No. 168. It continues along the ridge, traversing several gaps, and then drops into the deep Lehigh Gap and crosses the Lehigh River before climbing into State Game Lands No. 217. Elevations are around 1,400 feet here, with many exceptional views. The trail may be accessed at many points in this area.

The trail continues another 28 miles along the Blue Mountain Ridge, passing through State Game Lands No. 106, then takes an eastern turn and climbs to the Pinnacle (1,450 feet) for one of the best views along the trail. It drops steeply to cross the Schuylkill River at Port Clinton, then climbs again into State Game Lands No. 110, where it connects with several side trails.

At PA Route 183, the trail enters State Game Lands No. 80, which it traverses, still along the ridge, dropping again to cross the Swatara Gap and Swatara Creek before climbing into the St. Anthony's Wilderness and State Game Lands No. 211. On top of Sharp Mountain, the trail meets the northern terminus of the Horseshoe Trail, coming in from the east.

The Appalachian Trail ascends Peters Mountain and follows its ridgeline to the Susquehanna River, where it drops to cross the river at 250 feet elevation. Then the trail climbs to the ridge once more, entering State Game Lands No. 170 over Cove Mountain and Blue Mountain, where it meets the Tuscarora Trail on the west and the Darlington Trail on the east.

The trail then descends to cross the rural Cumberland Valley on farm roads. Leaving the valley, it meets the Mason-Dixon Trail at Whiskey Spring. It then climbs Piney Mountain and enters Michaux State Forest. Following the ridgeline of Piney Mountain, the trail traverses Pine Grove Furnace State Park, which is located in the forest.

The trail continues through the forest toward Maryland, traversing Caledonia State Park and following the contours of the plateaulike South Mountain Ridge, at elevations ranging between 1,000 and 2,000 feet. It enters Maryland at Pen Mar Park on the state line.

Most of the Appalachian Trail follows high, remote ridges; when the trail crosses lowlands and rivers, however, it is often routed along roads and bridges. The scenery is continually impressive. The route is also historic. Shelters are located at convenient intervals.

The **Donut Hole Trail** is a 56-mile trail crossing much of the northern part of Sproul State Forest. It is appealing for its remoteness and solitude. Along the way, it follows a convoluted, roughly east-west route, crossing Hyner Run and Kettle Creek State Parks. It connects with several other trails and joins the Susquehannock Trail for a short distance. The trailheads are in Hyner Run State Park in the east and at Montour Road at Route 120 near Sinnemahoning in the west.

The 130-mile-long **Horseshoe Trail** is the northernmost of two trails that, together, form a 334-mile great eastern loop connecting at both ends with the Appalachian Trail in Pennsylvania. From its trailhead at Valley Forge National Historical Park, the Horseshoe Trail heads north and west through forests, fields, and orchards to join the Appalachian Trail on top of Sharp Mountain near Hershey. At Ludwigs Corner, a few miles north of Valley Forge, it meets the Mason-Dixon Trail, which follows a circuitous route roughly southwest, and it connects with the Appalachian Trail at Whiskey Springs, thus completing the loop. As the name indicates, hikers share this trail with equestrians.

The 70-mile **Laurel Highlands Hiking Trail** is a designated section of the Potomac Heritage National Scenic Trail. An exceptional hiking trail, it extends south and west from the upper end of the 1,000-foot-deep Conemaugh River Gorge south of Seward to the rugged Youghiogheny Gorge in Ohiopyle State Park. The trail follows the ridge of Laurel Mountain at an average altitude of 2,700 feet, except where it drops 1,000 feet or so to wind its way across the plateau of Fayette and Somerset Counties. Along the way, it traverses a string of state parks (Laurel Mountain, Laurel Hill, and Laurel Ridge), Forbes State Forest, and State Game Lands Nos. 111 and 42.

Views are spectacular no matter what the season: blooming laurel and rhododendron in spring, blazing foliage in the fall, varied greens in summer, and snow for the skier in winter. Some sections of the trail are rugged, particularly in the southern end. Eight overnight areas, somewhat apart from the trail, are located at convenient intervals. Reservations are handled by Laurel Ridge State Park.

The 204 miles of the **Mason-Dixon Trail** in Pennsylvania are the southern section of a great eastern loop (334 miles) connecting at both ends to the Appalachian National Scenic Trail. Beginning at the Appalachian Trail connection at Whiskey Springs near Mount Holly Springs, the trail at first follows a southeastern route for about 50 miles, roughly paralleling the west bank of the Susquehanna River through a corner of eastern Maryland to its mouth at Havre de Grace. It then heads northeast through western Delaware and crosses back into Pennsylvania to meet the Horseshoe Trail at Ludwigs Corner. The Horseshoe Trail goes north and west to connect with the Appalachian Trail on top of Sharp Mountain in State Game Lands No. 211, thus completing the loop.

The Mason-Dixon Trail is an easy one, traversing stream valleys, woods, and fields through mostly rural countryside and lovely historic areas. The southern section passes through Gifford Pinchot State Park. Along the high banks of the Susquehanna, the climber is rewarded with beautiful views of the river. On its return to Pennsylvania in its northern swing, the trail traverses Maryland's Elk Neck State Forest.

The **Mid-State Trail System** is one of Pennsylvania's longest internal trail systems, connecting with over 75 side trails. It extends 168 miles from Bohen Run north of Blackwell in Tioga County southward, then westward to Route 22 at the town of Water Street in Huntingdon County. At its northern end, it connects with the West Rim Trail, which traverses the western rim of Pennsylvania's Grand Canyon. Almost entirely on public land, the Mid-State Trail System traverses and connects four state forests, six state parks, and eight natural areas, as well as the Stone Valley Recreation Area. The ridges afford splendid views of the surrounding countryside, both rural and wild, depending on the location. Primitive campsites are located along the trail.

The Susquehannock Trail System is an 85-mile broad loop through the Susquehannock State Forest via old logging roads, footpaths, and abandoned railroad rights-of-way. The trailheads are in the Ole Bull State Park in the south and Patterson State Park in the north. The trail also can be accessed at Prouty Place, Lyman Run, and Denton Hill State Parks. Ten miles traverse the Hammersley Wild Area; this is the longest section without a road crossing. The trail connects with the Donut Hole Trail and the North and South Link Trails, as well as many forest trails. The northern section in the Denton Hill area offers excellent cross-country skiing.

A third National Scenic Trail, the **North Country Trail,** is a work in progress. This 3,200-mile trail will extend from the western shore of Lake Champlain to the Badlands of North Dakota and connect there with the Lewis and Clark Trail. About 220 miles of this trail will traverse Pennsylvania, proceeding south through the Allegheny National Forest and Cook Forest State Park, and then westward into Ohio. A 100-mile section through these two forests and a 20-mile section through Moraine and McConnells Mill State Parks are already completed.

Pennsylvania also offers many trails on a smaller scale to be enjoyed. Some of the best of these include the following, all designated National Recreational Trails:

Baptism Creek Trail, an 0.8-mile hiking and equestrian trail at Hopewell Village National Historic Site in Berks County.

East Impoundment Trail, a 3-mile hiking and biking trail at Tinicum National Environmental Center in Philadelphia.

Fairmount Park Bikeway, an 8.5-mile foot and bicycle trail in Philadelphia. Also in the park, **Wissahickon Trail,** a 5.4-mile multipurpose trail.

Friendship Hill Trail, a 5.4-mile trail near New Geneva traversing the 675-acre Friendship Hill National Historic Site on the east bank of the Monongahela River, 3 miles north of Point Marion in Fayette County.

Harrisburg River Front Bicycle Trail, a 4-mile bike and foot path along the Susquehanna River.

John Bartram's Garden Trail, a 1-mile footpath and interpretive trail in Philadelphia.

Kellys Run–Pinnacle Trail, located near the Holtwood Dam on the Susquehanna River in Lancaster County. This 4.7-mile hiking and horse trail has some rugged spots.

Lehigh Parkway Heritage Trail, a 7-mile hiking, biking, and equestrian trail in the city of Allentown.

Towpath Bike Trail, a 7.8-mile hiking and biking trail in Bethlehem and Palmer Townships in Northampton County.

Union Canal Walking and Bicycle Trail, a 2.3-mile trail in the city of Reading.

BIKING

Pennsylvania, with its diverse and interesting terrain, is one of the best places in the country for cyclists. Gov. Tom Ridge is a cyclist, and the state has made an effort to increase drivers' awareness of the need to share the road with cyclists. The Department of Transportation has published the *Bicycling Directory of Pennsylvania, 1995–96,* which covers every aspect of cycling. Numerous books on the bike trails and tours in the state are also available.

A 180-mile section of the 2,440-mile Maine-to-Florida Bicycle Route enters Pennsylvania west of the Susquehanna River at Delta and runs south to north. At Columbia, the route crosses the river and heads north and northeast into Philadelphia, following the Susquehanna and Schuylkill River Valleys. From Philadelphia, the route turns north to New Hope, where it crosses the Delaware River into New Jersey.

The route generally follows rural and suburban roads over rolling piedmont terrain. It passes through or near many parks and trail systems, including Hopewell Village National Historic Site, the Mason-Dixon and Horseshoe Trails, Valley Forge National Historical Park, and the Delaware Water Gap National Recreation Area.

There are three cross-state bike tours: in July, the ALA Bike H.O.P., which benefits the American Lung Association, and Pedal Pennsylvania, both over 450 miles and crossing Pennsylvania from Pittsburgh to Philadelphia; in August, the Perimeter Ride against Cancer, which benefits the Lehigh Valley Cancer Society, covers over 500 miles from Allentown.

Bicycling is permitted in 20 state parks, and bike rentals are available in five of them: Bald Eagle, Moraine, Ohiopyle, Oil Creek, and Pine Grove Furnace. Many trails are multipurpose, and responsible bicyclists are welcome.

Pennsylvania law requires all cyclists under age 12 to wear an approved bicycle helmet; prudent riders of all ages do so.

HORSEBACK RIDING

Twenty-four state parks have a total of 224 miles of bridle paths. The longest, 60 miles, is in the Delaware Canal State Park. The other parks are as follows:

Big Pocono (5 miles)
Blue Knob (8 miles)
Canoe Creek (5 miles)
Codorus (7 miles)
Cook Forest (5 miles)
Evansburg (15 miles)
French Creek (16 miles)
Gifford Pinchot (4 miles)
Jacobsburg (5 miles)
Kettle Creek (5 miles)
Keystone (2 miles)
Laurel Hill (3 miles)
Marsh Creek (6 miles)
Moraine (16 miles)
Nockamixon (15 miles)
Prince Gallitzin (2 miles)
Raccoon Creek (17 miles)
Ricketts Glen (5 miles)
Ridley Creek (5 miles)
Susquehannock (1 mile)
Tyler (9 miles)
White Clay Creek Preserve (6 miles)
Worlds End (4 miles)

Extensive bridle paths also exist in Sproul, Tuscarora, and Wyoming State Forests.

The Horseshoe Trail, a combination equestrian and hiking path, passes through French Creek State Park on its northwesterly route, 130 miles from Valley Forge National Historical Park through five counties to Denhart Dam, near Harrisburg.

BIRD-WATCHING

The state of Pennsylvania offers scores of great places for bird-watching. State game lands (off-season), parks, and forestlands provide opportunities to watch birds in their natural habitat. And migrating waterfowl love Pennsylvania's great water environment.

In two national wildlife refuges, birding is a major activity. The John Heinz National Environmental Center at Tinicum, near the Philadelphia Airport, is on the Atlantic Flyway. About 280 species of migrating birds and ducks have been counted here. The seasons are March and April and September through November. The center has about 1,350 acres of tidal wetlands crossed by 10 miles of trails.

At the Erie National Wildlife Refuge, near Guys Mills in Crawford County, 35 miles south of Lake Erie, birders have sighted 236 species of birds; 112 species nest here. Major duck and goose migrations pass through here in March and April and September through November. The refuge also attracts marsh birds and waterbirds, as well as songbirds. State Game Lands No. 69 is adjacent to the refuge, has similar terrain, and also attracts migrating birds.

Presque Isle State Park is a big migratory bird stopover. Over 300 species have been recorded here. Migration peaks in the area in May and September. Gull Point, a critical habitat for nesting and migrating birds, is closed from April through November.

The migration of hawks is a special annual event in the commonwealth. Hawk Mountain Sanctuary was the first refuge for birds of prey in the world. It is on a major migratory bird route; an average of 20,000 hawks, eagles, ospreys, and falcons soar over Kittatinny Ridge between August 15 and December 15 each year. There are numerous lookouts in the 2,380-acre preserve. Be prepared for weekend crowds; over 80,000 bird-watchers visit annually. There is a trail fee. The sanctuary is located north of I-78, between Drehersville and Eckville at the Berks-Schuylkill County border.

Waggoners Gap is on PA Route 74 8 miles north of Carlisle, at the crest of Blue Mountain. Thousands of raptors— bald eagles, ospreys, and many kinds of hawks—pass over on their way south; golden eagles join the migration in October through mid-November.

State Game Lands No. 97, in Huntingdon County near Everett, offers hawk-watching on a ridge of Tussey Mountain. The hawks are less numerous here, but so are the humans, as a minimum 1-mile walk from the road to the lookout discourages many viewers. September is prime time.

The main attraction at Middle Creek Wildlife Management Area, State Game Lands No. 46, off Hopeland Road from PA Route 897 near Kleinfeltersville in Lebanon and Lancaster Counties, is tundra swans, thousands of which stop here briefly in mid-February en route to Canada and Alaska. Other migrating birds use the area during periods when hunting is prohibited—March through mid-September. The elegant visitors center has many exhibits.

Delaware Water Gap National Recreation Area is the place to see eagles, especially in January and February, and especially in the north end of the area, near Milford. Migrating hawks fly over Mount Minsi, at the south end, in autumn. The area is also on a major flyway of migrating waterfowl and shorebirds.

Pymatuning State Park in Jamestown attracts some 20,000 Canada geese and many ducks each autumn. Bald eagles nest here; active nests can be observed in early spring. Birders should visit on

Sundays, if possible, when hunting is prohibited.

There is a sanctuary for little brown bats in an old church near the main entrance of Canoe Creek State Park. Up to 10,000 bats roost here on summer days. The thrill comes at dusk, when thousands of bats leave the church to feed on insects.

Raccoon Creek State Park is best known as the site of a wildflower reserve, with over 500 species of flowering plants. But it is also the place to see warblers, both migrating and resident. Woodpeckers and other songbirds abound. Flowers and birds both peak in the springtime.

The Brucker Great Blue Heron Sanctuary of Thiel College in Greenville, Mercer County, is a unique habitat of these dramatic birds. Over 250 nests can be observed on about 50 acres of land. The nests are 4 feet wide and are located about 50 to 75 feet above the ground. There is an observation shelter on the grounds. No walking around is permitted during the nesting season, February to September.

Mill Grove, the Audubon Wildlife Sanctuary in Montgomery County, home of John James Audubon from 1804 to 1806, provides the opportunity to spot some of the 175 species of birds that have been observed in the 130 acres of fields and woods. Visitors may also view prints from Audubon's *Birds of America* in a museum in the stone farmhouse, built in 1762 and once owned by John Penn. Murals depict Audubon's life and various scenes of bird life. Porcelain birds by Edward Boehm are also on display. The building is open Tuesday to Sunday, 10:00 A.M. to 4:00 P.M.; the grounds are open from dawn to dusk.

ENVIRONMENTAL ORGANIZATIONS

Pennsylvania Environmental Council
1211 Chestnut St., Suite 900
Philadelphia, PA 19107
Works on issues of land use, growth management, transportation, and air and water pollution

Pennsylvania Wildlife Federation
2426 N. 2nd St.
Harrisburg, PA 17110
Helps organizations and industry conserve wildlife and natural resources

Western Pennsylvania Conservancy
316 Fourth St.
Pittsburgh, PA 15222
The largest private land conservation agency in the state; has saved 200,000 acres and acquired the land for five state parks

The Nature Conservancy
1211 Chestnut St., 12th Floor
Philadelphia, PA 19107
Has purchased 36,000 acres of threatened habitat in Pennsylvania

Sierra Club
623 Catherine St.
Philadelphia, PA 19147
The country's most visible environmental group; concerned with every aspect of the environment

National Audubon Society
Mid-Atlantic Regional Office
1104 Fernwood Ave.
Camp Hill, PA 17011
Promotes ecology, energy conservation, and restoration of natural resources, with emphasis on wildlife habitat

4

Plants and Wildlife

PLANT LIFE

There are 2,076 native plant species in Pennsylvania. About 350 of them are currently at risk of being lost due to habitat destruction and degradation. The clearing of land for agriculture and for residential and industrial development is the greatest threat. Secondary impacts include pollution and the introduction of aggressive, non-native species that invade native habitats.

There are 108 species of native trees and many others that were introduced from Europe and Asia. The species described here represent the most common trees in the state.

Trees

Butternut, also called white walnut, is a small to medium-size tree, 30 to 50 feet tall, found in rich bottomlands and on fertile hillsides. It is more common in Northern Tier counties. The wood is used chiefly for furniture, instrument cases, and boxes. The nuts are an important wildlife food. A fungal disease has recently killed many butternut trees throughout their range.

Black walnut is found mainly in the southern part of the state. The wood is valuable for quality furniture, veneer, gunstocks, and musical instruments.

Eastern hemlock is the official state tree of Pennsylvania. A large, long-lived tree, it is used in construction and as a source of tannic acid for tanning leather. It is found in cool, moist woods throughout the commonwealth. Ruffed grouse, wild turkey, and songbirds find food (seeds) and shelter in this tree. Deer browse it heavily during winter snows.

Eastern red cedar is adaptable to a variety of conditions. It is common in abandoned farm fields in the southern tier counties and on rocky bluffs. It reaches heights of 40 feet. The wood is used for fence posts, and mothproof chests. Cedar waxwings and other song and game birds eat the fruits.

Colorado blue spruce is a widely planted ornamental in Pennsylvania. It is native to the Rocky Mountains and can reach 150 feet in height.

Norway spruce is a European species that is extensively planted as an ornamental. The wood is used chiefly for paper pulp, boxes and crates, and lumber.

Red pine is a valuable timber tree in the northern part of the state; its wood is used chiefly for construction lumber. The red pine is native on the dry slopes of Luzerne, Wyoming, Tioga, and Centre

Counties and is planted extensively by the Bureau of Forestry and the Pennsylvania Game Commission. Songbirds, mice, and chipmunks feed on the seeds.

Scotch pine is native to Europe and thrives anywhere, except in shade. It typically reaches 70 feet, but it can attain 120 feet with a diameter of 3 to 5 feet. It is widely planted for reforestation and landscaping.

Table mountain pine typically attains a height of 30 to 40 feet and, consequently, is too small for lumbering. It thrives on the dry, rocky, gravelly slopes and ridgetops in the south-central and southeastern counties, where it helps to prevent erosion.

Virginia pine is a southern species that reaches its northern limit in Pennsylvania. It is valuable as a cover for worn-out farmland and is harvested for pulpwood. Also called scrub pine, this small tree attains a height of 30 to 40 feet on sandy or poor rocky soils of barrens and ridgetops.

Pitch pine is a medium-size tree, 40 to 50 feet high, that is widespread in Pennsylvania except in the northwestern counties. It thrives in poor, sandy soils and areas where forest fires have killed most other trees. Its wood has a high resin content and is used for railroad ties, construction timber, pulpwood, and fuel. Pitch pine seeds are eaten by nuthatches, pine grosbeaks, and black-capped chickadees, and deer and rabbits browse the seedlings.

Eastern white pine is a large tree that usually reaches 50 to 90 feet in height. It is one of the most valuable timber trees, found in moist or dry woodlands throughout the state. Porcupines, deer, rodents, and many birds feed on the seeds and twigs of this tree.

American larch is a medium-size tree also known as eastern larch or tamarack. It is the only cone-bearing tree native to Pennsylvania that loses its needles annually, and it likes moist locations. The wood is used chiefly for paper pulp, lumber, posts, and railroad ties.

Flowering dogwood is a small native tree with a low, spreading crown, especially valued as an ornamental. The wood is used primarily for textile weaving shuttles.

Catalpa is native to southern states and is usually planted for its shade and flowers. The wood is durable and useful for posts.

Norway maple was imported from northern Europe and extensively planted along city streets and in parks. It typically reaches 50 feet in height.

Red maple, an excellent ornamental tree, is found in a variety of habitats, although it grows best in wet soils. It typically reaches 50 feet but can exceed 100 feet. It is heavily browsed by deer and rabbits, and its seeds are consumed by rodents.

Silver maple is found in moist woodlands and on streambanks, where it typically reaches heights of 50 to 60 feet. Many mammals and birds eat the seeds.

Striped maple has distinctive white stripes that make it an attractive ornamental species. It usually reaches 10 to 25 feet in height and is common in the mountains on moist, cool, shaded slopes and in deep ravines.

Sugar maple, also called the rock maple for its hard wood, is an important timber tree used for furniture, musical instruments, and flooring. The sap is tapped for maple syrup production. This tree is found on moist, wooded slopes throughout the state and typically reaches 60 to 80 feet high. Birds and rodents eat the seeds; deer, squirrels, porcupines, and other mammals browse the twigs, buds, and bark.

Box elder is typically found in low, moist areas, floodplains, and on streambanks. A medium-size tree, it occasionally reaches 70 feet in height. It is valued as an ornamental.

White ash is a large tree, often reaching 80 feet or more, with a long, straight trunk. The wood is used for baseball bats, handles, agricultural tools, and furniture. The juice from the leaf is reputedly effective in relieving the itch of mosquito bites. It is a fall foliage delight.

Black ash, sometimes called swamp ash, is found in cool swamps, wet woods, and bottomlands throughout the commonwealth. This medium-size tree is generally lighter in weight and weaker than white ash but is used for the same purposes. Wood ducks, game birds, songbirds, and many mammals eat the seeds; white-tailed deer browse the twigs and young foliage.

Buckeyes. Three buckeye species are found in Pennsylvania: Horsechestnut, or European buckeye, is a native of Greece planted as a shade tree in towns; yellow buckeye, or sweet buckeye, and Ohio buckeye are native to moist woods along streams in southwestern Pennsylvania.

Cucumbertree magnolia is a medium-size tree native to rich upland woods and slopes in western Pennsylvania. Its wood is used mainly for interior finish, furniture, and containers. Songbirds, squirrels, and mice eat the seeds.

Black gum, also called black tupelo, usually grows to 40 feet in height on dry slopes and ridgetops but can reach 100 feet in moist areas near streams. It is most common in southeast and south-central counties and rarer in the Northern Tier. The wood is used for boxes, fuel, and railroad ties. The fruit, twigs, and foliage provide food for many birds and animals. Its brilliant red autumn color and abundant blue fruits make the species an interesting ornamental.

Redbud is usually a small tree, 15 to 20 feet high with a trunk diameter of 6 inches, although it has been known to reach 30 feet. It is prized for its bright, rose-colored flowers in early spring. Wild populations are limited to the southern half of the commonwealth, but the tree is successfully cultivated farther north.

Common sassafras is a small to medium-size tree that grows to 50 feet high, with crooked branches. It has a spicy odor, and its oil is used for a tea, in medicines, and in perfumes. The wood is used for fuel and fence posts.

Bigtooth aspen is important for regenerating forest cover, protecting soil and slower-growing species. The seeds sprout best in open areas after cutting or fire and spread rapidly by sending up suckers from the roots. Many animals browse the twigs and buds in winter and spring. The wood is used chiefly for making paper.

Quaking aspen grows quickly to 30 to 40 feet tall, but it is shortlived. It is important for revegetating recently cut or burned areas. The wood is used chiefly for pulp in manufacturing paper and cardboard. Many animals browse the twigs, and it is a favorite food of beaver.

American beech is found in moist, rich soils throughout the state but is most abundant in the north. It is an important timber species typically reaching 50 to 60 feet and often higher. Its nuts are very important food for wildlife, including bears, squirrels, turkeys, and grouse. Beech is a handsome shade tree for large, open areas in parks and golf courses.

Paper birch grows to 50 to 75 feet high on upland woods and slopes in north-central and northeastern Pennsylvania. Its seeds and buds are eaten by the ruffed grouse, and its twigs are browsed by deer. Native Americans used the bark for constructing canoes, shelters, and containers.

Sweet birch, also known as black birch or cherry birch, normally attains a height of 50 to 60 feet and is found in a variety of sites from rich, fertile lowlands to rocky ridges throughout the state. The wood is used for fuel, furniture, and boxes, Distillation of the bark and twigs produces an oil sold as a substitute for wintergreen. Fermented sap can be used to make birch beer. Ruffed grouse feed on buds and seeds, and deer and rabbits browse the twigs.

Yellow birch is a medium to large tree, commonly 60 to 75 feet tall, occasionally 100 feet. It prefers moist, cool soils and cool summer temperatures. It is often found on north-facing slopes and swamps. The wood is used for furniture, flooring, doors, and cabinets. Ruffed grouse feed on its buds and seeds, and deer and rabbits browse the twigs.

Black cherry grows throughout the state to 50 to 75 feet. It thrives in fertile alluvial soil but also grows on dry slopes. The hard, reddish brown wood is highly prized for quality furniture and interior trim. Many game birds, song-birds, and mammals, including black bears, eat the fruits and seeds.

Chokecherry is a fast-growing but short-lived shrub or small tree that rarely exceeds 25 feet. It is found in a variety of habitats and is more abundant in the western counties. It is one of the first species to revegetate cleared areas. The chokecherry is attractive in spring flower and provides food to several dozen species of birds and mammals.

Fire cherry, also called pin cherry, is common in the mountains but rare in the southeast and southwest corners. It is a valuable reforestation species after fire or lumbering clears the land. It provides shade for seedlings of other tree species that follow it in succession. The fruits are food for many small mammals, and deer browse the twigs and young leaves.

Serviceberry is a small tree, typically under 40 feet tall. It is also called shadbush or shadblow, referring to its blooming as the shad ascend rivers to spawn. Snowy white flowers of service-berry, seen through the still-naked oaks, provide one of the first floral displays of spring on Pennsylvania ridges. The fruits are excellent food for birds, bears, and other wildlife, and humans eat the berries as well. Seven shrub species of serviceberry are also found in Pennsylvania.

American elm is a large and highly prized shade tree found throughout Pennsylvania, mainly in moist areas. The hard, tough wood is used in the manufacture of boxes, barrels, and furniture.

Slippery elm is a medium-size tree usually found near streams. The crown does not droop like that of the American elm. The wood is commonly marketed with American elm.

Common hackberry is a small tree 20 to 35 feet tall, larger in southern Pennsylvania in moist limestone soils. A second, smaller species, dwarf hackberry, is found on dry slopes in southeastern Pennsylvania. Fruits of both species are an important wildlife food.

American linden, also called basswood, is usually found mixed with other hardwoods in moist, rich valley soils. The wood is used for a variety of products, including boxes, venetian blinds, doors, picture frames, and furniture.

Red mulberry is typically found in rich, moist alluvial soils and lower slopes and reaches a height of 35 to 50 feet with a 12- to 18-inch diameter. The fruit is eaten by birds, animals, and humans.

Black oak is one of the most common oaks on dry, upland sites. The acorns are eaten by wildlife but are not preferred. The young stems and twigs are browsed by deer. The wood is sold as red oak for general construction lumber and furniture.

Northern red oak is a dominant forest tree throughout the state. It grows to 90 feet in moist to dry soils. Deer, bears, and many other mammals and birds eat the acorns. The hard, strong wood is used for furniture, flooring, millwork, railroad ties, and veneer.

Pin oak is typically found in wet sites and grows to 60 feet tall. It is a desirable street tree because of its beautiful form and ability to withstand the low oxygen content of urban soils. Its acorns are valuable food for birds and mammals. The wood is of limited commercial value because it tends to warp and split when dried.

Scarlet oak is a medium to large tree found on dry upland sites. The acorns are important food for many mammals and larger birds. The tree is often infected by fungus, which rots the wood.

Chestnut oak, also called rock oak or basket oak, grows to 80 feet on dry slopes and ridgetops throughout the state. Large crops of acorns produced every four to seven years are important food for deer, bears, turkeys, and many other birds and animals. The wood is used for furniture, flooring, millwork, and railroad ties.

White oak is a dominant forest tree that grows to 80 to 100 feet tall on dry to moist sites throughout the state. The acorns are important wildlife food. Traditional uses of white oak wood include hardwood flooring, whiskey barrels, and boatbuilding. The famous Revolutionary War frigate USS *Constitution,* "Old Ironsides," was made of white oak.

American chestnut was formerly the most common and arguably the most valuable tree in Pennsylvania for both its wood and its nuts but the species was nearly wiped out by a bark disease called chestnut blight. It persists as stump sprouts and small trees, however. Chinese chestnut, which is resistant to the blight, is planted for its 1-inch nuts.

Sycamore, also called buttonwood or American planetree, is a massive tree typically found on streambanks and floodplains, where it attains heights of 70 to 125 feet. The wood is used for furniture, butcher blocks, and flooring.

Tulip tree, also known as yellow poplar, white poplar, whitewood, or tulip poplar, is the tallest of the eastern hardwoods. The wood is used for veneer. Songbirds and game birds, rabbits, squirrels, and mice feed on the seeds, and white-tailed deer browse the young growth.

Black willow is the largest of our native willows, typically reaching 30 feet in height. It is found on streambanks and in wet meadows throughout the state, most commonly in the east and south. The wood is used in wickerwork, and the bark contains medicinal compounds. Deer browse the shoots. Weeping willow is a commonly cultivated species originally from china.

Witch hazel is a small tree or large shrub found in moist, rocky locations. It occasionally ascends slopes to rather dry sites. A medicinal extract is distilled from the bark.

Black locust is found in open woods, floodplains, thickets, and fencerows, where it grows to 45 feet high. The wood is in demand for posts, poles, railroad ties, and mine timbers. Trees growing in poor soils are heavily damaged by several insects and wood rot. Squirrels eat the seeds, and bees make honey from the nectar of the flowers.

Common honeylocust is found naturally in rich, moist bottomlands in southwestern Pennsylvania and is widely planted as an ornamental throughout the state. The wood is used for fence posts and general construction, but it is not widely available. Many animals, including cattle, feed on the pods and seedlings.

Bitternut hickory normally attains heights of 60 to 70 feet when growing in moist, fertile bottomland soils, but it can also be found on well-drained uplands throughout the state. The wood of this species is somewhat more brittle than other hickories, and the nuts are too bitter to eat. It is reported to be the best wood for smoking ham and bacon, giving a rich flavor.

Mockernut hickory is so named because the nuts are large but have thick shells and very small kernels. Found in moist, open woods and slopes mostly in the southern part of the state, the tree usually reaches 50 to 75 feet high. The wood is heavy, hard, and strong and is used for tool handles and furniture.

Pignut hickory reaches 50 to 60 feet high on dry ridgetops and slopes throughout the southern half of the state. The nuts are too bitter for humans, but they are an important food for squirrels and chipmunks. The wood is principally used for tool handles.

Shagbark hickory is found in rich soils on slopes and valleys throughout the state. The nuts are much relished by both humans and wildlife. Native Americans crushed the kernels and used the oil for cooking and the resulting flour for bread. The wood is used principally for tool handles and for smoking meat.

Shellbark hickory, also known as kingnut hickory, is found in moist to wet fertile bottomlands across southern Pennsylvania. The nuts are enjoyed by both humans and wildlife.

Tree of heaven is originally from China and was first planted in America near Philadelphia by English settlers. It is now found in disturbed woods, roadsides, vacant lots, and railroad banks across southern Pennsylvania. It is almost impossible to eradicate once established.

WILDLIFE
Mammals
The very diverse physical environment of the state of Pennsylvania provides the different habitats within which more than 60 species of mammals live.

MAMMALS

Pouched Mammals	Virginia opossum
Shrews and Moles	*Shrews:* masked, Maryland, water, smoky, long-tailed, pygmy, northern short-tailed, and least *Moles:* hairy-tailed, eastern, and star-nosed
Bats	*Myotis:* little brown, Keen's, Indiana, small-footed, and eastern pipistrelle *Bats:* silver-haired, big brown, red, seminole, hoary, and evening
Rabbits and Hares	eastern and New England cottontail rabbits, and snowshoe hare
Gnawing Mammals	gray, fox, red, southern flying, and northern flying squirrels; eastern chipmunk; woodchuck; beaver; porcupine; southern bog lemming; muskrat; marsh rice, Norway, and eastern wood rats; white-footed deer, house, meadow jumping, and woodland jumping mice; southern red-backed, meadow, rock, and woodland voles
Carnivores	coyote, red and gray foxes, black bear, raccoon, ermine, least and long-tailed weasels, mink, eastern spotted and striped skunks, river otter, and bobcat
Even-Toed Hoofed Mammals	white-tailed deer, elk

Black Bear. The black bear is the largest carnivore in the state. Adults weigh between 200 and 400 pounds on average and are usually 5 to 5½ feet long. (The largest bear killed in the 1995 bear season weighted 605 pounds.) Bears are most common in the heavily forested hills and valleys of the northern counties, where the thick underbrush provides shelter and protection. There are many color variations in black bears. The face and muzzle are tan, and a white spot may appear on the breast.

Black bears travel alone and spend enormous amounts of time eating everything from berries and plants to insects, small animals (dead or alive), fish, garbage, and the occasional picnic lunch. Based on Game Commission field reports from 1995, bears also ate the contents of 77 beehives, 35 head of livestock, 27 pet rabbits, and 20 chickens or ducks.

Black bears establish dens in logs, caves, or holes in the ground. They sleep through the cold weather but do not truly hibernate. Generally good-natured and mild-tempered, they avoid confrontations with humans—especially during the three-day bear-hunting season in August. In 1995, 2,180 of them, from a total estimated preseason population of 8,525, paid the supreme penalty for not being alert enough.

Bears have a wide home range. They cover up to 16 miles in a single night along well-developed bear trails, marking trees as they go. This marking may be territorial or may be part of stretching exercises.

Bears have poor eyesight, moderately good hearing, and an excellent sense of smell. They are great swimmers, can climb trees, and can run at speeds up to 28 miles per hour. They have few enemies—only humans, with their guns and cars, dogs, and forest fires.

Elk. Once so numerous in Pennsylvania that a county was named for them in 1843, the elk was exterminated by 1867, a victim of hunters and diminished habitat. The Pennsylvania Game Commission reintroduced the species in 1913, and a single herd of about 250 elk now roams Elk and Cameron Counties. Although the elk is classified as big game, there has been no open hunting season since 1931.

Elk are members of the deer family. They weigh from 400 to 1,100 pounds, with an average of 600 to 700. They range in length from about 7 to 9 feet and in height to 5 feet. The elk is a dark reddish brown in summer and gray in winter, with a dark mane and a white rump patch. Males are about 25% larger than females and have large, wide branching antlers that sweep upward and back. The antlers may weigh up to 25 pounds and have a 5-foot spread.

Males use elaborate mating rituals to acquire large harems. The female usually gives birth in June to a single calf weighing about 30 pounds. The life expectancy of elk in the wild is 15 years.

White-Tailed Deer. The white-tailed deer is the official state mammal. Its name is derived from a 6- to 12-inch fluffy tail that is white beneath and tan and black above and covers a white rump. When running, at speeds up to 40 miles per hour, the deer lifts the tail, exposing the white underside and rump. Other characteristic features are big ears, spindly legs, and, in males, antlers. Coats are reddish tan in summer and covered by a gray-brown prelage in winter that acts as an insulating blanket against the cold. The throat and underside of the adults are white, as are the areas across the nose, around the eyes, and inside the ears. The white-tailed deer stands about 3 feet tall at the rump and shoulders and is 5 to 6 feet long. Adults weigh between 100 and 300 pounds. They are herbivores.

The antlers on males grow through spring and summer and into early autumn. Growth is stimulated by a secretion of the pituitary gland. Antlers are initially covered with live skin and a short coat of hair, and have blood vessels. When the blood flow stops, the antlers begin to dry and peel. The buck scrapes away the dead skin and polishes the antlers against trees and plants. In winter, the antlers fall off and are eaten by small forest animals. Antler size is an indication of general health, availability of food, and heredity, not of age.

Although it is a prolific breeder, the white-tailed deer was hunted to the brink of extinction near the end of the 19th century. The Pennsylvania Game Commission, established in 1896, came to the rescue by banning the worst of the hunting practices. A century later, biologists estimated the deer population at 1,152,000. In 1995, 430,000 deer were killed by hunters and another 43,000 by automobiles. Cold and lack of food in severe winters, forest fires, and numerous predators, including dogs, foxes, bobcats, and coyotes, also extract a toll.

Cottontail Rabbit. Cottontail rabbits breed prolifically. They produce five to seven litters annually, totaling up to 35 young per pair. Many die quickly, about 35% within a month. The cottontail has many enemies, particularly hunters, who kill them by the hundreds of thousands each year. Consequently, the cottontail has a life expectancy of less than a year.

Cottontails prefer farmlands and suburbs to dense forest and are hated by farmers and gardeners because they love to nibble on green beans, peas, lettuce, cabbage, and other garden plants in addition to clover, grasses, and dandelions.

The cottontail has gray or brown fur, sprinkled with black on the back, and white underparts. Other characteristics are eyes with white rings, furry feet with four toes on the hind feet and five toes on the forefeet, and long, pointed ears. The trademark tail is dark above and white beneath. The cottontail weighs 2 to 3 pounds. When threatened, it can reach speeds of 18 miles per hour.

Snowshoe Hare. The snowshoe hare has large, heavily furred hind feet with four long toes that can be widely separated. This permits the hare to travel on top of snow, hence its name. The snowshoe hare's fur is rusty brown sprinkled with black in summer and turns white in winter. The head and legs are light brown, and the ears have black tops.

The snowshoe hare prefers the mountainous region of northern Pennsylvania and is rarely seen elsewhere in the state. In summer and in winter it eats grasses, herbs, and shrubs, young trees, bark, and twigs. On this diet, adults reach 3 to 5 pounds. The snowshoe has basically the same diet as the white-tailed deer. Consequently, its numbers and fortune are the converse of the deer's: The more prominent species will consume the majority of the other's food. Also, the number of snowshoe ebbs and flows dramatically in cycles for reasons not totally known. It also has many enemies, which limit its numbers despite prolific breeding.

Woodchuck (Groundhog). The most famous rodent in Pennsylvania, and perhaps in America, is a woodchuck named Punxsutawney Phil, who is called upon to predict the coming of spring every February 2, Groundhog Day. Phil's cohorts are hibernating then and will awaken when spring arrives. Neither they nor Phil has a clue as to when that might be.

The woodchuck is a brown rodent, a member of the squirrel family, dark on the back, lighter brown underneath. It weights from 4 to 11 pounds and measures 20 to 25 inches long. The woodchuck is built to suit its major activity, burrowing. The forefeet have toes with long, curved claws and a thumb that is a short stump with a blunt claw. The head is blunt and flat with small eyes and ear flaps for keeping dirt out. Large front incisors are used to cut through roots.

Woodchuck borrows can be 2 to 6 feet deep and 50 feet long. They dig in open fields, forests, hayfields, and pastureland. They are the bane of gardeners, farmers, and golf course maintenance people. Nor only do they burrow in the garden, but they also eat the vegetables therein. Other favorite foods include alfalfa, clover, and fruit, especially apples.

Young woodchucks appear in April and May, usually two to four to a litter. Natural enemies include man, dogs, and the red fox; owls and hawks take only the young.

Squirrels. The adult **gray squirrel** measures about 18 inches, including about 8 inches of tail, and weighs about 1 pound. The squirrel uses its tail as a sunshade bent up over its back, as a counterbalance when climbing, and shakes it to accompany its bark when it is excited. In the northern part of the state, the gray squirrel may be black. All of the various shades of black and gray may occur in a litter.

The adult **fox squirrel**, the least common of the Pennsylvania squirrels, averages 21 inches in length, of which about 9 inches is tail, and weighs about 2 pounds. The fox squirrel prefers pastured woodlots and open fields at the edge of the woods because it spends most of its time on the ground. It loves to forage in cornfields to supplement its diet of the nuts and seeds of trees.

The **red squirrel** is a small tree squirrel that weighs just ¼ to ½ pound and averages about 12 inches in length, about half of which is tail. It has a distinctive white eye ring. It is known as the "watchdog of the woodlands," because its shrill warning cry announces every intruder.

The three types of squirrels live in a certain harmony in the woods in somewhat different habitats and with different habits. The red squirrel establishes a food cache in one spot, in contrast to the gray and fox squirrels, which bury food items singly at random. The reputation of the red squirrel as aggressive may be related to its need to protect this cache from potential intruders. Squirrels find their stored food using a keen sense of smell and a good memory. Gray squirrels share their food. Squirrels do not hibernate; however, some curl up in their nests and wait out the worst storms of winter.

Squirrels have a legion of enemies. In good hunting years, a million or more squirrels are harvested. Thousands more are killed by motor vehicles, and they are preyed upon by hawks, owls, bobcats, snakes, and raccoons. Nevertheless, their life expectancies range from four to seven and a half years for the fox, up to 10 years for the red, and from nine to 13 years for the gray.

Birds

The Pennsylvania Ornithological Committee lists 418 species of birds that have been observed in the commonwealth. Of these, the average birder would be fortunate to observe half during a lifetime of bird-watching. In *Birds of Pennsylvania,* by James and Linda Wakeley, a beautifully illustrated guide for the amateur birder published by the Pennsylvania Game Commission, a checklist of Pennsylvania birds lists 294 species.

Whatever the actual number of species of birds, the variety and the different habitats in the state provide a marvelous venue for bird-watching.

The state and the U.S. governments protect all of the birds in the commonwealth except the English sparrow and the European starling. Birds that stay within the commonwealth and do not migrate with the seasons are protected by state game laws. Birds that migrate across state lines are protected by the U.S. Fish and Wildlife Service.

Three birds of prey, the bald eagle, peregrine falcon, and osprey, are benefiting from efforts of the Game Commission and other interested organizations to increase their numbers in the state. Despite increases in their populations, however, they retain their status as endangered.

Ruffed Grouse. The ruffed grouse is Pennsylvania's official state bird. It is known for its navigational skills under pressure through thick foliage with great beating wings. The grouse's mating call, a low rolling thunder that it produces by flapping its wings while perched on a log or a stone, is a familiar forest sound, especially in spring. The young are hatched on the forest floor, raised solely by the female, and become independent quickly.

Wild Turkey. The Pennsylvania Game Commission, which saved the wild turkey from almost certain extinction in the 19th century, classifies the bird as big game. With a wingspan of 4 to 5 feet, this bird can fly for short distances, but it mostly wanders about on foot with other turkeys looking for food. They eat fruits, buds, seeds, insects, nuts, and acorns. Turkeys nest on the ground but roost at night in large trees.

During the spring mating dance, males fan out their beautiful tales to attract females to a clearing. Usually three to five females respond. The male spends no time rearing the young. Fortunately for the females that must raise them, young turkeys can forage almost immediately and can fly to tree roosts in a month.

Ring-Necked Pheasant. In 1994, the Game Commission raised and released 265,257 ring-necked pheasants, mostly on state game lands, just prior to and during fall open season. There is a permanent wild population of these birds as well. They forage on the ground for grains and seeds around open fields and farms and nest in grassy areas.

Mourning Doves. Very common in farm fields and suburban areas, these plump, brown birds nest in trees. They are most noticeable on the ground during mating season when the male puffs up his body and walks quickly after the female while cooing a low-pitched song.

Bald Eagle. The bald eagle was selected as the central figure of the National Emblem of the United States when it was adopted by Congress in 1782. (Ben Franklin, however, argued for the wild turkey as the national bird.) The bald eagle was once a common sight in the state, but their number declined precipitously until their future presence in Pennsylvania was doubtful. But aggressive intervention by the Game Commission has increased the number of eagles in the state. The commission established the world's first bald eagle sanctuary on Mount Johnson Island in the Susquehanna River in southern Lancaster County.

Bald eagle nests are mansionlike structures that may be as large as 5 to 7 feet across, 12 feet deep, and weigh as much as 1,000 pounds. They are the playrooms of the maturing young eaglets for two or three months as they grow to 3 feet in length. Then the young leave the nest. Their parents, who mate for life, will return to the same nest for many years.

Bald eagles were so named for the

adult's white-feathered head, which starkly contrasts with the dark-feathered body.

Peregrine Falcon. The Game Commission and various organizations are trying to reestablish this amazing hunter in Pennsylvania. The falcon's dive has been estimated at 200 miles per hour when the bird is in pursuit of prey.

The peregrine projects are being conducted in cities. The rationale for a city habitat is that there are no wild predators, pigeons are plentiful, and the ledges of buildings are similar to cliffs. Also, the urban public gets a rare chance to observe an endangered species recovery project at work. In 1995, 23 young peregrines were released in Allentown, Harrisburg, Reading, and Williamsport; previously, birds had been released in Philadelphia. In addition to the released falcons, six young have fledged from natural nests since 1995.

Osprey. A third bird of prey being reestablished in the state is the osprey. A beautiful dark brown and white fishing bird with a 5-foot wingspan, the osprey flies low over water, legs dangling, searching for fish. Sighting one, it swoops down and goes briefly beneath the surface of the water to seize its prey. It returns to its perch before dining.

Amphibians and Reptiles

Pennsylvania has a diverse population of amphibians and reptiles despite the fact that the cold winter temperatures limit their distribution. The state is home to 38 species and subspecies of amphibians, including 16 frogs and toads and 22 salamanders, and 38 species and subspecies of reptiles, including 13 turtles, four lizards, and 21 snakes. The table found on the next page lists the amphibian and reptile species and subspecies found in the state. For a complete and beautifully illustrated description of each of these species, the reader is directed to *Pennsylvania Amphibians and Reptiles,* by Larry Shaffer, published by the Pennsylvania Fish and Boat Commission, Harrisburg.

Poisonous Snakes. Of the 21 species of snakes considered to be native to Pennsylvania, three are venomous: the northern copperhead, eastern massasauga snake, and timber rattlesnake. Reports of venomous snakebites are rare. The snakes are usually nonaggressive and prefer to avoid confrontation, and any bites usually occur while people are trying to catch or carelessly handle one of these snakes.

In the movies, victims of poisonous snakebites die quickly and horribly. In reality, the bite may be painful, but it is not life-threatening if treated properly. In the event of a snakebite, keep the victim calm and immobile, call 911, and apply a light constricting band *above* the bite (you should be able to insert a finger under the band), and take the victim to a medical facility without delay. Do not use ice, cold packs, or sprays; do not incise and suction; do not use a tourniquet; do not give the victim alcohol or drugs; and do not wait to see if symptoms develop—take the victim to a doctor immediately.

The three poisonous snakes in Pennsylvania are all pit vipers, so named for the deep pit located on each side of the head between the eye and the nostril. These pits are heat-sensitive organs, able to detect and locate warm bodies, which the snake uses to find its prey.

AMPHIBIANS AND REPTILES

Frogs and Toads eastern spadefoot toad; eastern American toad; Fowler's toad; northern cricket frog; northern spring peeper frog; eastern gray treefrog; mountain chorus frog; upland chorus frog; New Jersey chorus frog; western chorus frog; bullfrog; northern green frog; pickerel frog; northern leopard frog; wood frog; coastal plain leopard frog

Salamanders eastern hellbender salamander; mudpuppy salamander; Jefferson salamander; spotted salamander; marbled salamander; eastern tiger salamander; red-spotted newt; green salamander; northern dusky salamander; appalachian seal salamander; mountain dusky salamander; northern two-lined salamander; longtail salamander; northern spring salamander; four-toed salamander; redback salamander; slimy salamander; valley and ridge salamander; ravine salamander; Wehrle's salamander; eastern mud salamander; northern red salamander

Turtles common snapping turtle; eastern mud turtle; stinkpot turtle; midland painted turtle; spotted turtle; wood turtle; bog turtle; Blanding's turtle; map turtle; redbellied turtle; eastern box turtle; midland smooth softshell turtle; eastern spiny softshell turtle

Lizards northern fence lizard; northern coal skink; five-lined skink; broadhead skink

Snakes *Colubrid Snakes:* eastern worm snake; Kirtland's snake; northern black racer snake; northern ring-neck snake; black rat snake; eastern hognose snake; eastern king snake; eastern milk snake; northern water snake; rough green snake; eastern smooth green snake; queen snake; northern brown snake; northern redbelly snake; shorthead garter snake; ribbon snake; eastern garter snake; earth snake

Pit Vipers: northern copperhead snake; timber rattlesnake; eastern massasauga rattlesnake

The pit vipers have well-defined heads. Their eyes are vertically elliptical (shaped like a cat's pupil). They are equipped with fangs—long, hollow, modified teeth located near the front of the upper jaw. Each fang is connected by a duct to a gland on the side of the head where venom is stored. The venom attacks the victim's circulatory system; it destroys tissue and affects the blood's ability to clot properly. The nervous system might also be affected. Interestingly, these snakes have been known to bite humans but not inject venom.

Northern Copperhead. This snake's head may be covered with copper-colored scales. Overall, it is copper or hazel-brown with pink or orange tinges. It has chestnut or reddish brown cross-bands on its back and sides; the bands may have small, dark spots between them. The belly is a mottled pattern of white to gray. The copperhead reaches an average adult size of 24 to 36 inches.

The northern copperhead is found in the lower two-thirds of Pennsylvania. It prefers wooded hillsides and rock out-croppings near streams and swamps. It likes decaying logs and sawdust and large, flat stones for basking in the sun. This snake eats insects when young, then graduates to rodents. Birds, cicadas, caterpillars, frogs, and lizards are occasional foods.

Eastern Massasauga Rattlesnake. This small rattlesnake, which does not grow longer than 30 inches, is also called the swamp rattler, reflecting its preferred habitat. Unfortunately, the habitat is shrinking, and the snake is now found only in portions of some western counties. It is on Pennsylvania's list of endangered species. This snake prefers to feed on frogs and other amphibians but will eat the occasional lizard, rodent, or bird.

The massasauga is brownish gray to black on its back and sides, with a row of brown or black blotches running down the middle of its back. Dark bars, bordered with a lighter color, mark the head and neck. The belly is black with scattered white or yellow markings.

Timber Rattlesnake. This snake, sometimes called the banded rattle-snake, is found only in central Pennsylvania. It reaches an adult size of 36 to 54 inches. It has two different color phases, black and yellow; each is permanent. Black is the more common phase. In this phase, there is a flecking of very dark brown or black that covers most of the yellowish pigment. Some specimens are completely black. On a yellow specimen, black or dark brown crossbands contrast with the yellow background. These crossbands tend to break up near the rear of the body and form a row of dark spots down the back and along each side. The tail is black regardless of body color.

This snake prefers timber-covered hillsides with rock outcroppings, preferably facing south. It hibernates in winter. Mice and other rodents are diet staples; squirrels, chipmunks, and birds are eaten as available.

Fish

Pennsylvania has a large number of lakes and ponds of all sizes and descriptions. Three major and two smaller river systems, fed by a huge network of streams, brooks, and runs—in all, about 45,000 miles of waterways—cut through a diverse countryside. In these waters can be found about 160 species of fish.

FISH

Sturgeons	shortnose, lake, Atlantic
Gars	longnose, spotted
Bowfin	bowfin
Freshwater eels	American
Herrings	American shad, hickory shad, gizzard shad, alewife, blueback herring, skipjack herring
Trout and salmon	lake, brown, rainbow-steelhead, palomino, and brook trout; chinook, coho, pink, kokanee, and land-locked salmon
Smelts	rainbow
Pikes	northern, amur pike; muskellunge, tiger muskellunge; chain, redfin-grass pickerel
Minnows	carp, river chub, golden shiner, common shiner, creek chub, fallfish
Suckers	quillback carpsucker; white, hog, and redhorse suckers
Catfishes	white, channel, and flathead catfish; black, brown, and yellow bullheads
Temperate basses	white perch, white bass, striped bass
Sunfishes	largemouth, smallmouth, spotted, and rock basses; redbreast sunfish, green sunfish, pumpkinseed, bluegill, redear sunfish; white and black crappie
Perches	yellow perch, walleye sauger
Drums	freshwater drum
Sculpins	mottled sculpin, slimy sculpin

The table above lists the species, subspecies, and varieties in 16 families found in the state.

The following are descriptions of some of the state's favorite game fish species.

Smallmouth bass. A golden green fish with bronze overcast, darker vertical bars, and a mouth that does not extend to the rear of the eye. This bass prefers flowing waters, especially dropoffs, weed beds, and riffle areas.

Largemouth bass. In addition to having a larger mouth that extends beyond the rear of the eye, this bass is nearly black to dark green above, with lighter sides and belly, and dark bars along its sides. It prefers lakes or sluggish backwaters of streams. In lakes, it likes dropoffs, underwater structures, and, especially, aquatic plants.

Muskellunge and tiger muskellunge. Both of these fish are light gray to greenish, with irregular dark vertical bars. On the tiger, the bars are more evenly spaced. A solitary fish, it prefers slow-moving river water edged with vegetation. In lakes, it likes to lie in shadows or cruise along structures and dropoffs.

Northern pike. The pike has yellow-green sides with yellowish, bean-shaped spots and dark-spotted fins. It prefers weed beds in the shallow areas of lakes.

Chain pickerel. This fish gets its name from the dark, chainlike pattern on its sides. It has a bronze back, dark yellow-green or brassy sides, and a whitish belly. The pickerel likes shallow shoals of lakes heavy with vegetation and sluggish areas of clear streams.

Walleye and sauger. These two fish differ only in that the walleye has a dark spot on the dorsal fin. Both fish are yellow-olive to brassy yellow, with darker mottlings over the back, and large glassy or milky eyes. The sauger is found only in the Ohio River Basin. They both like lakes and rivers with rock ledges and gravelly bottoms in moderately deep, clear water.

Striped bass and hybrid. Both fish have dark backs with silvery sides and seven or eight distinct black stripes running gill to tail, but the stripes on the hybrid are less distinct and are broken and irregular. These fish travel in schools in the deep, open waters of lakes and rivers.

American shad. This shad has silvery sides, light olive to bluish above, with a row of several dark spots behind the gill cover. It prefers rivers and large streams with access to the ocean.

Brook trout. The official state fish, the brook trout is the only trout native to Pennsylvania. It has a brilliant orange belly, and its dark olive green back is laced with darker, wormlike markings. Red spots with bluish halos highlight the body. Wild brook trout are most likely to be found in smaller, high-gradient streams flowing off mountain ridges.

Brown trout. The brown trout is a golden brown above, shading to a lighter tone on the sides and silver or dusky yellow below. The back, sides, and dorsal fin are marked with large, dark spots outlined with pale halos. Reddish orange or yellow spots also dot the sides. Wild brown trout are found in limestone streams in the central part of the state and in larger streams flowing through the valleys separating mountain ridges.

Rainbow trout. Only a few streams in the state support sufficient numbers of wild rainbow trout to support a wild trout fishery. The rainbow trout is silver gray to dark greenish, with a pink or reddish streak along the sides. Its tail is covered with dark spots; small spots pepper the head, sides, and belly.

Endangered Species

The Federal Endangered Species Act of 1973 defines an endangered species as "any species which is in danger of extinction throughout all or a significant portion of its range" and threatened species as "any species that is likely to become an endangered species within the foreseeable future."

Currently in Pennsylvania, three mammal species are endangered: the Delmarva fox squirrel, the Indiana bat, and the least shrew. Three species are threatened: the West Virginia water shrew, the eastern wood rat, and the small-footed myotis.

Endangered birds in the state include the bald eagle, peregrine falcon, osprey, black tern, king rail, loggerhead shrike, and short-eared owl. Birds classified as threatened include the American bittern, great egret, least bittern, sedge wren, upland sandpiper, yellow-billed flycatcher, and yellow-crowned night heron.

Six amphibians and reptiles are classified as endangered in Pennsylvania: the bog turtle, the coastal plain leopard frog, the eastern massasauga rattlesnake, the eastern mud salamander, Kirtland's snake, and the New Jersey chorus frog. Three species are threatened: the green salamander, the red-bellied turtle, and the rough green snake. Unfortunately, scientists believe that three species have already been lost from the state: the eastern mud turtle, the midland softshell turtle, and the eastern tiger salamander.

Endangered fish in the state are the eastern sand darter, gravel chub, lake sturgeon, longhead darter, longnose sucker, northern brook lamprey, shortnose sturgeon, spotted darter, and tippecanoe darter. Threatened fish are the Atlantic sturgeon, bluebreast darter, burbot, channel darter, gill darter, mountain brook lamprey, mountain madtom, northern madtom, and Ohio lamprey.

5

Geology, Weather, and Climate

THE GEOLOGY OF PENNSYLVANIA

Pennsylvania is an eastern state on a western scale—not only in sheer size, but also in the variety and grandeur of its landscape. Its geological history has been active, with repeated subsidences, foldings, upthrusts, weatherings, and ice ages. These forces have created a land of long mountains and stream valleys covered by forests, with great mineral resources.

The state is divided into seven areas called physiographic provinces, each of which has a particular type of landscape and geology.

The Atlantic Coastal Plain

The state's southeasternmost physiographic province, the Atlantic Coastal Plain, includes all except the northwestern part of Philadelphia, as well as the southeastern parts of Bucks and Delaware Counties. The province is situated along the Delaware River, which provides access to the Atlantic Ocean. Elevations of the land surface range from sea level to about 60 feet above. The land is gently rolling and slopes gradually toward the river.

The Coastal Plain ends in the northwest at the Fall Line, a line of contact between its poorly consolidated beds of sand and gravel and the consolidated rock of the Piedmont Province. The line is marked by falls and rapids in the streams, including the Schuylkill and the Lehigh Rivers, flowing to the Delaware. The falls prohibit transportation upriver and make Philadelphia the only city in Pennsylvania with access to the Atlantic Ocean.

The outstanding geological feature of this province is Tinicum Marsh, a National Natural Landmark in a very urban area, near the Philadelphia International Airport.

The Piedmont Province

The Piedmont is a plain with elevations ranging from 100 to 500 feet. It includes rolling, undulating uplands, low hills, fertile valleys, and well-drained soils. These features, combined with the prevailing climate, have made this area of southeastern Pennsylvania the leading agricultural section of the state, particularly in dairy farming and fruit.

The Piedmont consists of two main regions: the Conestoga Lowlands and the Piedmont Uplands. The lowlands are underlain by shale and carbonate rocks, limestone and dolomite. The rich limestone soil in the Lancaster County area makes it the most productive non-irrigated farmland in the United States. The uplands are underlain with harder rocks, primarily quartzite, and have a thin, sandy soil. The main topography is a series of northeast-southwest-trending uplands of rounded hills dissected by relatively narrow valleys. The Honeybrook Upland is typical, consisting of the Welsh Mountains, Mine Ridge, and South Valley Hills. These hills have a gentle rise in elevation of 150 to 200 feet above the surrounding valleys.

Some outstanding geological features of the Piedmont Province include Chickies Rock, 1 mile north of Columbia on PA Route 441, an anticline of Lower Cambrian Chickies quartzite exposed along the Susquehanna River at the west end of Chickies Ridge; the Conowingo Islands, 60 islands in the Susquehanna River that can be viewed from various overlooks, including Susquehannock State Park and Face Rock Overlook, located at the substation on the cliff above Holtwood Dam; and the 12-mile view of the Susquehanna River Valley afforded from the Samuel S. Lewis State Park near Wrightsville, York County.

The Triassic Lowland, also known as the Gettysburg-Newark Lowland Section, is the north and west section of the Piedmont Province. (It is often identified as a separate province.) The term "lowland" is a misnomer; the area is characterized by hills and mountains that are much higher than the adjacent limestone valleys. The landscape is very similar to that of the other sections of the Piedmont, with fertile lowlands and rugged uplands. It is the bedrock of the Triassic that is quite different.

The Triassic Lowland is an uplifted plain of relatively soft red sandstone and shale. Higher ridges mark the location of sheets of hard, dense volcanic rock on lenses of quartz conglomerate.

The general level of this rolling plain lies between elevations of 400 and 600 feet above sea level.

Nockamixon Cliffs in Bucks County, along PA Route 32 and the Delaware River, a half mile northeast of Kintnersville, are almost vertical cliffs of shales, sandstone, and siltstone of the Triassic Age.

Gettysburg National Military Park has a mass of diabase boulders facing Little Round Top and Round Top called the Gettysburg sill. The sill intruded the Triassic red sandstones and shales that floor the Gettysburg Valley 180 million years ago. The geology of the region had great influence on the battle fought there.

The Blue Ridge Province

The Blue Ridge Province consists of two segments of mountain range, each of which is called South Mountain. It is bounded on the west by the Great Valley Section of the Ridge and Valley Province and on the east primarily by the Triassic Lowland. The southernmost segment, called the Carlisle Prong, is an extension of the Blue Ridge Mountains of the southeastern United States, which it does not resemble at all. It is more ridge than mountain in Pennsylvania. A series of northeast-trending ridges of South Mountain dominates the topography. Individual ridges are separated by narrow valleys. Because many of the ridges have almost flat-topped summits and concordant summit levels, they form a broad, moderately dissected surface.

Mountaintop elevations range from 1,500 feet above sea level near Mount Holly Springs to 2,100 feet atop Big Pine Flat Ridge, north of Caledonia State Park. The lowest elevation is 675 feet, and the maximum relief is about 1,425 feet.

The northern segment of the Blue Ridge Province is called the Reading Prong. This highland is an extension of the crystalline rocks of New England that continue across eastern New York, northern New Jersey, and into southeastern Pennsylvania. The region is a deeply dissected mountain range. The local relief is as much as 500 feet, and the ridge summits rise more than 800 feet above the Great Valley. The Reading Prong is represented by an east-west-trending belt of ridges that range from 6 to 8 miles in width and extend from the Delaware River to the Schuylkill River in the vicinity of Reading. South Mountain is the most prominent topographic feature.

There is an 80-mile gap between the two segments of the Blue Ridge Province. Settlers heading west from their debarkation site in Philadelphia poured through this gap. Railroads, highways, and the Susquehanna River also use it. Harrisburg was named capital of the state partly for its accessibility from both east and west through this gap.

Some outstanding geological features of the province can be observed in Michaux State Forest in Cumberland County, where Lewis Rocks, hard, tough, weather-resistant spires of quartzite, are spectacular. Hammonds Rocks, on the crest of South Mountain, 4 miles southwest of Mount Holly Springs in Cumberland County, provide a great view of the province. The Mount Penn Scenic Lookout, along Skyline Drive in the city of Reading and Lower Alsace Township, has an elevation of 800 to over 1,000 feet. It provides an excellent view of the Reading Prong and the Great Valley.

The Ridge and Valley Province

The Ridge and Valley Province is a series of long, parallel, sharp-crested ridges separated by long, narrow valleys that form a "backbone" across the center of the state from the southwest to the northeast. The mountain slopes are only slightly dissected, and the crest lines are almost uninterrupted and uniform.

The topography is the result of differences in the underlying rock. Limestone and limey shales, which weather rapidly by solution, underlie the lowest valleys. The more resistant quartzite and sandstone underlie the higher ridges. These differing weathering characteristics and upright folds have produced the typical topography of long valleys and ridges. This province is also the site of the great anthracite coal deposits.

The Susquehanna River flows south through the center of the Ridge and Valley Province, producing magnificent water gaps. Farther east, the Lehigh River flows south in a steep-sided gorge that cuts across the mountains. In many places, the gorge is over 1,000 feet deep. Mountains range in elevation from 1,400 to 2,800 feet above sea level; valley elevations vary between 200 and 1,500 feet above sea level. Generally, the relief between a ridge and the neighboring valley varies from 800 to 1,000 feet.

A major portion of the Ridge and Valley Province is the Great Valley, which constitutes its easternmost area. This valley is almost continuous from New York to Georgia. In south-central Pennsylvania, it is called the Cumberland Valley; to the north and east, it is known as the Lebanon Valley; and farther east, it is the Lehigh Valley. The Great Valley is an area of fertile soil within an area of generally poor soil.

Interesting geological features of the province include the Archbald Pothole, located in a state park of that name 6 miles northeast of Scranton; Bald Eagle Lookout, along U.S. Route 322, 8 miles north of State College, which provides a view of the Bald Eagle Valley, the Allegheny Front, and the junction of the Ridge and Valley Province and the Appalachian Plateaus Province; and the Delaware Water Gap, within the borough of the same name just south of the toll-bridge on I-80 over the Delaware River.

The Appalachian Plateaus Province

The largest topographical province, the Appalachian Plateaus Province, covers about half of the state. It extends from Greene and Somerset Counties in the southwest to Erie County in the northwest (excluding Lake Erie), and to Wayne and Pike Counties in the northeast.

This province is a highland that has been eroded by streams that have created deep valleys and hilly topography. The northern sections, which were overridden by glaciers, also have lakes, swamps, peat bogs, and extensive deposits of loose sediment.

The word *plateau,* meaning flat, may seem inappropriate here—the landscape is the most rugged in the state. But it applies because the rock layers are flat. The different rock types are stacked on top of each other rather than tilted and lying next to each other, as is the case in the Ridge and Valley Province. When streams cut through, they find different rocks and leave behind either cliffs or rounded benches, according to the hardness of the rock. If streams cut into a weak rock, such as shale, which then undermines a harder rock, such as sandstone, steep-sided gorges develop. Pine Creek Gorge, the Grand Canyon of Pennsylvania, is the result of such activity.

The Appalachian Plateaus Province ends to the east in a large, rounded cliff, the Allegheny Front. The horizontal rocks of the plateau cease and the Ridge and Valley Province begins. The division is very pronounced in the area between Lock Haven and Williamsport.

The deeply scored landscape of the plateau is difficult to cross, its soils are too rocky for farming, and in places the area is uninhabitable. But the woodland is valuable for recreation, and bituminous coal underlies the region.

The Appalachian Plateaus Province is broken into six subregions, according to the differences in the height of the land or its erosional history.

The Pittsburgh Plateau is a section in the southwest corner of the state that is more than 50% shale, along with sandstone and bituminous coal. The land has been deeply cut by the Ohio, Allegheny, and Monongahela Rivers and is characterized by rounded hills and open valleys. From Washington north to Pittsburgh, the undulating uplands reach elevations of 1,200 feet above sea level. South and west of Washington, the ridges reach a maximum point of about 1,600 feet in Greene County. The Pittsburgh Plateau is best observed on Minnie Knob, one of the highest points in Greene County, about 3 miles east of Blacksville, Pennsylvania, on the Pennsylvania–West Virginia state line. Other counties in this section are Allegheny, Beaver, Butler, and Clarion; most of Clearfield, Fayette, Indiana, Westmoreland, and Venango; and parts of Forest and Jefferson.

The High Plateau Section, in north-central Pennsylvania, is the highest land in the commonwealth. Elevations reach 2,500 feet above sea level. It is a very rugged plateau, deeply dissected by numerous streams. The total relief of the section exceeds 1,600 feet. Valley walls tend to be steep along the streams and numerous hollows. It can best be appreciated on PA Route 44, a scenic highway between U.S. Route 6 at Sweden Valley and U.S. Route 220 near Jersey Shore. The 55-mile route has vistas, scenic areas, and narrow and flat plateau divides. Counties in the High Plateau include Cameron, McKean, Potter, and parts of Clinton, Forest, Lycoming, Tioga, and Warren.

The Allegheny Mountain Section is the southern portion of the High Plateau. It is bounded on the west by Chestnut Ridge, whose crest is 2,778 feet above sea level, and Laurel Hill, 3,000 feet above sea level, and on the east by the Allegheny Front. All of Somerset County, most of Cambria, and small parts of Centre, Fayette, Indiana, and Westmoreland counties make up this section.

Loyalhanna Gorge in Westmoreland County, 3 miles southeast of Latrobe on U.S. Route 30, is a 3-mile-long gorge cut through Chestnut Ridge by the Loyalhanna Creek. The geological record of hundreds of millions of years is recorded in this rock.

The Low Plateau is a glaciated section in the extreme northeast corner of the state underlain by soft rock—thick layers of reddish shales and sandstone. It is an area of smooth, rolling hills, glacial lakes, and swamps. The western portion slopes gently toward the Susquehanna River, and the eastern portion toward the Delaware River. Elevations range from 2,100 feet in western Wayne County to as low as 500 feet along the Delaware River in Pike County. Overlook

Cliff in Wayne County, near the village of Balls Eddy and the New York state line, along the west side of the Delaware River, provides a breathtaking view of the Delaware River Gorge. A series of red siltstones and gray sandstones are exposed in massive cliffs formed by the river as it eroded these rocks. Susquehanna County, most of Bradford, and parts of Lackawanna, Monroe, Tioga, and Wyoming are also in this section.

The Pocono Plateau is located in the extreme southeastern corner of the Appalachian Plateau and is known as the Pocono Mountains. It includes parts of Carbon, Lackawanna, Luzerne, Monroe, Pike, and Wayne Counties. The topographic relief within the plateau is low; it seldom exceeds 100 feet. Slopes are generally low. The entire area has been glaciated. The main topographic interruptions are stream valleys and occasional bedrock ridges; swamps and peat bogs are common.

Camelback Mountain, in Big Pocono State Park, is the highest point in the area—2,133 feet—and is a striking projection marking the edge of the Pocono Plateau in Monroe County.

The Glaciated Northwest Section, also known as the Glaciated Pittsburgh Plateau Section, is an area of low relief and glacial settlement, covered with deposits of drift carried by the continental ice sheets. The deposits lie north of a line from Ellwood City in Beaver County to the center of the northern boundary of Butler County. It includes Crawford, Erie (excluding the lake plain), Lawrence, Mercer, and parts of Venango and Warren Counties.

Slippery Rock Creek, flowing through McConnells Mill State Park, is the result of the glaciation of this area. It is a National Natural Landmark.

The Lake Erie Plain

The waters of early lakes in the Erie basin worked upon the existing sediments and upon the rocks where they were exposed to produce a narrow, 40-mile strip of flat, rich land 3 to 4 miles wide called the Lake Erie Plain, which lies along the southern shore of present-day Lake Erie.

Low elevations and relief are characteristic of the plain. Elevations start slightly above the lake level of 572 feet and rise to approximately 800 feet above sea level. The surface is flat except for abrupt rises to former beaches created by higher levels of the lake in the past. Each time the level of the lake dropped, a new shoreline was cut.

Bedrock underlies the entire region. It is concealed by a thick cover of unconsolidated glacial deposits, which vary in thickness from 10 to 75 feet, although depths of 100 feet exist. Rocks in the area include sand, gravel, alternating sandstone, and shale.

The level slopes of the terraces provide good drainage for farming and are attractive sites for railroads and highways. It was geology that made the city of Erie a transportation center and the surrounding countryside a major fruit and vegetable production area.

Presque Isle, along the southern shore of Lake Erie, is a 3,200-acre sandy peninsula jutting into the lake. This National Natural Landmark is one of the rare spots in the world where one can study the action of winds, currents, and waves upon glacial sand.

WEATHER AND CLIMATE

Dr. Benjamin Rush shared his very subjective observations about Pennsylvania weather with the readers of *A Gazetteer of the State of Pennsylvania 1832:*

The coldest weather is from the middle of January to the tenth of February. . . . The spring in Pennsylvania is generally unpleasant. In March, the weather is stormy, variable, and cold. In April, and sometimes far into May, it is moist and accompanied by a degree of cold, which has been called rawness. The month of June is the only month in the year, which resembles a spring month in the southern countries in Europe. The weather is generally temperate, the sky is serene, and the verdure of the country is universal and delightful.

The autumn is the most agreeable season of the year in Pennsylvania. The cool evenings and early mornings which generally begin about the first week in September, are succeeded by a moderate temperature of the air during the day. This species of weather continues with an increase of cold scarcely perceptible til the middle of October, when the autumn is closed by rain. . . . These rains are the harbingers of winter.

Frost and ice appear about the latter end of October, or the beginning of November. But, intense cold is rarely felt until around Christmas. . . . The depth of the snow is sometimes between two and three feet; in 1829–30, it was near four, but in general, it is from six to nine inches. Hail frequently falls with snow in the winter. At intervals of years, heavy showers of hail fall in the spring and summer.

From this account of the temperature of the air, it is apparent that there are seldom more than four months in which the weather is agreeable without a fire.

In 1996, five declared disasters set an annual record. Rain and snowstorms cost Pennsylvania an estimated $1 billion in damages and 109 lives in 1996. It was the worst year since 1972, when Hurricane Agnes caused $2 billion in flood damage.

Pennsylvania's Five Disasters:

1. A blizzard in January closed state roads for 32 hours.
2. Subsequent flooding forced the evacuation of thousands of residents along the Susquehanna River and caused 100 deaths.
3. Flooding occurred in Philadelphia and four suburban counties in June.
4. Flooding occurred in 10 western counties in July.
5. Flooding occurred in central Pennsylvania in September.

Approximately 42,000 individuals and businesses received more than $355 million in federal and state aid.

Of course, Dr. Rush's observations were limited to the Philadelphia area. In the macroweather sense, the areas of the state are more alike than different. Each falls within the weather classification "continental humid." They have similar average temperature ranges, precipitation levels, prevailing winds, cloudiness, and sky cover conditions. But each has a few unique climatic conditions that set it apart. Five climatic regions can be identified.

The Southeast Region is the warm, wet area of the Atlantic Coastal Plain and the Piedmont Region. Philadelphia is the representative city. The area has the longest and hottest summers; high humidity and light winds often provide oppressive summer heat waves. It is the sunniest region—rather, the least cloudy. Clear skies appear about twice a week. The region also has the mildest winters.

The Central Region includes the relatively dry Ridge and Valley Region. The ridgetops have a more extreme climate— lower temperatures, more snow and wind—than the adjacent valleys, where most of the towns are located. The skies are cloudier here than in the southeast. In Williamsport, the representative city, the winds always come from the west.

The Southwest Region endures a continual succession of storms coming from the southwest. The storms generally produce less precipitation than storms in other areas. This is the cloudiest area in the state—indeed, one of the cloudiest areas in the United States— with less than 60 clear days annually. Pittsburgh is the representative city.

The Northwest Region is the coldest, snowiest region in the state. It is only slightly less cloudy than the Southwest Region, although during the summer, the Erie area has more clear days. This is offset by the total overcast in the late fall and winter. The sun usually appears only one or two days per month from November through February.

The Northeast Region, represented by Wilkes-Barre and Scranton, has a wide range of temperatures and precipitation, making it more continental than the rest of the state. Because of their higher elevation, the Pocono Mountains, in the extreme northeast area, are snowier in winter and cooler in summer than the rest of the region.

The average annual temperature in Pennsylvania is 49°F, with an average of 32° in January and 77° in July. The southern part of the state is about 4° to 6° warmer than the north. The average annual precipitation is 41 inches.

The most dramatic variations from the average include a high temperature of 111° in Phoenixville on July 10, 1936, and a low of −42° in Smethport on January 5, 1904. The heaviest rainfall occurred on July 17, 1942, when 34.5 inches fell in Smethport. The greatest annual rainfall recorded was 81.6 inches at Mount Pocono in 1952. The greatest daily snowfall occurred in Morgantown on March 20, 1958, 38 inches, part of a three-day storm that produced 50 inches. The state record snowfall was 225 inches on Blue Knob in the winter of 1890–91; 86 inches fell in December 1890.

The most destructive weather event in Pennsylvania history was Hurricane Agnes in 1972. The storm killed 122 people and caused $2 billion in property damage, mostly from massive flooding along the Susquehanna River.

In a state with 45,000 miles of rivers and streams, floods are the most common disasters. A flood museum in Johnstown commemorates the flood of 1889, which killed 2,209 people.

TEMPERATURE, PRECIPITATION, AND SNOWFALL (1995)

Pocono Mountains
Stroudsburg

	Jan.	Feb.	Mar.	Apr.	May	Jun.	Jul.	Aug.	Sep.	Oct.	Nov.	Dec.
Avg. temp.	31	22	38	45	56	68	72	70	60	54	34	23
+ or - norm.	8	-3	4	0	-1	3	3	3	-1	4	-5	-5
Precip. (in.)	3	2	2	2	3	3	4	2	3	8	5	2
+ or - norm.	0	-1	-1	-1	-1	-2	0	-3	-1	5	1	-1
Snowfall (in.)	3	11	4	1	0	0	0	0	0	0	18	20

East-Central Mountains
Allentown

	Jan.	Feb.	Mar.	Apr.	May	Jun.	Jul.	Aug.	Sep.	Oct.	Nov.	Dec.
Avg. temp.	33	28	42	49	59	70	76	74	64	57	38	28
+ or - norm.	8	0	5	1	1	2	4	3	1	5	-4	-3
Precip. (in.)	4	2	3	2	3	2	6	1	3	8	4	2
+ or - norm.	1	-1	0	-1	-1	-2	1	-3	-1	4	0	-1
Snowfall (in.)	1	9	2	0	0	0	0	0	0	0	6	18

TEMPERATURE, PRECIPITATION, AND SNOWFALL *(continued)*

Southeast Piedmont
Lancaster

	Jan.	Feb.	Mar.	Apr.	May	Jun.	Jul.	Aug.	Sep.	Oct.	Nov.	Dec.
Avg. temp.	35	28	43	49	60	70	76	75	66	58	40	29
+ or - norm.	6	-3	3	-2	-2	0	1	2	-1	3	-5	-5
Precip. (in.)	4	2	2	2	4	2	5	1	4	7	4	2
+ or - norm.	0	-1	-1	-2	0	-2	0	-3	0	4	0	-1
Snowfall (in.)	0	8	1	0	0	0	0	0	0	0	4	13

Lower Susquehanna
York

	Jan.	Feb.	Mar.	Apr.	May	Jun.	Jul.	Aug.	Sep.	Oct.	Nov.	Dec.
Avg. temp.	33	28	43	50	60	70	76	75	64	57	38	29
+ or - norm.	5	-2	3	-1	-1	0	1	2	-1	3	-6	-4
Precip. (in.)	4	2	1	2	4	6	5	1	3	6	4	2
+ or - norm.	1	-1	-2	-1	0	2	2	-2	-1	3	1	-1
Snowfall (in.)	0	7	2	0	0	0	0	0	0	0	8	8

Middle Susquehanna
Williamsport

	Jan.	Feb.	Mar.	Apr.	May	Jun.	Jul.	Aug.	Sep.	Oct.	Nov.	Dec.
Avg. temp.	32	26	42	47	59	69	75	76	63	56	37	27
+ or - norm.	7	-1	4	-1	0	2	3	5	0	4	-5	-4
Precip. (in.)	4	2	1	2	3	4	3	1	1	8	4	2
+ or - norm.	2	-1	-2	-1	-1	0	-1	-3	-2	5	1	-1
Snowfall (in.)	0	8	2	0	0	0	0	0	0	0	10	25

Upper Susquehanna
Montrose-Wellsboro

	Jan.	Feb.	Mar.	Apr.	May	Jun.	Jul.	Aug.	Sep.	Oct.	Nov.	Dec.
Avg. temp.	28	20	37	41	53	66	71	70	57	52	33	21
+ or - norm.	7	-3	3	-3	-2	3	3	3	-2	4	-6	-6
Precip. (in.)	4	2	1	3	2	3	3	2	4	7	4	2
+ or - norm.	1	0	-1	0	-1	-2	0	-1	0	4	1	-1
Snowfall (in.)	6	12	4	2	0	0	0	0	0	0	18	26

TEMPERATURE, PRECIPITATION, AND SNOWFALL *(continued)*

Central Mountains
Ridgway-Philipsburg

	Jan.	Feb.	Mar.	Apr.	May	Jun.	Jul.	Aug.	Sep.	Oct.	Nov.	Dec.
Avg. temp.	28	22	38	43	55	66	71	73	60	54	35	25
+ or - norm.	5	-3	3	-3	-1	2	2	5	0	4	-5	-4
Precip. (in.)	3	2	1	3	4	3	3	1	2	6	4	2
+ or - norm.	1	-1	-2	0	0	-1	-2	-3	2	3	1	-1
Snowfall (in.)	3	6	4	0	0	0	0	0	0	0	15	21

South-Central Mountains
Altoona-Ebensburg

	Jan.	Feb.	Mar.	Apr.	May	Jun.	Jul.	Aug.	Sep.	Oct.	Nov.	Dec.
Avg. temp.	29	24	40	45	57	68	72	73	61	54	35	26
+ or - norm.	3	-5	2	-4	-2	1	1	3	-2	2	-7	-5
Precip. (in.)	3	2	1	2	4	6	3	1	2	6	4	2
+ or - norm.	0	-1	-2	-1	0	2	-1	-2	-2	3	1	-1
Snowfall (in.)	4	8	3	0	0	0	0	0	0	0	22	13

Southwest Plateau
Butler-Donora-Confluence

	Jan.	Feb.	Mar.	Apr.	May	Jun.	Jul.	Aug.	Sep.	Oct.	Nov.	Dec.
Avg. temp.	30	25	41	47	58	69	73	75	62	55	37	27
+ or - norm.	4	-3	3	-2	0	3	2	6	-1	3	-5	-4
Precip. (in.)	3	2	2	3	5	4	3	2	2	4	4	2
+ or - norm.	0	0	-2	-1	0	0	-1	-1	-2	1	0	-1
Snowfall (in.)	8	8	5	0	0	0	0	0	0	0	14	15

Northwest Plateau
Brookville-Corry-Franklin

	Jan.	Feb.	Mar.	Apr.	May	Jun.	Jul.	Aug.	Sep.	Oct.	Nov.	Dec.
Avg. temp.	28	21	37	42	55	68	71	72	59	53	35	24
+ or - norm.	5	-4	3	-3	-1	3	2	5	-1	3	-5	-4
Precip. (in.)	3	2	2	3	4	4	4	2	2	5	4	3
+ or - norm.	1	-1	-2	0	0	-1	-1	-2	-2	2	1	-1
Snowfall (in.)	12	15	6	2	0	0	0	0	0	0	20	28

Source: U.S. Weather Bureau

NORMAL DATES OF FIRST AND LAST FROST
SELECTED PENNSYLVANIA STATIONS

Area and Station	Minimum of 32°F	
	Last Spring	First Fall
Pocono Mountains		
Stroudsburg	May 8	September 29
East-Central Mountains		
Allentown	May 5	October 9
Southeast Piedmont		
Lancaster	May 3	October 10
Lower Susquehanna		
York	April 30	October 9
Middle Susquehanna		
Williamsport	May 2	October 11
Upper Susquehanna		
Montrose	May 15	October 3
Wellsboro	May 22	September 25
Central Mountains		
Ridgway	May 26	September 24
Philipsburg	April 27	October 12
South-Central Mountains		
Altoona	May 8	October 8
Ebensburg	May 15	October 3
Southwest Plateau		
Butler	May 18	October 2
Donora	April 21	October 28
Confluence	April 29	October 15
Northwest Plateau		
Brookville	May 25	September 23
Corry	May 24	September 25
Franklin	May 13	October 6

Source: U.S. Department of Agriculture.

PLANTING AND HARVESTING DATES
PENNSYLVANIA FIELD AND VEGETABLE CROPS

Crop	Planting	Harvesting
Winter wheat and rye	Sept. 15–Oct. 15	July 1–Aug. 15
Spring oats	Apr. 15–May 30	August
Fall barley	Sept. 10–30	June 15–July 15
Corn (grain)	May 10–June 21	Sept. 21–Nov. 21
Corn (silage)	May 10–July 1	Sept. 21–Oct. 10
Soybeans	May 15–July 1	Oct. 21–Dec. 1
Tobacco	May 25–July 1	Aug. 15–Oct. 1
Potatoes (fall)	Apr. 15–June 15	July 25–Nov. 15
Vegetables, processing		
Snap beans	May 1–July 7	July 7–Sept. 21
Sweet corn	May 1–July 7	Aug. 1–Oct. 15
Tomatoes	May 1–June 21	Aug. 1–Oct. 25
Vegetables, fresh market		
Cabbage (summer)	Apr. 21–June 21	June 21–Oct. 15
Cabbage (fall)	June 1–July 30	Sept. 1–Nov. 30
Snap beans	Apr. 15–June 21	June 21–Oct. 15
Sweet corn	Apr. 15–June 15	July 15–Oct. 15
Tomatoes	Apr. 21–June 21	July 1–Nov. 1
Strawberries	Apr. 1–May 30	May 30–July 1

Source: U.S. Department of Agriculture.

6

Industry and Commerce

AGRICULTURE

Agriculture is Pennsylvania's leading industry. Cash receipts from farm marketing totaled $3.74 billion in 1995. Income from crop sales was $1.18 billion; from livestock and livestock products, $2.61 billion. Pennsylvania ranked 19th of the 50 states in farm sales.

The top five agricultural commodities in the state are dairy products, cattle and calves, greenhouse and nursery products, mushrooms, and chicken eggs. Dairy products account for about half of the total cash receipts. Pennsylvania farms ranked fourth in the nation in milk production, producing about 7% of the country's milk and earning $1.4 billion in the process. Pennsylvania also ranked in the top six states in each of the manufactured dairy product categories—butter, cheese, and ice cream.

The state's cattle inventory was valued at $1.28 billion, accounting for 94% of the total value of all livestock. (Sheep account for 1%, hogs for 4%.) Pennsylvania ranked 18th in the nation in cattle inventory and fourth in milk cow inventory. Pennsylvania ranked tenth in red meat products, and gross income from meat products was $4.76 million. The state has 201 slaughter plants, which slaughtered 1.3 billion pounds of cattle in 1995.

Pennsylvania ranked seventh nation-

ally in wholesale sales of floriculture crops. The 665 growers produced $7 million in cut flowers, $27 million in potted plants, $37 million in foliage plants, and $57 million in bedding plants in 19.8 million square feet of growing area.

The commonwealth is the number one producer of agaricus mushrooms, the conventional button variety, in the United States, accounting for 45% of domestic production.

The state's fourth-place ranking in chicken egg production was achieved by 26.5 million chickens, which laid an average of 266 eggs each during the year, producing 5.7 billion eggs valued at $265 million.

The state had 50,000 farms and 7.7 million acres of farmland in 1995. (In 1955, there were 85,000 farms and 11.3 million acres of farmland.) Average farm size is 154 acres. There are 33,000 cattle operations, 10,800 dairy farms, 5,500 hog farms, 3,200 sheep farms, and 5,700 poultry farms. (Many farms have more than one operation.)

By almost any measure—livestock inventory, number of farms, acreage, total cash receipts, or poultry, milk, and egg production—the leading farm county is Lancaster. This county is also the leading producer of corn (both for grain and for silage), barley, hay, and alfalfa hay and ranks second in the production of soybeans and wheat (York County ranks first) and fourth in potatoes.

Lancaster County has the most farms, 4,940, and the most farmland, 419,000 acres. It also has the third smallest average farm size, 85 acres. But Lancaster County farmers, many of them Amish, who have a spiritual aspect guiding their stewardship of the land, make the most of the available resources. For example, the 95,000 cows in Lancaster County produce an average of 18,600 pounds of milk per cow annually; in the other 66 counties of the state, the average production of milk per cow ranges from 12,900 to 17,800 pounds. Also helping the farmers are the facts that Lancaster County has the best limestone soils and the best climate for farming in the commonwealth.

PENNSYLVANIA FARM STATISTICS, 1995

County	Number	Acres	Average Size
Northwestern Region			
Crawford	1,235	227,000	184 Acres
Erie	1,295	180,000	139
Forest	40	5,000	125
Mercer	1,160	173,000	149
Venango	390	56,000	144
Warren	430	72,000	167
Total	4,550	713,000	—
North-Central			
Bradford	1,500	336,000	224
Cameron	30	2,500	83
Clinton	285	42,000	147
Elk	170	17,500	103
Lycoming	900	142,000	158
McKean	235	42,000	179
Potter	330	96,000	291
Sullivan	160	32,000	200
Tioga	920	228,000	248
Total	4,530	938,000	—
Northeastern			
Lackawanna	265	40,000	151
Susquehanna	790	190,000	241
Wayne	660	130,000	197
Wyoming	335	67,000	200
Total	2,050	427,000	—

PENNSYLVANIA FARM STATISTICS *(continued)*

County	Number	Acres	Average Size
West-Central			
Armstrong	725	127,000	175 Acres
Beaver	565	62,000	110
Butler	1,110	138,000	124
Clarion	490	101,000	206
Indiana	820	153,000	187
Jefferson	460	85,000	185
Lawrence	690	92,000	133
Total	4,860	758,000	—
Central			
Blair	465	82,000	176
Cambria	590	82,000	139
Centre	810	150,000	185
Clearfield	410	59,000	144
Columbia	720	109,000	151
Dauphin	675	96,000	142
Huntingdon	630	138,000	219
Juniata	600	91,000	152
Mifflin	680	87,000	128
Montour	295	44,000	149
Northumberland	660	117,000	177
Perry	665	111,000	167
Snyder	740	93,000	126
Union	510	67,000	131
Total	8,450	1,326,000	—
East-Central			
Carbon	160	20,000	125
Lehigh	480	88,500	184
Luzerne	435	53,000	122
Monroe	160	22,500	141
Northampton	435	87,000	200
Pike	40	6,000	150
Schuylkill	650	95,000	146
Total	2,360	372,000	—

PENNSYLVANIA FARM STATISTICS *(continued)*

County	Number	Acres	Average Size
Southwestern			
Allegheny	370	35,000	95 Acres
Fayette	855	114,000	133
Greene	700	135,000	193
Somerset	1,095	236,000	216
Washington	1,500	218,000	145
Westmoreland	1,270	165,000	130
Total	5,790	903,000	—
South-Central			
Adams	1,060	184,000	174
Bedford	1,040	214,000	206
Cumberland	1,030	152,000	148
Franklin	1,420	252,000	177
Fulton	490	95,000	194
York	1,890	271,000	143
Total	6,930	1,168,000	—
Southeastern			
Berks	1,720	239,000	139
Bucks	755	82,000	109
Chester	1,505	190,000	126
Delaware	75	5,500	73
Lancaster	4,940	419,000	85
Lebanon	980	112,000	114
Montgomery	505	47,500	94
Philadelphia	0	0	0
Total	10,480	1,095,000	—
State Total	**50,000**	**7,700,000**	—

COUNTY RANK IN CROP PRODUCTION (1995)

Crop	1	2	3
Wheat	York	Lancaster	Berks
Corn (grain)	Lancaster	York	Berks
Corn (silage)	Lancaster	Franklin	Lebanon
Oats	Somerset	Crawford	Cambria
Barley	Lancaster	York	Franklin
Soybeans	York	Lancaster	Chester
Hay (all)	Lancaster	Bradford	Franklin
Alfalfa hay	Lancaster	Franklin	Bedford
Potatoes	Erie	Cambria	Schuylkill
Apples	Adams	Franklin	Berks
Peaches	Adams	Franklin	York

COUNTY RANK IN LIVESTOCK AND POULTRY INVENTORY (1995)

Crop	1	2	3
Cattle, calves	Lancaster	Franklin	Bradford
Hogs, pigs	Lancaster	York	Lebanon
Sheep, lambs	Washington	Greene	Lancaster
Chickens	Lancaster	Lebanon	Franklin
Milk cows	Lancaster	Franklin	Bradford

County Rank in Production

	1	2	3
Broilers	Lancaster	Lebanon	Juniata
Milk	Lancaster	Franklin	Bradford
Eggs	Lancaster	Lebanon	Franklin

County Rank in Cash Receipts

	1	2	3
	Lancaster	Chester	Berks

PRINCIPAL CROPS HARVESTED (1995)

Crop	Acres Harvested	Production		Value	National Ranking
Winter wheat	185,000	10M	bu	$42M	24
Rye	10,000	330,000	bu	$1M	13
Oats	160,000	9M	bu	$16M	6
Barley	75,000	5M	bu	$9M	13
Soybeans	315,000	10M	bu	$58M	22
Corn (grain)	980,000	94M	bu	$348M	14
Corn (silage)	390,000	6M	ton	$129M	4
Hay (all)	1,910,000	4M	ton	$416M	15
Hay (alfalfa)	780,000	2M	ton	$235M	17
Hay (other)	1,130,000	2M	ton	$180M	9
Tobacco	7,900	16M	lbs	$22M	9
Potatoes	17,000	4M	cwt	$30M	14
Mushrooms	—	354M	lbs	$274M	1
Fresh vegetables					
Sweet corn	17,200	800,000	cwt	$16M	7
Tomatoes	4,200	462,000	cwt	$9M	9
Cabbage	2,000	440,000	cwt	$5M	12
Processing vegetables					
Sweet corn	2,900	14,800	ton	$776,000	9
Tomatoes	1,400	36,600	ton	$3M	5
Snap beans	8,200	18,450	ton	$4M	6
Strawberries	1,400	64,000	cwt	$6M	9
Pears	—	6,300	ton	$2M	5
Cherries (sweet)	—	900	ton	$1M	7
Cherries (tart)	—	10M	lbs	$1M	5
Grapes	—	63,000	ton	$11M	5
Apples	—	493M	lbs	$47M	5
Peaches	—	90M	lbs	$25M	4
Cantaloupes	1,300	156,000	cwt	$3M	8

RECORD HIGHS AND LOWS IN PENNSYLVANIA AGRICULTURE

Field Crops and Vegetables

Corn (grain)	High	151,800,000	bu	1985
	Low	19,074,000	bu	1930
Corn (silage)	High	7,448,000	ton	1982
	Low	1,326,000	ton	1923
Wheat	High	26,565,000	bu	1901
	Low	7,095,000	bu	1978
Oats	High	44,165,000	bu	1918
	Low	8,480,000	bu	1994
Barley	High	9,900,000	bu	1967
	Low	130,000	bu	1914
Rye	High	4,368,000	bu	1891
	Low	186,000	bu	1951
Soybeans	High	13,230,000	bu	1994
	Low	33,000	bu	1935
Hay (all)	High	5,302,000	ton	1985
	Low	2,255,000	ton	1866
Hay (alfalfa)	High	2,772,000	ton	1985
	Low	65,000	ton	1919
Potatoes	High	19,662,000	cwt	1934
	Low	3,500,000	cwt	1991
Tobacco	High	72,275,000	lbs	1918
	Low	3,390,000	lbs	1867
Mushrooms	High	370,113,000	lbs	1993
	Low	93,000,000	lbs	1966
Sweet corn	High	1,250,000	cwt	1944
	Low	545,000	cwt	1972
Tomatoes	High	800,000	cwt	1989
	Low	27,000	cwt	1926
Snap beans	High	24,900	ton	1990
	Low	300	ton	1921

Fruits

Strawberries	High	125,300	cwt	1937
	Low	2,700	cwt	1945
Apples	High	1,114,000	mlbs*	1896
	Low	78,000	mlbs	1921

*MLBS = million pounds

RECORD HIGHS AND LOWS IN PENNSYLVANIA AGRICULTURE
(continued)

Cherries (tart)	High	35,000 mlbs	1964
	Low	3,200 mlbs	1977
Cherries (sweet)	High	2,200,000 ton	1940
	Low	50,000 ton	1990
Grapes	High	80,000 ton	1994
	Low	6,000 ton	1945
Pears	High	21,125 ton	1920
	Low	1,900 ton	1973
Peaches	High	148,800 mlbs	1954
	Low	0	1994

Livestock Inventory

Cattle, calves	High	2,100,000	1982
	Low	1,250,000	1927
Milk cows	High	1,039,000	1956
	Low	639,000	1995
Hogs, pigs	High	1,265,000	1919
	Low	386,000	1966
Sheep	High	2,985,000	1867
	Low	88,000	1984
Chickens	High	27,700,000	1992
	Low	13,850	1975
Turkeys	High	11,500,000	1995
	Low	192,000	1929
Broilers produced	High	127,700,000	1989
	Low	2,500,000	1939

Livestock Production

Milk	High	10,600 mlbs	1995
	Low	2,242 mlbs	1929
Eggs	High	5.6 b*	1993
	Low	1.6 b	1924
Wool	High	4.5 mlbs	1911
	Low	560,000 mlbs	1995

*b =billion

NONFARM EMPLOYMENT IN PENNSYLVANIA (1990–1995)

Thirty-four of Pennsylvania's 43 labor market areas showed increases in the number of nonagricultural jobs from 1990 to 1995, with the Potter County market area showing the best growth, 21%. Two labor market areas maintained their level of jobs, while seven areas had fewer jobs. Of these seven areas, six are rural. Philadelphia, with a job loss of 2%, is the only area to show a decline, although slow growth has been the trend of the past three years.

The long-term shift from a goods-producing to a service economy continued in most Pennsylvania market areas from 1990 to 1995. Only eight of the state's 43 areas added goods-producing jobs over this period. The goods-producing sector (mining, construction, and manufacturing) declined by 9%. Goods-producing industries accounted for 22% of total nonagricultural jobs.

Service-producing industries gained 5% since 1990 and accounted for 78% of all nonfarm jobs in 1995.

In the Pittsburgh area, job growth has been slow but steady in each of the last four years. Large-scale layoffs due to corporate downsizing have decreased.

The Philadelphia area has not regained all of the jobs lost in the last recession. Goods-producing jobs decreased 15% from 1990 to 1995. The phasing out of the Philadelphia Naval Shipyard led to a loss of 15% of federal government jobs over this period. However, state and local government jobs grew 3%. Service jobs increased 4% over the last three years. Philadelphians are definitely living in post-industrial America.

EMPLOYEES ON NONFARM PAYROLLS BY MAJOR INDUSTRIES IN PENNSYLVANIA (1996)

Service	1,651,200
Wholesale and retail trade	1,205,300
Manufacturing	929,100
Government	720,900
Finance, insurance, real estate	308,700
Transportation and public utilities	271,900
Construction	201,700
Mining	19,400
Total employees	5,308,200
State unemployment rate, December 1996	4.3%

Manufacturing Workers' Hours and Earnings

Average weekly hours, December 1996	42.6
Average hourly earnings	$13.64
Average weekly earnings	$581.06

Source: Pennsylvania Department of Labor and Industry, Bureau of Research and Statistics

MANUFACTURING ESTABLISHMENTS AND EMPLOYEES

County	Establishments	Employees
Allegheny	1,759	89,394
Montgomery	1,505	98,705
Philadelphia	1,498	73,694
Bucks	1,144	47,888
Lancaster	897	60,954
York	701	53,129
Chester	650	34,214
Erie	643	40,182
Berks	601	46,882
Westmoreland	590	25,100
Delaware	589	38,837
Luzerne	479	30,159
Lehigh	425	35,717
Northampton	378	25,583
Washington	338	16,056
Lackawanna	335	22,259
Butler	296	14,833
Dauphin	260	18,978
Schuylkill	257	18,912
Crawford	253	9,595
Cumberland	239	16,094
Lycoming	236	17,630
Lebanon	231	11,597
Beaver	225	10,716
Mercer	218	11,633
Franklin	201	14,295
Lawrence	186	6,372
Cambria	181	7,993
Blair	153	11,541
Centre	151	12,450
Fayette	151	6,200
Indiana	148	5,461
Northumberland	145	11,241
Somerset	145	5,853
Adams	133	7,792

MANUFACTURING ESTABLISHMENTS AND EMPLOYEES
(continued)

County	Establishments	Employees
Clearfield	132	5,892
Columbia	128	10,201
Monroe	120	5,409
Armstrong	117	6,105
Elk	108	9,288
Warren	105	5,328
Jefferson	103	5,224
Venango	101	4,702
McKean	85	6,431
Mifflin	76	7,406
Snyder	74	4,849
Carbon	67	4,195
Wayne	67	1,619
Bradford	66	6,865
Huntingdon	64	4,204
Susquehanna	59	1,836
Bedford	57	3,070
Clarion	57	2,619
Clinton	54	4,237
Tioga	52	3,115
Union	47	4,329
Juniata	41	2,341
Greene	40	2,359
Wyoming	35	3,158
Perry	33	730
Potter	32	1,315
Cameron	22	1,348
Pike	22	328
Fulton	20	1,369
Montour	15	1,409
Sullivan	13	313
Forest	4	122

Source: Pennsylvania Department of Commerce

PENNSYLVANIA FORTUNE 500 CORPORATIONS (1996)

Rank in PA	Rank	Revenues (in millions)	Profits (in millions)	HQ
1. USX	42	$21,076.0	$943.0	Pittsburgh
2. CIGNA	54	18,950.0	1056.0	Philadelphia
3. ALCOA	97	13,128.4	514.9	Pittsburgh
4. Bell Atlantic	99	13,081.4	1,881.5	Philadelphia
5. Ikon Office Solutions	121	11,122.6	210.7	Wayne
6. Union Pacific	142	10,051.0	904.0	Bethlehem
7. Sun	148	9,875.0	(115.0)	Philadelphia
8. Westinghouse Electric	156	9,401.0	30.0	Pittsburgh
9. H. J. Heinz	161	9,112.3	659.3	Pittsburgh
10. Crown Cork & Seal	179	8,331.9	284.0	Philadelphia
11. PPG Industries	199	7,218.1	744.0	Pittsburgh
12. Unisys	226	6,370.5	49.7	Blue Bell
13. PNC Bank	228	6,333.8	992.2	Pittsburgh
14. Aramark	235	6,122.5	109.5	Philadelphia
15. Amerisource Health	256	5,551.7	35.4	Malvern
16. AMP	261	5,468.0	287.0	Harrisburg
17. Rite Aid	262	5,446.0	158.9	Camp Hill
18. VF	276	5,137.2	299.5	Wyomissing
19. Mellon Bank Corp.	299	4,762.0	733.0	Pittsburgh
20. Bethlehem Steel	302	4,679.0	(308.8)	Bethlehem
21. PECO Energy	318	4,283.7	517.2	Philadelphia
22. CoreStates Financial Corporation	323	4,197.3	649.1	Philadelphia
23. Comcast	339	4,038.4	(53.5)	Philadelphia
24. Air Products & Chemicals	340	4,033.0	416.0	Allentown
25. Hershey Foods	344	3,989.3	273.2	Hershey
26. Rohm & Haas	345	3,882.0	363.0	Philadelphia
27. Allegheny Teledyne	359	3,815.6	213.0	Pittsburgh
28. CNG	360	3,794.3	298.3	Pittsburgh
29. Conrail	365	3,714.0	342.0	Philadelphia
30. Intelligent Electronics	384	3,547.8	(103.8)	Exton
31. York International	419	3,218.5	147.9	York
32. PP&L Resources	472	2,805.0	329.0	Allentown
Total		226,637.3	12,860.2	

PENNSYLVANIA CHAMBERS OF COMMERCE

Pennsylvania Chamber of Business
  and Industry
  One Commerce Square
  417 Walnut St.
  Harrisburg, PA 17101
  (717) 255-3252
Albion
  P.O. Box 7
  Albion, PA 16401
  (814) 756-4133
Allegheny Valley
  2858 Old Freeport Rd.
  Natrona Heights, PA 15061
  (412) 224-3400
Allentown–Lehigh County
  462 Walnut St.
  Allentown, PA 18102
  (610) 437-9661
Altoona–Blair County
  1212 12th Ave.
  Altoona, PA 16601
  (814) 943-8151
Ambridge
  719 Merchant St.
  Ambridge, PA 15003
  (412) 266-3040
Armstrong County
  2 Butler Rd.,
  Kittanning, PA 16201
  (412) 543-1305
Beaver County
  1008 Seventh Ave.
  Beaver Falls, PA 15010
  (412) 846-6750
Bedford County
  37 E. Pitt St.
  Bedford, PA 15522
  (814) 623-2233
Bellefonte
  320 W. High St.
  Bellefonte, PA 16823
  (814) 355-2917

Bensalem
  Box 125
  Bensalem, PA 19020
  (215) 245-6575
Berks County
  645 Penn St.
  Reading, PA 19601
  (610) 376-6766
Berwick
  120 E. 3rd St.
  Berwick, PA 18603
  (717) 752-3601
Bethel Park
  2823 Park Rd.
  Bethel Park, PA 15102
  (412) 833-1177
Bethlehem
  509 Main St.
  Bethlehem, PA 18018
  (610) 867-3788
Bloomsburg
  238 Market St.
  Bloomsburg, PA 17815
  (717) 784-2522
Boyertown
  238 E. High St.
  Pottstown, PA 19464
  (610) 367-5300
Bradford
  10 Main St.
  Bradford, PA 16701
  (814) 368-7115
Bridgeville
  990 Washington Pike
  Bridgeville, PA 15017
  (412) 221-4100
Broad Top
  Box 188
  Saxton, PA 16678
  (814) 635-2913
Brookville
  233 Main St.
  Brookville, PA 15825
  (814) 849-8448

Brownsville
  Union Station Building
  Market St.
  Brownsville, PA 15417
  (412) 785-4160
Butler County
  Box 1082
  Butler, PA 16003
  (412) 283-2222
California
  153 Third St.
  California, PA 15419
  (412) 938-8333
Canton
  Box 222
  Canton, PA 17724
  (717) 673-5500
Capitol Region
  114 Walnut St.
  Harrisburg, PA 17108
  (717) 232-4121
Carbondale
  1 N. Main St.
  Carbondale, PA 18407
  (717) 282-4110
Carlisle
  212 N. Hanover St.
  Carlisle, PA 17013
  (717) 243-4515
Carmichaels
  Box 93
  Carmichaels, PA 15320
  (412) 276-8080
Castle Shannon
  935 Park Ave.
  Pittsburgh, PA 15234
  (412) 343-6100
Central Bucks
  115 W. Court St.
  Doylestown, PA 18901
  (215) 348-3913
Central Chartiers
  13 W. Pike St.
  Canonsburg, PA 15317
  (412) 745-1812

Central Chester
  Box 314
  Exton, PA 19341
  (610) 363-7746
Central Fayette
  11 Pittsburgh St.
  Uniontown, PA 15401
  (412) 437-4571
Central Montgomery
  Lafayette Place One
  Norristown, PA 19401
  (610) 277-9500
Central Susquehanna Valley
  Box 10
  Shamokin Dam, PA 17876
  (717) 743-4100
Central Westmoreland
  R.D. 1
  Greensburg, PA 15601
  (412) 834-2900
Centre County
  200 Innovation Blvd.
  State College, PA 16803
  (814) 234-1829
Chambersburg
  72 S. 2nd St.
  Chambersburg, PA 17201
  (717) 264-7101
Charleroi
  Box 127
  Charleroi, PA 15022
  (412) 483-3508
Chester County
  17 E. Gay St.
  West Chester, PA 19380
  (610) 436-7696
Clarion County
  41 S. 5th Ave.
  Clarion, PA 16214
  (814) 226-9161
Clearfield County
  125 E. Market St.
  Clearfield, PA 16830
  (814) 765-7560

Clinton County
151 Susquehanna Ave.
Lock Haven, PA 17745
(717) 748-5782
Connellsville
923 W. Crawford Ave.
Connellsville, PA 15425
(412) 628-5500
Conshohocken
Two Tower Bridge
Conshohocken, PA 19428
(610) 828-3660
Corry
112 N. Center St.
Corry, PA 16407
(814) 665-9925
Cranberry
2700 Rochester Rd.
Mars, PA 16046
(412) 776-4949
Danville
206 Walnut St.
Danville, PA 17821
(717) 275-5200
Delaware County
602 E. Baltimore Pike
Media PA 19603
(610) 565-3677
Donora
638 McKean Ave.
Donora, PA 15033
(412) 379-5929
Downingtown
38 W. Lancaster Ave.
Downingtown, PA 19335
(610) 269-1523
DuBois
33 N. Brady St.
DuBois, PA 15801
(814) 371-5010
Eastern Montgomery County
Box 172
Jenkintown, PA 19046
(215) 887-5122

East Liberty
5972 Baum Blvd.
Pittsburgh, PA 15206
(412) 661-9660
East Suburban
2069 Route 286
Pittsburgh, PA 15239
(412) 325-2500
Elizabethtown
23 S. Market St.
Elizabethtown, PA 17022
(717) 367-5126
Ellwood City
5th St. & Bell Ave.
Ellwood City, PA 16117
(412) 758-5501
Emlenton
Main St. & 5th
Emlenton, PA 16373
(412) 867-1855
Emmaus
244 Main St.
Emmaus, PA 18049
(610) 965-5070
Emporium–Cameron County
33 E. 4th St.
Emporium, PA 15834
(814) 486-4314
Ephrata
23 Washington Ave.
Ephrata, PA 17522
(717) 738-9010
Erie
1006 State St.
Erie, PA 16501
(814) 454-7191
Franklin County
1256 Liberty St.
Franklin, PA 16323
(814) 432-5823
Freeland
Box 31
Freeland, PA 18224
(717) 636-0670

Fulton County
Box 141
McConnellsburg, PA 17233
(717) 485-4064
Galeton
Box 176
Galeton, PA 16922
(814) 435-2321
Gettysburg–Adams County
33 York St.
Gettysburg, PA 17325
(717) 334-8151
Glenside
Box 22
Glenside, PA 19038
(215) 887-3110
Greater Pittsburgh
3 Gateway Circle, 14th Floor
Pittsburgh, PA 15222
(412) 392-4500
Greater West Shore
4211 Trindle Rd.
Camp Hill, PA 17011
(717) 761-0702
Great Valley Regional
70 Valley Stream Parkway
Malvern, PA 19335
(610) 993-1790
Greencastle-Antrim
Box 175
Greencastle, PA 17225
(717) 597-4610
Greenville
Box 350
Greenville, PA 16125
(412) 588-7150
Grove City
111 W. Pine St.
Grove City, PA 16127
(412) 458-6410
Hanover
146 Broadway
Hanover, PA 17331
(717) 637-6130

Hatboro
Box 244
Hatboro, PA 19040
(215) 956-9540
Hawley–Lake Wallenpaupack
Box 150
Hawley, PA 18428
(717) 226-3191
Hazleton
1 S. Church St.
Hazleton, PA 18201
(717) 455-1508
Hellertown–Lower Saucon
Box 33
Hellertown, PA 18055
(610) 838-1808
Horsham Township
Box 141
Horsham, PA 19044
(215) 443-7154
Huntingdon County
241 Mifflin St.
Huntingdon, PA 16652
(814) 643-4322
Indiana County
1019 Philadelphia St.
Indiana, PA 15701
(412) 465-2511
Indian Valley
Box 77
Telford, PA 18969
(215) 723-9472
Jersey Shore
Box 231
Jersey Shore, PA 17740
(717) 398-0201
Johnsonburg
501 High St.
Johnsonburg, PA 15845
(814) 965-4793
Johnstown
111 Market St.
Johnstown, PA 15901
(814) 536-5107

Juniata Valley
3 W. Monument Square, #208
Lewistown PA 17044
(717) 248-6713

Kane
14 Greeves St.
Kane, PA 16735
(814) 837-6565

King of Prussia
1150 First Ave.
King of Prussia, PA 19406
(610) 265-1776

Kutztown
276 W. Main St.
Kutztown, PA 19530
(610) 683-8860

Lake City–Girard
Box 118
Lake City, PA 16423
(814) 774-9666

Lancaster
Box 1558
Lancaster, PA 17608
(717) 397-3531

Latrobe
10 Lloyd Ave.
Latrobe, PA 15650
(412) 537-2671

Lawrence County
138 Washington St.
New Castle, PA 16101
(412) 658-1648

Lebanon Valley
252 N. 8th St.
Lebanon, PA 17042
(717) 273-3727

Lehighton
364 First St.
Lehighton, PA 18235
(610) 377-2191

Ligonier Valley
120 E. Main St.
Ligonier, PA 15658
(412) 238-4200

Linesville
Box 651
Linesville, PA 16424
(814) 683-5839

Lower Bucks County
409 Hood Blvd.
Fairless Hills, PA 19030
(215) 943-7400

Main Line
155 E. Lancaster Ave.
Wayne, PA 19087
(610) 687-6232

Manheim
210 S. Charlotte St.
Manheim, PA 17545
(717) 665-6330

Mansfield
Box 401
Mansfield, PA 16933
(717) 662-3442

Mars
Box 65
Mars, PA 16046
(412) 625-3571

Meadville
211 Chestnut St.
Meadville, PA 16335
(814) 337-8030

Mercer County
Box 473
Mercer, PA 16137
(412) 662-4185

Mercersburg
Box 61
Mercersburg, PA 17236
(717) 328-5827

Mifflinburg
451 Chestnut St.
Mifflinburg, PA 17844
(717) 966-2721

Milton
1 S. Arch St.
Milton, PA 17847
(717) 742-7341

Monessen
125 Sixth St.
Monessen, PA 15062
(412) 684-3200
Monongahela
173 W. Main St.
Monongahela, PA 15063
(412) 258-5919
Monroeville
2790 Mosside Blvd., #295
Monroeville, PA 15146
(412) 856-0622
Montgomery County
420 W. Germantown Pike
Eagleville, PA 19403
(610) 272-5000
Mon Valley
Eastgate Eleven
Monessen, PA 15062
(412) 684-3381
Mon-Yough
633 Long Run Rd.
McKeesport, PA 15132
(412) 754-6000
Mount Carmel
25 S. Oak St.
Mount Carmel, PA 17851
(717) 339-0370
Mount Joy
Box 73
Mount Joy, PA 17552
(717) 653-0773
Mount Oliver
Box 59272
Pittsburgh, PA 15210
(412) 381-1929
Mount Pleasant
Municipal Bldg., #201
Mount Pleasant, PA 15666
(412) 547-7521
Mount Union
Box 12
Mount Union, PA 17066
(814) 542-9413

Nanticoke
179 S. Market St.
Nanticoke, PA 18634
(717) 735-6990
Nazareth
Box 173
Nazareth, PA 18064
(610) 759-9188
New Bethlehem
Box 107
New Bethlehem, PA 16242
(814) 275-3929
New Kensington
858 Fourth Ave.
New Kensington, PA 15068
(412) 339-6616
New Oxford
Box 152
New Oxford, PA 17350
(717) 624-2342
Northampton County
Box 355
Northampton, PA 18067
(610) 262-6780
North East
21 S. Lake St.
North East, PA 16428
(814) 725-4262
Northeast Philadelphia
8601 Roosevelt Ave.
Philadelphia, PA 19152
(215) 332-3400
Northern Allegheny County
9401 McKnight Rd.
Pittsburgh, PA 15237
(412) 367-3920
Northern Lehigh County
125 S. Walnut St.
Slatington, PA 18080
(610) 767-2131
North Penn
Box 97
Montgomeryville, PA 18936
(215) 362-9200

Northside
512 Foreland St.
Pittsburgh, PA 15212
(412) 231-6500

North Suburban
547 Lincoln Ave.
Bellevue, PA 15202
(412) 761-2113

Norwin
8871 Route 30
North Huntingdon, PA 15642
(412) 863-0888

Oakmont
Box 384
Oakmont, PA 15139
(412) 828-3322

Oil City
Box 376
Oil City, PA 16301
(814) 676-8521

Oxford
Box 4
Oxford, PA 19363
(215) 932-0740

Panther Valley
Box 116
Lansford, PA 18232
(717) 645-7830

Penn Hills
Box 10640
Penn Hills, PA 15235
(412) 795-8741

Pennridge
1211 N. 5th St.
Perkasie, PA 18944
(215) 257-5390

Perkiomen
Box 176
Schwenksville, PA 19473
(610) 489-6660

Peters Township
Box 991
McMurray, PA 15317
(412) 941-6345

Philadelphia
1234 Market St., #1800
Philadelphia, PA 19107
(215) 545-1234

Phoenixville
Box 29
Phoenixville, PA 19460
(610) 933-3070

Pike County
Box 883
Milford, PA 18337
(717) 296-8700

Pittsburgh Airport Area
986 Broadhead Rd.
Moon Township, PA 15108
(412) 264-2670

Pittston
Box 704
Pittston, PA 18640
(717) 655-1424

Pocono Mountains
556 Main St.
Stroudsburg, PA 18360
(717) 421-4433

Port Allegany
Box 464
Port Allegany, PA 16743
(814) 642-2181

Punxsutawney
124 W. Mahoning St.
Punxsutawney, PA 15767
(814) 938-7700

Quarryville
Box 24
Quarryville, PA 17566
(717) 786-1911

Reynoldsville
Box 157
Reynoldsville, PA 15851
(814) 653-8270

Ridgway–Elk County
159 Main St.
Ridgway, PA 15853
(814) 776-1424

Schuylkill
91 S. Progress Ave.
Pottsville, PA 17901
(717) 622-1942

Scottdale
Box 276
Scottdale, PA 15683
(412) 887-6350

Scranton
Box 431
Scranton, PA 18501
(717) 342-7711

Selinsgrove
Box 84
Selinsgrove, PA 17870
(717) 374-2550

Sellersville
Box 85
Sellersville, PA 18960
(215) 257-2230

Shamokin
51 E. Lincoln St.
Shamokin, PA 17872
(717) 648-4675

Shenango Valley
1 W. State St.
Sharon, PA 16146
(412) 981-5880

Shippensburg
75 W. King St.
Shippensburg, PA 17257
(717) 532-5509

Slate Belt
5741 Shady Lane
Bangor, PA 18064
(610) 588-4411

Somerset County
829 N. Center Ave.
Somerset, PA 15501
(814) 445-6431

South Park Township
5700 Brownsville Rd.
Pittsburgh, PA 15236
(412) 653-8813

South Side
1411 E. Carson St.
Pittsburgh, PA 15203
(412) 481-0650

Southern Chester County
206 E. State St.
Kennett Square, PA 19348
(610) 444-0774

Southern Wayne County
Box 296
Hamlin, PA 18427
(717) 689-4199

St. Marys
126 Center St.
St. Marys, PA 15857
(814) 781-3804

Steel Valley
1705 Maple St., #213
Homestead, PA 15120
(412) 461-4141

Strongland
Box 10
Vandergrift, PA 15690
(412) 845-5426

Sullivan County
Box 269
Laporte, PA 18626
(717) 946-4160

Susquehanna Valley
Box 510
Columbia, PA 17512
(717) 684-5249

Tamaqua
114 W. Broad St.
Tamaqua, PA 18252
(717) 668-1880

Titusville
116 W. Central Ave.
Titusville, PA 16354
(814) 827-2941

Tri-County
238 High St.
Pottstown, PA 19464
(610) 326-2900

Two Rivers
Box 637
Easton, PA 18044
(610) 253-4211
Tyrone
1004 Logan Ave.
Tyrone, PA 16686
(814) 684-0736
Union County
219 Hafer Rd., #D
Lewisburg, PA 17837
(717) 524-2815
Upper Bucks County
Box 484
Quakertown, PA 18951
(215) 536-3211
Upper Perkiomen Valley
Box 52
Pennsburg, PA 18073
(215) 679-3336
Upper Saint Clair
71 Muray Rd., #201
Upper Saint Clair, PA 15241
(412) 833-9111
Verona
Box 276
Verona, PA 15147
(412) 828-7600
Warminster
575 Madison Ave.
Warminster, PA 18974
(215) 672-6633
Warren County
Box 942
Warren, PA 16365
(814) 723-3050
Washington
20 E. Beau St.
Washington, PA 15301
(412) 225-3010
Wayne County
742 Main St.
Honesdale, PA 18431
(717) 253-1960

Waynesboro
323 E. Main St.
Waynesboro, PA 17268
(717) 762-7123
Waynesburg
24–29 High St.
Waynesburg, PA 15370
(412) 627-5926
Wellsboro
Box 733
Wellsboro, PA 16901
(717) 724-1926
West Chester
40 E. Gay St.
West Chester, PA 19380
(610) 696-4046
Western Chester County,
Box 1171
Coatesville, PA 19320
(610) 384-9550
Whitehall Township
30 Alta Dr.
Whitehall, PA 18052
(610) 432-4130
Wilkes-Barre
67–69 Public Square, #600
Wilkes-Barre, PA 18701
(717) 823-2101
Wilkinsburg
718 Wallace Ave.
Wilkinsburg, PA 15221
(412) 242-0234
Williamsport–Lycoming County
454 Pine St.
Williamsport, PA 17701
(717) 326-1971
Willow Grove
Box 100
Willow Grove, PA 19090
(215) 657-2227
Wissahickon Valley
12 E. Butler Ave.
Ambler, PA 19002
(215) 646-7550

Wyoming County
  Box 568
  Tunkhannock, PA 18657
  (717) 836-7755
York County
  Box 1229
  York, PA 17405
  (717) 848-4000
Zelienople-Harmony
  Box 464
  Zelienople, PA 16063
  (412) 452-5232

PUBLIC UTILITIES

Regulation of utilities is the responsibility of the Pennsylvania Public Utilities Commission. The commission is an independent, quasijudicial agency created to establish and maintain reasonable rates and safe, adequate service. It is composed of five full-time members appointed by the governor for five-year staggered terms, and subject to confirmation by a majority vote of the Senate. The commission regulates 3,835 public utilities:

Transportation and related utilities:
Railroads	63
Trucking companies	2,279
Bus companies	336
Taxi companies	430
Airlines	2
Ferries	4

Other utilities:
Electric	12
Gas	42
Telephone	265
Telegraph	1
Radio-telephone	77
Water	228
Steam heat	4
Sewage disposal	83
Pipelines	9
Total	3,835

THE BUREAU OF CONSUMER SERVICES

Customers who are unhappy with their gas, electric, water, or telephone service may contact the Bureau of Consumer Services of the Public Utility Commission if they are unable to resolve the matter with the utility. The Bureau of Consumer Services was mandated in 1976 and began investigating customer complaints and writing decisions on service terminations in April 1977. The Bureau's phone number is (800) 692-7380.

ATOMIC POWER STATIONS IN PENNSYLVANIA

Plant Name	Location	First Operable
Susquehanna 1	Berwick	1982
Susquehanna 2	Berwick	1984
Three Mile Island	Middletown	1974
Peach Bottom 2	Lancaster	1974
Peach Bottom 3	Lancaster	1974
Limerick 1	Pottstown	1985
Limerick 2	Pottstown	1989
Beaver Valley 1	Shippingport	1976
Beaver Valley 2	Shippingport	1987

7

Pennsylvania Citizens

VITAL STATISTICS

Population

The population of Pennsylvania has remained relatively stable since 1970. The 1994 estimated population was 12,052,410, a 1.4% increase from the 1990 census figures. Between 1970 and 1990, the population increased by only about 87,000 residents. The demographic make-up of the state's residents is very different, however. The number of elderly and nonwhite residents has increased; the number of children under age 15 has decreased.

The percentage of senior citizens (age 65 and older) has almost doubled since 1950, from 8.4% to 15.8% of the population. Meanwhile, the number of children under age 15 has decreased from 27% in 1970 to 20% in 1994. Consequently, the median age of Pennsylvania residents has increased from 30.7 years in 1970 to 36.1 years. The median age for white residents was 36.9; for black residents, 29.8; and for Hispanic residents, 24.8.

There were an estimated 1,324,208 nonwhite residents in 1994, constituting about 11% of the population. (Nonwhites make up 19.7% of the U.S. population.) Blacks represent about 87% of the nonwhite population of Pennsylvania.

Births

There were 156,431 resident live births reported in Pennsylvania in 1994. The birth rate, 13 per 1,000, was the lowest annual figure recorded since 1978 (the U.S. rate was 15.7). Pennsylvania birth rates have been lower than the national rate since 1950, when the state rate was 21 and the national rate was 24.

The median age of a Pennsylvania woman giving birth was 28. The general fertility rate per 1,000 females aged 15 to 44 has decreased from 80.6 live births in 1970 to 59.4 in 1994.

Births to black mothers in 1994 accounted for 14.9% of all births, and to Hispanic mothers, 4%. In about 25% of these births, the mother was less than 20 years old. Among whites, the percentage of births to teenagers was 8.6.

About 62% of the births recorded in Philadelphia were to unmarried mothers; statewide, about 33% of births were to unmarried women.

The names most frequently given to female babies were Emily, Jessica, Ashley, Samantha, and Nicole; to males, Michael, Tyler, Matthew, Christopher, and Ryan.

Abortions

There were 39,628 abortions performed in the state in 1994, the lowest number

PENNSYLVANIA POPULATION (1995)		
County	Population	% of Total
Adams	83,998	.7
Allegheny	1,309,821	11.0
Armstrong	74,569	.6
Beaver	187,979	1.6
Bedford	49,192	.4
Berks	349,583	2.9
Blair	131,647	1.1
Bradford	62,260	.5
Bucks	573,901	4.7
Butler	165,557	1.3
Cambria	160,531	1.3
Cameron	5,707	*
Carbon	58,832	.5
Centre	131,968	1.1
Chester	404,945	3.3
Clarion	42,338	.3
Clearfield	79,724	.7
Clinton	37,215	.3
Columbia	64,492	.5
Crawford	89,173	.7
Cumberland	205,959	1.7
Dauphin	246,338	2.0
Delaware	548,708	4.5
Elk	35,125	.3
Erie	280,460	2.3
Fayette	146,287	1.2
Forest	5,001	*
Franklin	126,444	1.0
Fulton	14,362	*
Greene	41,114	.3
Huntingdon	44,933	.4
Indiana	90,604	.8
Jefferson	46,260	.4
Juniata	21,701	*
Lackawanna	215,688	1.8

PENNSYLVANIA POPULATION (continued)

County	Population	% of Total
Lancaster	447,521	3.7
Lawrence	96,604	.8
Lebanon	116,789	1.0
Lehigh	297,838	2.5
Luzerne	326,063	2.7
Lycoming	120,194	1.0
McKean	48,503	.4
Mercer	122,254	1.0
Mifflin	47,066	.4
Monroe	116,091	1.0
Montgomery	705,178	5.8
Montour	18,223	*
Northampton	256,796	2.1
Northumberland	96,260	.8
Perry	43,531	.4
Philadelphia	1,498,971	12.6
Pike	36,852	.3
Potter	17,090	*
Schuylkill	153,616	1.3
Snyder	37,845	.3
Somerset	80,113	.7
Sullivan	6,184	*
Susquehanna	41,800	.3
Tioga	41,534	.3
Union	40,928	.3
Venango	59,057	.5
Warren	44,928	.4
Washington	208,017	1.7
Wayne	44,070	.4
Westmoreland	376,501	3.1
Wyoming	29,316	*
York	362,793	3.0
Total	12,071,842	

*Less than .3
Source: U.S. Department of Commerce, Bureau of the Census

VITAL EVENTS (1994)

Events	Average Number per Day
Live births	429
Deaths	347
Abortions	109
Marriages	207
Divorces	110

By Age at Death

Less than 28 days	2
28–364 days	1
1–19 years	3
20–34 years	8
35–49 years	19
50–64 years	43
65–74 years	78
75 and over	193

By Cause of Death

Heart disease	120
Cancer	82
Stroke	23
Chronic obstructive pulmonary disease	14
Unintentional injuries	
Motor vehicle	4
Non–motor vehicle	8
Pneumonia and influenza	12
Diabetes	9
Septicemia	5
Nephritis, nephrosis	5
Suicide	4
HIV infection	4
Liver disease and cirrhosis	3
Aortic aneurysm	3
All other causes	53

Source: Pennsylvania Department of Health

since 1975, when the state began collecting these figures. The rate per 1,000 female residents aged 15 to 44 was 15, the lowest rate ever recorded. Eight counties accounted for 99% of all abortions performed: Philadelphia, Chester, Allegheny, Dauphin, Delaware, Lehigh, Montgomery, and York. Philadelphia residents accounted for 39% of the total, Allegheny County residents for 13.5%. Forty-seven counties reported no abortions performed; three reported only one.

Life Expectancy

The life expectancy of Pennsylvania residents in 1994 was 76.9 years, an increase of 3.7 years since 1980. Males live an average of 73.6 years and females 80.1 years. White females have the longest life expectancy, 80.3 years, followed by white males, 74.2 years. Nonwhites have a life expectancy of 68.1 years: females 72.6, and males 63.9.

Deaths

The leading cause of death of Pennsylvania residents is heart disease, which accounted for about 34% of all deaths in 1994. Cancer remained, by far, the second most frequent cause of death, 24%. Stroke was in third place, accounting for 6% of all deaths. The rank order of the top three causes of death remains consistent. Since 1950, however, the percentage of deaths from cancer has consistently increased, while the figures for the other two have generally declined.

The three leading causes of death are the same for all races; however, homicide and HIV infection are among the top ten causes of death for blacks, but not for whites. Instead, suicide

and nephritis/nephrosis appear in the top ten causes of death among whites. Causes of death with significantly higher rates for men include motor vehicle accidents, suicide, HIV infection, homicide, and pneumoconiosis.

Marriages and Divorces

In 1994, 75,703 marriages took place in the commonwealth, the lowest annual number since 1963. The marriage rate was 6.3 per 1,000 population, the lowest since 1964. Since 1950, Pennsylvania's marriage rate has been consistently lower than the national rate, usually trailing by about 2.5 per 1,000 population. October was the most popular month for marriage, followed by June, September, and May. January was the least popular.

The number of divorces and annulments occurring in Pennsylvania in 1994 was 40,049. The state's divorce rate of 3.3 per 1,000 population has varied by only .2 or less every year since 1980. Since 1950, Pennsylvania's divorce rate has been consistently lower than the national rate, usually trailing by 1.5 to 2.0 per 1,000 population each year.

ANCESTRY

In the 1990 U.S. Census, Pennsylvanians declared the following as their primary nationalities:

Arab	30,798
Austrian	43,549
Belgian	6,933
Canadian	6,956
Czech	28,356
Danish	11,941
Dutch	172,084
English	749,786

Finnish	5,471	Asian Indian	27,494
French	136,174	Korean	25,494
French Canadian	22,293	Vietnamese	14,961
German	3,485,436	Cambodian	5,301
Greek	44,265	Hmong	458
Hungarian	92,006	Laotian	2,139
Hispanic	1,161,953	Thai	1,222
Irish	1,270,330	Other Asian	7,038
Italian	1,047,893	Polynesian:	
Lithuanian	66,899	Hawaiian	1,017
Norwegian	18,777	Samoan	240
Polish	632,518	Tongan	52
Portuguese	9,209	Other Polynesian	12
Romanian	10,447	Micronesian:	
Russian	156,393	Guamanian	345
Scots-Irish	195,220	Other Pacific Islander	184
Scottish	132,813	Other race	119,821
Slovak	295,843	Total population	11,881,644
SubSaharan Africa	13,088		
Swedish	73,648	Persons of Hispanic origin	220,479
Swiss	40,610	Mexican	22,615
Ukrainian	89,780	Puerto Rican	143,872
United States; American	309,814	Cuban	7,390
Welsh	109,613	Dominican	3,678
West Indian	17,550	Central American:	
Yugoslavian	32,181	Guatemalan	806
Other groups	450,010	Honduran	837
Unclassified	911,105	Nicaraguan	876
		Panamanian	1,452

RACE

Revised 1990 U.S. Census Bureau data reveal the following racial breakdown for the commonwealth:

		Salvadoran	1,063
		Other Central American	697
		South American:	
		Colombian	5,417
		Ecuadorian	1,251
White	10,523,180	Peruvian	1,482
Black	1,087,570	Other South American	4,720
American Indian	15,557	Other Hispanic	24,314
Eskimo	227		
Aleut	193		
Asian or Pacific Islander:			
Chinese	29,469		
Filipino	12,901		
Japanese	6,769		

RELIGION

A 1992 study of religious affiliation in America identified 7,290,699 members of organized religion in the state—61 percent of the total population.

MEMBERSHIP IN LEADING DENOMINATIONS

Roman Catholics	3,675,250
Methodists	735,367
Lutherans	706,700
Presbyterians	404,616
Baptists	358,827
Jewish	329,651
United Church of Christ	284,275
Episcopalians	138,152
Mennonites	91,182
Assembly of God	74,616
Church of the Brethren	57,368
Christian & Missionary Alliance	37,006
Congregationalists	32,451
African Methodist Episcopal	28,041
Church of the Nazarene	26,626

Source: *Churches and Church Membership in the United States, 1990,*
ed. Martin B. Bradley. (Atlanta: Glenmary Research Center, 1992).

CRIME

The State Police compiles crime statistics annually from all law-enforcement agencies in the commonwealth. The latest available statistics are for 1995.

There were 927,601 crimes of all types reported, representing a rate of 7,696 crimes per 100,000 population. The number of crimes in 1995 was slightly lower than in 1994, and the rate for most serious crimes decreased.

Crimes in the major category include murder and manslaughter, rape, robbery, aggravated assault, burglary, larceny-theft, arson, and motor vehicle theft. Major crimes account for 40% of all crimes; 378,914 were reported in 1995.

The State Police uses a "crime clock" to illustrate the extent of serious crime. A major crime occurred every one minute and 23 seconds, a violent offense every 10 minutes and 35 seconds, and a property crime every one minute and 36 seconds. Also, there was a murder every 12 hours and 28 minutes, a rape every 2 hours and 55 minutes, a robbery every 23 minutes and 53 seconds, an aggravated assault every 21 minutes and 57 seconds, a burglary every 8 minutes and 17 seconds, a larceny-theft every 2 minutes and 31 seconds, a motor vehicle theft every 10 minutes and three seconds, and an act of arson every 2 hours and 37 minutes.

There were 548,650 crimes of a less serious nature committed in 1995. These include minor assaults, forgery and counterfeiting, fraud, embezzlement, stolen property, vandalism, weapons, sex offenses, gambling, liquor law violations, drunken driving, disorderly conduct, and vagrancy.

Arrests were made in 46% of all crimes reported. Arrests were made in 23% of serious crimes and 61% of lesser offenses. Law enforcement solved 72% of murders, 65% of aggravated assaults, 59% of rapes, and 24% of larceny-theft cases.

The percentage of stolen property that is recovered varies greatly. The overall recovery rate is 46%. Locally stolen motor vehicles are the items most often recovered; about two of three are found. Electronic equipment, such as TVs, radios, and cameras, is seldom recovered. Only 1 item in 20 is found. Other items with low recovery rates include office equipment (9%) and household goods (8%).

Crime in Pennsylvania is largely an urban phenomenon. The variation in rates between core cities and their suburbs is striking. Rates in the core cities are at least double those of their suburbs in the fifteen metropolitan statistical areas in the commonwealth. In Reading and Williamsport, however, the crime rate in the city was four times higher than that of the suburbs. In Allentown, Bethlehem, Harrisburg, Johnstown, Lancaster, Pittsburgh, and York, there was three times as much crime as in the suburbs.

In 1995, there were 25,926 full-time law-enforcement employees in 830 jurisdictions in the state. Full-time police officers make up 86% of departments, civilian employees 14%. There were 2,907 assaults on police officers reported, of which 898 (31%) resulted in injury to the officer. Firearms and dangerous weapons were used in 12% of these assaults. Two law-enforcement officers were killed feloniously and accidentally while performing official duties.

Murder

Murder claimed 736 victims in 1995. They were mostly male (79%), nonwhite (60%), and between the ages of 15 and 29 (46%). The killers were mostly male (92%) and nonwhite (64%), and half were ages 15 to 24. About half of the victims were related to or acquainted with their assailants. The murder weapon of choice was a handgun, used in 60% of the murders; knives were used in 13%.

Rape

Law-enforcement officials recognize rape as one of the most underreported crimes. There were 2,964 rapes reported to the police in 1995, 10% of which were determined to be unfounded. Of the 1,238 persons arrested for rape, 42% were under 25 years of age (20% were under 18) and 53% were white.

Robbery

There were 22,122 robberies reported in 1995, an average of 61 daily, in which $12.4 million was stolen. The average robbery nets the robber $561. There were 291 banks and 848 convenience stores robbed, and 72% occurred on the streets. Firearms were involved in half of the robberies. Robbers are mainly young (30% are under 18 and 67% under 25 years old), male (92%), and nonwhite (72%).

Aggravated Assault

There were 23,028 assaults reported in 1995, 18% of which involved a firearm, 14% a knife, and 21% other dangerous weapons, and 13,989 persons were arrested for the crimes. Offenders were mostly male (83%), young (half under 25 years old), and white (55%).

Burglary
There were 62,594 burglaries in 1995, in which property valued at $71 million was stolen—an average of $1,135 per offense. Seventy percent of burglaries involved private residences. The burglars were mostly young (almost 67% under 25 years old), male (91%), and white (72%).

Larceny-Theft
This crime is roughly defined as theft that does not involve force, violence, or fraud. There were 219,527 such thefts in 1995, and a total of $113 million worth of property was stolen. The number of these crimes has remained very stable over the past five years, from 209,000 to 218,000 cases annually.

Theft of property from motor vehicles was the most common offense, accounting for 26% of the total; another 11% involved theft of motor vehicle parts and accessories. Shoplifting accounted for 15%, and bicycle theft for 7% (15,227 bikes were stolen).

There were 46,199 persons arrested for larceny-theft. Almost 29% were females, by far the largest percentage of all offenses for females. Most of the thieves were under 25 years old (32% were under 18), and about two-thirds were white.

Motor Vehicle Theft
Of the 47,568 motor vehicle thefts reported, police made an arrest in only 17%, but 68% of the vehicles were recovered. About 80% of the recovered vehicles had remained in the local jurisdiction. Motor vehicle thieves tend to be young males: 77% were under 25 years old (42% were under 18).

Arson
There were 4,970 cases of arson reported, causing $115 million in property damage and seven deaths. About 94% of the fires involved structures, 5% mobile property, and 1% crops and timber. Of the 2,833 structure fires, 24% involved uninhabited or abandoned buildings.

Arrested arsonists were primarily young adults and juveniles: 70% were under 25 years old (54% under 18), 84% were male, and 78% were white.

Drug-Abuse Violations
Although generally considered less serious, drug offenses are considered to be the cause of many other criminal offenses. In 1995, there were 34,567 violations of laws concerning possession, sale, use, growing, and manufacturing or making narcotic drugs, representing an increase of 5.5% over 1994. Of those arrested, 86% were male, 55% white, and 51% under 25 years old.

Persons Charged and Dispositions
Of the 86,583 people charged with serious crimes in 1995, 74% were arrested and arraigned and 26% received citations. A total of 23,124 violent offenders were charged.

In court, 37% of persons charged with serious crimes were convicted of the charges, 11% were found guilty of a lesser offense, 23% were acquitted or charges were dismissed, and 29% were referred to juvenile court. Murder had the highest rate of conviction, 65%, followed by larceny-theft, 50%.

The disposition of persons charged with less serious crimes was distributed as follows: 126,162 (65%) were guilty as charged, 11,651 (6%) were guilty of a lesser offense, 35,523 (18%) were acquitted or charges were dismissed, and 21,577 (12%) were referred to juvenile court. The highest conviction rates for persons charged were reported for driving under the influence, 87%, and liquor law violations, 84%.

PUNISHMENT

Pennsylvania is the birthplace of the penitentiary concept. When Eastern State Penitentiary opened in 1829 outside Philadelphia, it was an innovation in humanitarian confinement. The penitentiary was a Quaker concept. The root word is *penitent*—one who is feeling regret for sins or offenses. Penitents in Eastern State had their own 8-by-12 cells in one of seven cell blocks that met at the hub of the cell block wheel. Guards could stand at the hub and watch all the cell blocks simultaneously. There were exercise yards in the prison, a radical concept.

Eastern State became the model for 19th- and early-20th-century prisons. Over 300 prisons worldwide are similarly constructed. Eastern State Penitentiary operated until 1950.

The Pennsylvania Department of Corrections oversees 22 state correctional institutions, 15 community correction centers, and one motivational boot camp. It has over 10,000 employees who deal with more than 33,000 inmates ranging in age from 14 to 87. Prisons are a growth industry in Pennsylvania. Since 1990, the state has added 10,000 beds to the system through the construction of six new institutions and the expansion of existing facilities. A new prison will open in Chester in 1998, and the department has plans to add another 10,000 beds over the next several years. In 1996, the cost of these institutions, excluding building costs, was almost $1 billion.

The state also has the responsibility to supervise juvenile criminals. As of January 1997, there were 761 juveniles in 11 state-operated institutions. Also, 79 inmates in state correctional facilities were under age 18. However, the majority of juvenile offenders are in private facilities operated by nonprofit agencies under state contracts.

Of the 67 Pennsylvania counties, 62 operate a county prison. Cameron, Forest, Fulton, Pike, and Sullivan Counties have closed their prisons and farm out their very few prisoners. In January 1997, county facilities housed 22,081 inmates. Inmate populations varied from 15 in Juniata County to 5,487 in Philadelphia County's four jails. For ten years, Philadelphia has been under a federal court order to reduce its inmate population. Squalor and overcrowding have spawned claims of cruel and unusual punishment. To comply, Philadelphia systematically releases nonviolent criminals early.

The most common serious offenses for which prisoners are remanded into county custody are theft and burglary. The most common lesser offenses are driving under the influence and narcotic drug law violations.

Most sentences fall in the one-to-two-year range; and the average maximum sentenced received is 15 months. Time served is another matter. Across all offenses, county offenders, on average, serve three months. Serious offenders serve approximately seven months, less serious offenders an average of three months.

PENNSYLVANIA CORRECTIONAL INSTITUTIONS

Institution	County	Population*
Albion	Erie	1,782
Cambridge Springs	Crawford	584
Camp Hill	Cumberland	2,815
Coal Township	Northumberland	1,608
Cresson	Cambria	1,326
Dallas	Luzerne	1,914
Frackville	Schuylkill	993
Graterford	Montgomery	3,522
Greene	Greene	1,417
Greensburg	Westmoreland	968
Houtzdale	Clearfield	1,526
Huntingdon	Huntingdon	1,888
Laurel Highlands	Somerset	167
Mahanoy	Schuylkill	1,776
Mercer	Mercer	1,116
Muncy	Lycoming	826
Pittsburgh	Allegheny	1,782
Quehanna Boot Camp	Clearfield	133
Retreat	Luzerne	868
Rockview	Centre	2,145
Smithfield	Huntingdon	1,216
Somerset	Somerset	1,785
Waymart	Wayne	1,159
Waynesburg	Greene	431
CCCs and group homes		892
Total		34,639

*As of February 1997
Source: Pennsylvania Department of Corrections

The federal government operates eight institutions in the commonwealth. All of the federal inmates are male. All figures given below are as of June 1994.

At the Allenwood site in White Deer, the Federal Bureau of Prisons has established a multi-institutional U.S. penitentiary complex. It consists of three separate facilities on a 55-acre site within one secure perimeter. It houses

851 inmates in maximum security, 1,107 inmates in a federal correctional institution, and 1,145 inmates in a low-security setting. A total of 878 correctional officers are employed in the complex.

Another U.S. penitentiary is located in Lewisburg. It houses 1,822 inmates in a maximum-security prison and 240 inmates in a minimum-security satellite facility that opened in 1992. There are 840 correctional officers working at Lewisburg.

Three more federal correctional institutions also operate in Pennsylvania: McKean, in Bradford, has 1,383 inmates and 346 correctional officers; Loretto has 550 inmates and 234 correctional offices; and Schuylkill, in Minersville, has 1,409 inmates and 340 correctional officers.

8

Transportation

DRIVER'S LICENSING

A driver's license is required for people living in Pennsylvania who are at least 16 years old and want to operate a motor vehicle; those who have moved to Pennsylvania and are establishing residency, even if they hold a valid driver's license from another state; and members of the armed forces whose legal residence is in Pennsylvania.

The quest for a license to drive in Pennsylvania beings with a phone call to the Bureau of Driver Licensing to request a *Pennsylvania Drivers Manual.* It contains a copy of the Medical Qualification Certificate (DL-180A) and a Parental Consent Form. It also contains all the information needed to prepare for the driving knowledge examination.

The bureau's automated telephone system has four 24-hour numbers: (800) 932-4600, (717) 787-3130, (215) 698-8100, and (412) 565-5670. Recorded information is available 24 hours a day; service representatives are available for further information from 7 A.M. to 6:30 P.M., Monday through Friday.

Aspiring new drivers must first obtain a learner's permit. Applicants must go to a Penn DOT Driver's License Office for a vision test and a Pennsylvania signs and knowledge test and must present a completed Medical Qualification Form (DL-180A), which must be signed by a physician; proof of identity and date of birth; and a social security card or acceptable proof of a social security number. Parental consent must be obtained for those under 18. There is a fee of $27, which includes $20 for a four-year license.

Upon passing the vision test and the signs and knowledge test, the applicant is issued a temporary learner's permit, valid for 60 days. This permit allows the holder to practice driving only when accompanied by a driver 18 years of age or older. Within this 60-day period, normally in about three weeks, a learner's permit is issued; the road test may not be taken until then.

Applicants under 18 years of age will be issued a junior license, which allows driving only between the hours of 5 A.M. and midnight, unless accompanied by a parent or a spouse 18 or older. Seventeen-year-olds may get a regular license by passing a driver training course, having a record clear of violations and accidents, and receiving parental consent.

All new drivers must take a road test at a Penn DOT Driver License Center. Applicants must provide the vehicle, which must be registered, insured, inspected, and, if required, have a valid emissions sticker. Do not drive to the center for the test; the examiner will ask for the driver's license of the person 18 or older who accompanied the applicant. Upon passing the road test, the applicant is issued a license that is valid for four years. The words "organ donor" will appear on the licenses of drivers who request that designation.

Motorcycles

A Class M license is required to operate a motorcycle. The cost is $37, which includes $7 for a learner's permit and $28 for a four-year license. A motorcycle rider course is offered by the Department of Transportation at sites throughout the commonwealth. The registration fee is $18. It is not mandatory.

Motorcyclists, both drivers and riders, must wear helmets and eye protection devices approved by the Department of Transportation. Using headlights during daylight hours is strongly recommended.

Mopeds, defined as cycles having pedals that operate an automatic transmission, a maximum design speed of 25 miles per hour, and a motor rated no higher than 1.5 horsepower and 50 cc displacement, do not require inspection, helmet and eye protection, or a special driver's license.

Sanctions

The Department of Transportation maintains a driving record of every licensed driver in Pennsylvania. The record is based upon a point system. Points are added to a driving record when a driver is found guilty of moving violations:

5 Points: passing a stopped school bus with flashing red lights and stop arm extended (this violation also carries an automatic 60-day license suspension); exceeding a maximum speed limit by 26 miles per hour.

4 Points: improper passing on a hill; exceeding a maximum speed limit by 16 to 25 miles per hour; leaving the scene of an accident involving property damage only.

3 Points: red light violations; improper passing; following too closely; failure to yield in various situations; stop sign violations; illegal U-turn; improper backing; and careless driving.

2 Points: driving too fast for conditions; violation of license restrictions (e.g., not wearing required glasses); failure to obey police.

Drivers who accumulate 6 points will be required to take a special written examination. Driving privileges are automatically suspended when 11 points are accumulated.

Driving Under the Influence

A driver with a blood alcohol level of .10 percent or higher is considered to be driving under the influence. A first conviction could result in a loss of license for up to one year, a jail sentence of up to two years, a fine of $300 or more, mandatory rehabilitation treatment, and attendance at an Alcohol Highway Safety Education Class.

Implied Consent Law

The law covering chemical testing states that drivers agree to testing by accepting a license to drive. Drivers who refuse to take any chemical test demanded by the police will automatically have driving privileges suspended for one year. Because an additional year-long suspension is imposed for conviction, a refusal plus conviction could result in a two-year suspension.

VEHICLE TITLE AND REGISTRATION

All vehicles based in Pennsylvania require a Pennsylvania title, registration plate, an registration card. Title and registration may be applied for simultaneously on Form MV-1. The form, available from the Bureau of Motor Vehicles, AAA, auto dealers, and notaries, must be notarized and have a tracing of the vehicle identification number attached. The title fee is $22.50; an additional $5 fee is required if there is an unpaid lien on the vehicle.

The registration fee is $36 for cars and $58.50 and up for trucks, depending on their weight. Proof of insurance is required for registration. Failure to maintain insurance will result in suspension of vehicle registration and, possibly, suspension of driving privileges of the owner for three months. Personalized registration plates are available for a one-time fee of $20. Individuals may select any combination of seven numbers or letters. Nonprofit organizations may order a special plate of their own design if 300 members or supporters preorder.

VEHICLE INSPECTION AND EMISSIONS TEST

Vehicles must be inspected every 12 months at an authorized inspection station. Equipment checked includes the lights, brakes, horns, tires, safety belts, exhaust system, mirrors, tag mounting, suspension, signals, steering, windshield glass, wipers, and other major parts.

An annual emissions test, performed at authorized stations, is required in areas of the state that do not meet federal air-quality standards. Currently, these areas include Pittsburgh, the five-county Philadelphia area, and the Allentown-Bethlehem-Easton area.

OTHER LAWS
Seat Belt Law

All drivers and front seat passengers in autos, light trucks, and motor homes must wear seat belts.

Child Restraint Law

Children under four years must be buckled into a federally approved safety seat no matter where they ride in a motor vehicle. Drivers are responsible for securing the children.

Bicycle Helmet Law

Children under the age of 12 must wear an ANSI or SNELL approved helmet when operating or riding as a passenger on any bicycle, tricycle, or other pedal cycle.

THE PENNSYLVANIA TURNPIKE

The Pennsylvania Turnpike, a 506-mile superhighway was America's first modern turnpike. Opened in 1940, it initially connected Irwin and Carlisle. Construction was interrupted by World War II; it did not reach Valley Forge until 1950. The Mainline Turnpike from Ohio to New Jersey was completed in 1956. A 110-mile Northeast Extension from Norristown into the anthracite region and Scranton opened in 1957. Three north-south extensions to the east-west Mainline were built in western Pennsylvania in the early 1990s: Turnpike 60 to New

TURNPIKE TOLLS AND MILEAGES

Interchange		Toll	Miles
1	Gateway to Ohio	.50	1.4
1A	New Castle	.50	9.4
2	Beaver Valley	.50	12.8
3	Cranberry	1.05	28.4
4	Butler Valley	1.45	39.1
5	Allegheny Valley	1.75	47.7
6	Pittsburgh	2.20	56.6
7	Irwin	2.55	67.4
8	New Stanton	3.00	75.5
9	Donegal	3.60	90.7
10	Somerset	4.30	109.9
11	Bedford	5.85	145.5
12	Breezewood	6.50	161.4
13	Fort Littleton	7.10	179.5
14	Willow Hill	7.55	188.6
15	Blue Mountain	8.05	201.3
16	Carlisle	9.05	226.3
17	Gettysburg Pike	9.35	236.1
18	Harrisburg–West Shore	9.55	242.0
19	Harrisburg–East Shore	9.80	247.4
20	Lebanon-Lancaster	10.40	266.4
21	Reading	11.05	285.5
22	Morgantown	11.50	298.3
23	Dowingtown	12.05	312.0
24	Valley Forge	12.75	326.3
25	Norristown	13.20	333.1
25A	Mid-County	13.20	333.7
26	Fort Washington	13.50	338.5
27	Willow Grove	13.80	342.9
28	Philadelphia	14.15	351.3
29	Delaware Valley	14.60	357.7
30	Delaware River Bridge	14.70	359.0

At Exit 25A, Mid-County, connection can be made to the Northeast Extension, I-476. The first exit is Lansdale.

TURNPIKE TOLLS AND MILEAGES *(continued)*

Interchange		Toll	Miles
31	Lansdale	13.70	10.3
32	Quakertown	14.15	23.9
33	Lehigh Valley	14.55	37.2
34	Mahoning Valley	15.40	55.7
35	Pocono	16.00	74.7
36	Wilkes-Barre	16.40	85.3
37	Wyoming Valley	16.70 (last tollbooth)	94.6
38	Keyser Avenue	.35 (exact change)	101.2
39	Clarks Summit	.35 (exact change)	110.6

Castle; Turnpike 66, the Greensburg bypass; and Turnpike 43, a 6-mile road in Washington County that is isolated from the Turnpike Mainline.

In 1994, an average of 274,355 cars and 38,918 trucks used the Turnpike daily; the total annual volume was 114.3 million cars and 2.4 million trucks. The State Police issued 84,276 citations to drivers on the Turnpike. The Turnpike Commission supports strict enforcement of speed limits as a way to keep the fatality rate far below the national average.

There are 32 tollbooths on the east-west Mainline of the Turnpike. The toll for the entire route is $14.70 for passenger cars and other two-axle vehicles under 7,000 pounds. Commercial vehicles weighing between 7,000 and 101,000 pounds pay 6 cents per mile; those over 101,000 pay $1.68 per mile.

Bright yellow emergency call boxes line both sides of the Turnpike at 1-mile intervals. There are four buttons in the box: police, medical, accident, and service. Response is instantaneous, and the proper vehicles are sent to the call box. Cellular phone owners can dial *11 (star-one-one) to contact emergency services. The call is free.

There are 22 service plazas on the Turnpike. All are open 24 hours a day and offer fuel, food, telephones, and restrooms. Many have picnic areas and gift shops. Welcome Centers are located at the Zelienople, Sideling Hill, and North Neshaminy Service Plazas. The centers provide directions, travel advice, and a free hotel reservation service.

THE INTERSTATE HIGHWAY SYSTEM

Turnpike construction was reduced by the Interstate Highway Act of 1956, which provided federal funding only for toll-free highways. Pennsylvania has built over 1,500 miles of interstate highways with those funds:

I-70 is part of the Turnpike from Exit 12 at Breezewood to Exit 8 at New Stanton. From there it continues west through Westmoreland and Washington

Counties, intersecting I-79 at the borough of Washington and crossing the West Virginia border into Wheeling. From Breezewood, I-70 runs southeast to Frederick, Maryland, continuing to Baltimore.

I-78 runs from Harrisburg to Allentown-Bethlehem-Easton and into New Jersey.

I-79 begins in Erie, intersecting I-90 in Erie County, and proceeds south through Pittsburgh to Charleston, West Virginia.

I-80, known as the Keystone Shortway in Pennsylvania, extends 313 miles east-west through the northern part of the state from New Jersey to Ohio.

I-81 extends from the end of the Northeast Extension of the Pennsylvania Turnpike at Scranton, crossing the New York border into Binghamton. Southbound from Scranton, it parallels the Turnpike until just north of Wilkes-Barre, then runs southwest through Hazleton, Harrisburg, and Carlisle, continuing into Maryland.

I-83 connects Harrisburg and Baltimore, via York.

I-84 runs from I-380 at Scranton east through Pike County and on into New York.

I-90, which crosses the northern part of the country, runs through Erie County on its way between Buffalo and Cleveland.

I-95, a north-south highway from Maine to Florida, crosses the southeastern tip of Bucks County, then runs along the Delaware River through Philadelphia and Delaware Counties.

I-176 runs from the Morgantown exit of the Turnpike to Reading.

I-180 runs from Exit 31 of I-80 in Northumberland County to Williamsport.

I-276 is a Turnpike connector road from King of Prussia through Willow Grove and Philadelphia, and on to the New Jersey Turnpike.

HIGHWAY STATISTICS

	1970	1995
Registered vehicles	5,947,000	9,255,714
Licensed drivers	6,200,000	8,100,000
Vehicle crashes	311,981	134,171
Deaths	2,255	1,440
Injuries	136,518	130,678
PennDOT employees	19,873	12,202
Cost of a gallon of gas	$.35	$1.22
State tax per gallon	$.08	$.22
Federal tax per gallon	$.04	$.18
Average fuel consumption (mpg)	13	28
Federal funds to Pennsylvania	$174,000,000	$871,000,000

HIGHWAY MILEAGES

	Allentown	Altoona	East Stroudsburg	Erie	Gettysburg	Harrisburg	Hazleton	Hershey	Johnstown	Lancaster
Allentown	—	199	19	320	124	82	43	82	223	73
Altoona	199	—	201	181	122	129	156	141	47	166
East Stroudsburg	19	201	—	332	161	119	54	119	246	110
Erie	320	181	332	—	299	273	287	285	186	310
Gettysburg	124	122	161	299	—	42	123	51	121	58
Harrisburg	82	129	119	273	42	—	81	12	143	37
Hazleton	43	156	54	287	123	81	—	75	201	90
Hershey	82	141	119	285	51	12	75	—	153	31
Johnstown	223	47	246	186	121	143	201	153	—	177
Lancaster	73	166	110	310	58	37	90	31	177	—
New Castle	314	130	315	96	228	248	271	260	116	285
Philadelphia	59	235	83	379	128	107	98	95	247	72
Pittsburgh	284	97	312	122	183	205	267	214	67	235
Reading	35	185	79	329	88	57	64	45	197	33
Scranton	74	184	47	294	158	115	41	116	229	124
State College	161	43	162	184	124	88	118	101	87	121
Warren	278	151	276	65	246	218	235	230	138	256
Wellsboro	169	130	161	180	180	142	125	154	176	171
Williamsport	117	99	118	230	129	91	74	103	146	119
York	96	153	133	297	32	25	106	34	153	25

I-279 is a loop off I-79 through Pittsburgh.

I-283 is a short portion of PA Route 283 near Harrisburg, a state highway that connects it with Lancaster.

I-376 is a short stretch through Pittsburgh connecting I-279 and the Turnpike.

I-380 connects I-80 and I-81 through Monroe and Lackawanna Counties.

I-476, known as the Blue Route, connects the Turnpike at Plymouth Meeting and I-95 in Delaware County. The Turnpike's Northeast Extension, formerly known as PA Route 9, is also designated as I-476. It is a toll road from Scranton

HIGHWAY MILEAGES *(continued)*

	New Castle	Philadelphia	Pittsburgh	Reading	Scranton	State College	Warren	Wellsboro	Williamsport	York
Allentown	314	59	284	35	74	161	278	169	117	96
Altoona	130	235	97	185	184	43	151	130	99	153
East Stroudsburg	315	83	312	79	47	162	276	161	118	133
Erie	96	379	122	329	294	184	65	180	230	297
Gettysburg	228	128	183	88	158	124	246	180	129	32
Harrisburg	248	107	205	57	115	88	218	142	91	25
Hazleton	271	98	267	64	41	118	235	125	74	106
Hershey	260	95	214	45	116	101	230	154	103	34
Johnstown	116	247	67	197	229	87	138	176	146	153
Lancaster	285	72	235	33	124	126	256	171	119	25
New Castle	—	354	52	305	299	168	120	219	214	260
Philadelphia	354	—	308	59	124	195	332	223	172	96
Pittsburgh	52	308	—	259	295	138	143	227	210	215
Reading	305	59	259	—	101	145	276	167	115	56
Scranton	299	124	295	101	—	145	229	115	88	140
State College	168	195	138	145	145	—	128	98	67	113
Warren	120	332	143	276	229	128	—	115	66	243
Wellsboro	219	223	227	167	115	98	115	—	52	166
Williamsport	214	172	210	115	88	67	166	52	—	115
York	260	96	215	56	140	113	243	166	115	—

to the Mid-County Exit, east of Valley Forge. The section of I-476 known as the Blue Route is toll free from the Turnpike to I-95 in Delaware County.

COUNTY MAPS

The following county maps include each county's major roadways, towns, and cities. County seats are specified by a circled dot. North points toward the top of the page throughout the maps, and each scale symbol represents 0–5 miles.

ADAMS COUNTY

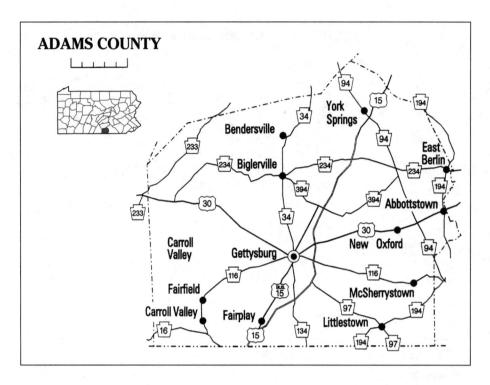

ALLEGHENY COUNTY

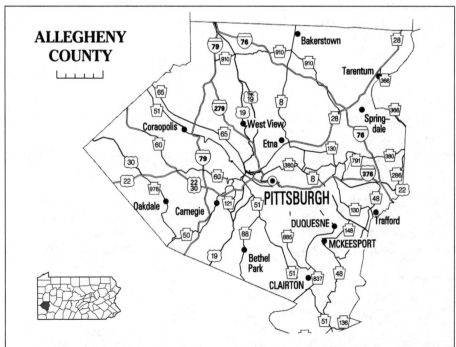

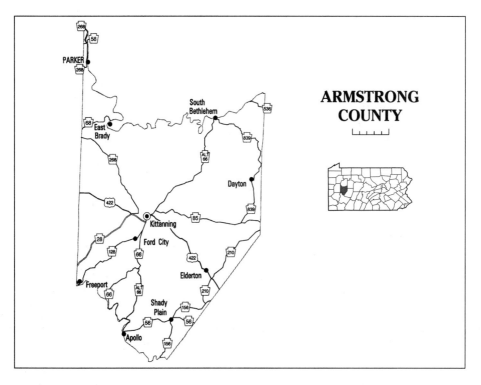

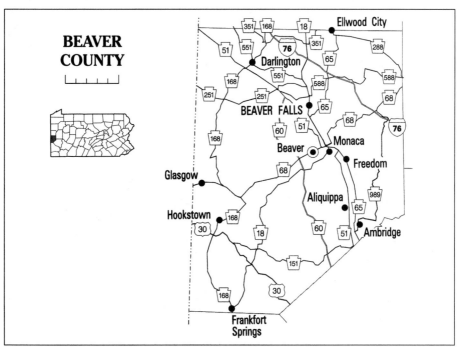

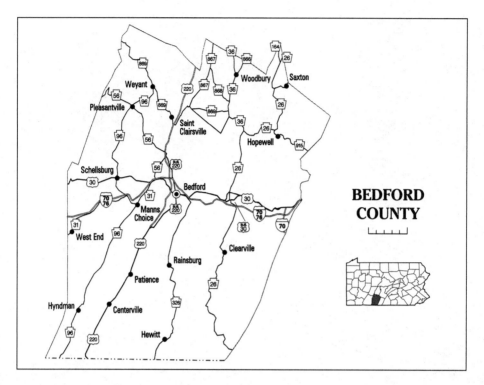

BEDFORD COUNTY

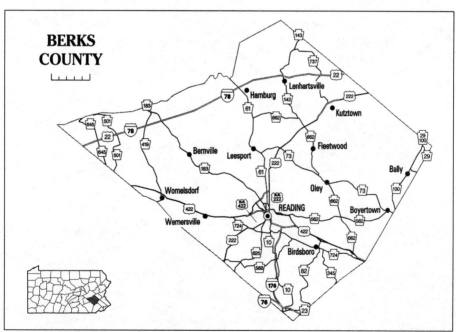

BERKS COUNTY

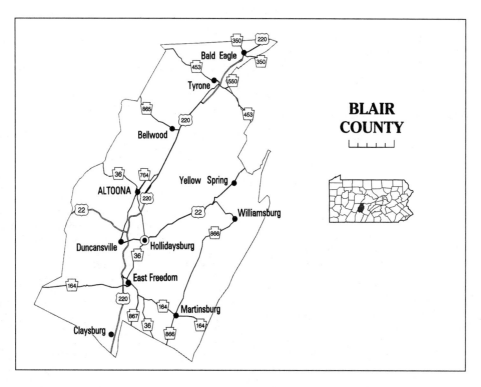

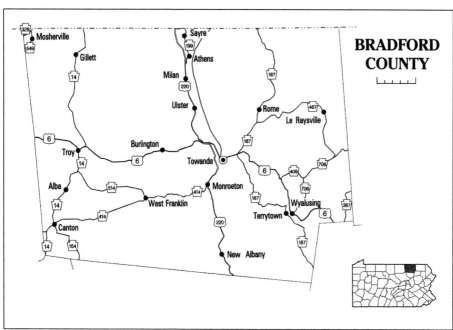

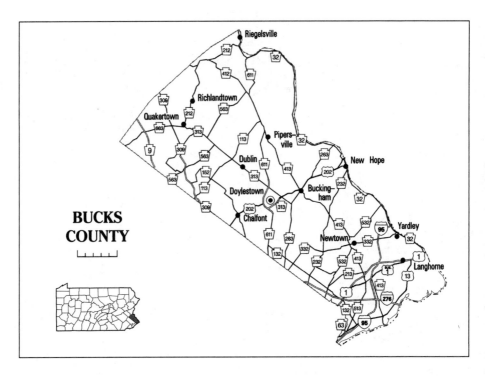

BUCKS COUNTY

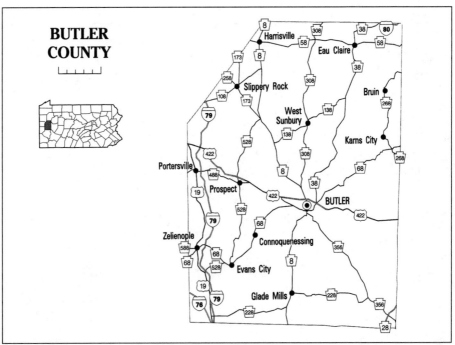

BUTLER COUNTY

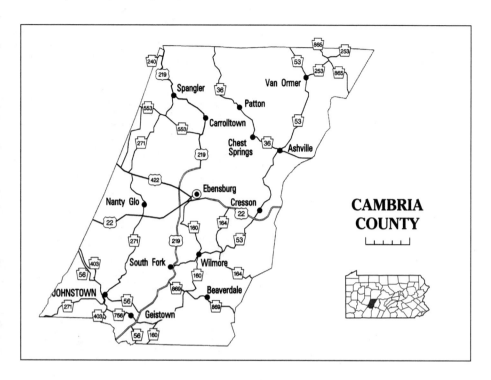

CAMBRIA
COUNTY

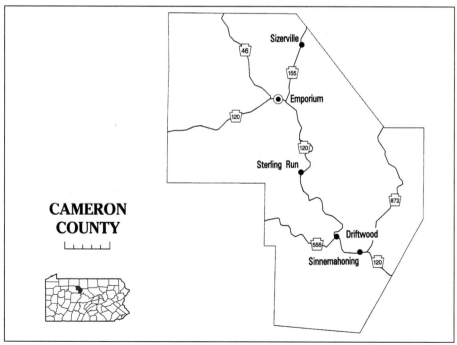

CAMERON
COUNTY

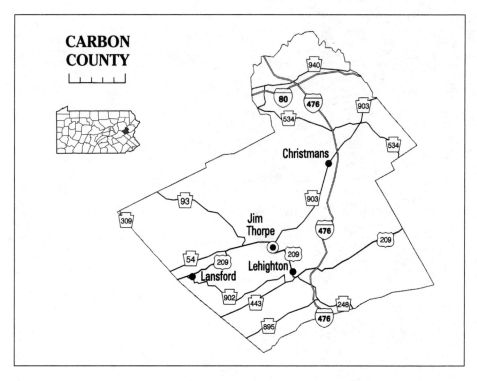

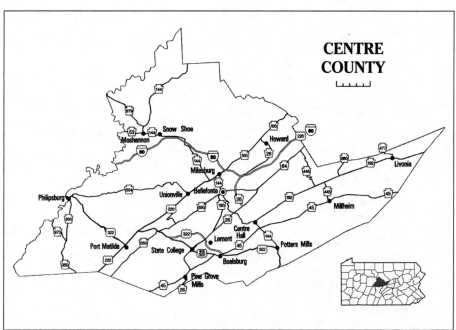

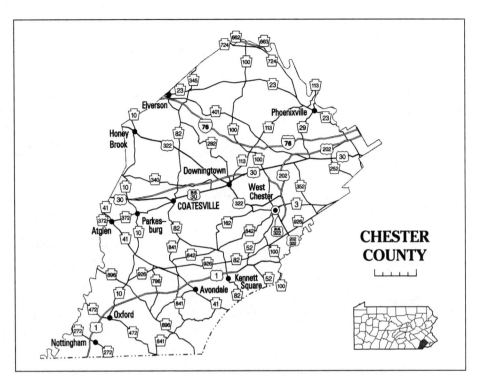

CHESTER
COUNTY

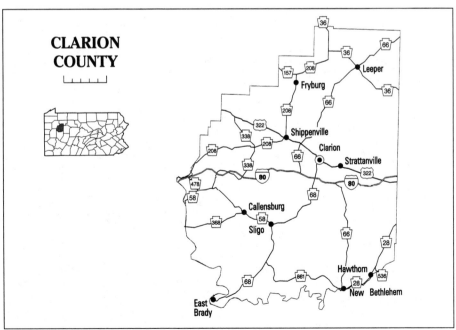

CLARION
COUNTY

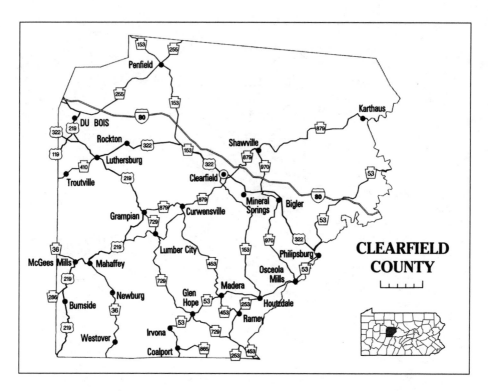

CLEARFIELD COUNTY

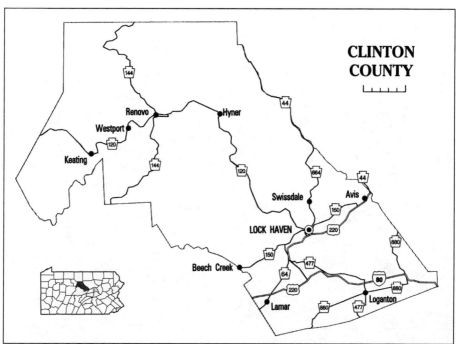

CLINTON COUNTY

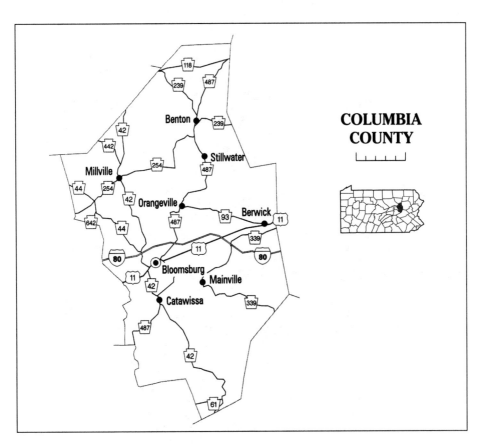

COLUMBIA COUNTY

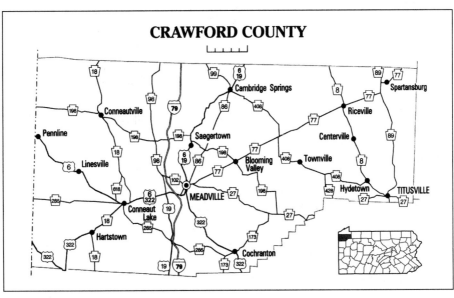

CRAWFORD COUNTY

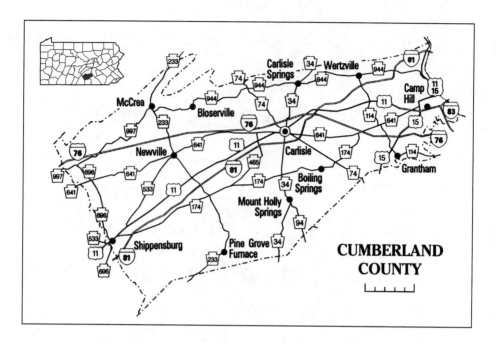

CUMBERLAND COUNTY

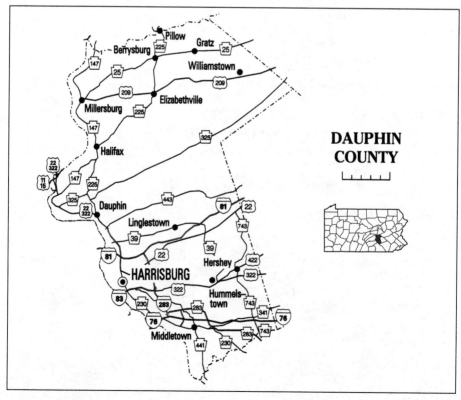

DAUPHIN COUNTY

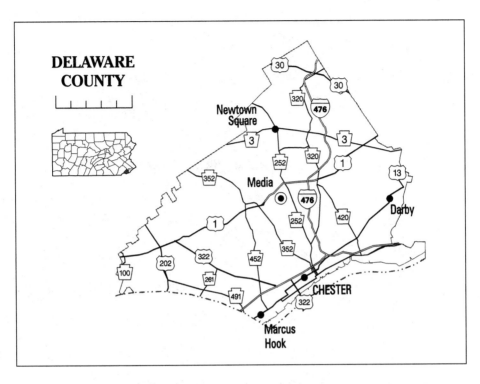

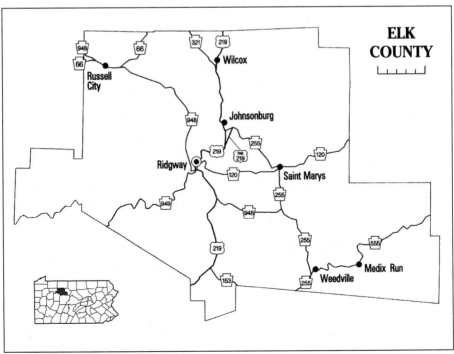

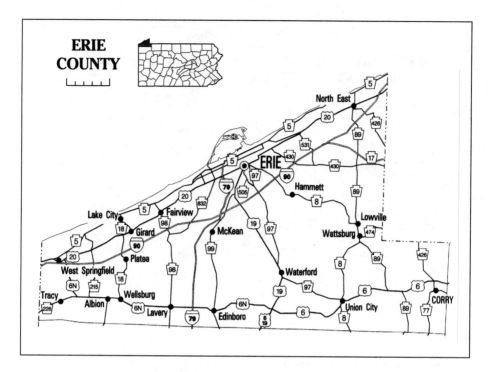

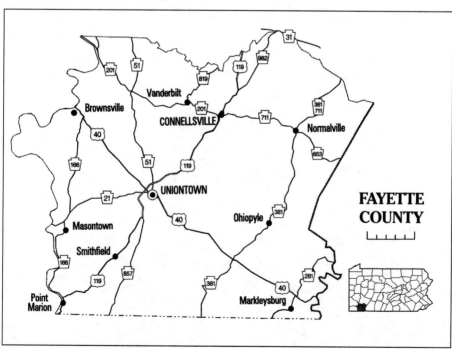

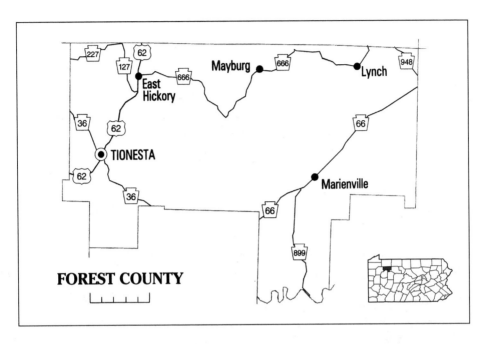

FOREST COUNTY

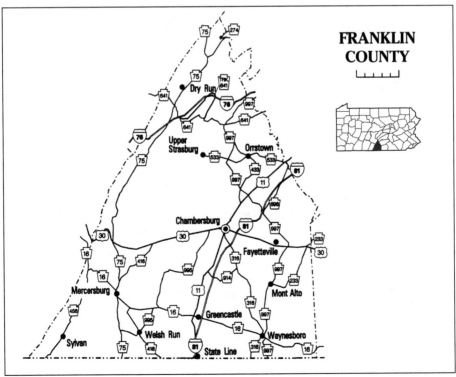

FRANKLIN COUNTY

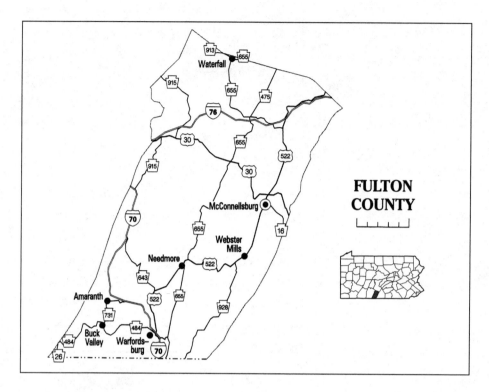

FULTON COUNTY

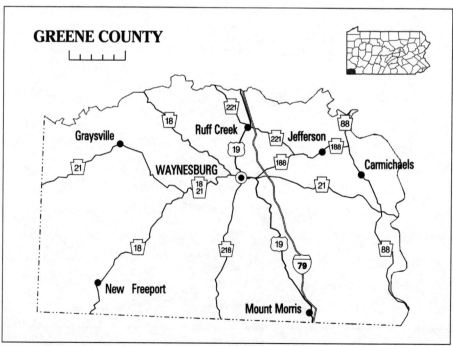

GREENE COUNTY

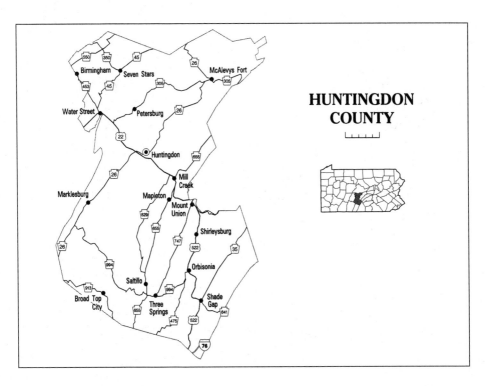

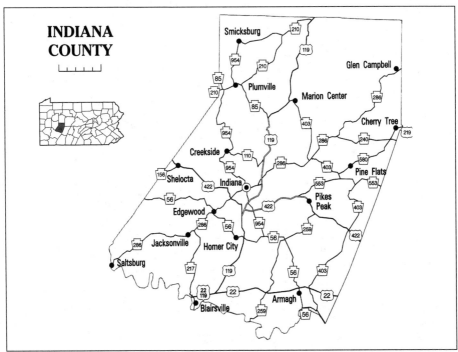

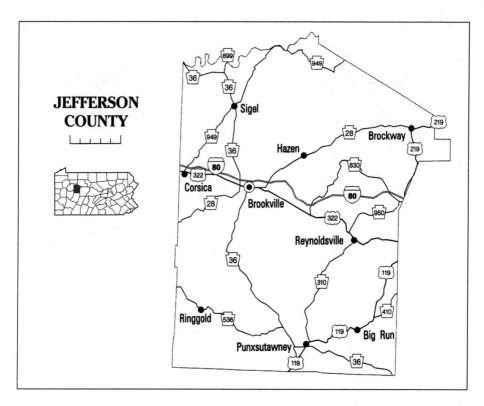

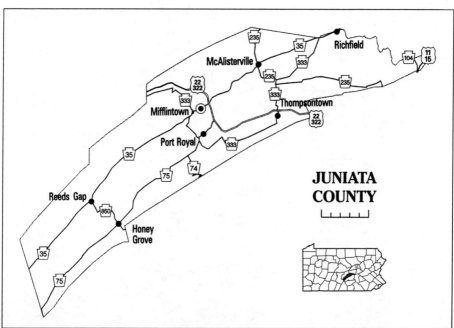

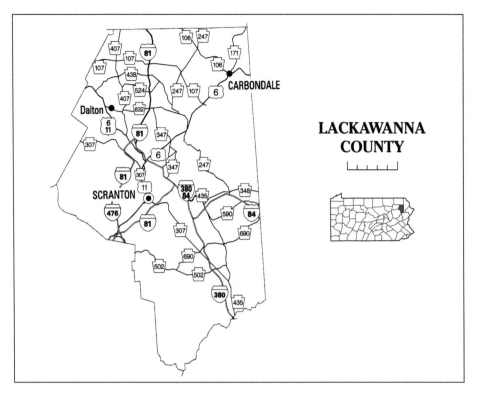

LACKAWANNA
COUNTY

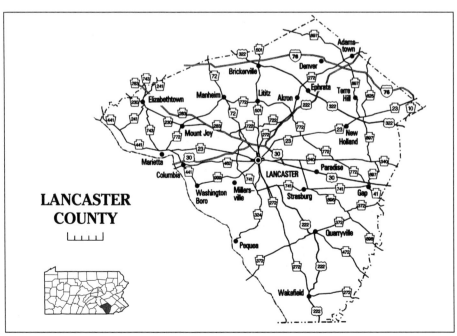

LANCASTER
COUNTY

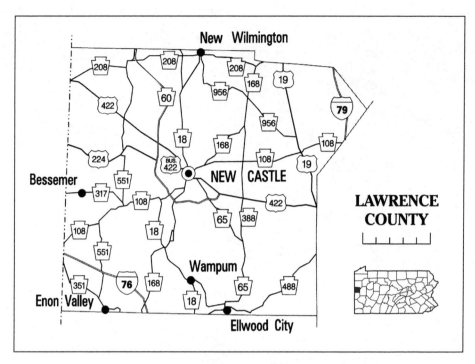

LAWRENCE
COUNTY

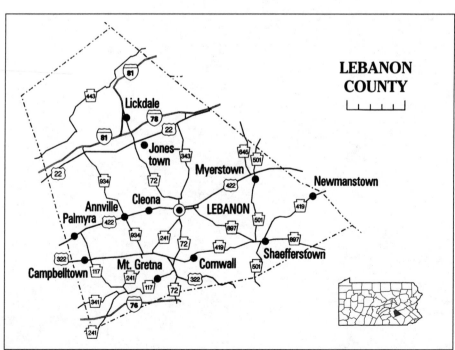

LEBANON
COUNTY

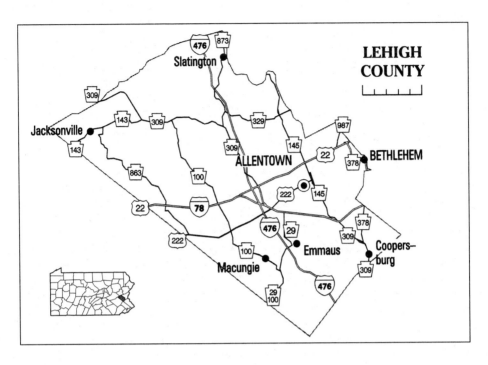

LEHIGH COUNTY

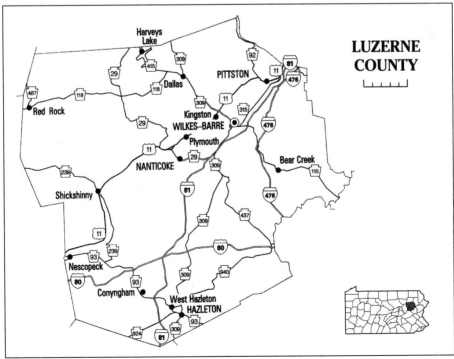

LUZERNE COUNTY

LYCOMING COUNTY

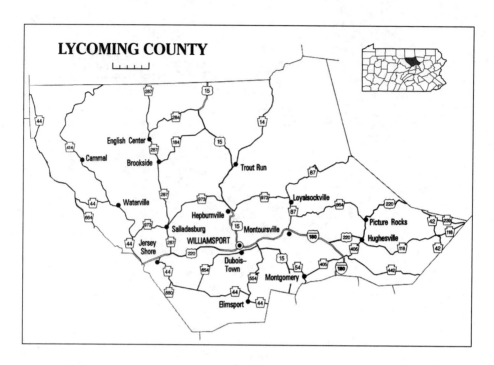

MCKEAN
COUNTY

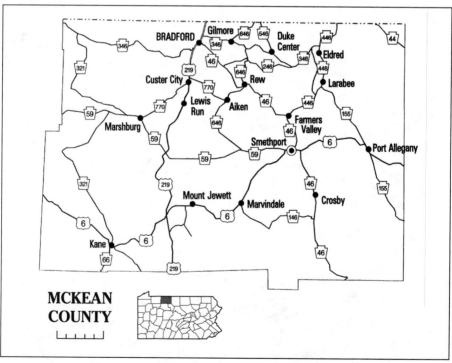

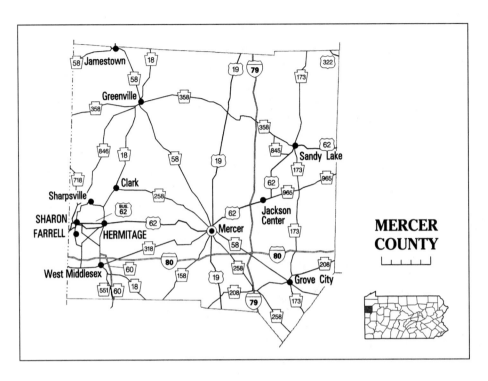

MERCER
COUNTY

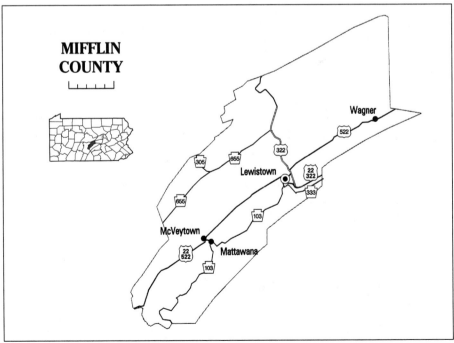

MIFFLIN
COUNTY

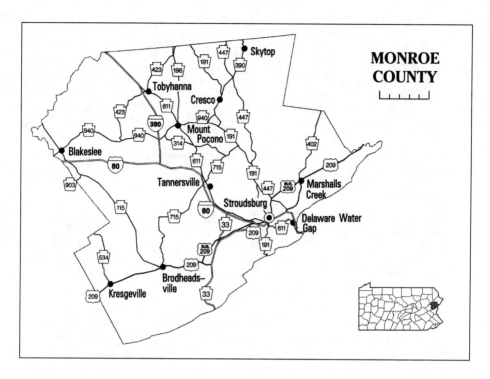

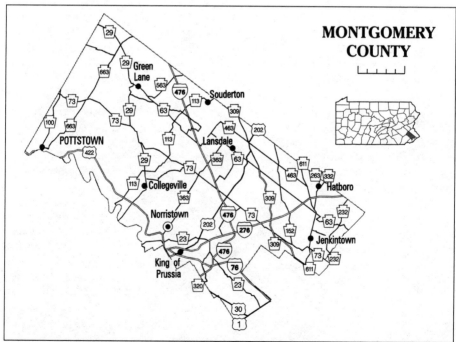

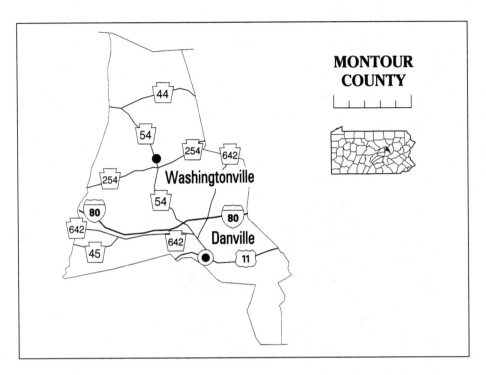

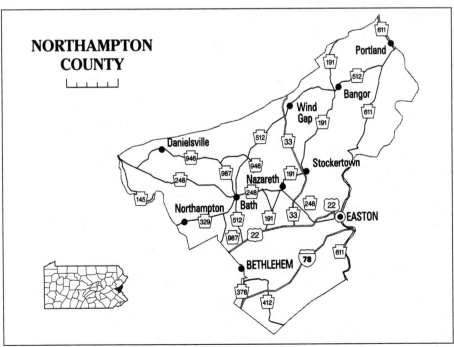

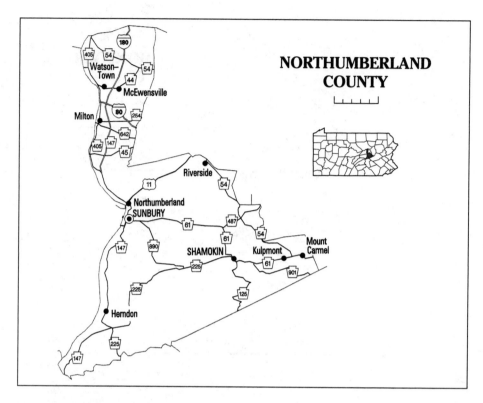

NORTHUMBERLAND COUNTY

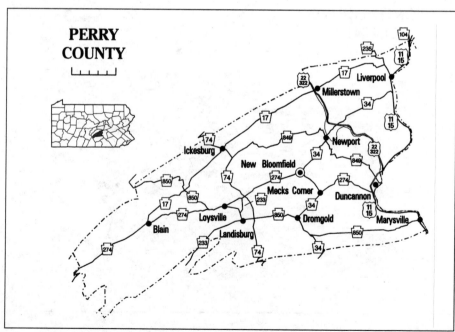

PERRY COUNTY

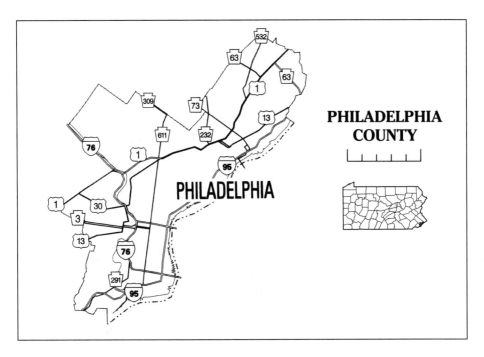

PHILADELPHIA
COUNTY

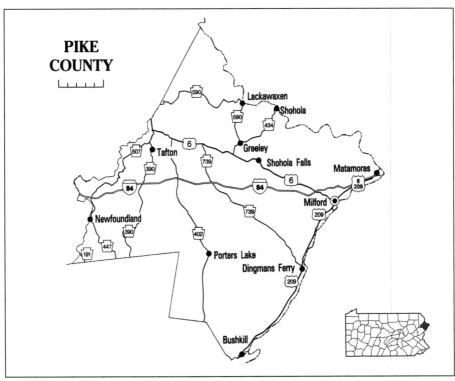

PIKE
COUNTY

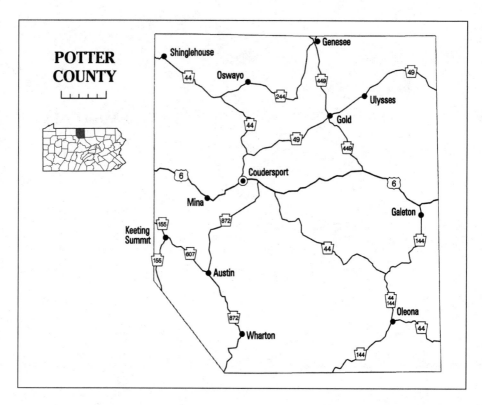

POTTER
COUNTY

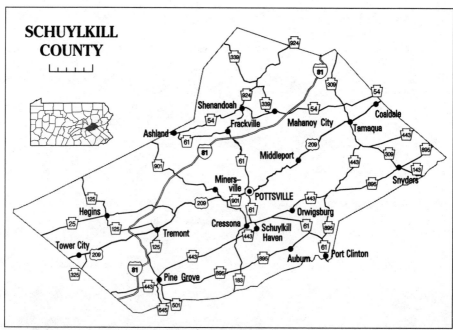

SCHUYLKILL
COUNTY

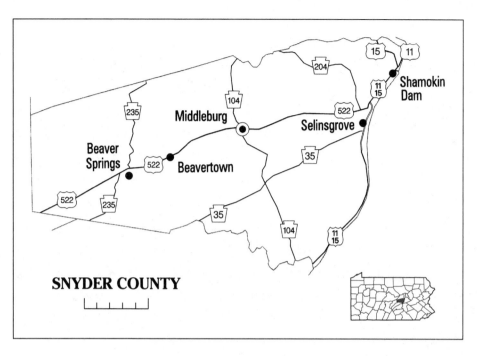

SNYDER COUNTY

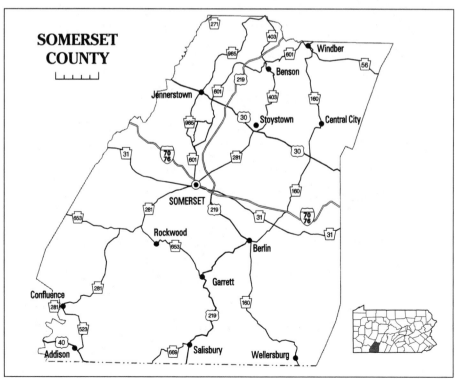

SOMERSET COUNTY

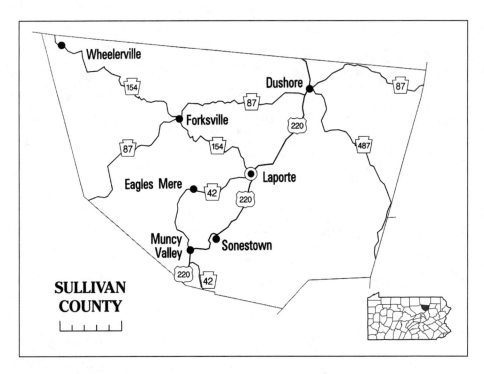

SULLIVAN
COUNTY

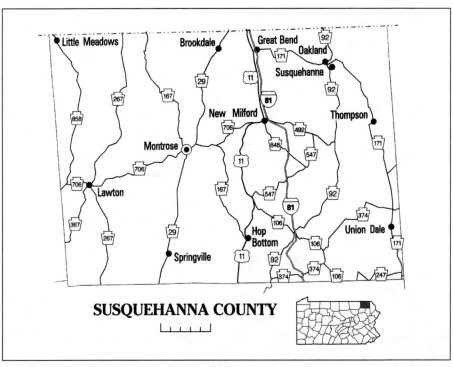

SUSQUEHANNA COUNTY

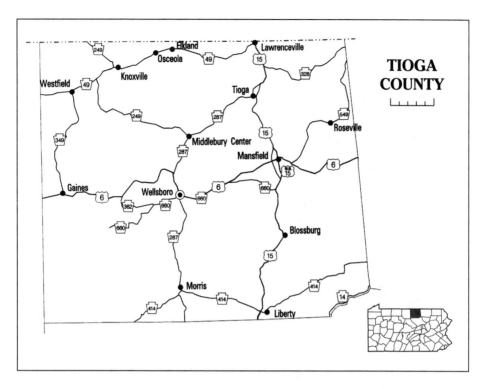

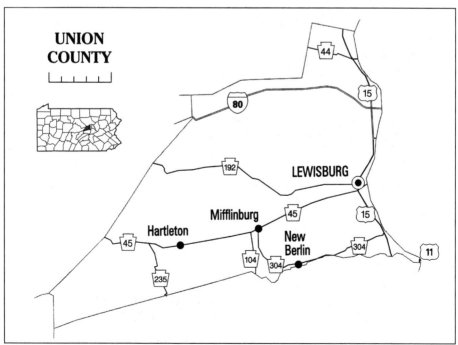

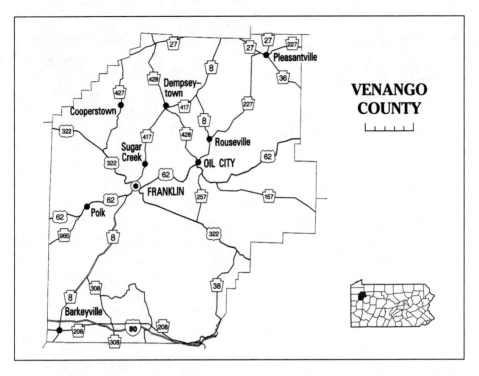

VENANGO COUNTY

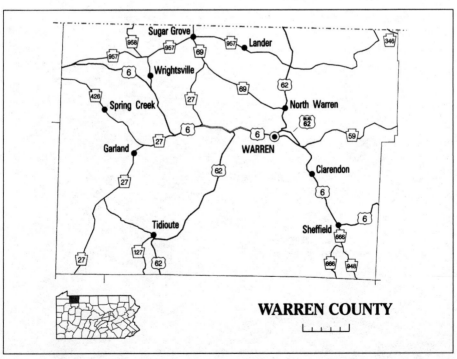

WARREN COUNTY

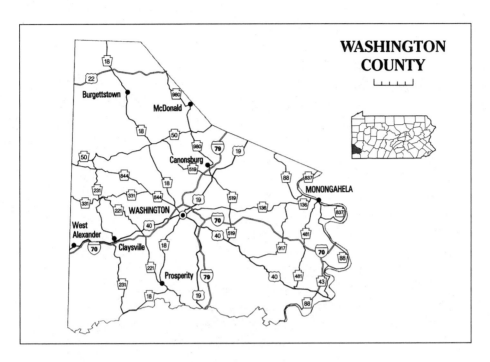

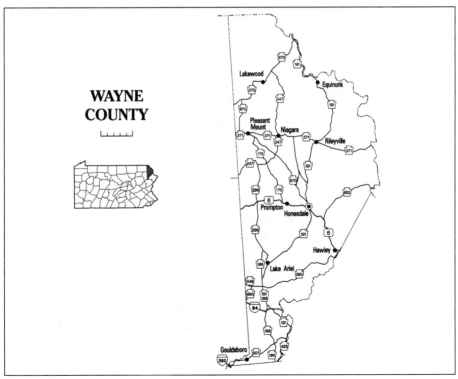

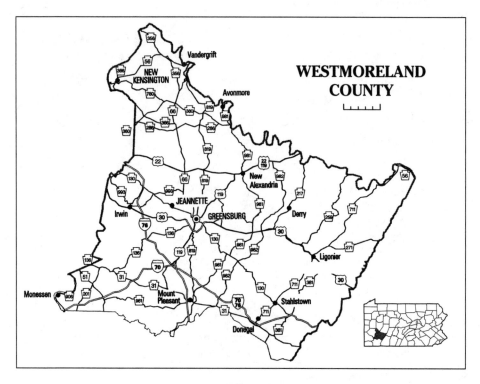

WESTMORELAND COUNTY

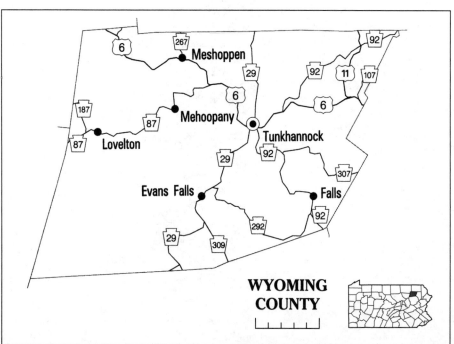

WYOMING COUNTY

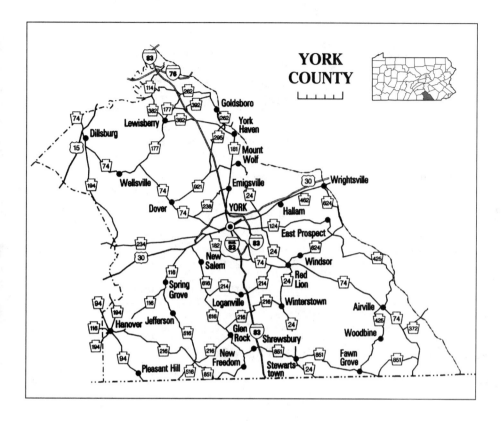

AIRPORTS

The airport network in Pennsylvania includes five international airports, 12 regional airports, 122 public-use airports, eight heliports, and a seaplane base.

Philadelphia International and the Greater Pittsburgh International Airport are the state's major aviation facilities, with millions of passengers being served by most of the major airlines, domestic and foreign. Pittsburgh is the major hub of operations for US Airways, as well as its corporate headquarters.

Erie, Harrisburg, and Wilkes-Barre–Scranton are international airports, but on a much smaller scale. They do not usually have international flights arriving or departing directly; however, they have the personnel and facilities available to provide U.S. customs services, if needed.

Twelve markets have regional airports. They have one or two carriers that provide flights to Philadelphia, Pittsburgh, Baltimore, New York City, or other major airports. In the era of deregulation, carriers, schedules, and fares change constantly. The regional airports also serve private aviation.

The public-use airports serve private aviation exclusively. They offer various services to private planes—among these services are fueling, repairs, storage, and tiedowns.

Eight heliports and a seaplane base in the Delaware River near Essington round out the public aviation facilities in the commonwealth.

REGIONAL AIRPORTS

Associated City	Facility Name
Allentown	Allentown-Bethlehem-Easton
Altoona	Altoona–Blair County
Bradford	Bradford Regional
DuBois	DuBois–Jefferson County
Franklin	Chess Lamberton
Johnstown	Johnstown–Cambria County
Lancaster	Lancaster
Latrobe	Westmoreland County
Meadville	Port Meadville
Reading	Reading Regional
State College	University Park
Williamsport	Williamsport–Lycoming County

PUBLIC-USE AIRPORTS

Associated City	Facility Name
Allentown	Queen City Airport
Annville	Millard Airport
Bally	Butter Valley Golf Port
Beaver Falls	Beaver County Airport
Bedford	Bedford County Airport
Bellefonte	Bellefonte Airport
Bessemer	Gwin Airport
Bethel	Grimes Airport
Bloomsburg	Bloomsburg Municipal Airport
Brogue	Baublitz Airport
Burgettstown	Miller Airport
Butler	Butler County Airport
Butler	Butler Farm Show Airport
Canadensis	Flying Dollar Airport
Carlisle	Carlisle Airport
Central City	Indian Lake Airport
Centre Hall	Centre Airpark
Centre Hall	Penn's Cave Airport

PUBLIC-USE AIRPORTS *(continued)*

Associated City	Facility Name
Chambersburg	Chambersburg Municipal Airport
Clarion	Clarion County Airport
Clearfield	Clearfield Lawrence Airport
Coatesville	Chester County–G. O. Carlson Airport
Collegeville	Perkiomen Valley Airport
Columbia	McGinness Field Airport
Connellsville	Connellsville Airport
Corry	Corry Lawrence Airport
Culmerville	Culmerville Airport
Danville	Danville Airport
Doylestown	Doylestown Airport
Easton	Easton Airport
East Stroudsburg	Stroudsburg-Pocono Airport
Ebensburg	Ebensburg Airport
Eighty Four	Bandel Airport
Erwinna	Van Sant Airport
Factoryville	Seamens Field
Fairfield	Mid-Atlantic Soaring Center
Finleyville	Finleyville Airpark
Fredericksburg	Farmers Pride Airport
Freeport	McVille Airport
Galeton	Cherry Springs Airport
Germansville	Flying M Aerodrome
Gettysburg	Doersom Airport
Greenville	Greenville Municipal Airport
Grove City	Grove City Airport
Hanover	Hanover Airport
Harrisburg	Capital City Airport
Hazleton	Hazleton Municipal Airport
Honesdale	Cherry Ridge Airport
Indiana	Indiana County–Jimmy Stewart Airport
Irwin	Inter-County Airport
Jeannette	Pittsburgh-Boquet Airpark
Jersey Shore	Jersey Shore Airport
Kralltown	Bermudian Valley Airpark

PUBLIC-USE AIRPORTS *(continued)*

Associated City	Facility Name
Kutztown	Kutztown Airport
Langhorne	Buehl Field
Lebanon	Keller Brothers Airport
Lehighton	Beltzville Airport
Lehighton	Jake Arnold Memorial Airport
Linesville	Merrys Pymatuning Airport
Lock Haven	William T. Piper Memorial Airport
Mars	Lakehill Airport
Mifflintown	Mifflintown Airport
Minersville	Chim Airport
Monongahela	Rostraver Airport
Monroeville	Pittsburgh-Monroeville Airport
Morgantown	Morgantown Airport
Mount Joy/Marietta	Donegal Springs Airport
Mount Pleasant	Mount Pleasant–Scottdale Airport
Mount Pocono	Pocono Mountains Municipal Airport
Mount Union	Huntingdon County Airport
Myerstown	Deck Airport
New Castle	New Castle Municipal Airport
New Hanover	New Hanover Airport
New London	New London Airport
Newry	Blue Knob Valley Airport
North East	Moorhead Airpark
Osterburg	Ickes Airport
Palmyra	Reigle Airport
Perkasie	Pennridge Airport
Philadelphia	Northeast Philadelphia Airport
Philadelphia	Wings Field
Philipsburg	Albert Airport
Philipsburg	Mid-State Airport
Pittsburgh	Allegheny County Airport
Pittsburgh	Pittsburgh Metro Airport
Pittsfield	Brokenstraw Airport
Pottstown	Pottstown Municipal Airport
Pottstown	Pottstown Limerick Airport

PUBLIC-USE AIRPORTS *(continued)*

Associated City	Facility Name
Pottsville	Schuylkill County–Joe Zerby Airport
Punxsutawney	Punxsutawney Airport
Quakertown	Quakertown Airport
Reedsville	Mifflin County Airport
Revere	Schneiders Field Airport
Russell	Scandia Airpark
Sayre	Blue Swan Airport
Selinsgrove	Penn Valley Airport
Seven Springs	Seven Springs Airport
Shamokin	Northumberland County Airport
Shippensburg	Shippensburg Airport
Slatington	Slatington Airport
Smoketown	Smoketown Airport
Somerset	Somerset County Airport
St. Marys	St. Marys Municipal Airport
Sterling	Spring Hill Airport
Sunbury	Sunbury Airport
Tarentum	West Penn Airport
Titusville	Titusville Airport
Toughkenamon	New Garden Flying Field
Towanda	Towanda Airport
Tower City	Bendigo Airport
Tunkhannock	Sky Haven Airport
Unionville	Keystone Gliderport
Washington	Washington County Airport
Wattsburg	Erie County Airport
Waynesburg	Greene County Airport
Wellsboro	Grand Canyon Airport
Wellsville	Kampel Airport
West Chester	Brandywine Airport
Wilkes-Barre	Wilkes-Barre–Wyoming Valley Airport
Williamsburg	Cove Valley Airport
York	York Airport
Zelienople	Zelienople Municipal Airport

9

Education

Home-based schooling was the order of the day in colonial America. Eventually, some of these parent-teachers established private schools by including the neighbors. Next, groups of families or churches would hire a teacher and establish a one-room school. When the Public School Act of 1834 was enacted, there were about 1,000 schools in the commonwealth with an enrollment of about 150,000 students. Motivated by the availability of public funds, half of these schools joined the state system immediately; by 1875, most had joined. The public system was a primary-school system. Secondary schools were privately funded until the 1920s.

In Pennsylvania, schools must be provided for children from age six to 21, or until graduation. Kindergarten is optional for children four to six, but each district has a kindergarten program.

The State Board of Education, created in 1911, establishes regulations, standards, policies, and guidelines for all public and private schools. The 22-member board consists of 17 citizens appointed by the governor, four members of the General Assembly, and the chairman of the Professional Standards and Practices Committee. The Pennsylvania Department of Education carries out the policies of the State Board and administers the school laws.

The 500 local school districts are governed by an elected nine-member school board, except in Philadelphia, where the mayor appoints the board. The local boards make the decisions on almost every aspect of school operations—curricula, staff, buildings, and textbooks—consistent with state law. All local school boards, except Philadelphia's, establish budgets and levy taxes to support their schools. In Philadelphia, the city council appropriates school funds. Local school boards appoint a district superintendent to administer the school district.

Schools are funded by a complicated state and local financial partnership established by the General Assembly. Districts receive subsidies based upon pupil population and the wealth of the district. The state funds special programs such as vocational education, special education, and transportation.

HIGHER EDUCATION

Higher education in Pennsylvania is available at 144 institutions, which had a total enrollment of 447,774 students in 1995–96. These institutions can be divided into eight general categories:

PUBLIC SCHOOL ENROLLMENT, GRADES K–12 (1995–96)

County	Pupils	County	Pupils
Adams	13,970	Lackawanna	28,070
Allegheny	171,650	Lancaster	67,202
Armstrong	12,292	Lawrence	16,314
Beaver	29,257	Lebanon	18,012
Bedford	8,606	Lehigh	42,777
Berks	60,188	Luzerne	42,294
Blair	21,260	Lycoming	20,570
Bradford	12,218	McKean	8,014
Bucks	86,347	Mercer	19,655
Butler	27,248	Mifflin	6,368
Cambria	21,910	Monroe	23,813
Cameron	1,185	Montgomery	91,888
Carbon	8,878	Montour	2,920
Centre	14,133	Northampton	40,030
Chester	60,039	Northumberland	14,644
Clarion	8,075	Perry	7,946
Clearfield	16,110	Philadelphia	211,658
Clinton	5,570	Pike	4,085
Columbia	11,906	Potter	3,407
Crawford	12,455	Schuylkill	21,033
Cumberland	27,738	Snyder	5,676
Dauphin	38,472	Somerset	13,444
Delaware	69,127	Sullivan	972
Elk	4,722	Susquehanna	9,069
Erie	43,389	Tioga	7,248
Fayette	22,345	Union	4,508
Forest	815	Venango	11,488
Franklin	18,622	Warren	7,261
Fulton	2,628	Washington	31,188
Greene	6,938	Wayne	9,276
Huntingdon	6,725	Westmoreland	58,418
Indiana	13,875	Wyoming	5,114
Jefferson	7,551	York	63,493
Juniata	3,434	Total	1,787,533

RELIGIOUS SCHOOL ENROLLMENT (1995–96)

	Pupils
Catholic Schools by Diocese	
Philadelphia	116,295
Allentown	18,635
Altoona-Johnstown	6,767
Erie	14,422
Greensburg	6,289
Harrisburg	14,456
Pittsburgh	32,876
Scranton	15,863
Independent	135
Total	225,738
Other Religious Schools	
Amish	10,410
Assembly of God	1,870
Baptist	8,127
Brethren	213
Church of God	94
Episcopal	2,002
God's Missionary	199
Islamic	768
Jewish	2,940
Lutheran	1,633
Mennonite	9,044
Methodist	1,564
Missionary Alliance	10
Pentecostal	194
Presbyterian	757
Seventh-Day Adventist	1,200
Society of Friends	6,325
Other Christian denominations	30,785
Other religions	94
Total	78,229

1. Fourteen state universities, which enrolled 82,636 students.

2. Four state-related commonwealth universities: Pennsylvania State University, its 21 branch campuses, and the Pennsylvania College of Technology, which is affiliated with Penn State; the University of Pittsburgh, with its four branch campuses; Temple University; and Lincoln University. These four institutions enrolled 116,758 students in 1995–96.

3. Fifteen community colleges, which enrolled 66,473 students.

4. Eight private, state-aided institutions (including the University of Pennsylvania), which enrolled 34,390 students.

5. Seventy-eight private colleges and universities, which enrolled 141,162 students.

6. Seventeen theological seminaries.

7. Seven private two-year colleges.

8. The Stevens State School of Technology.

In addition, there are 95 specialized associate degree granting institutions, primarily business and technical schools, along with a few art, music, and culinary arts institutes. To earn the associate degree, students must have a high school diploma and earn 60 units in a program approved by the secretary of education. In 1994–95, 47,289 students were enrolled in these institutions.

The State System of Higher Education

The state universities spent their first 100 years of existence training teachers for Pennsylvania's schools. The Normal School Act of 1857 established regional teacher training institutes throughout the commonwealth. The School Code of 1911 called for the purchase of all normal schools, and by 1921, the present configuration of 14 state-owned universities was established. The evolution of the normal schools included four name changes: normal schools, state normal schools, state teachers college, and state colleges. In 1982, Act 188 established the Pennsylvania System of Higher Education, and 13 state colleges joined Indiana University of Pennsylvania as universities.

The universities are located in rural, suburban, and small-town settings throughout the state. The Office of the Chancellor is located in Harrisburg, in the Dixon University Center. The Center in Harrisburg also offers academic programs through a consortium of the universities.

Universities in the system offer 217 undergraduate and 107 graduate degrees in 32 major academic areas. Prerequisite coursework and counseling are afforded students planning to enter professional schools of engineering, health-related sciences, and law. About 90% of the students are residents of Pennsylvania, and about 72% of the graduates remain in the state.

With about 11,600 professional and support staff, the system is the 17th-largest employer in the state.

LIBRARIES

The State Library of Pennsylvania is charged with developing, improving, and coordinating library services and systems. It provides statewide leadership in the development of libraries. As one of the largest research libraries in the commonwealth, the State Library has holdings in almost every area of hu-

ENROLLMENT, TUITION, AND FEES
PENNSYLVANIA INSTITUTIONS OF HIGHER
EDUCATION (FALL 1995)

	Enrollment	Tuition and Fees*
State Universities		
Bloomsburg	6,405	$3,915
California	5,278	4,136
Cheyney	1,194	3,729
Clarion	5,299	4,054
East Stroudsburg	4,647	4,016
Edinboro	6,741	3,924
Indiana	12,603	3,891
Kutztown	7,000	3,940
Lock Haven	3,352	3,822
Mansfield	2,653	3,804
Millersville	6,278	4,100
Shippensburg	5,877	4,010
Slippery Rock	6,584	4,013
West Chester	9,027	3,874
Total Enrollment	82,626	
State-Related Commonwealth Universities		
Lincoln	1,479	$3,956
Penn College/PSU Affiliate	4,044	5,838
Pennsylvania State	61,635	
Main Campus	36,644	5,258
Abington-Ogontz	2,362	5,094
Allentown	496	5,094
Altoona	2,690	5,094
Beaver	803	5,094
Berks	1,501	5,094
Delaware County	1,259	5,094
DuBois	759	5,094
Erie Behrend College	2,797	5,258
Fayette	824	5,094
Great Valley Graduate Center	613	—
Harrisburg Capital College	2,097	5,258

ENROLLMENT, TUITION, AND FEES
PENNSYLVANIA INSTITUTIONS OF HIGHER
EDUCATION *(continued)*

	Enrollment	Tuition and Fees*
Hazleton	1,252	5,094
Hershey Medical Center	568	—
McKeesport	748	5,094
Mont Alto	1,016	5,094
New Kensington	744	5,094
Schuylkill	833	5,094
Shenango	715	5,094
Wilkes-Barre	674	5,094
Worthington-Scranton	1,032	5,094
York	1,209	5,094
Pittsburgh	27,002	
Main Campus	21,734	5,638
Bradford	1,002	5,594
Greensburg	1,177	5,600
Johnstown	2,843	5,656
Titusville	245	5,414
Temple	22,599	5,514
Total Enrollment	**116,758**	

Community Colleges

Allegheny County	11,270	$2,020
Beaver County	1,760	1,910
Bucks County	5,782	2,034
Butler County	2,037	1,500
Cambria County	277	1,350
Delaware County	5,398	1,710
Erie County Technical Institute	1,035	1,950
Harrisburg Area	6,799	
Main Campus	5,609	1,748
Lancaster Campus	780	1,748
Lebanon Campus	411	1,748
Lehigh-Carbon	2,658	1,890

ENROLLMENT, TUITION, AND FEES
PENNSYLVANIA INSTITUTIONS OF HIGHER
EDUCATION *(continued)*

	Enrollment	Tuition and Fees*
Community Colleges (continued)		
Luzerne County	4,394	1,590
Montgomery County	5,130	2,040
Northampton County	3,450	
Main Campus	3,154	1,950
Monroe Campus	296	3,390
Philadelphia	10,087	2,055
Reading Area	2,000	1,890
Westmoreland County	4,126	1,313
Total Enrollment	66,473	
Private State-Aided Institutions		
Drexel University	6,818	$13,844
Medical College of Pennsylvania/ Hahnemann University	2,696	9,210
PA College of Optometry	635	—
PA College of Podiatry	446	—
Philadelphia College of Osteopathic Medicine	1,019	—
Thomas Jefferson University	2,030	14,350
University of the Arts	1,270	13,670
University of Pennsylvania	19,475	19,898
Total Enrollment	34,390	
Private Colleges and Universities		
Academy of the New Church	121	$4,400
Albright College	1,107	16,575
Allegheny College	1,818	18,020
Allentown College of St. Francis de Sales	1,552	10,440
Alvernia College	1,047	9,850
American College	163	—
Baptist Bible College	609	6,686

ENROLLMENT, TUITION, AND FEES
PENNSYLVANIA INSTITUTIONS OF HIGHER
EDUCATION *(continued)*

	Enrollment	Tuition and Fees*
Beaver College	1,703	13,970
Bryn Mawr College	1,643	19,780
Bucknell University	3,561	19,470
Cabrini College	1,466	11,600
Carlow College	1,460	10,588
Carnegie-Mellon University	6,782	18,700
Cedar Crest College	1,067	14,770
Chatham College	670	14,196
Chestnut Hill College	763	11,865
College Misericordia	1,484	12,190
Curtis Institute of Music	161	625**
Delaware Valley College	1,581	31,208
Dickinson College	1,795	19,750
Dickinson School of Law	532	—
Duquesne University	7,542	12,578
Eastern College	1,641	11,780
Elizabethtown College	1,588	15,490
Franklin & Marshall College	1,787	21,350
Gannon University	3,026	11,114
Geneva College	1,527	10,040
Gettysburg College	2,023	20,834
Gratz College	63	6,400
Grove City College	2,289	6,174
Gynedd-Mercy College	1,102	12,017
Haverford College	1,115	19,888
Holy Family College	1,687	9,500
Immaculata College	915	10,880
Juniata College	1,038	16,010
King's College	2,022	12,260
Lafayette College	2,070	19,261
Lancaster Bible College	478	7,700
La Roche College	1,016	9,426
La Salle University	3,743	12,600

ENROLLMENT, TUITION, AND FEES
PENNSYLVANIA INSTITUTIONS OF HIGHER
EDUCATION *(continued)*

	Enrollment	Tuition and Fees*
Private Colleges and Universities (continued)		
Lebanon Valley College	1,346	14,785
Lehigh University	5,462	19,650
Lycoming College	1,403	14,760
Marywood College	2,201	11,500
Mercyhurst College	2,236	11,016
Messiah College	2,381	10,954
Moore College of Art & Design	366	14,422
Moravian College	1,496	15,880
Mount Aloysius College	1,151	8,360
Muhlenberg College	1,926	17,550
Newmann College	819	11,090
Pennsylvania Academy of Fine Arts	283	8,050
Philadelphia College of the Bible	817	8,060
Philadelphia College of Pharmacy & Science	1,978	12,450
Philadelphia College of Textiles & Science	2,484	12,286
Point Park College	1,531	10,552
Robert Morris College	3,586	7,350
Rosemont College	485	12,405
Saint Francis College	1,464	11,850
Saint Joseph's College	4,236	14,025
Saint Vincent College	1,083	11,310
Seton Hill College	748	11,775
Susquehanna University	1,602	17,080
Swarthmore College	1,352	20,186
Thiel College	928	11,952
University of Scranton	2,244	12,570
Ursinus College	1,623	15,840
Valley Forge Christian College	495	4,692
Villanova University	8,422	16,520
Washington & Jefferson College	1,175	16,840

ENROLLMENT, TUITION, AND FEES
PENNSYLVANIA INSTITUTIONS OF HIGHER
EDUCATION *(continued)*

	Enrollment	Tuition and Fees*
Waynesburg College	1,244	9,600
Westminster College	1,540	13,950
Widener University	4,476	12,950
Wilkes University	2,108	12,473
Wilson College	483	12,117
York College of Pennsylvania	3,908	5,730
Total Enrollment	141,162	
Private Two-Year Colleges		
Harcum College	579	8,596
Keystone College	648	8,970
Lackawanna Junior College	640	6,370
Manor Junior College	497	6,990
Peirce College	952	6,752
Pennsylvania Institute of Technology	308	7,320
Valley Forge Military College	184	13,600
Total Enrollment	3,808	
Stevens State School of Technology***	427	4,295

* Annual tuition for undergraduate in-state students, excluding room and board.
** Registration fees only.
*** The only four-year state school of technology.

man concern. It provides information and materials from its collections and automated resources to state government, state institutions, and the general public. It also provides rapid access to other library collections around the state and the nation through the use of various computerized systems, networks, and databases.

The State Library coordinates a network of state-aided local, district, and regional public libraries. There are 622 public libraries in the commonwealth, including branches. Ninety-one percent receive some state financial aid, which accounts for 17 percent of total library revenues. About 60 percent of library funding comes from municipalities.

DISTRICT LIBRARY CENTERS

City	Library
Aliquippa	B. F. Jones Memorial Library
Allentown	Allentown Public Library
Altoona	Altoona Area Public Library
Bellefonte	Centre County Library
Bethlehem	Bethlehem Area Public Library
Brookhaven	Delaware County Library System
Chambersburg	Conococheague District Library
Doylestown	Bucks County Free Library
Easton	Easton Area Public Library
Erie	Erie County Public Library
Harrisburg	Dauphin County Library System
Johnstown	Cambria County Library System
Lancaster	Lancaster County Library
Monessen	Monessen Public Library
New Castle	New Castle Public Library
Norristown	Montgomery County–Norristown Public Library
Oil City	Oil Creek District Library Center
Philadelphia	Free Library of Philadelphia
Pittsburgh	Carnegie Library of Pittsburgh, Neighborhood & Outreach Services
Pottsville	Pottsville Free Public Library
Reading	Reading Public Library
Scranton	Scranton Public Library
Warren	Seneca District Center
Washington	Citizens Library
West Whiteland	Chester County Library
Wilkes-Barre	Osterhout Free Library
Williamsport	James V. Brown Library
York	Martin Memorial Library

PENNSYLVANIA DEPOSITORY LIBRARIES

City	Library
Allentown	Trexler Library, Muhlenberg College
Altoona	Altoona Area Public Library
Bethel Park	Bethel Park Public Library
Bethlehem	Fairchild/Martindale Library, Lehigh University
Bloomsburg	Andruss Library
Blue Bell	Learning Resources Center, Montgomery County Community College
Bradford	Hanley Library, University of Pittsburgh at Bradford
Broomall	Marple Public Library
Bryn Mawr	Canaday Library, Bryn Mawr College
California	Manderino Library, California University
Carlisle	Spahr Library, Dickinson College
	Sheely-Lee Library, Dickinson School of Law
Cheyney	Hill Library, Cheyney University
Collegeville	Myrin Library, Ursinus College
Coraopolis	Robert Morris College Library
Doylestown	Bucks County Free Library
East Stroudsburg	Kemp Library, East Stroudsburg University
Erie	Erie County Public Library
Greenville	Langenheim Library, Thiel College
Harrisburg	State Library of Pennsylvania
	Widener University School of Law Library
Haverford	Magill Library, Haverford College
Indiana	Stapleton Library, Indiana University of Pennsylvania
Johnstown	Glosser Memorial Library Building, Cambria County Library System
Lancaster	Shadek-Fackenthal Library, Franklin & Marshall College
Lewisburg	Bertrand Library, Bucknell University
Mansfield	Main Library, Mansfield University
Meadville	Pelletier Library, Allegheny College
Millersville	Ganser Library, Millersville University
Monessen	Monessen Public Library

PENNSYLVANIA DEPOSITORY LIBRARIES *(continued)*

City	Library
New Castle	New Castle Public Library
Newtown	Bucks County Community College Library
Norristown	Montgomery County–Norristown Public Library
Philadelphia	Free Library of Philadelphia–Logan Square
	Drexel Library, Saint Joseph's University
	Paley Library, Temple University
	Temple University Law Library
	U.S. Court of Appeals Library
	School of Law Library, University of Pennsylvania
Pittsburgh	Allegheny County Law Library
	Carnegie Library of Pittsburgh
	Carnegie Library, Allegheny Regional Branch
	Duquesne University Law Library
	Wright Library, La Roche College
	Hillman Library, University of Pittsburgh
	University of Pittsburgh Law Library
	Bureau of Mines Library, U.S. Department of Interior
Pottsville	Pottsville Free Public Library
Reading	Reading Public Library
Scranton	Scranton Public Library
Shippensburg	Ezra Lehman Memorial Library, Shippensburg University
Slippery Rock	Bailey Library, Slippery Rock University
Swarthmore	McCabe Library, Swarthmore College
University Park	Pennsylvania State University Libraries
Villanova	Pulling Law Library, Villanova University School of Law
	Falvey Library, Villanova University
Warren	Warren Public Library
West Chester	Green Library, West Chester University
Williamsport	Lycoming College Library
Youngwood	Learning Resources Center, Westmoreland Community College

The Pennsylvania Public Library System has designated twenty-eight district library centers, which provide library services to residents. In urban areas, the county library is the district library. In rural areas, a district library may serve several adjoining counties.

In order to make U.S. government documents accessible to the public, the government distributes them to designated libraries, called depository libraries. Due to the vast number of publications involved, the majority of depository libraries are college and university libraries and a few of the largest public libraries. Even they have difficulty keeping up with the cataloging of government publications.

10

Arts and Culture

SYMPHONY ORCHESTRAS

Allentown Symphony
Altoona Symphony
Ambler Symphony
Butler County Symphony (Butler)
Central Pennsylvania Symphony (Hummelstown)
Delaware Valley Philharmonic (Fairless Hills)
Edgewood Symphony (Pittsburgh)
Erie Philharmonic
European Women's Orchestra (Philadelphia)
Harrisburg Symphony
Hershey Symphony
Johnstown Symphony
Kennett Symphony (Kennett Square)
Landsdowne Symphony
Main Line Symphony (Wayne)
McKeesport Symphony
Nittany Valley Symphony (State College)
Northeastern Pennsylvania Philharmonic (Avoca)
North Penn Symphony (Lansdale)
North Pittsburgh Civic Symphony (Allegheny, Westmoreland, and Butler Counties)
Orchestra of the Pennsylvania Ballet (Philadelphia)
Pennsylvania Sinfonia Orchestra (Allentown)
Philadelphia Orchestra
Pittsburgh Civic Orchestra
Pittsburgh Symphony
Pottstown Symphony
Reading Symphony
Schuylkill Symphony (Pottsville)
Slovak Philharmonic (Jenkintown)
Westmoreland Symphony (Greensburg)
Williamsport Symphony
York Symphony

CHORAL GROUPS

Bach and Handel Chorale (Jim Thorpe)
Bach Choir of Bethlehem
Bach Choir of Pittsburgh
Bel Canto Singers of York
Chamber Singers of Harrisburg
Choral Arts Society of Philadelphia
Mendelssohn Choir of Pittsburgh
Mendelssohn Club of Philadelphia
Philadelphia Chamber Chorus
Philadelphia Singers
Pittsburgh Concert Chorale (Warrendale)
Pittsburgh Oratorio Society
Singing City (Philadelphia)
State College Chorale
Susquehanna Valley Chorale (Lewisburg)
Williamsport Civic Chorus
Wyoming County Chorale (Tunkhannock)

OPERA

Harrisburg Opera
Opera Company of Philadelphia

Opera Theatre of Pittsburgh
Pennsylvania Opera Theatre (Philadelphia)
Pittsburgh Civic Light Opera
Pittsburgh Opera

BALLET
Allegheny Ballet (Altoona)
Ballet Theatre of Pennsylvania (Kingston)
Ballet Northeast (Wilkes-Barre)
Bucks County Dance Company (Feasterville)
Civic Ballet (Scranton)
Cumberland Dance Company (Enola)
Harrisburg Ballet
Lehigh Valley Ballet Company (Bethlehem)
Pennsylvania Ballet (Philadelphia)
Pittsburgh Ballet

MAJOR ART MUSEUMS
Allentown Art Museum
European and American paintings,
period rooms, gems, and textiles
Andy Warhol Museum (Pittsburgh)
Art and artifacts of the pop culture's
best-known artist
Barnes Foundation (Merion)
Hundreds of paintings by renowned
artists displayed in an idiosyncratic
style
Carnegie Museum of Art (Pittsburgh)
Major holdings in Impressionist,
post-Impressionist, and 19th- and
20th-century American works;
Heinz Architectural Center
Frick Art and Historical Center (Pittsburgh)
Permanent collection of Italian
Renaissance and Flemish artists,
and rotating exhibits
Paley Design Center of Philadelphia College of Textiles and Science

Textiles from Coptic to contemporary,
costumes, fine arts, and crafts
Palmer Museum of Art (Penn State University)
Ten galleries of historic, modern, and
contemporary art
Pennsylvania Academy of the Fine Arts, Museum of American Art
The best collection of Pennsylvania
artists—Mary Cassatt, Benjamin
West, Thomas Eakins
Philadelphia Museum of Art
A world-class museum, with art
from all eras and schools: European
Renaissance, contemporary Ameri-
can, and modern
Rodin Museum (Philadelphia)
A major collection of the master's
work, both original and casts
Rosenbach Museum and Library (Philadelphia)
Rare books, 18th- and 19th-century
furniture, silver, paintings, and
decorative arts
Woodmere Art Museum (Philadelphia)
Arts of Philadelphia, past and
present, including paintings and
decorative arts; features 19th-century
American paintings

MAJOR NATURAL HISTORY MUSEUMS
Academy of Natural Sciences (Philadelphia)
Museum and research facility,
founded in 1812, dedicated to edu-
cation and promotion of the natural
sciences; major dinosaur exhibit
Carnegie Museum of Natural History (Pittsburgh)
One of the finest dinosaur collections
in the world, minerals and gems,
polar exhibit, and Egyptian artifacts
Museum of Archaeology and Anthropology–University of Pennsylvania

*Internationally renowned institution
with superb collections of artifacts
from ancient cultures*
State Museum of Pennsylvania (Harrisburg)
*This museum has a major natural
history aspect—earth science, natural
history, and archaeology*
Wagner Free Institute of Science (Philadelphia)
*A National Historic Landmark
Victorian building with thousands
of natural specimens*

MAJOR SCIENCE MUSEUMS

Carnegie Science Center (Pittsburgh)
*Traveling and permanent exhibits, a
World War II submarine, a four-story
domed Omnimax theater, and an
interactive planetarium*
Franklin Institute Science Museum
(Philadelphia)
*Museum with exhibits related to science, industry, mathematics, history,
communications, and Benjamin
Franklin; a planetarium; a futures
center; and an Omniverse theater*
Museum of Scientific Discovery (Harrisburg)
About 100 changing exhibits, demonstrations, special programs

GOVERNOR'S AWARDS FOR THE ARTS

Since 1980, governors of Pennsylvania have presented awards to recognize excellence in, or outstanding service to, the arts in the commonwealth. The first awards were named for Theodore L. Hazlett, Jr., the first chairman of the Pennsylvania Council on the Arts, who died in 1979.

Ten awards were presented in 1980, 1981, and 1982; six in 1984 and 1986; and five in 1985. No awards were made in 1987. A Distinguished Pennsylvania Artist Award was also established in 1980.

In 1988, Governor Casey established the Governor's Award for Excellence in the Arts, Humanities, and Sciences to recognize outstanding creativity and achievement by individuals with roots in, or current association with, Pennsylvania. One award was made in each of the three categories. No awards were made in 1995.

In 1996, Governor Ridge presented five awards for the Arts: Distinguished Artist, Artist of the Year (Hazlett Award), Corporate Patron Award, and two Arts Leadership and Service Awards.

AWARD RECIPIENTS

Distinguished Artist Award
1996   Paul Winter, Composer, Jazz Artist

Artist of the Year
1996   Tito Capobianco, Opera Director

Arts Leadership and Service Award
1996   Carol R. Brown, President, Pittsburgh Cultural Trust
        Robert Montgomery Scott, President and Chief Executive
            Officer, Philadelphia Museum of Art

Corporate Patron Award
1996   Binney & Smith, Inc., Easton

Governor's Awards for Excellence in the Arts
1994   Lorin Maazel, Conductor
1993   John Edgar Wideman, Author
1992   Paul Plishka, Opera Singer
1991   Gary Graffman, Pianist
1990   August Wilson, Playwright
1989   Riccardo Muti, Conductor
1988   Judith Jamison, Dancer

Distinguished Pennsylvania Artists
1986   Andrew Wyeth, Painter
1985   Byron Janis, Pianist
1984   Bill Cosby, Entertainer
1983   John Updike, Author
1982   Marian Anderson, Opera Singer
1981   James Michener, Author
1980   James Stewart, Actor

Theodore L. Hazlett Memorial Awards
1986   Lester Breininger, Jr., Crafts
        Joan Myers Brown, Dance
        Samuel Hazo, Literature
        Sidney Goodman, Painting
        Katherine Minehart, Theatre
        Edgar Kaufmann, Jr., Service to the Arts

AWARD RECIPIENTS *(continued)*

Theodore L. Hazlett Memorial Awards (continued)

1985   Mitchell & Giurogola, Architecture
        Anthony Buba, Media Arts
        Max Rudolf, Music
        Larry Fink, Photography
        Charles Fahlen, Sculpture
1984   Stanley Lechtzin, Crafts
        Hellmut Fricke-Gottschild, Dance
        Daniel Hoffman, Literature
        Charles Fuller, Theatre
        Dorothy Dressler, Service to the Arts
1983   Linda Blackaby, Film/Video
        Andre Previn, Music
        Emmet Gowin, Photography
        Jody Pinto, Sculpture
        Robert Ventura/Denise Scott Brown, Architecture
1982   Rudolph Staffel, Crafts
        Paul Draper, Dance
        Fred Rogers, Mister Rogers, Film/Video
        David Bradley, Literature
        George Crumb, Music
        Larry Day, Painting
        Mark Cohen, Photography
        Rafael Ferrer, Sculpture
        John Allen, Jr., Theatre
        Phillip I. and Muriel Berman, Service to the Arts
1981   George Nakashima, Crafts
        Barbara Weisberger, Dance
        Peter Rose, Film/Video
        Paul West, Literature
        Vincent Persichetti, Music
        Andrew Wyeth, Painting
        William Larsen, Photography
        Selma Burke, Sculpture
        Margo Lovelace, Theatre
        Gregory Gibson, Service to the Arts

AWARD RECIPIENTS *(continued)*

Theodore L. Hazlett Memorial Awards, continued

1980　Natale Rossi, Crafts
　　　Arthur Hall, Dance
　　　Dwinell Grant, Film/Video
　　　Gerald Stern, Literature
　　　Eugene Ormandy, Music
　　　Edna Andrade, painting
　　　Ray K. Metzker, Photography
　　　Harry Bertoia, Sculpture
　　　Dr. Alvina Krause, Theatre
　　　Sondra Myers, Service to the Arts

11

Communications

DAILY NEWSPAPERS

More than 250,000 circulation

Philadelphia Inquirer — 400 N. Broad St., Philadelphia, PA 19130

100,000–250,000 circulation

Philadelphia Daily News — 400 N. Broad St., Philadelphia, PA 19130

Pittsburgh Post Gazette — 34 Blvd. of the Allies, Pittsburgh, PA 15222

50,000–100,000 circulation

Beaver County Times — 400 Fair Ave., Beaver, PA 15009

Bucks County Courier Times — 8400 Route 13, Levittown, PA 19057

Daily Times — 500 Mildred Ave., Primos, PA 19018

The Express Times — 30 N. 4th St., Easton, PA 18042

Lancaster New Era — 8 W. King St., Lancaster, PA 17603

The Times Leader — 15 N. Main St., Wilkes-Barre, PA 18711

25,000–50,000 circulation

Altoona Daily Mirror — 301 Cayuga Ave., Altoona, PA 16602

Butler Eagle — 114 W. Diamond St., Butler, PA 16001

Centre Daily Times — 3400 E. College Ave., State College, PA 16801

Citizens Voice — 75 N. Washington St., Wilkes-Barre, PA 18711

The Daily Item — 200 Market St., Sunbury, PA 17801

Daily Local News — 215 N. Bradford Ave., West Chester, PA 19382

The Daily News — 401 Walnut St., McKeesport, PA 15132

The Derrick — 1510 W. 1st St., Oil City, PA 16301

DAILY NEWSPAPERS *(continued)*

Erie Daily Times	12th and Sassafras Sts., Erie, PA 16534
The Evening News	812 Market St., Harrisburg, PA 17105
The Herald	52 Dock St., Sharon, PA 16146
The Herald Standard	818 East Church St., Uniontown, PA 15401
The Intelligencer Journal	8 W. King St., Lancaster, PA 17603
The Mercury	Hanover and King Sts., Pottstown, PA 19464
Montgomery County Record	145 N. Easton Rd., Horsham, PA 19044
The Morning News	205 W. 12th St., Erie, PA 16534
North Hills News Record	137 Commonwealth Dr., Warrendale, PA 15086
The Observer Reporter	122 S. Main St., Washington, PA 15301
Pottsville Republican	111 Mahantongo St., Pottsville, PA 17901
Reading Eagle	345 Penn St., Reading, PA 19601
Reading Times	345 Penn St., Reading, PA 19601
Scranton Times	149 Penn Ave., Scranton, PA 18503
Scranton Tribune	149 Penn Ave., Scranton, PA 18503
Tarentum Valley News Dispatch	210 Fourth Ave., Tarentum, PA 15084
The Times Herald	410 Markley St., Norristown, PA 19401
The Tribune Democrat	425 Locust St., Johnstown, PA 15907
York Daily Record	1750 Industrial Hwy., York, PA 17402
York Dispatch	205 N. George St., York, PA 17405

10,000–25,000 circulation

Bedford Daily Gazette	424 W. Penn St., Bedford, PA 15009
Bradford Era	43 Main St., Bradford, PA 16701
Courier-Express	500 Jeffers St., DuBois, PA 15801
Daily American	334 W. Main St., Somerset, PA 15501
Daily Collegian	123 S. Burrows, University Park, PA 16801
Daily Courier	127 W. Apple St., Connellsville, PA 15425
Daily News	325 Penn St., Huntingdon, PA 16652
Daily News	718 Poplar St., Lebanon, PA 17042
Daily Pennsylvanian	4015 Walnut St., Philadelphia, PA 19104
The Evening Herald	Ringtown Blvd., Shenandoah, PA 17976
Evening Sun	135 Baltimore St., Hanover, PA 17331

DAILY NEWSPAPERS *(continued)*

The Express	9 W. Main St., Lock Haven, PA 17745
Gettysburg Times	18 Carlisle St., Gettysburg, PA 17325
Indiana Gazette	899 Water St., Indiana, PA 15701
Leader Times	115–21 N. Grant Ave., Kittanning, PA 16201
Meadville Tribune	947 Federal Court, Meadville, PA 16335
New Castle News	27–35 N. Mercer St., New Castle, PA 16101
News Item	707 Rock St., Shamokin, PA 17847
Pocono Record	511 Lenox St., Stroudsburg, PA 18360
Press-Enterprise	3185 Lackawanna Ave., Bloomsburg, PA 17815
The Progress	206 E. Locust St., Clearfield, PA 16830
Public Opinion	77 N. 3rd St., Chambersburg, PA 17201
Record Herald	30 Walnut St., Waynesboro, PA 15370
The Reporter	307 Derstine Ave., Lansdale, PA 19446
The Sentinel	Box 130, Carlisle, PA 17013
The Sentinel	375 Sixth St., Lewistown, PA 17044
Standard Observer	R.D. #1, Route 136, Greensburg, PA 15601
Standard Speaker	21 N. Wyoming St., Hazleton, PA 18201
The Times News	1st and Iron Sts., Lehighton, PA 18235
The Valley Independent	Eastgate 19, Monessen, PA 15062
Warren Times Observer	205 Pennsylvania Ave., Warren, PA 16365

Under 10,000 circulation

Corry Journal	28 W. South St., Corry, PA 16407
Daily Press	245 Brussels St., St. Marys, PA 15857
Daily Record	204 E. Lincoln Hwy., Coatesville, PA 19320
Daily Review	116 Main St., Towanda, PA 18848
Danville News	14 E. Mahoning St., Danville, PA 17821
Ellwood City Leader	835 Lawrence Ave., Ellwood City, PA 16117
Evening Times	210 N. Lehigh Ave., Sayre, PA 18840
Kane Republican	200 N. Fraley St., Kane, PA 16735
Latrobe Bulletin	1211 Ligonier St., Latrobe, PA 15650
Legal Intelligencer	1617 JFK Blvd., Philadelphia, PA 19103
Lewisburg Daily Journal	150 Buffalo Rd., Lewisburg, PA 17837

DAILY NEWSPAPERS *(continued)*

Milton Daily Standard	19 Arch St., Milton, PA 17847
The News Herald	631 Twelfth St., Franklin, PA 16323
Observer-Reporter	32 Church St., Waynesburg, PA 15370
The Phoenix	225 Bridge St., Phoenixville, PA 19460
The Record Argus	10 Penn Ave., Greenville, PA 16125
Ridgway Record	20 Main St., Ridgway, PA 15853
The Spirit	510 Pine St., Punxsutawney, PA 15767
Titusville Herald	209 W. Spring St., Titusville, PA 16354
Tyrone Daily Herald	1018 Pennsylvania Ave., Tyrone, PA 16686
Wayne Independent	220 Eighth St., Honesdale, PA 18431

WEEKLY NEWSPAPERS
Paid Circulation Publications

Allegheny County	*Aspinwall Herald*
	Bridgeville Area News
	Coraopolis Record
	McKees Rock Suburban Gazette
	Monroeville Advance Leader
	Monroeville Progress
	Monroeville Times Express
	New Pittsburgh Courier
	South Hills Record
Armstrong County	*Leechburg Advance*
Bedford County	*Bedford Inquirer*
	Broad Top Bulletin
Berks County	*Boyertown Area News*
	Hamburg Item
	Kutztown Patriot
Blair County	*Morrisons Cove Herald*
Bradford County	*Canton Independent Sentinel*
	Troy Gazette Register
	Wyalusing Rocket Courier

WEEKLY NEWSPAPERS *(continued)*
Paid Circulation Publications

Bucks County	*New Hope Gazette* *Newtown Advance* *Perkasie News Herald* *Quakertown Free Press* *Yardley News*
Cambria County	*Barnesboro Star* *Ebensburg Mountaineer Herald* *Ebensburg News Leader* *Patton Union Press Courier* *Portage Dispatch*
Cameron County	*Cameron County Echo*
Chester County	*Brandywine Chronicle* *Chester County Press*
Clarion County	*Clarion News* *New Bethelem Leader-Vindicator*
Clinton County	*Renovo Record*
Crawford County	*Conneautville Courier*
Cumberland County	*Newville Valley Times Star* *Shippensburg News Chronicle*
Dauphin County	*Hummelstown Sun* *Middletown Press and Journal* *Upper Dauphin Sentinel*
Delaware County	*County Press* (Newton Square) *Drexel Hill Press* (Newton Square) *El Hispano* *Garnet Valley Press* *Haverford Press* *Main Line Times* *Marcus Hook Press* *Ridley Press* *Springfield Press* *Upper Darby Press* *Wayne Suburban Advertiser* *Yeadon Times*
Erie County	*Albion News* *Edinboro Independent Enterprise*

WEEKLY NEWSPAPERS *(continued)*
Paid Circulation Publications

Erie County (continued)	*Girard Cosmoplite Herald* *North East Breeze* *Union City Times Leader*
Fayette County	*Masontown Centennial*
Forest County	*Tionesta Forest Press*
Franklin County	*Greencastle Echo Pilot*
Fulton County	*Fulton County News*
Indiana County	*Blairsville Dispatch*
Jefferson County	*Jefferson County* (Punxsutawney) *Jeffersonian Democrat* (Brookville) *Neighbors*
Juniata County	*Juniata Sentinel* (Mifflintown) *Port Royal Times*
Lackawanna County	*Abington Journal* *Carbondale News* *Moscow Villager* *Triboro Banner* (Taylor)
Lancaster County	*Elizabethtown Chronicle* *Ephrata Review* *Lititz Record Express* *Local Ledger* (Quarryville) *Public Ledger* (Quarryville) *Strasburg Weekly News*
Lawrence County	*New Wilmington Globe* *South County News*
Lehigh County	*Catasauqua Dispatch*
Luzerne County	*Dallas Post* *Pittston Dispatch* *White Haven Journal Herald*
Lycoming County	*Muncy Luminary*
McKean County	*Port Allegheny Reporter Argus*
Montgomery County	*Ambler Gazette* *Collegeville Independent*

WEEKLY NEWSPAPERS *(continued)*
Paid Circulation Publications

Montgomery County *(continued)*	Conshohocken Recorder Jenkintown Globe Jenkintown Times Chronicle Pennsburg Town and Country Royersford Reporter Souderton Independent
Northampton County	Bath Home News Bethlehem Bulletin Bethlehem Star
Perry County	Duncannon Record
Philadelphia County	Philadelphia Tribune
Pike County	Pike County Dispatch
Potter County	Potter Leader Enterprise
Schuylkill County	Pine Grove Press Herald Schuylkill Haven Call Valley View Citizen Standard West Schuylkill Herald (Tower City)
Snyder County	Middleburg Post Selinsgrove Times Tribune
Somerset County	Meyersdale New Republic
Sullivan County	Sullivan Review (Dushore)
Susquehanna County	Forest City News Susquehanna County Independent (Montrose)
Tioga County	Wellsboro Gazette Westfield Free Press Courier
Union County	Mifflinburg Telegraph
Washington County	Burgettstown Enterprise Claysville Weekly Recorder McDonald Record Outlook
Wayne County	Hawley News Eagle
Westmoreland County	Jeannette Spirit Ligonier Echo

WEEKLY NEWSPAPERS *(continued)*
Paid Circulation Publications

Westmoreland County *(continued)*	*Mount Pleasant Journal* *Murrysville Penn Franklin News* *Scottdale Independent Observer* *Vandergrift News Citizen* *West Newton Times Sun*
Wyoming County	*Tunkhannock New Age Examiner*
York County	*Delta Star*

TELEVISION STATIONS

City	Call Letters	Channel	Network
Allentown	WFMZ	69	Ind.
Altoona	WKBS	47	Ind.
	WTAJ	10	CBS
Bethlehem	WBPH	60	Ind.
	WLVT	39	PBS
Chambersburg	WJAL	68	Ind.
Erie	WETG	66	Fox
	WICV	12	NBC
	WJET	24	ABC
	WQLN	54	PBS
Harrisburg	WHP	21	CBS
	WHTM	27	ABC
	WITF	33	PBS
Johnstown	WATM	23	ABC
	WJAC	6	NBC
	WWCP	8	Fox
Lancaster	WGAL	8	NBC
Lebanon	WLYH	15	CBS
Monroeville	WPIT	22	Ind.
Moosic	WNEP	16	NBC
Philadelphia	KYW	3	CBS
	WPVI	6	ABC
	WCAU	10	NBC

TELEVISION STATIONS *(continued)*

City	Call Letters	Channel	Network
Philadelphia	WHYY	12	PBS
(continued)	WPHL	17	Ind.
	WTXF	29	Fox
	WYBE	35	PBS
	WGBS	47	Ind.
	WTGI	61	Telemundo
Pittsburgh	KDKA	2	CBS
	WTAE	4	ABC
	WPXI	11	NBC
	WQED	13	PBS
	WQEX	16	PBS
	WPCB	40	Ind.
	WPGH	53	Fox
	WNEV	63	Ind.
Pittston	WVLA	44	PBS
Reading	WTUE	51	Ind.
Scranton	WYOU	22	CBS
	WOLF	38	Fox/Ind.
	WWLF	56	Fox
University Park	WPSX	3	PBS
Wilkes-Barre	WBRE	28	NBC
York	WPMT	43	Fox/Ind.
	WGCB	49	Ind.

AREA CODES

There are five telephone area codes in Pennsylvania:

215 Southeastern Pennsylvania, including Philadelphia, Doylestown, and Bristol

610 Southeastern Pennsylvania, including Allentown, Coatesville, and Reading

717 Eastern and Central Pennsylvania, including Harrisburg, Hazleton, Lancaster, Lebanon, Scranton, Wilkes-Barre, Williamsport, and York

412 Southwestern Pennsylvania, including New Castle, McKeesport, and Pittsburgh

814 Western Pennsylvania, from Ohio to State College, and from New York to Maryland, except for the 412 area in the southwestern corner; includes Altoona, Erie, Johnstown, and State College

AREA CODES AND ZIP CODES
OF SELECTED TOWNS AND CITIES*

19001	Abington	215	19405	Bridgeport	610
15001	Aliquippa	412	15017	Bridgeville	412
**18101	Allentown	412	19007	Bristol	215
15101	Allison Park	412	15825	Brookville	814
**16601	Altoona	814	17508	Brownstown	717
19002	Ambler	215	15417	Brownsville	412
15003	Ambridge	412	19010	Bryn Mawr	610
17003	Annville	717	**16011	Butler	412
18403	Archbald	717	15419	California	412
19003	Ardmore	610	**17011	Camp Hill	717
17921	Ashland	717	15317	Canonsburg	412
18810	Athens	717	18407	Carbondale	717
16720	Austin	814	17013	Carlisle	717
19311	Avondale	610	15106	Carnegie	412
19004	Bala-Cynwyd	610	18032	Catasauqua	610
18013	Bangor	610	16404	Centerville	814
18014	Bath	610	17201	Chambersburg	717
16402	Bear Lake	814	15002	Charleroi	412
15009	Beaver	412	**19013	Chester	610
15010	Beaver Falls	412	19017	Chester Heights	610
17813	Beavertown	717	15828	Clarington	814
15522	Bedford	814	16214	Clarion	814
16823	Bellefonte	814	18411	Clarks Summit	717
18603	Berwick	717	16830	Clearfield	814
15102	Bethel Park	412	18218	Coaldale	814
**18016	Bethlehem	610	19320	Coatesville	610
15715	Big Run	814	19426	Collegeville	610
15717	Blairsville	412	17512	Columbia	717
17815	Bloomsburg	717	15425	Connellsville	412
17506	Blue Ball	717	19428	Conshohocken	610
19512	Boyertown	610	16317	Cooperstown	814
15014	Brackenridge	412	15108	Coraopolis	412
15104	Braddock	412	16319	Cranberry	814
16701	Bradford	814	19021	Croydon	215

*The zip codes given are for main post offices only.
**There is more than 1 zip code for this location.

AREA CODES AND ZIP CODES OF SELECTED
TOWNS AND CITIES *(continued)*

15427	Daisytown	412	16922	Galeton	814
17821	Danville	717	17325	Gettysburg	717
19023	Darby	610	19036	Glenolden	610
16115	Darlington	412	15116	Glenshaw	412
16222	Dayton	814	19038	Glenside	215
18519	Dickson City	717	17028	Grantville	717
15628	Donegal	412	15601	Greensburg	412
15033	Donora	412	16125	Greenville	412
19335	Downingtown	610	16127	Grove City	412
18901	Doylestown	215	19526	Hamburg	610
19026	Drexel Hill	610	17331	Hanover	717
15801	DuBois	814	**17105	Harrisburg	717
15110	Duquesne	412	19041	Haverford	610
19408	Eagleville	610	18201	Hazleton	717
**18045	Easton	610	18055	Hellertown	610
15112	E. Pittsburgh	412	17033	Hershey	717
18301	E. Stroudsburg	717	15340	Hickory	412
15931	Ebensburg	814	16648	Hollidaysburg	814
17022	Elizabethtown	717	15120	Homestead	412
19027	Elkins Park	215	18431	Honesdale	717
16117	Ellwood City	412	19344	Honey Brook	610
18049	Emmaus	610	16652	Huntingdon	814
**16515	Erie	814	15701	Indiana	412
19341	Exton	610	15447	Isabella	412
16415	Fairview	814	16134	Jamestown	412
19053	Feasterville	215	15644	Jeannette	412
17322	Felton	717	19046	Jenkintown	215
18921	Ferndale	610	17740	Jersey Shore	717
15332	Finleyville	412	18434	Jessup	717
19522	Fleetwood	610	18229	Jim Thorpe	717
19032	Folcroft	610	**15901	Johnstown	814
19033	Folsom	610	19347	Kemblesville	610
16226	Ford City	412	19348	Kennett Square	610
16323	Franklin	814	19406	King of Prussia	610

*The zip codes given are for main post offices only.
**There is more than 1 zip code for this location.

AREA CODES AND ZIP CODES OF SELECTED
TOWNS AND CITIES *(continued)*

16201	Kittanning	412	15061	Monaca	412
19530	Kutztown	610	15062	Monessen	412
**17604	Lancaster	717	15063	Monongahela	412
19350	Landenberg	610	15146	Monroeville	412
19446	Lansdale	215	18801	Montrose	717
19050	Lansdowne	610	19067	Morrisville	215
18232	Lansford	717	17851	Mount Carmel	717
18626	Laporte	717	15666	Mount Pleasant	717
15650	Latrobe	412	18634	Nanticoke	717
**17042	Lebanon	717	19072	Narberth	610
18235	Lehighton	610	15065	Natrona Heights	412
**19055	Levittown	215	18064	Nazareth	610
17837	Lewisburg	717	15066	New Brighton	412
17044	Lewistown	717	**16108	New Castle	412
19351	Lewisville	610	15068	New Kensington	412
16930	Liberty	717	18940	Newtown	215
15658	Ligonier	412	**19401	Norristown	610/215
17543	Lititz	717	18067	Northampton	610
17745	Lock Haven	717	16428	North East	814
17948	Mahanoy City	717	19704	Norwood	610
16933	Mansfield	717	15071	Oakdale	412
**15134	McKeesport	412	15139	Oakmont	412
16335	Meadville	814	16301	Oil City	814
17055	Mechanicsburg	717	18518	Old Forge	717
19063	Media	610	17859	Orangeville	717
19357	Mendenhall	610	19363	Oxford	610
16137	Mercer	412	17078	Palmyra	717
19066	Merion Station	215	19301	Paoli	610
17057	Middletown	717	19365	Parkesburg	610
15059	Midland	412	16668	Patton	814
17844	Mifflinburg	717	15849	Penfield	814
17060	Mill Creek	814	19104	Philadelphia	215
17062	Millerstown	717	19460	Phoenixville	610
17551	Millersville	717	**15290	Pittsburgh	412
17847	Milton	717	**18640	Pittston	717
17954	Minersville	717	18651	Plymouth	717

AREA CODES AND ZIP CODES OF SELECTED
TOWNS AND CITIES *(continued)*

18349	Pocono Manor	717	18360	Stroudsburg	717
**19464	Pottstown	610	17801	Sunbury	717
17901	Pottsville	717	18847	Susquehanna	717
19076	Prospect Park	610	19081	Swarthmore	610
15767	Punxsutawney	814	18252	Tamaqua	717
18951	Quakertown	215	15084	Tarentum	412
17247	Quincy	717	18517	Taylor	717
15104	Rankin	412	16946	Tioga	717
**19612	Reading	610	16354	Titusville	814
17356	Red Lion	717	18466	Tobyhanna	717
17764	Renovo	717	18848	Towanda	814
15853	Ridgway	814	15145	Turtle Creek	412
19078	Ridley Park	610	16686	Tyrone	814
18077	Riegelsville	610	15401	Uniontown	412
15074	Rochester	412	16802	University Park	814
19468	Royersford	610	19082	Upper Darby	610
15076	Russellton	412	**19481	Valley Forge	610/215
17970	St. Clair	717	19085	Villanova	610
18840	Sayre	717	18974	Warminster	215
15683	Scottdale	412	16365	Warren	814
**18505	Scranton	717	15301	Washington	412
15143	Sewickley	412	**19380	West Chester	610
17872	Shamokin	717	19390	West Grove	610
16146	Sharon	412	**18701	Wilkes-Barre	717
19079	Sharon Hill	610	**17701	Williamsport	717
16150	Sharpsville	412	19090	Willow Grove	215
17257	Shippensburg	717	16681	Woodland	814
18080	Slatington	610	19094	Woodlyn	610
16057	Slippery Rock	412	17368	Wrightsville	717
15501	Somerset	814	18853	Wyalusing	814
18964	Souderton	215	19095	Wyncote	215
18966	Southampton	215	19096	Wynnewood	610
15144	Springdale	412	**17402	York	717
**16801	State College	814	16063	Zelienople	412

*The zip codes given are for main post offices only.
**There is more than 1 zip code for this location.

12

Tourism

Tourism is the second-largest industry in Pennsylvania. Foreign and domestic travelers spent $10.3 billion in the commonwealth in 1993, according to a study conducted by the U.S. Travel Data Center. The expenditures were for public transportation, $2.7 billion; automobile transportation, $1.8 billion; lodging, $1.6 billion; food, $2.5 billion; entertainment and recreation, $901 million; and retail trade, $1 billion.

Pennsylvania ranked eighth in the United States in attracting tourist dollars. This spending provided jobs for 174,000 residents, 3.4 percent of the workforce in the state. About half of these jobs were in food service and lodging.

The major tourist destinations were Philadelphia, with revenues of $2.25 billion; Allegheny County (Pittsburgh), $2.17 billion; Monroe County, $522 million; and Montgomery County, $502 million. Philadelphia and Pittsburgh have the two major international airports, Monroe County is the center of the Pocono resort area, and Montgomery County benefits from its proximity to Philadelphia.

Three of these counties benefit from the presence of National Park sites within their boundaries: The Delaware Water Gap National Recreation Area attracted 4.7 million visitors to Monroe (and Pike) County; Independence National Historical Park attracted 3 million visitors to Philadelphia; and Valley Forge National Historical Park attracted 1.8 million visitors to Montgomery (and Chester) Counties. The fourth major National Park attraction, Gettysburg National Military Park, attracted 1.6 million visitors to Adams County.

The benefits of tourist spending are widespread. Nineteen of the state's 67 counties exceeded $100 million in tourist-related revenues; 25 reported that the number of jobs directly related to travel exceeded 1,000.

All of these figures are conservative. They include only direct-spending figures. Research studies have shown that the average travel dollar generates an additional 73 cents in secondary revenues. Using that formula, the total impact of travel spending in 1993 was $18.4 billion in revenues, which created 344,600 jobs and wages of $6 billion.

TOURIST PROMOTION

The Office of Travel and Tourism, Department of Commerce, is responsible for the state's advertising campaign designed to promote Pennsylvania as a travel destination. This office publishes the *Pennsylvania Visitors Guide,* a 235-

page travel planner. To obtain a free copy, call (800) VISIT-PA.

Each of the state's 67 counties is represented by a Tourist Promotion Agency, some of which serve two or more counties. They provide literature about attractions, events, lodging, dining, and places of interest in their county or region, and can provide the latest road and weather conditions.

TOURIST PROMOTION AGENCIES

County	Phone Number	County	Phone Number
Adams	(717) 334-6274	Lackawanna	(800) 22-WELCOME
Allegheny	(800) 366-0093	Lancaster	(800) PA-DUTCH
Armstrong	(412) 548-3226	Lawrence	(412) 654-5593
Beaver	(800) 342-8192	Lebanon	(717) 272-8555
Bedford	(800) 765-3331	Lehigh	(800) 747-0561
Berks	(800) 443-6610	Luzerne	(717) 825-1635
Blair	(800) 84-ALTOONA	Lycoming	(800) 358-9900
Bradford	(800) 769-8999	McKean	(814) 368-9370
Bucks	(800) 836-BUCKS	Mercer	(800) 637-2370
Butler	(800) 348-9393	Mifflin	(717) 248-6713
Cambria	(800) 237-8590	Monroe	(800) 762-6667
Cameron	(814) 546-2665	Montgomery	(888) VISIT-VF
Carbon	(800) JIM-THORPE	Montour	(800) VISIT-10
Centre	(800) 358-5466	Northampton	(800) 747-0561
Chester	(800) 228-9933	Northumberland	(800) 525-7320
Clarion	(800) 348-9393	Perry	(717) 582-2131
Clearfield	(800) 348-9393	Philadelphia	(800) 537-7676
Clinton	(717) 748-5782	Pike	(800) 762-6667
Columbia	(800) VISIT-10	Potter	(888) POTTER2
Crawford	(800) 332-2338	Schuylkill	(800) 765-7282
Cumberland	(800) 995-0969	Snyder	(800) 525-7320
Dauphin	(800) 995-0969	Somerset	(800) 925-7669
Delaware	(800) 343-3983	Sullivan	(800) 769-8999
Elk	(814) 834-3723	Susquehanna	(800) 769-8999
Erie	(814) 454-7191	Tioga	(800) 332-6718
Fayette	(800) 925-7669	Union	(800) 525-7320
Forest	(800) 624-7802	Venango	(800) 483-6264
Franklin	(717) 261-1200	Warren	(800) 624-7802
Fulton	(717) 485-4064	Washington	(800) 531-4114
Greene	(412) 627-TOUR	Wayne	(800) 762-6667
Huntingdon	(800) 269-4684	Westmoreland	(800) 925-7669
Indiana	(412) 463-7505	Wyoming	(800) 769-8999
Jefferson	(800) 348-9393	York	(800) 673-2429
Juniata	(717) 248-6713		

WINERIES

Pennsylvania's 48 wineries welcome visitors for tastings, tours, and sales. *Pennsylvania Wine and Wineries* is published quarterly by the Pennsylvania Wine Association, and is available free of charge in Pennsylvania wine and spirits shops. A calendar of special events includes concerts, art exhibits, grape stompings, hikes, arts and crafts shows, dancing, picnics, and a covered bridge festival.

Adams County Winery
251 Peach Tree Rd.
Orrtanna, PA 17353
(717) 334-4631
Mon.–Sat., 12:30–5
Allegro Vineyards
R.D. 2, Box 64
Brogue, PA 17309
(717) 927-9148
Mon.–Sun., 12–5
Big Creek Vineyard
R.R. 1, Box 1011
Kunkletown, PA 18058
(610) 681-3960
Mon.–Thur., 1–5; Fri. & Sat., 1–7; Sun., 2–5
Blue Mountain Vineyards
7627 Grape Vine Dr.
New Tripoli, PA 18066
(610) 298-3068
Sat. & Sun., 10–6; Weekdays, 4–7
Brookmere Farm Vineyards
R.D. 1, Box 53, Rt. 655
Belleville, PA 17004
(717) 935-5380
Mon.–Sat., 10–5; Sun., 1–4
Buckingham Valley Vineyards
1521 Route 413, P.O. Box 371
Buckingham, PA 18912
(215) 794-7188; fax (215) 794-3606
Tues.–Sat., 11–6; Sun., 12–4

Calvaresi Winery
107 Shartlesville Rd.
Bernville, PA 19506
(610) 488-7966
Thur. & Fri., 1–6; Sat. & Sun., 12–5
Chaddsford Winery
632 Baltimore Pike (U.S. 1)
Chadds Ford, PA 19317
(610) 388-6221
Apr.–Dec.: daily, 12–5; Jan.–Mar.: closed Mon.
Cherry Valley Vineyards
R.D. 5, Box 5100
Saylorsburg, PA 18353
(717) 992-2255
daily, 11–5; tours Sat. & Sun., 1–5
Clover Hill Vineyards and Winery
9850 Newtown Road
Breinigsville, PA 18031
(610) 395-2468
Mon.–Sat., 11–5:30; Sun., 12–5
Conneaut Cellars Winery
Route 322, Box 5075
Conneaut Lake, PA 16316
(814) 382-3999
daily, 10–6
Country Creek Winery
133 Cressman Rd.
Telford, PA 18969
(215) 723-6516
Sat. & Sun., 12–5
Evergreen Valley Vineyards
Evergreen Road
R.R. 1, Box 173D
Luthersburg, PA 15848
(814) 583-7575
summer: Thurs. & Fri., 12–6; Sat. & Sun., 12–5
Fox Ridge Vineyard & Winery
3528 East Market St.
York, PA 17402
(717) 755-3384
Wed., 12–5; Thurs., 2–6; Fri., 2–7; Sat., 11–4

Franklin Hill Vineyards
7833 Franklin Hill Rd.
Bangor, PA 18013
(610) 588-8708
Mon.–Sat., 11–4

French Creek Ridge Vineyards
200 Grove Rd.
Elverson, PA 19520
(610) 286-7754; fax (610) 286-7772
Sat. & Sun., 12–5

Glades Pike Winery
2706 Glades Pike
Somerset, PA 15501
(814) 445-3753
daily, 12–6

Heritage Wine Cellars
12162 E. Main Rd.
North East, PA 16428
(814) 725-8015
Mon.–Thur., 9–6; Fri. & Sat., 9–8; winter hours vary

Hunters Valley Winery
R.D. 2, Box 326D
Liverpool, PA 17045
(717) 444-7211
Thur. & Sat., 11–5; Fri., 11–7; Sun., 1–5

In & Out Vineyards
258 Durham Rd.
Newtown, PA 18940
(215) 860-5899
Sat. & Sun., 11–5

Christian W. Klay Winery
P.O. Box 309
412 Fayette Springs Road
Chalk Hill, PA 15421
(412) 439-3424
Mon.–Thur., Sun., 12–6; Fri. & Sat., 11–7

Lancaster County Winery
799 Rawlinsville Rd.
Willow Street, PA 17584
(717) 464-3555
Mon.–Sat., 10–4; Sun., 1–4

Lapic Winery
682 Tulip Dr.
New Brighton, PA 15066
(412) 846-2031
Mon.–Sat., 10–6; Sun., 1–5

Laurel Mountain Vineyard
R.D. 1, Box 238
Falls Creek, PA 15840
(814) 371-7022
Wed.–Sun., 10–6; closed in January

Mazza Vineyards
11815 E. Lake Rd.
North East, PA 16428
(814) 725-8695
summer: Mon.–Sat., 9–8; winter: Mon.–Sat., 9–5:30

Mount Hope Estate and Winery
83 Mansion House Rd.
Manheim, PA 17545
(717) 665-7021
Jan.–July: Mon.–Sat., 10–5, Sun., 12–5; Aug.–Dec.: Sun.–Thur., 10–6, Fri. & Sat., 10–7

Mount Nittany Vineyard and Winery
R.D. 1, Box 138
Centre Hall, PA 16828
(814) 466-6373; fax (814) 466-3066
Fri., 1:30–5; Sat., 10–5; Sun., 12:30–4

Naylor Wine Cellars
R.D. 3, Box 424
Stewartstown, PA 17363
(717) 993-2431
Mon.–Sat., 11–6; Sun., 12–5

Nissley Vineyards and Winery Estate
140 Vintage Dr.
Bainbridge, PA 17502
(717) 426-3514
Mon.–Sat., 10–5; Sun., 1–4

Oak Spring Winery
R.D. 1, Box 604
Altoona, PA 16601
(814) 946-3799
daily, 11–6

Oregon Hill Winery
R.D. 1, Box 604
Morris, PA 16938
(717) 353-2711
daily, 10–6:30
Peace Valley Winery
300 Old Limekiln Rd., Box 94
Chalfont, PA 18914
(215) 249-9058
Wed.–Sun., 12–6; Dec., daily, 10–6
Penn Shores Vineyards
10225 E. Lake Rd.
North East, PA 16428
(814) 725-8688
July & Aug.: Mon.–Sat., 9–8;
Sept.–June: Mon.–Sat., 9–5:30
Philadelphia Wine Company
3061 Miller St.
Philadelphia, PA 19134
(215) 482-3457
call for information
Pinnacle Ridge Winery
407 Old Route 22
Kutztown, PA 19530
(610) 756-4481
Sat., 10–5; Sun., 12–5
Presque Isle Wine Cellars
9440 Buffalo Rd.
North East, PA 16428
(814) 725-1314
Mon.–Sat., 8–5
Quaker Ridge Winery
211 S. Wade Ave.
Washington, PA 15301
(412) 222-2914
Thur. & Fri., 11–6; Sat. & Sun., 12–5
Ripepi Winery and Vineyards
93 Van Voorhis Lane
Monongahela, PA 15063
(412) 258-3395
Mon.–Sat., 11–6; Sun., 12–5
Rushland Ridge Vineyard and Winery
2665 Rushland Rd.

Rushland, PA 18956
(215) 598-0251
Apr.–Dec.: Sat., 12–6, Sun., 12–4;
closed Jan.–Mar.
Sand Castle Winery
Route 32, River Rd., Box 177
Erwinna, PA 18920
(800) 722-9463
Mon.–Sat., 10–6; Sun., 11–6
Seven Valleys Vineyard and Winery
R.D. 4, Box 4660
Glen Rock, PA 17327
(717) 235-6281
by appointment
Slate Quarry Winery
460 Gower Rd.
Nazareth, PA 18064
(610) 759-0286
Fri.–Sun., 1–6
Smithbridge Winery
159 Beaver Valley Rd.
Chadds Ford, PA 19317
(610) 558-4703
Wed.–Sun., 12–5
Susquehanna Valley Winery
802 Mount Zion Dr.
Danville, PA 17821
(717) 275-2364
Wed.–Sun., 1–6
Twin Brook Winery
5697 Strasburg Rd.,
R.D. 2, Box 2376
Gap, PA 17527
(717) 442-4915
Apr.–Dec.: Mon.–Sat., 10–6, Sun., 12–5;
Jan.–Mar.: Tues.–Sun., 12–5
Vynecrest Winery
172 Arrowhead Lane
Breinigsville, PA 18031
(610) 398-7525
Thur.–Sun., 1–6
Windgate Vineyards
R.D. 1, Box 213

Smicksburg, PA 16256
(814) 257-8797
daily, 12–5
The Winery at Wilcox
  Mefferts Run Rd., Box 39
  Wilcox, PA 15870
  (814) 929-5598
  daily, 12–6

GARDENS AND ARBORETUMS

The Philadelphia area is the center of Pennsylvania's garden attractions. Any of 15 sites will provide a pleasant visit on a spring or summer afternoon. Complete information about the gardens, and gardening in general, is available from the Pennsylvania Horticultural Society, 325 Walnut St., Philadelphia, PA (215) 625-8250.

The six major Pennsylvania gardens described here are destinations worth traveling some distance to visit.

Longwood Gardens is the state's premier horticultural display, with 11,000 types of plants on 1,050 acres. Longwood offers exquisite flowers, majestic trees, manicured gardens, opulent conservatories, illuminated fountains, an idea garden, and a children's garden with a maze, as well as over 300 events annually, including performances, festivals, concerts, and holiday displays. During the winter, 20 gardens in nearly 4 acres of heated greenhouses are the main attraction. U.S. Route 1 and PA Route 52, Kennett Square, (610) 388-1000. Open every day of the year, 9 to 5, and many evenings. Admission is $10.

The **Tyler Arboretum** is a 650-acre historic arboretum with woods, open fields, special plant collections, extensive rhododendron and holly areas, an herb garden, butterfly garden, bird habi-

tat, and 20 miles of walking paths. 515 Painter Rd., Media, (610) 566-5431. Open 8 A.M. to dusk. Admission is $3.

Fairmount Park, an 8,579-acre park along the Schuylkill River, is the largest landscaped city park in the world. Within the park, there are some special areas for garden enthusiasts. The Horticulture Center, in West Fairmount Park, has a landscaped arboretum, a reflecting pool, a 32,000-square-foot greenhouse, and seasonal gardens. It is open daily from 9 to 3. Within the Horticulture Center there is a Japanese House and Garden, open Tues. to Sun., 11 to 4. Admission to the center is $2; to the Japanese House, $2.50.

Bartram's Garden is America's oldest botanical garden, begun in 1731 by botanist John Bartram, and is a National Historic Landmark. In addition to the 200 native American trees and shrubs on 44 acres, the park has a restored 18th-century house, barn, stable, and carriage house. 54th St. and Lindbergh Blvd., (215) 729-5281. Open Wed. to Sun., 12 to 4, May–October; Wed. to Fri., 12 to 4, November–April. Admissions is free; guided tour $4.

The **Morris Arboretum** of the University of Pennsylvania, in the Chestnut Hill section of Philadelphia, has over 3,500 kinds of trees and shrubs growing on 92 acres. It is a romantic Victorian landscape garden with a rose garden and a swan pond. 100 Northwestern Ave., Chestnut Hill, (215) 247-5777. Open Mon. to Fri., 10 to 4; during the summer, also open Sat. and Sun., 10 to 5. Admission is $3.

The **Phipps Conservatory** is the premier garden attraction in western Pennsylvania. Located in Pittsburgh, it is a 100-year-old, 13-room Victorian tropical plant conservatory with a Japanese courtyard garden, rose garden, perennial garden, aquatic garden, and children's garden. The conservatory sponsors numerous flower shows and a special show during the Christmas season. One Schenley Park, (412) 622-6914. Open Tues.-Sun., 9 to 5. Admission is $3.

The **Philadelphia Flower Show,** an event that the *New York Times* called "the nation's oldest, biggest, and most prestigious indoor floral exhibit," is held in late February or early March at the Philadelphia Convention Center. More than 2,500 individuals enter the show's competitive division. The 1997 show featured gardens from Japan, Holland, and Belgium and 60 full-size home and garden settings, fountains, pondscapes, and an array of exotic flowers and plants on a 10-acre site.

AMUSEMENT PARKS

Pennsylvania has two major-league amusement parks: Dorney Park and Wildwater Kingdom in Allentown, and Hersheypark in Hershey. These destination parks can fulfill every expectation visitors have and are big and varied enough to warrant repeat visits.

There are other amusement parks in the commonwealth well worth a visit, but they are on a smaller scale and their appeal is more regional. They are not in themselves destinations, but they are good entertainment for those who live in the area or are enjoying other attractions nearby.

All of the parks are open daily from Memorial Day to Labor Day. Most are open weekends during the remainder of May and September, unless otherwise noted. Admission prices may vary according to the age of buyer, time of year,

time of day, and activities selected. Some parks offer free admission, with a pay-as-you-play system.

Dorney Park and Wildwater Kingdom is the prototypical modern American amusement park. It includes one of the largest waterparks in the country, with waterslides, whitewater raft rides, a wave pool, and a super wave splashdown ride. In addition, it has 100 major rides, plus children's rides and a Berenstain Bear Country Adventure Land. 3700 Hamilton Blvd., Allentown, (610) 395-3724. Take Exit 16B of I-78.

Hersheypark is a 100-acre theme park featuring 50 rides and attractions, including an all-new wooden roller coaster. The park is divided into theme areas, such as Pennsylvania Dutch and Pioneer Frontier. A visit to ZooAmerica, a North America wildlife park, is included in the admission fee. Daily live entertainment includes a dolphin show, and frequent concerts are held. 100 W. Hersheypark Dr., (800) HERSHEY. PA Turnpike, Exit 18.

Conneaut Lake Park is an old-fashioned—in the best sense of the world—amusement park. It is related, as most such parks once were, to a natural body of water. It has traditional rides, water activities, and a beach. The Jazz Festival in August is a prime attraction. On PA Route 618, off U.S. Route 6, (800) 828-9619.

Dutch Wonderland Family Fun Park has 25 rides, shows, and exhibits on 44 acres in the heart of Pennsylvania Dutch country. 2249 Route 30 East, Lancaster, (717) 291-1888.

Idlewild Park is home to Mister Rogers's Neighborhood of Make-Believe, via a trolley ride, and Story Book Forest, where nursery rhyme characters live.

The park also has amusement rides, miniature golf, water slides, a swimming pool, and live entertainment. U.S. Route 30, Ligonier, (412) 238-3666.

Kennywood Park bills itself as America's finest traditional park, and it has the National Historic Landmark status to back the claim. It has buildings that date from 1898. It also has four roller coasters, a water coaster, 30 amusement rides, and daily live entertainment. 4800 Kennywood Blvd., West Mifflin, (412) 461-0500. Take Swissdale Exit of I-376.

Knoebels Amusement Resort, Pennsylvania's largest free amusement park, uses a pay-by-the-ride system for its 41 rides, including a major roller coaster, waterslides, miniature golf, and a show with animated bears. PA Route 487, near Elysburg, in Northumberland County, (800) ITS-4FUN.

Lakemont Park has a waterpark, 30 rides, a go-cart track, and miniature golf. Admission is free; various pay-by-the-ride options exist. 700 Park Ave., Altoona, (814) 949-PARK.

Sandcastle, a waterpark on the Monongahela River, has 15 waterslides, miniature golf, go-carts, and a swimming pool. 1000 Sandcastle Dr., West Homestead, (412) 462-6666. On PA Route 837.

Sesame Place is a children's play-and-learn theme park, with the Muppets and other "Sesame Street" characters. It has 13 waterslides, a wave pool, science exhibits, electronic games, and an al-phabet parade. 100 Sesame Rd., Langhorne, (215) 752-7070. Thirty minutes from Philadelphia via I-95, Exit 29A.

Shawnee Place Play and Water Park is a children's participatory play park with 15 play elements for children aged three to 13. Attractions include a chairlift ride, waterslide, video and other games, and a daily magic show. Shawnee-on-Delaware, (717) 421-7231. On U.S. Route 209, 5 miles north of I-80, Exit 52.

Waldameer Park and Water World is located at the entrance to Presque Isle State Park on Lake Erie. It has rides, shows, games, videos, and a 16-slide water park. Admission is free, with many ticket price options for rides. PA Route 832, Peninsula Dr., (814) 838-3591.

COMMUNITY FAIRS

Community fairs are a tradition that dates back to colonial times. In 1996, 113 fairs were held in the commonwealth. Each fair is generally held during the same week or weekend each year. Call to confirm exact dates of each event.

In addition, the Pennsylvania Renaissance Faire, a re-creation of a 16th-century English county fair, is held on weekends in August and September in the 30-acre formal garden of a Victorian mansion at the Mount Hope Estate and Winery in Lancaster County. Over 200 costumed performers create the sights and sounds of the period. Come in costume.

FAIRS*

Month	Fair	Location	Telephone
January			
10–16	PA State Farm Show	Harrisburg	717-783-3071
April			
20–21, 26–28	PA Maple Festival	Meyersdale	814-634-0213
May			
16–27	PA Fair at Philadelphia Park	Bensalem	800-749-3247
30–June 9	Philadelphia County Fair	Philadelphia	800-749-3247
June			
25–29	Schnecksville Fair	Schnecksville	610-799-2609
28–July 6	Butler Fair	Butler	412-283-9861
July			
8–13	Derry Township Fair	New Derry	412-459-8781
11–20	Lycoming County Fair	Hughesville	717-784-0487
12–20	Wilkes-Barre/Scranton Fair	Pocono Downs Raceway	800-749-3247
14–20	Jefferson County Fair	Brookville	814-265-0640
21–27	Clarion County Fair	New Bethlehem	814-275-3929
21–27	Shippensburg Community Fair	Shippensburg	717-532-2797
22–27	Jefferson Township Fair	Mercer	412-962-9823
22–27	Kimberton Community Fair	Kimberton	610-933-4566
22–27	Troy Fair	Troy	717-297-2823
23–27	Jacktown Fair	Wind Ridge	412-428-3843
23–27	Plainfield Farmers Fair	Plainfield	610-759-4365
25–Aug. 3	Fayette County Fair	Uniontown	412-628-3360
27–Aug. 2	Lebanon Area Fair	Lebanon	717-273-3670
28–Aug. 3	Mercer County Grange Fair	Mercer	412-748-4007
28–Aug. 3	Potter County Fair	Millport	814-698-2368
29–Aug. 2	Morrison Cove Dairy Show	Martinsburg	814-793-2111
29–Aug. 3	Clearfield County Fair	Clearfield	814-765-4629

*Dates listed are from 1996.

FAIRS *(continued)*

Month	Fair	Location	Telephone
August			
29–Aug. 3	Goshen County Fair	West Chester	610-430-1555
30–Aug. 3	New Stanton Farm and Home Fair	New Stanton	412-925-2788
2–10	Wayne County Fair	Honesdale	717-253-1847
3–10	Clinton County Fair	Mackeyville	717-726-4148
3–10	Greene County Fair	Waynesburg	412-627-9459
4–10	Union County West End Fair	Laurelton	717-966-2435
4–10	Bedford County Fair	Bedford	814-623-9011
4–10	Schuylkill County Fair	Summit Station	717-943-2637
5–10	Butler Farm Show	Butler	412-283-9861
5–10	Cochranton Community Fair	Cochranton	814-425-2463
5–10	Dawson Grange Community Fair	Dawson	412-736-2943
5–10	Sewickley Township Community Fair	West Newton	412-872-6521
5–10	Tioga County Fair	Whitneyville	717-549-8176
5–10	Warren County Fair	Pittsfield	814-757-8668
6–9	Carlisle Fair	Carlisle	717-249-8434
6–10	Elk County Fair	Kersey	814-885-8296
6–10	Harrold Fair	Greensburg	412-446-9779
7–10	Cumberland Ag Fair	Newville	717-240-6500
11–17	Bullskin Township Community Fair	Mount Pleasant	412-887-7056
11–17	Huntingdon County Fair	Huntingdon	814-643-4452
12–17	Kutztown Fair	Kutztown	610-683-3458
11–17	Montour-DeLong Community Fair	Washingtonville	717-437-2178
11–17	McKean County Fair	Smethport	814-837-6447
11–18	Washington County Agricultural Fair	Washington	412-225-7718
12–17	Dayton Fair	Dayton	814-257-8332
12–17	Lawrence County Fair	New Castle	412-336-5403
12–17	Venango County Fair	Franklin	814-437-7607
15–17	Mount Nebo Grange Fair	Mount Nebo	412-741-5407

FAIRS *(continued)*

Month	Fair	Location	Telephone
August			
15–17	Findlay Township Fair	Clinton	412-695-0500
15–17	Middletown Grange Fair	Wrightstown	215-968-2321
17–24	Crawford County Fair	Meadville	814-333-7300
18–24	Fulton County Fair	McConnellsburg	717-485-5730
18–24	Cameron County Fair	Emporium	814-486-1775
18–24	Somerset County Fair	Meyersdale	814-634-0916
18–25	Westmoreland Agricultural Fair	Greensburg	412-423-5005
18–24	Franklin County Fair	Chambersburg	717-369-4100
19–24	Harford Fair	Harford	717-289-4405
19–24	Mountain Area Community Fair	Farmington	412-438-4270
19–24	Sykesville Agricultural and Youth Fair	Sykesville	814-371-3180
19–26	Williamsburg Community Farm Show	Williamsburg	814-832-2405
20–24	Blue Valley Farm Show	Bangor	610-588-9504
20–24	Elizabethtown Community Fair	Elizabethtown	717-367-7256
20–24	Hookstown Fair	Hookstown	412-573-4512
20–24	Perry County Community Fair	Newport	717-567-6260
20–24	Transfer Harvest Home Fair	Greenville	412-962-0448
23–29	Centre County Grange Fair	Centre Hall	814-355-2943
25–31	Indiana County Fair	Indiana	412-465-6703
26–31	West End Fair	Gilbert	610-681-4293
27–31	Big Knob Grange Fair	Rochester	412-843-7863
27–Sept. 2	Allentown Fair	Allentown	610-433-7541
27–Sept. 2	Greene-Dreher-Sterling Fair	Newfoundland	717-698-9373
27–Sept. 2	Wattsburg/Erie County Fair	Wattsburg	814-739-2952
28–Sept. 2	South Mountain Fair	Arendtsville	717-677-9663
28–Sept. 2	Stoneboro Fair	Stoneboro	412-376-2852
28–Sept. 2	Sullivan County Fair	Forksville	717-924-3843
28–Sept. 2	Wyoming County Fair	Tunkhannock	717-836-5502
31–Sept. 7	Juniata County Fair	Port Royal	717-527-4825

FAIRS *(continued)*

Month	Fair	Location	Telephone
September			
1–7	Cambria County Fair	Ebensburg	814-472-7491
1–7	Spartansburg Community Fair	Spartansburg	814-654-7250
2–7	Ox Hill Community Fair	Home	412-397-4449
2–7	Waterford Community Fair	Waterford	814-796-4490
2–7	West Alexander Fair	West Alexander	412-484-7340
3–7	Claysburg Area Farm Show	Claysburg	814-239-2079
3–7	Jamestown Community Fair	Jamestown	412-932-3526
4–7	Bellwood-Antis Farm Show	Bellwood	814-742-8121
4–8	Luzerne County Fair	Dallas	717-675-FAIR
5–8	Pike County Fair	Matamoras	717-296-8790
6–14	York Interstate Fair	York	717-848-2596
9–14	Green Township Community Fair	Commodore	412-254-4613
10–14	Albion Area Fair	Albion	814-756-4883
10–14	Sinking Valley Fair	Altoona	814-684-4379
10–14	Denver Community Fair	Denver	717-336-4072
15–21	Beaver Community Fair	Beaver Springs	717-658-3318
15–21	Gratz Fair	Gratz	717-365-3175
17–21	Harmony Grange Fair	Westover	814-743-6716
18–21	Berlin Brothers Valley Fair	Berlin	814-267-4622
18–20	Southern Lancaster County Fair	Quarryville	717-786-1054
19–21	North East Community Fair	North East	814-725-9187
19–21	Oley Valley Community Fair	Oley	610-944-7862
21–28	Bloomsburg Fair	Bloomsburg	717-784-4949
23–28	Reading Fair	Reading	610-370-3473
24–27	Morrison Cove Community Fair	Martinsburg	814-793-2972
24–28	Ephrata Fair	Ephrata	717-733-4451
25–27	West Lampeter Community Fair	Lampeter	717-687-0351
26–29	Tri-Valley Community Fair	Hegins	717-682-3125

FAIRS *(continued)*

Month	Fair	Location	Telephone
October			
2–5	New Holland Farmers Fair	New Holland	717-354-5880
7–10	Hollidaysburg Community Fair	Hollidaysburg	814-695-2179
7–11	Manheim Community Farm Show	Manheim	717-664-3710
10–12	Unionville Community Fair	Unionville	610-869-8716
15–19	Dillsburg Community Fair	Dillsburg	717-432-7361
18–20	Uniontown Poultry & Farm Show	Uniontown	412-439-5253

13

Military

PENNSYLVANIA NATIONAL GUARD

The citizen-soldier concept of defense had its beginning in Pennsylvania with Benjamin Franklin's Associators. The idea was that the farmer, the merchant, and the ironmaster would leave their work and take up arms whenever it was necessary to defend their community. That simple idea has evolved into the Pennsylvania National Guard, which is organized into Army and Air Units, including infantry, armor, cavalry, field artillery, air defense artillery, engineers, maintenance, transportation, public affairs, medical, and every type of aviation group.

In times of national emergency, the president of the United States orders units of the Pennsylvania Army and Air National Guard into the active military service of the United States. Recent federal missions have included Panama, Haiti, and Operation Desert Storm. In February 1992, 13 members of the 14th Quartermaster Detachment from Greensburg were killed by a missile while serving during Operation Desert Storm.

When not in the service of the United States, the National Guard is a state force, with the governor as commander-in-chief. He delegates this command to the adjutant general, the head of the Department of Military Affairs.

The best-known role of the National Guard is performed during emergencies: When catastrophic weather, civil unrest, or man-made calamities strike the commonwealth, the Guard is called upon to help. Troops often perform public-service work in their communities. Recently, they have been enlisted in the war on drugs.

The aviation program of the Army National Guard has three support facilities: Muir Army National Guard Airfield at Fort Indiantown Gap, Washington County Airport in Washington, and the Mid-State Airport in Philipsburg. The 57 Pennsylvania Air National Guard Units are located at Fort Indiantown Gap, Harrisburg and Pittsburgh International Airports, Willow Grove Air Reserve Station, and State College.

VETERANS HOSPITALS

The Bureau of Veterans Affairs manages four veterans hospitals:

Pennsylvania Soldiers and Sailors Home, Erie, founded in 1885
Hollidaysburg Veterans Home, founded in 1976, expanded in 1992
Southeastern Pennsylvania Veterans

Center, Spring City, founded in 1986, expanded in 1993

Northeastern Pennsylvania Veterans Center, Scranton, founded in 1993

INDIANTOWN GAP NATIONAL CEMETERY

The 667-acre Indiantown Gap National Cemetery, which opened September 20, 1982, is the only open National Cemetery in Pennsylvania. As of February 1996, there were 11,365 veterans and their dependents buried there, including one veteran of the Spanish-American War and two veterans of the Persian Gulf War. According to a 1948 law, burial in a National Cemetery is restricted to those who die while in the service, honorably discharged veterans, honorably dis-

charged war veterans of allied nations, and the spouses and minor children of eligible servicemembers and veterans.

MILITARY BASES

Military bases in the state include the following:

Carlisle Barracks
Fort Indiantown Gap (Annville)
Letterkenny Army Depot (Chambersburg)
Naval Ship Parts Control Center (Mechanicsburg)
New Cumberland Army Depot
Tobyhanna Army Depot
Warminster Naval Air Development Center
Willow Grove Air Reserve Station

14

Spectator Sports

PROFESSIONAL SPORTS
Major League Baseball

Pittsburgh Pirates Founded in 1882 as the Pittsburgh Alleghenys of the American Association, the League in which they played from 1882 to 1886. Joined the American League in 1887. Changed name to Pirates in 1891. Won seven National League Championships and five World Championships.

WORLD SERIES RECORD

1903:	Red Sox	5	Pirates	3
1909:	Pirates	4	Tigers	3
1925:	Pirates	4	Senators	3
1927:	Yankees	4	Pirates	3
1960:	Pirates	4	Yankees	3
1971:	Pirates	4	Orioles	3
1979:	Pirates	4	Orioles	3

NATIONAL LEAGUE MOST VALUABLE PLAYERS

1927: Paul Waner
1960: Dick Groat
1966: Roberto Clemente
1978: Dave Parker
1979: Willie Stargell
1990: Barry Bonds
1992: Barry Bonds

Philadelphia Phillies Founded in 1883, when the Worcester, Massachusetts, Ruby Legs moved to Philadelphia and changed their name to the Philadelphia Quakers. They played under that name until 1890. They have been the Phillies ever since. They have won five National League Championships and one World Championship.

WORLD SERIES RECORD

1915:	Red Sox	4	Phillies	1
1950:	Yankees	4	Phillies	0
1980:	Phillies	4	Royals	2
1983:	Orioles	4	Phillies	4
1993:	Blue Jays	4	Phillies	2

NATIONAL LEAGUE MOST VALUABLE PLAYERS

1932: Chuck Klein
1950: Jim Konstanty
1980: Mike Schmidt
1981: Mike Schmidt
1986: Mike Schmidt

Philadelphia Athletics Charter members of the American League in 1901, the Athletics were founded in 1891 and played in the Players League until 1901. The A's moved to Kansas City after the

1954 season; they ultimately left Kansas City for Oakland, California, where they are still known as the A's. The Philadelphia Athletics won eight American League Championships and five World Championships between 1901 and 1954.

WORLD SERIES RECORD

1905:	N.Y. Giants	4	Athletics	1
1910:	Athletics	4	Cubs	1
1911:	Athletics	4	N.Y. Giants	2
1913:	Athletics	4	N.Y. Giants	1
1914:	Braves	4	Athletics	0
1929:	Athletics	4	Cubs	1
1930:	Athletics	4	Cardinals	2
1931:	Cardinals	4	Athletics	3

AMERICAN LEAGUE MOST VALUABLE PLAYERS

1914: Eddie Collins

1928: Mickey Cochran

1931: Lefty Grove

1932: Jimmie Foxx

1933: Jimmie Foxx

1952: Bobbie Schantz

Minor League Baseball
　Erie Seawolves A farm team of the Pittsburgh Pirates
　Harrisburg Senators AA farm team of the Montreal Expos
　Johnstown Steal Class A, Independent
　Reading Phillies AA farm team of the Philadelphia Phillies
　Scranton/Wilkes-Barre Red Barons AAA farm team of the Phillies
　Williamsport Cubs A farm team of the Chicago Cubs

National Football League
　Pittsburgh Steelers Founded in 1939 as the Pirates; changed name to Steelers in 1940.

SUPER BOWL WINS

1974: 16–6 vs. Vikings

1975: 21–17 vs. Dallas

1978: 35–31 vs. Dallas

1979: 31–19 vs. Rams

SUPER BOWL LOSSES

1995: 27–17 vs. Dallas

Philadelphia Eagles Founded in 1933. In 1943, due to World War II, the Eagles and the Steelers merged operations for one season.

NATIONAL FOOTBALL LEAGUE CHAMPIONS

1948: 7–0 vs. Chicago Cardinals

1949: 14–0 vs. Los Angeles Rams

SUPER BOWL LOSSES

1981: 27–10 vs. Raiders

NFL MOST VALUABLE PLAYER

1960: Norm Van Brocklin

National Basketball Association
　Philadelphia Warriors The Philadelphia Warriors represented the city from 1946–47 to 1961–62, when the franchise moved to San Francisco and was renamed the Golden State Warriors. The

Warriors won the NBA championship in 1946–47 and 1955–56.

Philadelphia 76ers In 1963, the Syracuse Nationals franchise was moved to Philadelphia and renamed the 76ers. The team won the NBA championship in 1966–67 and 1982–83.

NBA MOST VALUABLE PLAYERS

1980–81: Julius Erving

1982–83: Moses Malone

Pittsburgh Franchises Professional basketball in Pittsburgh has had three unsuccessful franchises: In 1946–47, the Pittsburgh Ironmen folded after one season in the NBA. In 1967–68, the Pittsburgh Condors played only one season in the new American Basketball Association. In 1970–72 a new franchise, the Pittsburgh Condors, played two seasons in the ABA before folding.

National Hockey League
Pittsburgh Penguins Founded in 1967–68, the Penguins were league champions in 1990–91 and 1991–92.

MOST VALUABLE PLAYERS

1988–89 and 1993–94: Mario Lemieux

Philadelphia Flyers Founded in 1967–68, the Flyers were league champions in 1973–74 and 1974–75.

MOST VALUABLE PLAYERS

1974–75 and 1975–76: Bobby Clarke
1995–96: Eric Lindros

Minor League Hockey
Hershey Bears American Hockey League

Erie Otters Ontario Hockey League
Johnstown Chiefs East Coast Hockey League

INTERCOLLEGIATE ATHLETICS
NCAA Division I
National Collegiate Athletic Association (NCAA) Division I is for large, highly competitive athletic programs. Competition is bound by a complex body of rules and regulations. Schools in this division field teams in every sport. Temple University, the University of Pittsburgh, and Penn State University compete on this level. The following are some football highlights from Division I competition.

Penn State has been playing football since 1887 and has played 1,030 games, of which it has won 695, lost 294, and tied 41, for a winning percentage of .695. The team has appeared in 32 postseason bowl games, compiling a record of 20–10–2, the last 26 of these appearances under Coach Joe Paterno.

The University of Pittsburgh has been playing football since 1890 and has played 1,015 games, of which it has won 572, lost 401, and tied 42, for a winning percentage of .584. It has appeared in 18 postseason bowl games, winning 8.

Temple University has been playing football since 1900 and has played 832 games, of which it has won 370, lost 410, and tied 52, for a winning percentage of .476. It won one of its two bowl games.

In the first six seasons of the 1990s, Penn State compiled the seventh best winning percentage in the country; the other two programs were doing poorly:

Penn State	W 58	L 15	.795
Pittsburgh	W 20	L 46	.306
Temple	W 14	L 52	.212

Penn State joined the Big 10 Conference in 1994. The Penn State–Pitt game, one of college football's great rivalries, was lost in the scheduling shuffle, but resumed in 1997.

NCAA Division I-AA

Division I-AA competition is at a much lower level of intensity. Schools in this division do not field teams in all sports, and they award fewer scholarships (Bucknell, Lafayette, and Lehigh do not award any). Ten Pennsylvania institutions compete at this level: Bucknell, Drexel, Duquesne, Lafayette, La Salle, Lehigh, St. Francis, St. Joseph's, Penn, and Villanova. The following are some highlights of Division I-AA competition.

Lafayette and Lehigh have played in 106 consecutive football games since 1890, the longest uninterrupted rivalry in the country. Pennsylvania and Cornell have played a football game every year since 1893.

La Salle won the National Collegiate Athletic Association basketball championship in 1954 and was runner-up in 1955. Villanova won the tournament in 1985, finished second in 1971, and fourth in 1939. St. Joseph's finished third in the NCAA tournament in 1961; Penn finished in fourth place in 1979.

NCAA Division II

Institutions in Division II grant only partial scholarships to athletes. Thirteen of the 14 state universities compete on this level (Lincoln University of Pennsylvania competes on the Division III level). Kutztown competes on the Division I level in wrestling. The four other Division II schools are Erie, Gannon, Philadelphia Textile, and the University of Pittsburgh at Johnstown. The following are some highlights of Division II competition.

Indiana University of Pennsylvania earned the right to compete in seven football championship tournaments: 1987, 1988, 1989, 1990, 1991, 1993, and 1994. The school won 12 and lost seven tournament games, finishing second in 1990 and 1993.

Philadelphia Textile won the 1970 basketball tournament; Cheyney was the 1978 champion. Cheyney's women's team was runner-up in the 1982 tournament.

Division III

At the Division III level, no scholarships are awarded to athletes. Some Division III schools compete in one sport at the Division I or II level. Pennsylvania's District III schools are Albright, Allegheny, Carnegie-Mellon, Delaware Valley, Dickinson, Elizabethtown, Franklin & Marshall, Gettysburg, Grove City, Juniata, King's College, Lebanon Valley, Lincoln, Lycoming, Marywood, Muhlenberg, Scranton, Susquehanna, Swarthmore, Ursinus, Washington & Jefferson, Waynesburg, Widener, Wilkes, and York College. The following are some highlights of Division III competition.

In 1990, the football championship playoff was an all-Pennsylvania affair, with Allegheny College defeating Lycoming College. Widener University won the football championship in 1977 and 1981; Washington & Jefferson College was the runner-up in the 1992 and 1994 football championships; Juniata College was runner-up in 1973. In basketball, Scranton won the national championship in 1976 and 1983, and Lebanon Valley College won the title in 1994.

Division III institutions with limited athletic programs and women's colleges include Allentown College of St. Francis de Sales, Alvernia, Beaver, Bryn Mawr,

Cabrini, Cedar Crest, College Misericordia, Haverford, Immaculata, Messiah, Moravian, Neumann, and Penn State at Erie-Behrend Campus.

Although teams in this group do not ordinarily compete for championships, Immaculata College won the AIAW (Association of Intercollegiate Athletics for Women) basketball championship in 1972, 1973, and 1974 and finished second in 1975 and 1976. The AIAW was the forerunner of the NCAA, when women's sports were considered inferior.

Other Collegiate Athletic Associations
There are four additional very small collegiate athletic associations in which a few Pennsylvania institutions compete:

National Association of Intercollegiate Athletics Schools competing in this organization are Carlow, Geneva, Holy Family, La Roche, Philadelphia College of Pharmacy and Science, Point Park, St. Vincent, and University of Pittsburgh–Bradford.

National Small College Athletic Association Schools competing in this organization are Academy of the New Church, Chatham, Hahnemann, Penn State–Harrisburg, Rosemont, and Wilson.

National Junior College Athletic Association Lackawanna, Manor, and Mount Aloysius Junior Colleges compete in this organization.

National Christian College Association Schools competing in this organization are Baptist Bible College of Pennsylvania, Eastern College, Lancaster Bible College, Philadelphia College of the Bible, and Valley Forge Christian College.

HORSE RACING
Horse racing in Pennsylvania includes both harness racing and Thoroughbred racing. Both types of racing are regulated by the Pennsylvania Department of Agriculture. Separate commissions oversee the two types of racing, which are held at separate tracks and conducted by different licensees.

Thoroughbred Racing
Thoroughbreds race at Penn National Racetrack in Grantville, 13 miles from Harrisburg, off Exit 28 of I-81, on 210 racing days; and at the Philadelphia Park Racetrack in Bensalem, off Exit 28 of the Pennsylvania Turnpike, on 218 racing dates.

In addition, Thoroughbred racing licensees operate nine off-track betting sites: Penn National at Chambersburg, Reading, York, Lancaster, and Muncy; Turf Clubs in Philadelphia, South Philadelphia, Oaks, and Upper Darby.

In 1995, the total wagering at all sites, on- and off-track, was $955 million.

Harness Racing
Harness racing is held at Ladbroke at The Meadows, 10 miles south of Pittsburgh at the intersection of U.S. Route 19 and I-79, on 230 racing days; and at Pocono Downs, on PA Route 315, off Exit 47 of I-81, north of Wilkes-Barre, on 143 racing dates.

In 1996, 23 Pennsylvania fairs had harness-racing meetings of one to four days' duration.

Harness-racing licensees operate eight off-track wagering sites: The Downs at Erie, The Downs at Lehigh Valley (Allentown), Greenburg, Harmar Township (Pittsburgh), Johnstown, Moon Township (Coraopolis), New Castle, and West Mifflin.

In 1995, the total wagering at all sites, on- and off-track, was $471 million.

GOLF

No discussion of sports and athletes in Pennsylvania would be complete without mention of Latrobe native Arnold Palmer, the dominant player on the Professional Golfers' Association tour in the 1960s. Palmer won his first tournament at the 1958 Masters, and followed it in 1960 with victories in eight major tournaments, including the Masters and the United States Open. In 1961 and 1964, Palmer won two Masters and two British Open titles. He resurrected interest in the British Open, which had been declining in popularity until he competed in it.

Between 1965 and 1970, he won 12 tournaments but no major titles. He finished second in the PGA Championship three times but never won it. In the 1970s, he faded as a major player but did win a few domestic and international titles. Palmer was a modest, well-loved figure who was encouraged in his play by "Arnie's Army," the name given to the hordes of fans who followed him around the course and the millions of television viewers who cheered him on to his come-from-behind finishes. His victories over—and losses to—his nemesis, Jack Nicklaus, during the prime of both golfers are the stuff of golf legends.

Bibliography

That great English man of letters, Dr. Samuel Johnson, wrote, "To write a book, one must read a library." Fortunately, when writing a book about Pennsylvania, the library that one must read is filled with interesting, informative, well-written books.

Barnes, J. H., and W. D. Sevon. *The Geological Story of Pennsylvania.* Harrisburg: Buchart-Horn, 1968.

Beers, Paul B. *Pennsylvania Politics Today and Yesterday.* University Park, PA: The Pennsylvania State University Press, 1980.

———. *The Pennsylvania Sampler.* Harrisburg: Stackpole Books, 1970.

———. *Profiles from the Susquehanna Valley.* Harrisburg: Stackpole Books, 1973.

Beyer, George. *Guide to the State Historical Markers of Pennsylvania.* Harrisburg: Pennsylvania Historical and Museum Commission, 1991.

Common Trees of Pennsylvania. Harrisburg: Department of Conservation and Natural Resources, Bureau of Forestry, 1995.

Cuff, D. J., et al., eds. *The Atlas of Pennsylvania.* Philadelphia: Temple University Press, 1989.

Cupper, Dan. *The Pennsylvania Turnpike: A History.* Lebanon, PA: Applied Arts Publishers, 1995.

Davis, A. A., and K. A. Miller. *Pennsylvania Recreation Plan 1991–1997.* Harrisburg: Department of Environmental Resources, Bureau of State Parks, 1995.

DeCoster, Lester A. *The Legacy of Penn's Woods.* Harrisburg: Department of Conservation and Natural Resources, Bureau of Forestry, 1995.

Finkel, Kenneth, ed. *The Philadelphia Almanac and Citizen's Manual 1994.* Philadelphia: The Library Company of Philadelphia, 1993.

Geyer, Alan R., and William Bolles. *Outstanding Scenic Geological Features of Pennsylvania.* Harrisburg: Bureau of Topographic and Geologic Survey, 1979.

Gille, Frank. *The Encyclopedia of Pennsylvania.* St. Clair Shores, MI: Somerset Publishers, 1983.

Gordon, Thomas. *A Gazetteer of the State of Pennsylvania.* Philadelphia: T. Belknap, 1832.

Gutkind, Lee. *Our Roots Grow Deeper Than We Know.* Pittsburgh: University of Pittsburgh Press, 1985.

Hill, Robert J. *Poisonous Plants of Pennsylvania.* Harrisburg: Pennsylvania Department of Agriculture, 1986.

Hoy, Mark. *1996 Pennsylvania Visitors Guide.* Harrisburg: Department of Commerce, Office of Travel and Tourism, 1996.

Hylton, Thomas. *Save Our Lands—Save Our Towns.* Harrisburg: RB Books, 1995.

Korber, H., and K. Korber. *A Viewer's Guide to Pennsylvania Wildlife.* Lemoyne, PA: Northwoods Publications, 1994.

McQuown, Lynn S., ed. *The Pennsylvania Manual,* Vol. 112. Harrisburg: Department of General Services, 1995.

Merritt, Joseph F. *Guide to the Mammals of Pennsylvania.* Pittsburgh: University of Pittsburgh Press, 1991.

Miller, E. W. *A Geography of Pennsylvania.* University Park, PA: The Penn State University Press, 1995.

My Pennsylvania. Harrisburg: Pennsylvania Department of Commerce, 1946.

The National Parks: Index 1995. Washington, DC: United States Department of Interior, 1995.

Palmer, Tim. *Rivers of Pennsylvania.* University Park, PA: The Penn State University Press, 1980.

Pennsylvania Vital Statistics 1994. Harrisburg: Pennsylvania Department of Health, 1994.

Reynolds, Patrick M. *Pennsylvania Profiles.* Willow Street, PA: Red Rose Studio, 1977.

Secor, Robert, et al., eds. *Pennsylvania 1776.* University Park, PA: The Penn State University Press, 1975.

Shaffer, Larry L. *Pennsylvania Amphibians & Reptiles.* Harrisburg: Pennsylvania Fish and Boat Commission, 1995.

Shank, William H. *Great Floods of Pennsylvania.* Harrisburg: Buchart-Horn, 1968.

Shiffer, Clark. *Identification Guide to Pennsylvania Fishes.* Harrisburg: Pennsylvania Fish and Boat Commission, 1990.

Stranahan, Susan. *Susquehanna, River of Dreams.* Baltimore: Johns Hopkins University Press, 1993.

Trials of the Mid-Atlantic Region. Washington, DC: United States Department of Interior, 1989.

Van Diver, B. B. *Roadside Geology of Pennsylvania.* Missoula, MT: Mountain Press, 1996.

Wakeley, James, and Linda Wakeley. *Birds of Pennsylvania.* Harrisburg: Pennsylvania Game Commission, 1995.

Water Quality Assessment. Harrisburg: Department of Environmental Resources, Bureau of Water Quality Management, 1996.

Index